Accounting
for Business Studies

Aneirin Sion Owen

Manchester Metropolitan University

Routledge
Taylor & Francis Group

LONDON AND NEW YORK

First published by Butterworth-Heinemann

This edition published 2011 by Routledge
2 Park Square, Milton Park, Abingdon, Oxon OX14 4RN
711 Third Avenue, New York, NY 10017, USA

Routledge is an imprint of the Taylor & Francis Group, an informa business

Copyright © 2003, Taylor & Francis

British Library Cataloguing in Publication Data
A catalogue record for this book is available from the British Library

Library of Congress Cataloguing in Publication Data
A catalogue record for this book is available from the Library of Congress

ISBN 978-0-7506-5834-8

Dedicated to Kathy Marshall

Contents

Preface

This book explains the role of accounting in modern business and management and shows you how to confidently evaluate business ideas using profit and loss accounts, spreadsheets and cash flow forecasts, etc. It illustrates financial models and concepts enabling you to write professional reports and prepare presentations on complex business problems. It gives you sufficient breadth of vision and commercial awareness to make recommendations on operational and strategic issues.

The approach adopted will be particularly relevant to undergraduate business students and the text will also serve as an introduction to MBA studies as well as professional accounting and management courses. No prior knowledge of accounting is assumed.

Business is an exciting and fast changing environment in which globalisation and e-business have created many new opportunities and fresh challenges. This book brings accounting up to date with the fast changing business world, integrating insights from strategy, marketing and operations with financial concepts and disciplines. No one involved in modern business and management can afford to miss this book.

*The author is a Chartered Accountant and Senior Lecturer
in Accounting at Manchester Metropolitan University*

1 Introducing accounting

This chapter establishes the main concepts and issues, which are fully explored later.

Objectives	• Understanding profit; • Circuit of capital model; • Types of assets & liabilities.

Introduction

Business context

Business is an exciting and fast changing environment. 'Globalisation' and e-business have created new opportunities and fresh challenges. Accounting concepts, definitions and frameworks need reformulating to make them more relevant and applicable to a high technology, global environment as well as traditional business sectors.

Activities

This chapter introduces the concepts of capital and profit using a worked example and a 'circuit of capital' model. When you have completed this chapter, attempt the two questions at the end, checking your answers against the solutions given. Once the relationship between capital and profit is understood, we progress to accounting terms and definitions (Chapter 2) which are then placed in an overall framework for understanding accountancy and finance (Chapter 3).

Businesses are run for profit; without it they do not survive. Profit is generated by selling a product or service for *more* than the total cost of making or buying it. The more a company sells, the more profit it should make. Measuring the exact amount of profit, however, is not easy. Measuring profit is the main purpose of accounting.

Just making a profit is not enough. Profit has to be sufficient to justify the capital invested in the business. Making a £100,000 profit seems, at first glance, a good result; however, if £10,000,000 (£10 million) of capital had been invested, the profit is not sufficient. The profit only represents a 1% return on the capital. A better return can be earned by simply putting the money in a bank. As well as measuring profit, accounting also measures the amount of capital invested in a business.

Capital is used to buy the equipment, such as computers, and materials, such as stationery, needed to run a business. Capital, therefore, is invested in a range of different types of assets, some of which are long term and some short term. Accounting keeps a record of all the different types of assets a business owns. As well as owning assets, businesses also owe money, e.g. to suppliers. These are termed liabilities. Accounting is a useful tool for managers because it measures:

- Profit
- Capital
- Assets and liabilities

Profit is shown on the profit and loss account. All assets and liabilities are listed on the year-end balance sheet.

> Companies sometimes sell goods for less than cost. Retailers, for example, occasionally sell at a loss in order to gain publicity and attract new customers. On the Internet, DVDs are sometimes sold at a loss to attract new subscribers to a web service. Evan Schwartz (Digital Darwinism, Penguin, 1999, p. 10) reports the fact that copies of the Oscar-winning 'Titanic', which cost the company $15.00, were sold for $9.99. Losses reduce the company's capital.

Circuit of capital

Managing a business can be broken down into four stages:

- Put money into the business;
- Use the money to buy the materials, equipment and people needed;
- Make the product or provide the service;
- Sell the product for more than it cost to make it.

The total amount of money put into the business by the owner is known as **capital**. The first transaction (Step 1) in any new business is the injection of **capital** into the business, usually in the form of cash. Step 2 is using the **capital** to get the resources (materials, people, equipment, etc.) the business needs. Step 3 is making the product. Step 4 is when the **profit** is made, because the goods are sold for more than it cost to make them. At the end of Step 4, the initial **capital** invested has come back and, because of the **profit**, there will be more **capital** than at the start.

Because **capital** comes around in a circle, the four stages are called the 'circuit of capital' (see Figure 1.1).

Step 1

Investing in the business

There are three main sources of finance for business:

- Cash from the owner(s) of the business;
- Reinvesting profit earned by the business;
- Borrowing money from a bank.

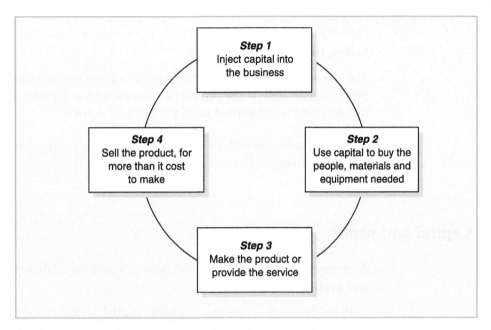

Figure 1.1 The circuit of capital

Most small firms start up with an injection of cash from the owner. This cash may come from the owner's savings or from a redundancy payout. Larger businesses work on a combination of finance from banks and shareholders.

Step 2

Buying what the company needs

Every business needs materials, equipment and people. New businesses usually have to pay cash for materials, but eventually suppliers will offer credit terms. This means the firm does not have to pay for goods immediately. The difficulty with recruiting people is getting those with the right skills and attitude. Employees might be on permanent or short-term contracts, either full or part time.

Equipment can be rented or bought. If it is bought then it becomes an asset, which the business owns. This is called a fixed asset. If it is rented it is not owned, so it cannot be an asset of the business.

Step 3

Making the product or service

A range of industries, including retailing, wholesaling, business services and manufacturing, will be considered. Accounting is applicable in all industries as well as in government, hospitals, schools and charities.

Selling the product or service

The aim is to sell the product for more than it cost the firm to make it. This is how profit is generated. If the product cannot be sold at a profit, the business has no future. Profit is not earned until the product is sold.

> It is better to invest £10 for a year and earn a profit of £1 than to invest £100 million and earn a profit of £1 million.

Capital and profit

As a result of the circuit of capital, there is a definite relationship between **capital** and **profit**:

- If the business is making a **profit**, **capital** at the end of the circuit will be greater than at the start.
- If the business is making a **loss**, **capital** at the end of the circuit will be less than at the start.
- If the company is **breaking even**, **capital** at the end of the circuit will be the same as at the start.

Businesses can be classified into sole traders, partnerships or limited companies. The **profit** earned by a business is owned by the proprietor or shared among the partners or shareholders. The owner(s) may choose to take all or some or none of the profit out of the business. For example, if a small business makes a £50,000 profit, the owner can choose to take all the £50,000, or just £20,000 or even none. Money taken out of the business by a sole trader or partner is called **drawings**, because it is drawn out of the business. Profit taken out of the business by shareholders in a limited company is termed **dividends**.

- If the owner takes all the **profit**, the **capital** at the end is the same as at the start.
- If the owner takes none of the **profit**, the **capital** at the end is higher than at the start.

Because the business is separate from its owner, **capital** and **profit** held by the business are 'owed to the owner' and are both, therefore, liabilities.

Example

Type of business	Starting capital	Profit or loss	Drawings	Finishing capital
Making a small loss	5000	−500	0	4500
Breaking even	5000	0	0	5000
Making a small profit	5000	1000	0	6000
Making a larger profit	5000	3000	500	7500

Many e-businesses have reported losses and, consequently, their capital has decreased rather than increased. Colin Barrow (How To Survive the e-Business Downturn, John Wiley, 2000, p. 172) reports that during the year 2000 Amazon.com, the Internet-based bookseller, made a net loss of $308 million. This reduced shareholders' capital from around $266 million to just $25 million.

Circuit of capital in action

Here is an example of how the circuit of capital works for a fruit & veg. street trader called Mark Flowers. This business does not need a lot of specialist equipment and the overheads are low, so it is not risky.

Follow the four stages of the 'circuit of capital' every day.

Monday

Mark Flowers has a fruit & veg. stall on Albert Square. He puts £500 start-up capital into the business. On the first morning he buys £300 worth of fruit & veg. By the end of the day he has sold all of this for £400.

1. Mark starts with £500 **capital** in cash.
2. All he has to buy is fruit & veg., which costs £300.
3. He offers this product throughout the day.
4. He manages to sell it all for £400, making £100 profit.

He ends the day with £600 capital, made up of the original £500 + £100 profit.

At the end of the first day of trading, Mark's position is as follows:

Assets		*Workings*
Cash	600	(£500 − £300 + £400)
Liabilities		
Opening capital	500	
Profit	100	(£400 − £300)
Closing capital	600	

Make sure you understand where every figure comes from. Note the total of the assets equals the total of the liabilities.

Tuesday

Mark buys a new stall for £100 and £300 of fruit & veg. He sells all the fruit & veg. for £400. He draws out £20.

1. Starts off with £600 **capital**.
2. Buys fixed assets £100 and purchases £300.
3. Works the stall all day (and doesn't employ anyone).
4. Sells all the fruit & veg. for £400 and draws out £20 for his own use.

He ends Tuesday with capital of £680, invested in £100 fixed assets and £580 in cash.

At the end of the second day, Mark's position is as follows:

Assets		Workings
Fixed assets	100	
Cash	580	(£600 − £100 − £300 + £400 − £20)
	680	
Liabilities		
Opening capital	600	*From Monday*
Add: profit	100	(£400 − £300)
Less: drawings	20	
Closing capital	680	*Note:* capital is **not** the same as cash

Make sure you are happy with every figure; if not, go back. *Note:* **Capital** has only gone up £80.

Wednesday

Mark purchases £300 of fruit & veg. and sells it for £350 (Wednesday is a half-day). Draws another £20 out of the business.

1. Starts with £680 c**apital**.
2. Purchases £300.
3. Works all morning.
4. Sells all the fruit & veg. for £350, making a profit of £50, but draws out £20.

He ends up with capital of £710, invested in £100 fixed assets and £610 in cash.

Assets		Workings
Fixed assets	100	
Cash	610	(£580 − £300 + £350 − £20)
	710	
Liabilities		
Opening capital	680	*From Tuesday*
Add: profit	50	(£350 − £300)
Less: drawings	20	
Closing capital	710	

Understand every figure? If not, go back.

Thursday

Mark persuades his supplier to grant him one week of credit. He purchases £300, all on credit, and sells it for £400.

1. Starts with **capital** of £710.
2. Purchases £300 on credit.
3. Works all day.
4. Sells all the goods for £400, making a profit of £100.

He ends the day with capital of £810, invested in fixed assets £100 and cash £1110, and owes creditors £300.

Assets		*Workings*
Fixed assets	100	*Stall*
Cash	1010	*(£610 + £400)*
	1110	*Total*
Liabilities		
Opening capital	710	*From Wednesday*
Profit	100	*(£400 − £300)*
Less: drawings	0	
Closing capital	810	*Subtotal*
Creditors	300	*Owed to supplier*
	1110	*Grand total*

Friday

A very busy day, Mark purchases £500 of fruit & veg. on credit and sells it for £600. He takes out £150 for the weekend.

Assets		*Workings*
Fixed assets	100	
Cash	1460	*(£1010 + £600 − £150)*
	1560	
Liabilities		
Opening capital	810	*From Thursday*
Profit	100	
Less: drawings	150	*Ready for the weekend*
Closing capital	760	
Creditors	800	*Two days' worth*
	1560	

Summarising these five days in numbers gives the following figures, all in £'s.

How much profit has been made?

Sales	2150	*(£400 + £400 + £350 + £400 + £600)*
Less: cost of sales	1700	*(£300 + £300 + £300 + £300 + £500)*
Gross profit	450	

How much capital has been invested in the business?

Opening capital	500	*From day 1*
Add: profit	450	*See above*
Less: drawings	190	*(£20 + £20 + £150)*
Closing capital	760	*(£500 + £450 − £190)*

How has that capital been used?

Assets		
Fixed assets	100	*Stall*
Cash	1460	
Total	1560	

Liabilities		
Creditors	−800	*Two days' worth*
	760	

It is also a useful skill to be able to summarise these figures in words that are clear and easy to understand.

1. Mark Flowers bought a total of £1700 worth of fruit & veg. over the five days. He sold it all for £2150, making a **profit** of £450.
2. Mark started trading with £500 **capital**, which had been increased by £450 of **profit**, but reduced by £190 **drawings**. The resulting closing **capital** was therefore £760.
3. By Friday Mark owned a fixed asset (a stall) which cost £100 and had £1460 in cash. He also owed £800 to creditors.

Note: We have measured the profit, capital, assets and liabilities.

Conclusions

Keep in mind there is more than one issue in business. Not only how much profit, but also how much **capital** was invested to earn that profit, and what was it invested in? Profit is not a difficult concept to understand, but **capital** is more difficult. **Capital** invested in a business is spent on materials and equipment, etc. When goods are sold, the cash spent comes back. If the business is profitable, the **capital** and cash will increase. The **capital** is owed by the business to the owner, so it is a liability. If the owner draws out all the profit, the amount of **capital** at the end of the year is the same as at the start. If all the profit is left in the business, the **capital** at the end is greater than at the start.

There are two questions below for you to attempt. You will probably notice that the answers to the questions are given. Have a quick look at the answer before trying the question. Make sure you attempt the question at least twice, so that you can do it without looking at the answer.

> The amount of capital invested by global companies is huge. For instance Colin Barrow (How to Survive the e-Business Downturn, John Wiley, 2000, p. 17) reports that during 1999 IBM made a net profit of $7712 million on the basis of investing $20,511 million. The sales generated by global companies are also substantial. Major oil companies regularly exceed $200 billion sales per year.

Retro

An entrepreneurial student starts a new business buying second-hand clothes and selling them at a local street market.

Friday

Injects £100 cash into the business. Uses this to buy £100 worth of 'Starsky and Hutch' 1970s style open-collar shirts. Sells all the shirts for £200.

Buys a good-quality clothes rail for £50 and £150 of 'Paul McCartney' T-shirts. Sells the T-shirts for £300.

Buys some second-hand platform shoes for £100. Sells them for £110.

Buys a batch of 'Tom Jones' style frilly shirts for £100 and sells them for £200.

Buys a batch of flared denim jeans for £200. Sells them for £250. Draws out £25.

Buys a batch of cheesecloth shirts for £100 and sells them for £90.

All of the transactions, sales and purchases, are in cash. The student intends to develop the business by selling clothes to university lecturers.

Your task

1. Show the value of assets and liabilities at the end of every day, using the box format we used in the Mark Flowers example.
2. Summarise the week's trading in terms of the amount of profit made, the amount of capital invested in the business and the detail of what the capital was invested in (the assets and liabilities, etc.).
3. Summarise the week's trading in words.

Suggested layout

Friday

Assets   *Workings*
  Fixed assets
  Cash

Liabilities
  Opening capital
  Add: profit
  Less: drawings
  Closing capital

Saturday

Assets   *Workings*
  Fixed assets
  Cash

Liabilities
  Opening capital
  Add: profit
  Less: drawings
  Closing capital

Monday

Assets   *Workings*
  Fixed assets
  Cash

Liabilities
  Opening capital
  Add: profit
  Less: drawings
  Closing capital

Tuesday

Assets   *Workings*
  Fixed assets
  Cash

Liabilities
  Opening capital
  Add: profit
  Less: drawings
  Closing capital

Wednesday

Assets   *Workings*
  Fixed assets
  Cash

Liabilities
  Opening capital
  Add: profit
  Less: drawings
  Closing capital

Thursday

Assets   *Workings*
  Fixed assets
  Cash

Liabilities
  Opening capital
  Add: profit
  Less: drawings
  Closing capital

During the week purchases amounted to £   .
These were all sold for £   .
This gives a gross profit of £   .
At the end of the week fixed assets amounted to £   .
Cash amounted to £   .
The start-up capital was £   .
To this is added profit of £   .
Drawings amounted to £   .
Closing capital at the end of the week was £   .

Carlo Bianchi

Carlo sells slices of melon to tourists in Rome during July and August. Sales are best on hot days when there are many tourists about. All the figures in this question are in €'s.

Monday

Carlo started the business with €100 he earned working as a waiter. He uses this money to buy watermelons, which he sells on the streets.

1. Carlo starts with €100 capital in cash.
2. Buys ready sliced watermelons costing €100.
3. Sells slices of melons all day.
4. Sells all the watermelon for €200, making €100 profit.

Tuesday

Carlo buys catering knives and a chopping board for €75 and learns how to chop the pieces of melon himself.

1. Carlo starts with €200.
2. Buys equipment for €75.
3. Learns how to prepare the product.
4. No melons sold.

Wednesday

1. Carlo starts with €125.
2. Buys watermelon costing €125.
3. Slices it and sells it.
4. Sells all the watermelon for €400, making €275 profit.

Your task

Show the value of assets and liabilities at the end of every day, using the format used in the Mark Flowers example.

Solutions

Retro

Friday

Assets		*Workings*
Fixed assets		
Cash	200	(£100 − £100 + £200)
Liabilities		
Opening capital	100	
Add: profit	100	(£200 − £100)
Less: drawings	0	
Closing capital	200	

Saturday

Assets		Workings
Fixed assets	50	
Cash	300	(£200 − £50 − £150 + £300)
Total	350	

Liabilities		
Opening capital	200	*From Friday*
Add: profit	150	(£300 − £150)
Less: drawings	0	
Closing capital	350	

Monday

Assets		Workings
Fixed assets	50	
Cash	310	(£300 − £100 + £110)
Total	360	

Liabilities		
Opening capital	350	*From Saturday*
Add: profit	10	(£110 − £100)
Less: drawings	0	
Closing capital	360	

Tuesday

Assets		Workings
Fixed assets	50	
Cash	410	(£310 − £100 + £200)
Total	460	

Liabilities		
Opening capital	360	*From Monday*
Add: profit	100	(£200 − £100)
Less: drawings	0	
Closing capital	460	

Wednesday

Assets		Workings
Fixed assets	50	
Cash	435	(£410 − £200 + £250 − £25)
Total	485	

Liabilities		
Opening capital	460	*From Tuesday*
Add: profit	50	(£250 − £200)
Less: drawings	25	
Closing capital	485	

Thursday

Assets		Workings
Fixed assets	50	
Cash	425	(£435 − £100 + £90)
Total	475	

Liabilities		
Opening capital	485	*From Wednesday*
Less: loss	10	(£90 − £100)
Less: drawings	0	
Closing capital	475	

Summarising these five days in numbers gives the following figures, all in £'s.

How much profit has been made?

Sales	1150	(£200 + £300 + £110 + £200 + £250 + £90)
Less: cost of sales	750	(£100 + £150 + £100 + £100 + £200 + £100)
Gross profit	400	

How much capital has been invested in the business?

Opening capital	100	*From day 1*
Add: profit	400	*See above*
Less: drawings	25	Wednesday
Closing capital	475	

How has that capital been used?

Assets	
Fixed assets	50
Cash	425
Total	475

Liabilities	
Creditors	0
	475

During the week, goods worth £750 have been bought. These have been sold for £1150, giving a gross profit of £400.

By the end of the week the business had fixed assets worth £50 and had accumulated cash of £425. The total assets were, therefore, £475.

The business was started with an injection of £100 **capital** in the form of cash. **Profit** of £400 has been added to this, and the owner has drawn £25 for personal use. The closing **capital** was, therefore, £475.

Carlo Bianchi

Monday

Assets   *Workings*
Fixed assets (equipment)
Cash   200   (€100 − €100 + €200)

Liabilities
Opening capital   100
Add: profit   100   (€200 − €100)
Less: drawings   0
Closing capital   200

Tuesday

Assets   *Workings*
Fixed assets   75
Cash   125   (€200 − €75)
                      200
Liabilities
Opening capital   200
Add: profit   0   *No sales*
Less: drawings   0
Closing capital   200

Wednesday

Assets   *Workings*
Fixed assets (equipment)   75
Cash   400   (€125 − €125 + €400)
                          475
Liabilities
Opening capital   200
Add: profit   275   (€400 − €125)
Less: drawings   0
Closing capital   475

2 The language of accounting

This chapter sets out the definitions needed to understand profit and loss accounts and balance sheets.

Objectives	
	● Defining key terms; ● Understanding supply chain; ● Distinguishing cash and credit.

Introduction

Importance of definitions

This chapter focuses on the key definitions needed to understand modern business. As well as learning these definitions, their relevance in particular business contexts needs to be understood. The focus of this chapter is the retail sector and the 'supply chain'. The profit and loss account and the balance sheet are used to illustrate the importance of these key definitions.

Activities

Study the key accounting terms carefully and make sure you understand the significance of the distinction between cash and credit. After completing the in-chapter exercise, use the multiple choice questions at the end of the chapter to test your understanding.

Key accounting terms

The keywords are listed below along with their definitions:

Income	Most **income** is earned from selling goods or services, but there are other sources of **income** like interest received and profit on sale of fixed assets.
Sales	The value of goods and services sold to customers in a year.
Cash sales	**Sales**, which are paid for immediately using notes, coins, cheques, switch cards or credit cards.
Credit sales	**Sales**, which will be paid for by the customer within an agreed period of time, e.g. 60 days.

Debtors	A customer to whom **credit sales** have been made, who has not yet paid for the goods, i.e. a customer who owes the company money.
Expenditure	The costs of running the business week to week and month to month. **Expenditure** does not include long-term investments, i.e. anything lasting more than one year. These are classified as **fixed assets**. **Expenditure** is split into **purchases** and **expenses**.
Purchases	Goods bought to sell at a profit, rather than bought for use in the business.
Cash purchases	**Purchases** of goods for resale, which are paid for immediately in cash or by cheque.
Credit purchases	**Purchases** of goods for resale, which may be paid for within an agreed time limit, e.g. one week or four weeks.
Cost of sales	The cost of purchasing the goods sold. Often referred to as costs of goods sold (COGS).
Expenses	All the **expenditures**, which are not **purchases**. Everything bought not to sell at a profit but to support the profit-making activity, e.g. rent, insurance, management salaries, advertising, promotions, bank charges, overdraft interest, travel expenses, postage, stationery, etc. **Expenses** are often referred to as overheads.
Assets	Items which the business owns. Normally split into **fixed** and **current assets**. **Fixed assets** are retained for more than one year, e.g. motor vehicles, computers, etc. **Current assets** get used up much more quickly, e.g. stock. The most important **current asset** is **cash**. **Debtors** are also a **current asset**.
Liabilities	Items owed by the business. There are long-term liabilities such as bank loans and short-term liabilities (**current liabilities**) such as creditors, overdrafts and loans.
Capital	Money invested in the business by the owner, and hence owed by the business to the owner, i.e. a **liability**.
Drawings	Money or goods drawn out of the business by the owner. **Drawings** reduce **capital**.
Creditors	Suppliers to whom the business owes money. These may be for purchases or expenses. Like **capital**, creditors are a particular type of **liability**.
Stock	The value of the **purchases** left in the warehouse at the end of the year. Goods bought but not yet sold.
Cash	The total of all the money in the current account, on deposit, in foreign banks and in the petty cash tin.

Overdraft	When money goes out faster than it comes in, the amount of **cash** in the bank reduces. Eventually the company will run out of cash and become overdrawn. An overdraft is a **liability** because the company owes money to the bank.
Petty cash	Small amounts of notes and coins kept on business premises to meet **expenses** such as tea, coffee, birthday cakes.
Fixed assets	Equipment bought by the company to use in the business for more than one year. Can also include intangibles such as patents, trademarks and software. Sometimes referred to as 'capital expenditure'.
Current assets	**Stock + debtors + cash** (the total of the three figures).
Current liabilities	**Creditors** + overdraft.
Net current assets	**Current assets** less **current liabilities**. Sometimes referred to as 'working capital'.
Gross profit	The difference between **sales** and the cost of goods sold (cost of sales). The profit generated from buying and selling.
Net profit	**Gross profit** less **expenses**, which is the same as the excess of **income** over **expenditure**.

The impact of taxation is ignored in all these definitions. Within some companies slightly different definitions are used. For instance, the acquisition of a fixed asset is sometimes referred to as a 'capital expenditure'. The term expenditure should be reserved for transactions with a one-year impact. Capital expenditure will be referred to as fixed assets.

Supply chain

Goods pass through many firms before they reach consumers. This is referred to as the 'supply chain'. A simple model of the supply chain is as follows:

- Manufacture
- Distribution
- Wholesale
- Retail

Manufacturers make goods and sell them to distributors. Distributors transport the goods around the country and sell them to wholesalers. Wholesalers sell to retailers, who in turn sell to consumers (see Figure 2.1).

When retailers sell goods to consumers, it is usually a **cash sale**. The goods are paid for using notes, coins, cheques, switch cards or credit cards. These are all different forms of **cash**. All the other sales in the supply chain are usually **credit sales**. When manufacturers sell to distributors, this is usually a **credit sale**. When distributors sell to wholesalers, this is usually a **credit sale**. Sales to consumers are **cash sales**, while business to business (b2b) sales are **credit sales**. **Credit sales**

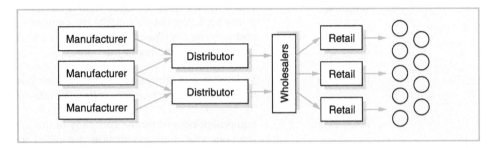

Figure 2.1 Supply chain

are, therefore, more common than **cash sales**. **Cash sales** usually only happen when retailers sell to consumers.

Credit sales always lead to **debtors**. This is because a customer does not pay **cash** for a **credit sale**. As a result, the customer owes the money for the goods. The amount the customer owes is referred to as **debtors**. Because **credit sales** are common, **debtors** are also common. **Debtors** have to be carefully monitored because some **debtors** are slow payers, or will not pay at all.

As well as **credit sales**, **credit purchases** are also common. When retailers buy from wholesalers they usually do not have to pay **cash**, they can take goods on credit. These have to be paid for in, say, one month's time. When wholesalers buy goods from distributors, they do not have to pay **cash**, they can take goods on credit. In the same way that **credit sales** lead to **debtors**, **credit purchases** lead to **creditors**. Most companies have both **debtors** and **creditors**.

The 'supply chain' is an important idea. It focuses attention on the difference between an immediate customer and the ultimate consumer of goods, further down the supply chain. It also focuses attention on the difference between an immediate supplier and the original manufacturer of materials, components and equipment. One strategy for increasing profit is cutting out the intermediaries. If a firm can deal directly with the ultimate consumer, and/or the original manufacturer, profits will be higher. The Internet makes it easier to deal direct with ultimate consumers and original manufacturers.

> Airlines have used the Internet to sell direct to customers, cutting out travel agents. Some airlines offer a lower price for a ticket bought on the Internet. Others refuse to sell through agents and only sell through the Internet.

Some supply chains are more complex than others. Compact discs go through the following supply chain before getting to your CD player:

- Polymer production
- Blank disc manufacture
- Disc recording
- Packaging
- Distribution
- Wholesale
- Retail

Although consumers pay **cash** when they buy CDs, all the other stages of the supply chain are on credit.

Cash and credit

Some businesses make **cash sales**, e.g. retailers, others **credit sales**. **Cash sales** are best because the **cash** is received immediately. Some businesses have to make **cash purchases**, others are able to negotiate **credit purchases**. **Credit purchases** are best because the company does not have to pay immediately. There are four possible situations:

- **Cash sales** and **cash purchases**;
- **Cash sales** and **credit purchases**;
- **Credit sales** and **cash purchases**;
- **Credit sales** and **credit purchases**.

Most businesses make **credit sales** and **credit purchases** and, as a result, they are owed money by customers (**debtors**) and they owe money to suppliers (**creditors**). Retailers are in a strong position, they make **cash sales** and **credit purchases**. They receive **cash** immediately, and do not have to pay suppliers for a few weeks. This is beneficial for cash flow, but profit margins are tight, e.g. 2%.

The worst position is to make **credit sales** and have to pay **cash** for **purchases**. This is often the position new businesses find themselves in, because suppliers will not offer credit to new firms (because they have no trading history) and customers insist on getting credit (because this is normal practice in the b2b sector). New businesses, therefore, start off at a disadvantage.

It is quite difficult to think of an example of an established business that has to pay **cash** for **purchases** and has to give credit to customers. If you can think of a business in this position, make a note of it in the space below.

Did you try? If not, go back. You should not be thinking of a retail business, because these usually have **cash sales**. Concentrate on the b2b sector. Another clue is that wages and salaries always have to be paid in cash, weekly or monthly. Can you think of a business that buys people's time, pays them week by week, and sells that time to companies?

A recruitment agency supplying temporary staff fits the criteria. The 'temps' have to be paid weekly, but the companies to which the staff are supplied only pay at the end of the month, or even two months. Money goes out every week and doesn't come back in for a month or two. Although these agencies have to wait for cash, the profit margin can be substantial, e.g. 25%. Most companies have both **debtors** and **creditors**, i.e. **credit sales** and **credit purchases**.

Profit and loss account and balance sheet

The definitions detailed above play an important role in the profit and loss (P&L) account and balance sheet. Consider the example below relating to a 'high street' retailer with stores in all major towns and cities in the UK. The stores sell a full range of food, drink and other household items, to consumers who pay in cash.

Klick Stores

Trading and P&L Account
Year Ended 31st December 200X

	£ million	£ million
Sales		2800.0
Cost of sales		2403.6
Gross profit		396.4
Less: expenses		
Distribution	246.6	
Administration	38.0	
		284.6
Net profit		111.8

During the year the company has made a profit of £111.8 million. Cash of £2800 million was received from customers and £2403.6 million was spent buying goods to sell at a profit. The total overheads (expenses) were £284.6 million.

The balance sheet below shows all the different types of assets and liabilities.

Klick Stores

Balance Sheet
As at 31st December 200X

	£ million	£ million
Fixed assets		527.4
Current assets		
Stock	148.4	
Debtors	7.9	
Cash	56.3	
	212.6	
Current liabilities		
Creditors	285.4	
Net current assets		−72.8
Net assets		454.6

The company has £56.3 million in the bank, as well as £148.4 million in stock. Equipment owned by the company is worth £527.4 million. The only liability seems to be to suppliers. These are owed £285.4 million.

To test your understanding of the definitions, answer the following questions about the Klick Stores figures in the space provided.

Question	Answer
How much are Klick Stores' **sales** in the year?	
Are the sales **cash sales** or **credit sales**?	
How much are Klick Stores' total **expenses** in the year?	
How much **profit** has been made in the year?	
Are **purchases** cash or credit?	
What do you think are the main **fixed assets** of the company?	
How much **cash** has the company accumulated over the years?	
You would expect **debtors** in a retail business to be much lower than **stock** (true or false)?	
Who are the **debtors**? Have a guess.	
Are Klick Stores' **fixed assets** greater than its **current assets** (yes or no)?	

Answers are given at the end of this chapter.

Conclusions

Accounting uses specific definitions of certain words, like **capital**. These specific definitions have to be learned in order to understand accounting. The definitions fit together under four main headings, as follows:

Income	Expenditure	Assets	Liabilities
Sales	Purchases	Fixed assets	Creditors
Others	Expenses	Current assets	Capital
		Stock	
		Debtors	
		Cash	

Use the multiple choice questions below to test your understanding. Do not start Chapter 3 until you have mastered all of these definitions.

Multiple choice questions

Tick the box next to your answer.

1. **Expenditure** includes?
   - ☐ Purchases and fixed assets
   - ☐ Drawings and capital
   - ☐ Purchases and expenses
   - ☐ Capital and profits
   - ☐ Cash purchases and liabilities

2. Which of the following is not a **cash sale?**
   - ☐ Sales paid for by cheque
   - ☐ Sales paid for in notes and coins
   - ☐ Sales paid for with a credit card
   - ☐ Sales paid for with a switch card
   - ☐ Sales paid for at an agreed future date

3. **Stock** is?
   - ☐ The quantity of goods at the end of the year
   - ☐ The total value of all the goods purchased during the year
   - ☐ Items purchased to sell at a profit
   - ☐ The value of goods left over at the end of the year
   - ☐ Fixed assets acquired during the year

4. Which of the following is not an **asset?**
   - ☐ Creditors
   - ☐ Fixed assets
   - ☐ Cash
   - ☐ Debtors
   - ☐ Petty cash

5. **Capital** is?
   - ☐ The total amount of cash in the business
   - ☐ The amount the bank has invested in the business
   - ☐ Total of the fixed assets and current assets
   - ☐ The total amount the owner has invested in the business
   - ☐ The total amount owed by the business to the bank

6. Which of these is the most favourable combination?
   - ☐ Cash purchases and credit sales
   - ☐ Credit purchases and no sales
   - ☐ Credit purchases and credit sales
   - ☐ Credit purchases and cash sales
   - ☐ Cash purchases and cash sales

7. **Credit purchases** always lead to?
   - ☐ Fixed assets
   - ☐ Debtors
   - ☐ Drawings
   - ☐ Creditors
   - ☐ Expenditure

8. **Interest paid** to a bank is an example of?
   - ☐ Income
   - ☐ Liabilities
   - ☐ Expenses
   - ☐ Drawings
   - ☐ Fixed assets

9. **Debtors** are?
   - ☐ The owner
   - ☐ The bank
   - ☐ Suppliers
   - ☐ Employees
   - ☐ Customers

10. **Purchases** are?
   - ☐ Goods bought to give to charity
   - ☐ Goods bought to sell at a profit
   - ☐ Fixed assets
   - ☐ Materials used in production
   - ☐ Anything the company buys

11. Which of the following is not a **liability**?
   - ☐ Bank loan
   - ☐ Creditor
   - ☐ Overdraft
   - ☐ Capital
   - ☐ Debtors

12. The impact of **drawings** is to?
   - ☐ Increase purchases
   - ☐ Increase capital
   - ☐ Reduce capital
   - ☐ No impact on capital
   - ☐ Increase fixed assets

13. What is meant by the term 'capital expenditure'?
   - ☐ Buying fixed assets
   - ☐ Selling fixed assets
   - ☐ Increasing capital
   - ☐ Increasing purchases
   - ☐ Borrowing money

14. Which of the following sells to the final consumer of goods?
   - ☐ Manufacturer
   - ☐ Distributor
   - ☐ Wholesaler
   - ☐ Retailer
   - ☐ Foreign suppliers

15. Which of these is not a particular type of **cash**?
   - ☐ Money in the bank
   - ☐ Petty cash
   - ☐ Money in a deposit account
   - ☐ Money in a foreign bank
   - ☐ Stock

16. What is the definition of **gross profit**?
   - ☐ Sales less expenses
   - ☐ Sales less cost of sales
   - ☐ Sales less purchases
   - ☐ Sales less cash
   - ☐ Capital less drawings

17. What is the difference between a **fixed** and **current asset**?
- ☐ Current assets are a type of liability
- ☐ Current assets appear on the balance sheet
- ☐ Current assets last for more than one year
- ☐ Fixed assets last for less than one year
- ☐ Fixed assets last for more than one year, current assets last for less than one year

18. **Credit sales** always lead to?
- ☐ Creditors
- ☐ Debtors
- ☐ Stock
- ☐ Fixed assets
- ☐ Capital

19. Working capital is?
- ☐ Stock + debtors + cash
- ☐ Creditors + overdraft
- ☐ Current assets less current liabilities
- ☐ Fixed assets + current assets
- ☐ Current liabilities + long-term loans

20. Which of these is not a type of **fixed asset**?
- ☐ Delivery van owned by the business
- ☐ IT equipment owned by the business
- ☐ Retail premises owned by the business
- ☐ Stock owned by the business
- ☐ Filing cabinet owned by the business

Tip: Take your time with multiple choice questions and pay attention to detail.

Multiple choice answers

	Correct answer	Comment
1	Purchases and expenses	This was an easy one. If you were not sure of the answer, go back and look at the definitions again.
2	Sales paid for at an agreed future date	The definition of **cash** includes some items that you might not be accustomed to think of as **cash**. Sales paid for by cheque, credit card or switch card are **cash sales**, as far as the company selling the goods is concerned. If a customer buys goods using a credit card, the shop receives **cash** from the credit card operator immediately. The customer owes the credit card operator, not the retailer.
3	The value of goods left over at the end of the year	**Stock** is not the quantity of the goods, it is the value of them. **Stock** is the portion of purchases not sold during the year.
4	Creditors	**Creditors** are suppliers to whom the company owes money. Because the company owes money, **creditors** are a **liability**. All the others are **assets** of different types.

5	The total amount the owner has invested in the business	If you thought the answer was **cash**, you have missed an important point. **Cash** is not **capital**. Go back to Chapter 1 if you are unclear about this.
6	Credit purchases and cash sales	Because money is received immediately, but not paid out for a while. Most retail businesses are in this situation.
7	Creditors	**Credit purchases** means that a company buys goods to sell at a profit, but does not have to pay for them immediately. Goods which are not paid for immediately are a **liability**, termed **creditors**.
8	Expenses	Interest is a very common example of an overhead or **expense**. The loan or overdraft relating to the interest is a **liability**.
9	Customers	**Debtors** are customers who owe the company money.
10	Goods bought to sell at a profit	You might have been tempted by 'materials' here. At the moment we are dealing with retail and wholesale companies. When we get on to manufacturing you will see where materials fit in.
11	Debtors	**Debtors** are an **asset** because they reflect the right to receive **cash** from a customer.
12	Reduce capital	**Drawings** are the opposite of putting money into the business.
13	Buying fixed assets	A confusing term because 'expenditure' should be a term reserved for transactions impacting in less than one year.
14	Retailer	All the others sell to companies rather than consumers.
15	Stock	All the others are different forms of **cash**.
16	Sales less cost of sales	**Cost of sales** is the cost of buying the goods, which have been sold. **Purchases**, on the other hand, is the amount that has been bought.
17	Fixed assets last for more than one year, current assets last for less than one year	Any piece of equipment which lasts for more than one year is a **fixed asset**.
18	Debtors	An easy one.

19	Current assets less current liabilities	Working capital is another term for **net current assets**.
20	Stock owned by the business	All the others are types of equipment which last more than one year.

Read my comments carefully. You can learn a lot from where you went wrong. Make sure you are clear about all the definitions before you progress to Chapter 3.

Klick Stores answers

Question	Answer
How much are Klick Stores' **sales** in the year?	£2,800,000,000, which can also be termed £2.8 billion. A substantial figure.
Are the sales **cash sales** or **credit sales**?	All retail businesses make **cash sales**.
How much are Klick Stores' total **expenses** in the year?	£284,600,000, the figure from the right-hand column, is the total **expenses**.
How much **profit** has been made in the year?	The bottom line figure, £111,800,000.
Are **purchases** cash or credit?	**Credit purchases** because of the large **creditors** on the balance sheet.
What do you think are the main **fixed assets** of the company?	Shops, warehouses, delivery lorries, shop fixtures, tills, computer hardware and software, etc.
How much **cash** has the company accumulated over the years?	£56,300,000.
You would expect **debtors** in a retail business to be much lower than **stock** (true or false)?	True, there are little or no **debtors** in a retail business, but there is always **stock** in the shops.
Who are the **debtors**? Have a guess.	Customers pay **cash**, so they do not owe the company any money. Many retailers grant concessions, which are like shops within the shop. **Debtors** probably relate to concessions owing rent to Klick Stores.
Are Klick Stores' **fixed assets** greater than its **current assets** (yes or no)?	Yes, **fixed assets** are greater: £527 million compared to £212 million.

3 The accounting framework

This chapter sets out a framework for understanding and calculating profits, assets and liabilities.

Objectives

- Accounting framework;
- Trial balance format;
- Spreadsheet format;
- Opening and closing balances;
- Loans and interest.

Introduction

Importance of the framework

If you are in a business meeting or giving a presentation, you need a picture in your mind of how company finances work. This picture will give you the confidence to ask and answer questions logically and professionally. The picture you need is termed the 'accounting framework', which consists of four elements: **income**, **expenditure**, **assets** and **liabilities**. All the definitions given in Chapter 2 fit logically into the accounting framework.

Activities and outcomes

This chapter contains a number of worked examples illustrating the application of the accounting framework. The link between the accounting framework and information technology is also examined here. As well as multiple choice questions, there are some end of chapter questions applying the accounting framework to different types of business situations. After completing this chapter you will have a robust framework for understanding the role of accounting in modern business.

The accounting framework

Modern accounting is based on four elements: income, expenditure, assets and liabilities. These make up the accounting framework as follows:

Income	Expenditure
Sales	Purchases
Other	Expenses
Assets	**Liabilities**
Fixed assets	Capital
Current assets	Loans
Stock	Creditors
Debtors	
Cash	

To keep the four elements in balance, every business transaction has two aspects. For example, when **capital** is injected into a new business, **cash**, an **asset**, increases and **capital**, a **liability**, also increases.

If some **cash** is used to make **purchases**, **cash**, an **asset**, decreases and **purchases**, an **expenditure**, increases. If a **cash sale** is made, **cash**, an **asset**, increases and **sales**, an **income**, increases. No transaction ever has just one aspect: there must always be two.

When a new business is started, it needs **cash** to buy materials, people and equipment, etc. When an entrepreneur invests money in a new business, **cash**, an **asset**, increases. Can you say which **liability** also increases when an entrepreneur puts money into a business? Write your answer in the space below.

Did you have a go? The answer was **capital**. **Capital** is a liability because it is owed to the person who started the business.

Accounting framework in action

Consider these 12 transactions for a new company, called Mr. H. Bean Winesellers:

No.	Date	Details
1	1st March	Mr. H. Bean paid a £5000 cheque into a business bank account
2	2nd March	Bought goods (wine) for £200, paid by cheque
3	3rd March	Bought goods on credit £1200 from H. Lomax
4	4th March	Sold goods (wine) for £800, cheque received
5	5th March	Sold goods on credit £1200 to Oliver Reed
6	6th March	Paid rent £955 by cheque
7	9th March	Bought a cash register for £1200 on credit from CBM Ltd.
8	10th March	Paid wages £780 by cheque
9	11th March	Bought goods on credit £5920 from W. Gould
10	12th March	Oliver Reed pays for goods with a £1200 cheque
11	15th March	Bought goods £1650 on credit from H. Lomax
12	16th March	Made payment £750 by cheque to H. Lomax

Take a fresh piece of paper and map out a box format like this:

Income	Expenditure
Assets	**Liabilities**

Try to fit each of the 12 transactions into the accounting framework. Make sure you work out the *two* sides of each transaction.

The answers are all given below, but attempt the task yourself, before looking at the solutions.

Transaction 1

Income	Expenditure
None	None
Assets	**Liabilities**
Cash = £5000	Capital = £5000

Notes

(a) This is Step 1 of the circuit of capital (see Chapter 1). **Capital** is a **liability** because the business owes the money back to the owner.

(b) **Cash**, an **asset**, increases by £5000 and **capital**, a **liability**, increases by £5000. This shows the two aspects of the transaction. The good side is that the business has got the money (**asset**) it needs and the bad side is that it has to pay it back (**liability**). The total of **assets** is equal to the total of **liabilities**.

(c) This is the only time at which **capital** = **cash**. Straight away the **cash** will be used to buy what the company needs, Step 2 of the circuit of capital. **Capital** will never again be the same as **cash.**

Transaction 2

Income	Expenditure
None	Purchase = £200
Assets	**Liabilities**
Cash = £4800	Capital = £5000

Notes

(a) This transaction results in money flowing out of the business. As a result, **cash** decreases by £200 to £4800 and **liabilities** are not affected. Because money is flowing out of the business, some sort of **expenditure** is going on. Because the goods are being bought for resale, it is a **purchases** type of **expenditure**.

(b) **Cash** decreases by £200 and **purchases** increases by £200.

(c) These goods have been bought, to sell at a profit. Because the goods have not yet been sold, we are unsure if a profit will be earned. The intention is to quickly dispose of these goods at a profit; therefore, the goods do not get classified as **stock**. There is little point recording them as **stock** today, when they may come straight out of **stock** tomorrow.

(d) The total of the **assets** no longer equals the total of the **liabilities** because profit has not yet been calculated. When profit is calculated and added to capital, the **assets** and **liabilities** will be equal.

Transaction 3

Income	Expenditure
None	Purchase = £200
	Purchase = £1200
Assets	**Liabilities**
Cash = £4800	Capital = £5000
	Creditor = £1200

Notes

(a) Mr. H. Bean seems to have persuaded a supplier to provide him with credit. He has taken advantage of this and has made **purchases** without having to pay for them. Because the goods are not paid for yet, Mr. H. Bean stills owes the supplier, which means a **liability, creditors**.

(b) This is a **purchase**, rather than an **expense**, because the goods are bought to sell at a profit. No money changes hands in this transaction, so **cash** is not altered.

(c) **Purchases** increases by £1200 and **creditors** increases by £1200.

Transaction 4

Income	Expenditure
Sale = £800	Purchase = £200
	Purchase = £1200

Assets	Liabilities
Cash = £5600	Capital = £5000
	Creditor = £1200

Note

(a) This sale is received in **cash**, so **cash** increases by £800 and **sales** increases by £800.

Transaction 5

Income	Expenditure
Sale = £800	Purchase = £200
Sale = £1200	Purchase = £1200

Assets	Liabilities
Cash = £5600	Capital = £5000
Debtor = £1200	Creditor = £1200

Note

(a) No **cash** is received, so it is unchanged, but a new asset called **debtors** appears. Mr. H. Bean seems to be making a healthy profit.

(b) **Sales**, an **income**, increases by £1200 and **debtors**, an **asset**, increases by £1200.

Income	Expenditure
Sale = £800	Purchase = £200
Sale = £1200	Purchase = £1200
	Rent = £955

Assets	Liabilities
Cash = £4645	Capital = £5000
Debtor = £1200	Creditor = £1200

Note

(a) Rent is **expenditure**, but it is an **expense** rather than a **purchase**. **Cash** decreases by £955 and **expenses** (**rent**) increases by £955.

Income	Expenditure
Sale = £800	Purchase = £200
Sale = £1200	Purchase = £1200
	Rent = £955

Assets	Liabilities
Cash = £4645	Capital = £5000
Debtor = £1200	Creditor = £1200 (H. Lomax)
Cash register = £1200	Creditor = £1200 (CBM)

Note

(a) Because Mr. H. Bean has not paid **cash** for the equipment, **creditors** increases by £1200. Another **asset**, a **fixed asset**, has also been created. This is a **fixed asset**, rather than **expenditure**, because a cash register is bound to last more than one year.

(b) **Purchases** are not affected because the cash register has been bought to use in the business, not to be sold at a profit.

Transaction 8

Income	Expenditure
Sale = £800	Purchase = £200
Sale = £1200	Purchase = £1200
	Rent = £955
	Wages = £780

Assets	Liabilities
Cash = £3865	Capital = £5000
Debtor = £1200	Creditor = £1200 (H. Lomax)
Cash register = £1200	Creditor = £1200 (CBM)

Note

(a) **Cash** decreases by £780 and **expenses** (wages) increases by £780.

Transaction 9

Income	Expenditure
Sale = £800	Purchase = £200
Sale = £1200	Purchase = £1200
	Rent = £955
	Wages = £780
	Purchase = £5920

Assets	Liabilities
Cash = £3865	Capital = £5000
Debtor = £1200	Creditor = £1200 (H. Lomax)
Cash register = £1200	Creditor = £1200 (CBM)
	Creditor = £5920 (W. Gould)

Note

(a) **Creditors** increase by £5920, and **purchases** increase by £5920. **Cash** does *not* change, because no **cash** has been paid.

Transaction 10

Income	Expenditure
Sale = £800	Purchase = £200
Sale = £1200	Purchase = £1200
	Rent = £955
	Wages = £780
	Purchase = £5920

Assets	Liabilities
Cash = £5065	Capital = £5000
Debtors = £0	Creditor = £1200 (H. Lomax)
Cash register = £1200	Creditor = £1200 (CBM)
	Creditor = £5920 (W. Gould)

Note

(a) Oliver Reed is paying for the goods that he acquired during transaction 5 on 5th March. These goods have already been accounted for as a **sale**. All we have to do now is account for the receipt of the **cash** relating to this **sale**. **Cash** increases by £1200 and **debtors** decreases by £1200. Both aspects of this transaction are within the **assets** heading.

Transaction 11

Income	Expenditure
Sale = £800	Purchase = £200
Sale = £1200	Purchase = £1200
	Rent = £955
	Wages = £780
	Purchase = £5920
	Purchase = £1650

Assets	Liabilities
Cash = £5065	Capital = £5000
Debtors = £0	Creditor = £1200 (H. Lomax)
Cash register = £1200	Creditor = £1200 (CBM)
	Creditor = £5920 (W. Gould)
	Creditor = £1650 (H. Lomax)

Note

(a) Mr. H. Bean is buying some more wine on credit. Cash does not change hands. **Creditors** increase by £1650 and **purchases** increases by £1650.

Transaction 12

Income	Expenditure
Sale = £800	Purchase = £200
Sale = £1200	Purchase = £1200
	Rent = £955
	Wages = £780
	Purchase = £5920
	Purchase = £1650
Assets	**Liabilities**
Cash = £4315	Capital = £5000
Debtors = £0	Creditor = £450 (H. Lomax)
Cash register = £1200	Creditor = £1200 (CBM)
	Creditor = £5920 (W. Gould)
	Creditor = £1650 (H. Lomax)

Note

(a) This represents a part payment for the goods acquired during transaction 3 on 3rd March. **Cash** decreases by £750 and **creditors** decreases by £750.

Go over the transactions again, and make sure you know where *every* figure comes from. The running totals up to transaction 12 are as follows:

Running totals up to transaction 12

Income	Expenditure
Sales = £2000	Purchases = £8970
	Expenses = £1735
Assets	**Liabilities**
Cash = £4315	Capital = £5000
Debtors = £0	Creditors = £9220
Cash register = £1200	

Trial balance format

Businesses deal with large numbers of transactions. In a busy store there may be over 1000 sales transactions in an hour. It can become difficult to list all of these transactions individually. It is much easier to keep a running total. Similarly, businesses also deal with a large number of **purchases** and **expenses** transactions. It is much easier to keep a running total of **purchases** and **expenses** than to list the individual transactions.

Computerised accounting is much easier and faster than bookkeeping, especially when dealing with large volumes of transactions. Accounting software presents the user with choices such as:

- Cash sales
- Credit sales
- Cash purchases
- Credit purchases
- Expenses
- Fixed assets

These are presented on easy-to-use screens.

The user selects the transaction type and inputs the value of the transaction, date and reference number, e.g. cheque number or invoice number. The computer automatically updates the accounting framework. It is possible to print a list of transactions; however, it is time-consuming and not particularly useful. It is simpler to print the totals of all the different transaction types. This is termed the trial balance. It displays the total **sales**, total **purchases** and total **expenses**, etc.

Look back at Mr. H. Bean's transaction 12 and match up the figures with the trial balance below:

Mr. H. Bean Winesellers

Trial Balance

	£ Debit	£ Credit
Sales		2,000
Purchases	8,970	
Expenses	1,735	
Fixed assets	1,200	
Stock	0	
Debtors	0	
Cash	4,315	
Creditors		9,220
Capital		5,000
Total	**16,220**	**16,220**

Another benefit of the computerised trial balance is that it gives all the information needed to prepare the **trading and profit and loss account** and the **balance sheet**. It provides a link between the accounting framework and the presentation of the company's results in the profit and loss account and the balance sheet.

The columns of the trial balance are headed up 'debit' and 'credit'. This refers to the double entry bookkeeping system, which underpins accounting. The increase of an **asset**, or an **expenditure**, is referred to as a debit and an increase of a **liability**, or **income**, is referred to as a credit. **Sales** and **liabilities**, such as **creditors**, are credits and **purchases**, **expenses** and **assets**, like **debtors** and **cash**, are debits.

Spreadsheet format

As well as the box format and trial balance, spreadsheets can be used to keep a record of business transactions. This is achieved by placing every accounting definition in a column of its own and putting each transaction in a row of its own. This is how Mr. H. Bean Winesellers' transactions would be set out:

Mr. H. Bean Winesellers

Solution

Ref.	Type	Income		Expenditure		Assets				Liabilities	
		Sales	Other	Purchases	Expenses	Equip.	Stock	Debtors	Cash	Capital	Creditors
1	Start up								5000	5000	
2	Cash purchase			200					−200		
3	Credit purchase			1200							1200
4	Cash sale	800							800		
5	Credit sale	1200						1200			
6	Rent				955				−955		
7	Cash register					1200					1200
8	Wages				780				−780		
9	Credit purchase			5920							5920
10	Cash received							−1200	1200		
11	Credit purchase			1650							1650
12	Cash paid								−750		−750
	Total	2000	0	8970	1735	1200	0	0	4315	5000	9220

The figures in the trial balance and the totals of the spreadsheet are the same. They represent different ways of presenting the same data.

Opening and closing balances

Assets and liabilities are cumulative, whereas sales, purchases and expenses relate to one year. At the beginning of the next financial year sales, purchases and expenses start from zero. If a business owns some equipment, e.g. a computer, it does not stop owning it at the end of the year. An asset is something a business has until it is sold off or worn out. Assets and liabilities are, therefore, cumulative. At the end of the financial year cash, fixed assets, loans, etc. do not disappear; rather, they get carried forward to the next financial year.

Income and expenditure are the opposite, they always relate to a particular year. Sales are the sales for the year, purchases are the purchases for the year. *Everything* on the trading and profit and loss account relates to a specific year. When the financial year comes to an end, income and expenditure go back to zero. They are not carried forward to the following year.

On the first day of a new business, all **income, expenditure, assets** and **liabilities** are zero. In every subsequent year, **income** and **expenditure** start from zero, and **assets** and **liabilities** start from the figure brought forward from the previous year. A computerised accounting system will automatically transfer the closing **asset** and **liability** balances into the new financial year. These are called the opening balances or the balances brought forward:

- Balance carried forward = the amount at the end of the year;
- Balance brought forward = the amount at the beginning of the year.

Loans and interest

The only source of finance so far considered is **capital**. Bank loans are another important source of finance. This is how loans and interest are dealt with in the accounting framework:

Bank loan	An **asset, cash** increases	A **liability, loan** increases
Loan interest paid	An **asset, cash** decreases	An **expenditure, expenses** (interest) increases
Interest charged (not yet paid)	A **liability, loan** increases	An **expenditure, expenses** (interest) increases
Loan capital repaid	A **liability, loan** decreases	An **asset, cash** decreases
Interest received	An **asset, cash** increases	An **income, other** increases

Consider starting up a new company with capital of £5000 and a loan of £1000:

Ref.	Type	Income		Expenditure		Assets				Liabilities	
		Sales	Other	Purchases	Expenses	Equip.	Stock	Debtors	Cash	Capital	Loans
1	Capital								5000	5000	
2	Loan								1000		1000
	Total								6000	5000	1000

An **asset, cash**, increases by £6000, while a **liability, capital**, increases by £5000 and a **liability, loans**, increases by £1000.

The bank charges the first month's interest of £25, which the business pays in cash:

Ref.	Type	Income		Expenditure		Assets				Liabilities	
		Sales	Other	Purchases	Expenses	Equip.	Stock	Debtors	Cash	Capital	Loans
	Start balance								6000	5000	1000
3	Interest paid				25				−25		
	Total				25				5975	5000	1000

An **asset, cash**, decreases by £25, and **expenditure, expenses** (interest), increases by £25.

The bank charges the second month's interest of £25, which the business has not yet paid:

Ref.	Type	Income		Expenditure		Assets				Liabilities	
		Sales	Other	Purchases	Expenses	Equip.	Stock	Debtors	Cash	Capital	Loans
	Start balance								6000	5000	1000
3	Interest paid				25				−25		
4	Interest charged				25						25
	Total				50				5975	5000	1025

A **liability, loan**, increases by £25, and **expenditure, expenses** (interest), increases by £25.

The bank pays the business interest of £120:

Ref.	Type	Income		Expenditure		Assets				Liabilities	
		Sales	Other	Purchases	Expenses	Equip.	Stock	Debtors	Cash	Capital	Loans
	Start balance								6000	5000	1000
3	Interest paid				25				−25		
4	Interest charged				25						25
5	Interest received		120						120		
	Total		120		50				6095	5000	1025

An **asset, cash**, increases by £120, and **income, other**, increases by £120.

Conclusions

Here is a summary of the two aspects of some common business transactions within the accounting framework:

1. *Cash sale*
An **asset, cash** increases — An **income, sales** increases

2. *Credit sale*
An **asset, debtors** increases — An **income, sales** increases

3. *Cash purchase*
An **asset, cash** decreases — An **expenditure, purchases** increases

4. *Purchases on credit*
A **liability, creditors** increases — An **expenditure, purchases** increases

5. *Expense paid in cash, e.g. wages*
An **asset, cash** decreases — An **expenditure, expenses** (wages) increases

6. *Receipt of cash from debtor*
An **asset, cash** increases — An **asset, debtors** decreases

7. *Pay cash to creditors*
An **asset, cash** decreases — A **liability, creditors** decreases

8. *Drawings in cash*	
An **asset, cash** decreases	A **liability, capital** decreases
9. *Injection of capital*	
An **asset, cash** increases	A **liability, capital** increases
10. *Acquiring a new fixed asset for cash*	
An **asset, cash** decreases	An **asset, fixed assets** increases
11. *Paying loan interest*	
An **asset, cash** decreases	An **expenditure, expenses** (interest) increases
12. *Taking out a loan*	
An **asset, cash** increases	A **liability, loan** increases
13. *Interest received*	
An **asset, cash** increases	An **income, other** increases
14. *Repayment of loan capital*	
An **asset, cash** decreases	A **liability, loans** decreases

If the Managing Director asks your opinion about investing £1,000,000 in a new computer system, you can answer as follows using the accounting framework:

- **Cash** will decrease by £1,000,000 and **fixed assets** will increase by £1,000,000.
- If the company has enough **cash**, no problem; if not, the money will have to be borrowed.
- If the money is borrowed an **asset** called **cash** increases by £1,000,000 and a **liability** called loan increases by £1,000,000.
- Borrowing leads to interest charges, which are an **expense**, and, therefore, reduce profit. The amount depends on the interest rate, e.g. 10% per year.
- Borrowing also means regular repayments of the loan, so the company will need to ensure it has sufficient **cash** to make the repayments.
- The computer system is a long-term commitment; once the money is spent it cannot be retrieved. Buying the computer represents a risk.
- Borrowing is also a long-term commitment and a risk.

The framework enables you to give a comprehensive and professional answer to a difficult question. If you were subsequently asked to work out detailed figures, you could switch to the spreadsheet format, making use of the benefits of IT. To become confident you will need to practise working with the accounting framework. Attempt the multiple choice questions, Mr. H. Bean Winesellers continued, Flintlock family and Hannibal Schlecter. Take your time with each question.

Multiple choice questions

Tick the box next to your answer.

1. As a result of a **cash sale**, which of the following goes up?
   - ☐ Creditors
   - ☐ Drawings
   - ☐ Debtors
   - ☐ Cash
   - ☐ Fixed assets

2. Which of the following is not a **liability**?
   - ☐ Profit
   - ☐ Capital
   - ☐ Loan
   - ☐ Petty cash
   - ☐ Creditors

3. When wages are paid in **cash**, which of the following goes up?
   - ☐ Purchases
   - ☐ Fixed assets
   - ☐ Profit
   - ☐ Expenses
   - ☐ Drawings

4. When **cash** is received from a **debtor**, which of the following goes down?
   - ☐ Sales
   - ☐ Creditors
   - ☐ Cash
   - ☐ Debtors
   - ☐ Profit

5. When goods are bought on credit, which of the following goes up?
   - ☐ Profit
   - ☐ Debtors
   - ☐ Expenses
   - ☐ Creditors
   - ☐ Income

6. Which of the following defines a **fixed asset**?
   - ☐ The amount owed to suppliers
   - ☐ Capital
   - ☐ What the company owns
   - ☐ The amount customers owe the company
   - ☐ Assets owned for more than one year

7. When the owner puts money into the business, what goes up?
   - ☐ Profit
   - ☐ Capital
   - ☐ Loan
   - ☐ Sales
   - ☐ Creditors

8. Motor vehicle insurance is paid in **cash**, which goes up?
   - ☐ Purchases
   - ☐ Fixed assets
   - ☐ Profit
   - ☐ Expenses
   - ☐ Drawings

9. At the end of the financial year, which of the following is set to zero?
☐ Purchases
☐ Creditors
☐ Equipment
☐ Debtors
☐ Capital

10. When a loan is repaid, which of the following goes down?
☐ Capital
☐ Bad debt
☐ Interest received
☐ Expenditure
☐ Cash

Multiple choice answers

	Correct answer	Comment
1	Cash	If a company receives money from a customer, an asset called cash increases.
2	Petty cash	If you selected capital, this means you do not understand capital is a liability. You may have been tempted by profit. Profit is owed to the owner so it is, in fact, a liability. The answer is petty cash which, being a type of cash, must be an asset.
3	Expenses	Wages is a good example of an expense. The answer cannot be purchases, because a company cannot buy people to sell at a profit.
4	Debtors	If a debtor settles an outstanding account, the amount the company is owed must decrease.
5	Creditors	Credit purchases always leads to creditors. If a company buys goods, and does not pay immediately, it owes the supplier for the goods. The term for what is owed is creditors.
6	Assets owned for more than one year	An asset is something the company owns. If it is owned for more than one year, it is a fixed asset.
7	Capital	When the owner of a business puts money into the business, this is termed capital.
8	Expenses	Motor vehicle insurance is an example of an expense.
9	Purchases	All assets and liabilities are carried forward, not set to zero. Purchases are an expenditure, so they are set to zero at the end of every financial year.
10	Cash	When a loan is repaid, an asset called cash (as well as a liability called loan) goes down.

Flintlock family

The Flintlock family started a business with $20,000. In the first month they bought $10,000 of **purchases** and sold all of it for $25,000. They incurred **expenses** of $7000, which they have not yet paid for. All the **sales** and **purchases** were for cash. Using the accounting framework box format, draw a diagram representing the company's financial position.

Mr. H. Bean Winesellers continued

The next few transactions during March are as follows:

No.	Date	Details
13	17th March	Cash purchase = £30
14	18th March	Credit purchase = £1000
15	20th March	Cash sale = £1000
16	21st March	Credit sale = £12,000
17	22nd March	Cash paid to creditors = £5220
18	30th March	Cash received from debtors = £2000

Your task

1. Using the spreadsheet format, show both sides of each of the transactions above (see the pro forma below).
2. Prepare a trial balance up to 30th March 20X0 (see the pro forma below).
3. Calculate the gross profit for the month of March (assume stock is zero).
4. Calculate the net profit for March.

Tip:

Gross profit = sales *less* purchases
Net profit = gross profit *less* expenses

Mr. H. Bean Winesellers continued

Pro Forma

Ref.	Type	Income		Expenditure		Assets				Liabilities	
		Sales	Other	Purchases	Expenses	Equip.	Stock	Debtors	Cash	Capital	Creditors
1	Start up								5000	5000	
2	Cash purchase			200					−200		
3	Credit purchase			1200							1200
4	Cash sale	800							800		
5	Credit sale	1200						1200			
6	Rent				955				−955		
7	Cash register					1200					1200
8	Wages				780				−780		
9	Purchase credit			5920							5920
10	Cash from debtors							−1200	1200		
11	Purchase credit			1650							1650
12	Payment creditors								−750		−750
13	Cash purchase										
14	Credit purchase										
15	Cash sale										
16	Credit sale										
17	Payment creditors										
18	Cash from debtors										
	Total										
	Profit										

START HERE

Mr. H. Bean Winesellers continued

Trial Balance Pro Forma

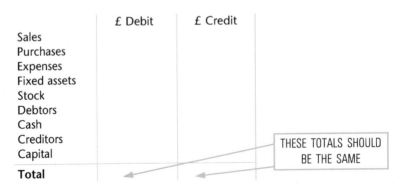

	£ Debit	£ Credit
Sales		
Purchases		
Expenses		
Fixed assets		
Stock		
Debtors		
Cash		
Creditors		
Capital		
Total		

THESE TOTALS SHOULD BE THE SAME

Tip: Incomes and liabilities are credits, expenditures and assets are debits.

Hannibal Schlecter

Hannibal Schlecter is a serial entrepreneur. He loves to start up new businesses, but he gets bored after about two months and moves on to something new. Hannibal was born in Denmark, but lives in Galveston, GA.

Hannibal's latest venture is buying used BMW cars in Germany, and driving them to Moscow, Prague, Warsaw and Budapest to sell at a profit. He started this business by depositing $50,000 in a bank account in Frankfurt.

The results of the first month's trading have been as follows (all in $):

Model	Selling price	Purchase price	Profit (loss)	Reference
3 Series Saloon	30,000	42,000	(12,000)	1
3 Series Convertible	50,000	40,000	10,000	2
5 Series Saloon	25,000	25,000	0	3
7 Series Estate	30,000	29,000	1,000	4
7 Series AMG	50,000	20,000	30,000	5
Total	185,000	156,000	29,000	

Hannibal incurred the following expenses (all in $) during the first month:

Insurance	5,000
Transport costs	10,000
Travel and hotel expenses	2,000
Commission	5,000
Entertaining	5,000
Total	**27,000**

All the transactions were undertaken in US$ and they were all cash sales and cash purchases. However, the bank has notified Hannibal of its intention to charge $1000 interest and currency charges for the first month. This should be included as an expense and a creditor.

Your task

1. Using the spreadsheet format, show both sides of each of the transactions above (see pro forma below).
2. Prepare a trial balance at the end of the first month (see pro forma below).
3. Write a paragraph comparing the profit earned to the amount of capital invested. State the profit in £'s if £1 = $2.

Hannibal Schlecter

Pro Forma

Ref.	Type	Income	Expenditure		Assets				Liabilities	
		Sales	Purchases	Expenses	Equip.	Stock	Debtors	Cash	Capital	Creditors
1										
1										
2										
2										
3										
3										
4										
4										
5										
5										

Hannibal Schlecter

Trial Balance Pro Forma

Capital		
Sales		
Purchases		
Expenses		
Interest		
Cash		
Creditors		
Total		

Solutions

Flintlock family

Income	Expenditure
Sales $25,000	Purchases $10,000
	Expenses $7000
Assets	**Liabilities**
Cash $35,000	Capital $20,000
	Creditors $7000

Mr. H. Bean Winesellers continued (£)

Ref.	Type	Income		Expenditure		Assets				Liabilities	
		Sales	Other	Purchases	Expenses	Equip.	Stock	Debtors	Cash	Capital	Creditors
1	Start up								5,000	5,000	
2	Cash purchase			200					−200		
3	Credit purchase			1,200							1,200
4	Cash sale	800							800		
5	Credit sale	1,200						1,200			
6	Rent				955				−955		
7	Cash register					1,200					1,200
8	Wages				780				−780		
9	Purchase credit			5,920							5,920
10	Cash from debtors							−1,200	1,200		
11	Purchase credit			1,650							1,650
12	Payment creditors								−750		−750
13	Cash purchase			30					−30		
14	Credit purchase			1,000							1,000
15	Cash sale	1,000							1,000		
16	Credit sale	12,000						12,000			
17	Payment creditors								−5220		−5,220
18	Cash from debtors							−2,000	2,000		
	Total	15,000	0	10,000	1,735	1,200	0	10,000	2,065	5,000	5,000
	Profit	3,265								3,265	

Trial Balance (£)

Sales		15,000
Purchases	10,000	
Expenses	1,735	
Fixed assets	1,200	
Stock	0	
Debtors	10,000	
Cash	2,065	
Creditors		5,000
Capital		5,000
Total	**25,000**	**25,000**

During the first month of trading **sales** have amounted to £15,000, made up of four transactions. The cost of buying the goods sold was £10,000 and, as a result, a **gross profit** of £5000 has been generated. **Expenses** for the period amounted to £1735, leaving a **net profit** of £3265.

Hannibal Schlecter ($)

Ref.	Type	Income	Expenditure		Assets				Liabilities	
		Sales	Purchases	Expenses	Equip.	Stock	Debtor	Cash	Capital	Creditors
	Start up							50,000	50,000	
1	Purchase 3 Series		42,000					−42,000		
1	Sale 3 Series	30,000						30,000		
2	Purchase 3 Series Conv.		40,000					−40,000		
2	Sale 3 Series Conv.	50,000						50,000		
3	Purchase 5 Series		25,000					−25,000		
3	Sale 5 Series	25,000						25,000		
4	Purchase 7 Series Est.		29,000					−29,000		
4	Sale 7 Series Est.	30,000						30,000		
5	Purchase 7 Series AMG		20,000					−20,000		
5	Sale 7 Series AMG	50,000						50,000		
	Expenses			27,000				−27,000		
	Interest			1,000						1,000
	Total	185,000	156,000	28,000				52,000	50,000	1,000
	Profit	1,000								

Trial Balance ($)

Capital		50,000
Sales		185,000
Purchases	156,000	
Expenses	27,000	
Interest	1,000	
Cash	52,000	
Creditors		1,000
Total	**236,000**	**236,000**

The profit earned during this venture was only $1000, on an original investment of $50,000. If £1 = $2, this profit is the equivalent of £500. Initially this seems a poor return on capital. The profit represents just 2% of the original **capital** after the first month. However, if the business continues for a year at the same rate of profit, it would yield a profit of $12,000 from a $50,000 investment.

The **expenses** ($28,000) wipe out most of the **gross profit** ($29,000), leaving only $1000 net profit. Hannibal should consider ways of reducing **expenses**.

4   Year end adjustments

This chapter explains the year end procedures for calculating profit, assets and liabilities.

Objectives	
	• Stock adjustment;
	• Depreciation adjustment;
	• The transfer of profit to capital.

Introduction

If a company is making a profit, capital will increase year on year. At the end of every financial year businesses need to know:

• How much profit has been earned during the year;
• The particular assets and liabilities of the business;
• The amount of capital invested in the business.

Importance of YEAs

To calculate these, three special year end procedures have to be carried out, as follows:

• Stock count,
• Depreciation calculation,
• Transfer of profit to capital.

These are termed the year end adjustments (YEAs). This chapter uses the accounting framework to illustrate the impact of YEAs and uses the spreadsheet format to calculate profits and capital, etc.

Stock

Stock is the **value** of the goods in the warehouse, shop or factory at the end of the financial year. Stock refers to the **value** of the goods, not the quantities. Be careful not to confuse stock with purchases. When a company buys goods to sell at a profit, these are purchases, not stock. Stock is what is left over at the end of the year. Look at the rectangle in Figure 4.1.

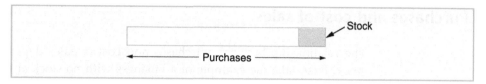

Figure 4.1 Purchases and stock

The whole of the rectangle represents purchases, while the shaded area represents stock. The value of stock at the end of the year is usually referred to as closing stock, because it is valued on the closing day of the financial year.

The 'circuit of capital' (Chapter 1) shows that profit is earned when goods are sold. Stock is made up of goods, which have been bought during the year (i.e. purchases) but not sold during the year. The goods will not be sold until next year. Profit cannot be earned on goods that have not been sold, so no profit is earned on stock. The profit will be earned next year when the goods are sold.

Because there is no profit earned on stock, there is no point including stock in the P&L account. The portion of purchases still in stock has to be taken out of the P&L account. On every P&L account, therefore, closing stock is subtracted from purchases. If stock is not subtracted from purchases, the profit figure will be wrong, because purchases will include goods that have not been sold during the year.

Stock should be *subtracted* from purchases at the end of the year, but this is only one aspect of the transaction. The other aspect is that an asset called stock increases. The reason an asset called stock increases is to reflect the fact that the business owns stock of a particular value at the end of the year. In summary, at the end of every year stock is counted and valued. The value of the stock is subtracted from purchases and added to an asset called stock.

This is not quite the end of the matter. Remember, all assets and liabilities are carried forward to the following year (see Chapter 3 if you are unsure about this). The closing stock at the end of year 1 will be carried forward to year 2. This will be referred to as the opening stock in year 2. The closing stock in year 1 becomes the opening stock in year 2. The closing stock in year 2 becomes the opening stock in year 3, etc.

Stock is valued at the end of a year, not during the year. Once year 2 starts, the opening stock figure is, therefore, no longer needed. To eliminate the opening stock, put it back into purchases. An asset called stock decreases to zero and purchases increase. In other words, the stock adjustment performed at the end of year 1 is reversed at the beginning of year 2. Because of the reversal, every year purchases have opening stock *added* and closing stock *subtracted*. The result is cost of sales:

$$\text{Cost of sales} = \text{opening stock} + \text{purchases} - \text{closing stock}$$

Cost of sales is the cost of buying the goods, which have been sold during the period.

Purchases and cost of sales

The relationship between purchases and cost of sales depends on the level of stock. First, take the example of a business with no stock at the beginning or at the end of the year. If a business has no stock, it must be buying goods every day and selling those goods before the end of the day. This is often referred to as 'turning over' every day. In a business like this, purchases are identical to cost of sales because everything purchased is also sold every day.

Daily turnover is quite an unusual situation. To develop our understanding, compare daily turnover to some other types of businesses, e.g. a new business, an established retail business and a high stock business. Consider, below, four different business situations:

- Daily turnover business, e.g. a fruit and veg. stall (no opening or closing stock).
- New business in any sector, e.g. an Internet-based business (no opening stock).
- Normal retail business, e.g. newsagents (both opening and closing stock).
- High stock business, e.g. jewellers (large opening and closing stock).

Look carefully at the cost of sales calculations below. The purchases figure is the same in each business:

	Opening stock	+	Purchases	−	Closing stock	=	Cost of sales
Daily turnover	0		100,000		0		100,000
New business	0		100,000		20,000		80,000
Normal stock	10,000		100,000		15,000		95,000
High stock	50,000		100,000		45,000		105,000

Make sure you understand every cost of sales figure.
The difference between purchases and cost of sales is that purchases is the total amount that is bought during the year, while cost of sales is the cost of buying the goods that have been sold during the year. Purchases include goods that have not been sold during the year (closing stock). Cost of sales includes goods that have been sold during the year, most of which were bought during the year (purchases) but some of which were bought in the previous year (opening stock).

In the space provided below, write a sentence explaining why the cost of sales in the 'high stock' business was greater than purchases:

Did you try? The key point is that stock has decreased from £50,000 to £45,000. The business has sold everything it purchased and also sold some of the goods that were in opening stock. Consequently, the cost of the goods sold (cost of sales) is greater than purchases.

Stock adjustment in action

The accounting framework illustrates the stock adjustment. A company has just finished the year end stock count and stock has been valued at £1000. Here are the two sides of the year end stock adjustment:

Two aspects of stock: year 1

Income	Expenditure
Sales	Purchases −£1000
Other	Expenses

Assets	Liabilities
Fixed assets	Creditors
Current assets	Loans
Stock +£1000	Capital
Debtors	
Cash	

Purchases decreases by £1000 and stock increases by £1000. Stock is subtracted from purchases at the end of the financial year because profit is not earned on goods, which have not been sold.

Recall that, because they are owned and owed, all assets and liabilities are carried forward to the following year. Sales, purchases and expenses are set back to zero at the end of every year, because they are figures that relate to one year. The first day of the next financial year can be presented as follows:

Balances brought forward: first day of year 2

Income	Expenditure
Sales	Purchases = 0
Other	Expenses

Assets	Liabilities
Fixed assets	Creditors
Current assets	Loans
Stock brought forward £1000	Capital
Debtors	
Cash	

Because purchases is an expenditure, it has been set back to zero. Stock is an asset so it has been brought forward to year 2.

The first transaction in the new financial year is to reverse the stock adjustment. This puts the stock back into purchases, where it is available to be sold.

Reverse adjustment in year 2

Income	Expenditure
Sales	Purchases +£1000
Other	Expenses

Assets	Liabilities
Fixed assets	Creditors
Current assets	Loans
Stock £1000 − £1000 = 0	Capital
Debtors	
Cash	

Stock goes down by £1000 and purchases goes up by £1000. The opening stock is added to purchases because the goods will now be sold. Stock is now zero, and will remain at zero until the end of year 2.

Fixed assets and depreciation

The second YEA is depreciation. Depreciation is a measure of the using up of a fixed asset, over its expected life. To calculate this, take the cost of a fixed asset and divide by its expected life. For example, a lorry costing £50,000 may be acquired with a view to using it for five years. Depreciation is, therefore, £10,000 per year for five years.

After the end of the first year, the lorry will have a net value of £40,000. After the second year it will only be worth £30,000. After five years it will be worth zero. Here are some examples of depreciation calculations:

Type of fixed asset	Cost of fixed asset	Expected life	Depreciation per year
Bought a computer	£1,500	3 yr	£500
Bought a car	£20,000	5 yr	£4,000
Bought a cash register	£1,200	10 yr	£120
Bought a photocopier	£2,500	10 yr	£250
Bought a factory	£1,000,000	50 yr	£20,000

Like all accounting transactions, depreciation has two aspects. One aspect of depreciation is similar to an expense. The expense represents the value of the fixed asset used up *in a year*. Think of the depreciation expense as the equivalent of a rental cost. If a company hires assets, it has to pay a monthly rental. Depreciation expense is the equivalent for fixed assets that are bought rather than hired or leased.

The amount of a fixed asset used up in a year reduces the value of a fixed asset. But, the original price paid for a fixed asset needs to be maintained in the books of account so, for example, in the event of an insurance claim, the original value is available. To avoid subtracting depreciation from the original cost, a new liability called the provision for depreciation is created, which is the second aspect of depreciation. Instead of the fixed asset being reduced, a liability called the provision for depreciation is increased. Because a liability is the opposite of an asset, an increase in a liability is equivalent to a reduction in an asset. In this way, the amount by which a fixed asset has reduced is recorded (as a liability), while at the same time not changing the original cost of the fixed asset.

Depreciation should be calculated at the end of every financial year. The expense depreciation will increase and the liability provision for depreciation will increase. The asset called fixed asset will remain unchanged. At the end of the financial year, assets and liabilities will be carried forward to the next year and income and expenditure, including expense depreciation, will be set back to zero. Consequently, the liability aspect of depreciation is cumulative while the expense aspect relates to one year. The liability provision for depreciation accumulates year on year, until it is equal to the fixed asset. When the liability provision for depreciation is equal to the fixed asset, they cancel each other out.

In summary, every fixed asset has three figures relating to it:

- Original cost, an asset termed fixed assets.
- This year's depreciation, an expenditure expense (depreciation).
- Cumulative depreciation, the liability provision for depreciation.

Each figure represents a different aspect of the fixed asset. In addition, there is a fourth figure, the net book value, which is the original cost less the cumulative depreciation.

Keywords

Fixed asset	The original cost of the fixed asset	Balance sheet
Expense depreciation	The annual figure	P&L account
Provision for depreciation	The cumulative depreciation	Balance sheet
Net book value	Cost less cumulative depreciation	Balance sheet

Depreciation adjustment in action

The accounting framework illustrates the depreciation adjustment. Take the example of a £50,000 lorry depreciated over five years giving depreciation of £10,000 per year:

Year 1 depreciation

Income	Expenditure
Sales	Purchases
Other	Expenses
	Depreciation = £10,000

Assets	Liabilities
Fixed assets = £50,000	Creditors
Current assets	Loans
Stock	Capital
Debtors	*Provision for depreciation = £10,000*
Cash	

A liability called provision for depreciation increases by £10,000 and expense (depreciation) increases by £10,000. The net book value of the fixed asset is £40,000 (£50,000 − £10,000).

Next consider the first day of the following year:

Balances brought forward: first day of year 2

Income	Expenditure
Sales	Purchases
Other	Expenses
	Depreciation = 0

Assets	Liabilities
Fixed assets = £50,000	Creditors
Current assets	Loans
Stock	Capital
Debtors	*Provision for depreciation = £10,000*
Cash	

The expense depreciation has been set back to zero at the beginning of year 2 because it is an expenditure. The fixed asset and the provision for depreciation, like all assets and liabilities, have been brought forward. Next consider the last day of year 2:

Last day of year 2

Income	Expenditure
Sales	Purchases
Other	Expenses
	Depreciation = £10,000
Assets	**Liabilities**
Fixed assets = £50,000	Creditors
Current assets	Loans
Stock	Capital
Debtors	*Provision for depreciation*
Cash	*£10,000 + £10,000 = £20,000*

The depreciation on the lorry is £10,000 per year. Expense depreciation increases by £10,000 and provision for depreciation increases by £10,000, giving a total liability of £20,000. The provision for depreciation is cumulative (like all liabilities), while the expense figure remains a one-year figure. The net book value at the end of the second year is £50,000 − £20,000 = £30,000.

Acquisition of a fixed asset

When a new fixed asset is acquired, an asset called cash decreases and an asset called fixed assets increases. The depreciation in the first year can become complicated. For the sake of simplicity, always give a full year of depreciation in the year of acquisition. Do not attempt to count the number of months in the year. Even if a fixed asset is acquired on 31st December, it is simpler and easier to give it a full year of depreciation.

Some companies take account of the fact that fixed assets may have a second-hand value. Motor vehicles, for instance, can always be sold because there is a ready market for second-hand cars. It is, therefore, possible to estimate what a motor vehicle might be worth in four or five years' time. This is called the residual value.

To take account of residual values, calculate depreciation as follows:

$$\text{(Cost} - \text{residual value)/expected life}$$

If a motor vehicle was acquired for £17,000 with an expected life of four years, after which it could be sold for £1000, depreciation would be calculated as follows:

$$£17,000 - £1000/4 \text{ years} = £4000 \text{ per year}$$

Residual values are best left at zero, unless it is certain that they can be estimated correctly. The inclusion of residual values always reduces depreciation and, as a result, tends to overstate profits.

Disposal of a fixed asset

A fixed asset can be sold at a profit or a loss. Recall that the original cost of a fixed asset, as well as its cumulative depreciation (the depreciation provision), is recorded. The difference between these two is net book value. A fixed asset sold for more than net book value generates a profit. It is much more likely, however, that a fixed asset will be sold for less than net book value, which is a loss:

Sell for **more** than net book value	Profit on disposal	Other income in P&L account
Sell for **less** than net book value	Loss on disposal	Expenses in P&L account
Sell for **exactly** net book value	No profit or loss	Nothing in P&L account

Within the accounting framework, follow these three stages when dealing with the disposal of a fixed asset:

1. Transfer the provision for depreciation to the fixed asset – a liability called cumulative depreciation decreases and fixed assets also decreases. This will leave the net book value.
2. Record the sale proceeds (how much the fixed asset was sold for) – cash increases and fixed assets decreases. This will leave a loss (in most cases).
3. Show the loss as an expense – the fixed assets decreases to zero, an expense called 'loss on disposal of fixed assets' increases. If the company happens to have made a profit, show it as other income.

Consider this example. A company bought a new computer network for £50,000, which included all the hardware and software as well as installation and initial training. It expected to use the system for five years, so it started to depreciate the system at 20% per year. After two years the system had to be scrapped, because competitors had introduced an Internet-based system that customers preferred. The company managed to get £6000 from selling off parts of the old system.

Take it step by step.

The original cost of buying the fixed asset was?

Depreciation in the first year would be?

Depreciation in the second year would be?

Accumulated depreciation over the two years would, therefore, be?

The net book value at the end of the second year would be?

The sale proceeds were?

The difference between the sales proceeds and the net book value is?

Is this a profit or a loss?

Did you have a go? If not, go back and attempt it yourself. The answers I was looking for are as follows:

Depreciation in the first year	£10,000
Depreciation in the second year	£10,000
Accumulated depreciation	£20,000
Net book value	£30,000
Sale proceed	£6,000
Loss on sale of fixed asset	£24,000

A substantial loss was incurred when this system was decommissioned.

Transfer of profit to capital

The final and simplest YEA is the transfer of profit to capital. This is necessary because profit is owed to the owner and is, therefore, part of capital. Within the accounting framework, this is dealt with as follows:

- Subtract total expenditure from income.
- This leaves the profit, under the income heading.
- Transfer profit from income to capital.

In the following section you will be able to observe this transfer in the spreadsheet format. You will also be able to see it in the 'financed by' section of the balance sheet in Chapter 5.

Year end adjustments in the spreadsheet format

Here is an example of how the YEAs are incorporated into the spreadsheet format. A new business, trading as 'Cassocks', is at the end of its first year of trading. During the first year, all transactions have been in cash.

Cassocks

First Year Transaction Summary (£)

Start up capital	10,000
Cash sales	450,000
Cash purchases	375,000
Wages	20,000
Bought a computer	1,500
Drawings	15,000

YEAs

Closing stock	25,000
Depreciation on computer	500

The figures above are the total figures for the year, e.g. **sales** £450,000 is the total **sales** for the year. Wages £20,000 is the total wages for the year.

The transactions during the year can be presented as follows:

Type	Income		Expenditure		Assets				Liabilities		
	Sales	Other	Purchases	Expenses	Equip.	Stock	Debt.	Cash	Capital	Credit.	Deprec.
Start up								10,000	10,000		
Cash sales	450,000							450,000			
Cash purchases			375,000					−375,000			
Wages				20,000				−20,000			
Computer					1,500			−1,500			
Drawings								−15,000	−15,000		
Total	450,000	0	375,000	20,000	1,500			48,500	−5,000	0	0

Make sure you understand all of this before you carry on.

The YEAs can be added as follows:

Type	Income		Expenditure		Assets				Liabilities		
	Sales	Other	Purchases	Expenses	Equip.	Stock	Debt.	Cash	Capital	Credit.	Deprec.
Start up								10,000	10,000		
Cash sales	450,000							450,000			
Cash purchases			375,000					−375,000			
Wages				20,000				−20,000			
Computer					1,500			−1,500			
Drawings								−15,000	−15,000		
Stock			−25,000			25,000					
Depreciation				500							500
Total	450,000	0	350,000	20,500	1,500	25,000	0	48,500	−5,000		500
Profit	79,500								79,500		
Total									74,500		

Stock is subtracted from purchases and added to stock. Depreciation for the year is added to the expenses column and the provision for depreciation column (on the extreme right-hand side). The profit is calculated in the income column and added to the capital column. The closing capital is £74,500.

Make sure you are clear about every figure before you carry on.

I have calculated the profit (£79,500) on my spreadsheet. This is how I calculated the figure:

Income

Sales	450,000
Other	0
	450,000

Expenditure

Cost of sales	350,000
Expenses	20,500
	370,500

Profit	79,500

Conclusions

The stock and depreciation adjustments have impacts over more than one year. It is important to be clear how stock and depreciation in year 1 roll over into year 2 and year 3, etc. The purpose of the stock and depreciation adjustments is to calculate the correct profit. Without the stock adjustment, the wrong profit figure would be shown on the P&L account. Without the depreciation adjustment, no account would be taken of the cost of using equipment.

Multiple choice questions

Tick the box next to your answer.

1. Which of the following defines a fixed asset?

   ☐ The amount owed to suppliers
   ☐ Cash in the bank
   ☐ What the company owns
   ☐ The amount customers owe the company
   ☐ Assets used in a business for more than one year

2. Which of the following is not **cash**?
   ☐ Petty cash
   ☐ Money in a deposit account
   ☐ Capital
   ☐ Money in the current account
   ☐ Money tied up for six months in a 'money market' account

3. When **interest** is received
   ☐ An asset called cash decreases
   ☐ A liability called loans increases
   ☐ An income called other increases
   ☐ Drawings increase
   ☐ An expenditure called expenses increases

4. What is **depreciation**?
- [ ] A current liability
- [ ] The revaluation of an asset
- [ ] A measure of the using up of a fixed asset
- [ ] Money put aside to replace fixed assets
- [ ] What is left of the value of a fixed asset

5. Why is **capital** a liability?
- [ ] Because it is owed by the business to the owner
- [ ] Because it is cash
- [ ] Because it is owed to suppliers
- [ ] Because there is an overdraft
- [ ] Because assets equal liabilities

6. Opening stock = £0, purchases = £100 and closing stock = £20
- [ ] Cost of sales = £0
- [ ] Cost of sales = £100
- [ ] Cost of sales = £20
- [ ] Cost of sales = £120
- [ ] Cost of sales = £80

7. Opening stock = £100, purchases = £900 and closing stock = £200
- [ ] Cost of sales = £100
- [ ] Cost of sales = £1000
- [ ] Cost of sales = £800
- [ ] Cost of sales = £1200
- [ ] Cost of sales = £1000

8. A computer costs £10,000 and has an expected life of five years
- [ ] Depreciation per year = £2500
- [ ] Depreciation per year = £2000
- [ ] Depreciation per year = £3000
- [ ] Depreciation per year = £10,000
- [ ] Depreciation per year = £1000

9. Cumulative depreciation of the above computer after three years?
- [ ] Cumulative depreciation = £300
- [ ] Cumulative depreciation = £30,000
- [ ] Cumulative depreciation = £3000
- [ ] Cumulative depreciation = £100
- [ ] Cumulative depreciation = £6000

10. Net book value of the above computer after four years?
- [ ] Net book value = £8000
- [ ] Net book value = £800
- [ ] Net book value = £200
- [ ] Net book value = £2000
- [ ] Net book value = £10,000

11. A company buys a patent for £1,000,000 that allows it the exclusive right to manufacture a drug for 10 years. Depreciation per year?
- [ ] £1,000,000
- [ ] £1000
- [ ] £100
- [ ] £10,000
- [ ] £100,000

12. A company started with an opening stock of £13,000 and purchased £55,000 during the year. The closing stock was only £7000. Cost of sales?
- [ ] £55,000
- [ ] £68,000
- [ ] £61,000
- [ ] £20,000
- [ ] £49,000

13. Closing stock is higher than opening stock when
- [ ] More goods have been purchased than sold
- [ ] Sales are higher than expected
- [ ] Purchasing department forget to order raw materials
- [ ] Suppliers refuse to deliver any more goods until all outstanding invoices are paid
- [ ] Fire destroys all the closing stock in the warehouse

14. A company buys a new factory for £2,000,000 and expects to use it for 50 years. Depreciation per year?
- [ ] £2,000,000
- [ ] £40,000
- [ ] £400,000
- [ ] £1,000,000
- [ ] £200,000

15. Purchases equals cost of sales when?
- [ ] Opening stock is zero
- [ ] Closing stock is zero
- [ ] Opening stock equals closing stock
- [ ] Sales are lower than expected
- [ ] Closing stock is higher than opening stock

Multiple choice answers

	Correct answer	Comment
1	Assets used in a business for more than one year	See definition in Chapter 2.
2	Capital	Capital is not cash.
3	Income called other increases	Another example of other income would be profit on sale of a fixed asset. This was a Chapter 3 question.
4	A measure of the using up of a fixed asset	Depreciation is not money put aside to replace the fixed asset.
5	Owed by the business to the owner	The owner is separate from the business.
6	Cost of sales = £80	Closing stock is subtracted from purchases.
7	Cost of sales = £800	£900 + £100 − £200. During the year stock has increased by £100. £100 of purchases has gone into stock rather than being sold.

8	Depreciation = £2000	£10,000/5.
9	Depreciation provision = £6000	£2000 × 3.
10	NBV = £2000	£10,000 − (4 × £2000).
11	£100,000	£1,000,000/10 years.
12	£61,000	£13,000 + £55,000 − £7000. Stock has decreased by £6000. So in addition to purchases, £6000 worth has been sold from stock.
13	More goods have been purchased than sold	If more is bought than sold, stock increases. All the other options reduce stock.
14	£40,000	£2,000,000/50 years.
15	Opening stock equals closing stock	If opening stock is the same as closing stock, the cost of the goods sold must be the same as purchases.

Call centre network

An Internet entrepreneur is considering buying a server and 25 monitors to provide the basis for a 'call centre' network. The total cost of the equipment will be £60,000. Because of the likely advances in IT, the network will probably have to be replaced after three years.

Your task

Using the 'box format' show the impact on company finances of buying the equipment and depreciating it over three years. Prepare a separate box for the acquisition, first year depreciation, second year depreciation and third year depreciation. Four 'boxes' in total.

The 'box format' should be presented as follows:

Income	Expenditure
Assets	Liabilities

Maelstrom

Maelstrom operates a letter delivery service specialising in legal correspondence. They own a fleet of vans which travel large distances every year. This year, 2003, they have disposed of six vans at a motor auction. Here are the details relating to the vans sold:

Registration	Original cost	Date acquired	Useful life	Selling price
L10 NDA	£12,000	1998	4 yr	Scrapped
M1 CKY	£13,000	1999	4 yr	£250
N1 CKY	£14,000	2000	4 yr	£4,000
P155 HEY	£16,000	2001	4 yr	£4,000
R1 CHY	£25,000	2002	5 yr	£10,000

Company policy is to give a full year's depreciation in the year of purchase and none in the year of disposal, e.g. a van bought in 2002 and sold in 2003 gets depreciated in 2002 only, for a full year not part of the year.

Your task

1. Calculate the net book value in the year of disposal.
2. Calculate the profit or loss on disposal.
3. Write a paragraph explaining why the loss on the P reg. is so much greater than on the N reg.

Jazz Club

By the end of the first year of trading the Jazz Club summarised its results as follows. Premises and sound equipment are leased.

	Sales	Purchases	Expenses	Fixtures & furniture	Stock	Cash	Capital	Creditors	Depreciation
Capital						50,000	50,000		
Fixed assets				150,000		−150,000			
Cash sales	1,223,795					1,223,795			
Credit purchases		645,000						645,000	
Cash paid						−551,274		551,274	
Expenses			434,796			−434,796			
Drawings						12,000	−12,000		
YEA									
Stock									
Depreciation									

The stock at the end of the year has been valued at £12,344. Depreciation on the fixtures and furniture should be calculated at the rate of 20%.

Your task

Show how the year end adjustments are dealt with in the spreadsheet format, calculate the net profit for the year and transfer the net profit to capital.

Solutions

Call centre network

Acquisition

Income	Expenditure
Assets Cash −£60,000 Fixed assets +£60,000	**Liabilities**

First year depreciation

Income	Expenditure Depreciation expenses £20,000
Assets Fixed assets £60,000	**Liabilities** Depreciation provision £20,000

*At the end of the first year all **expenses** are set to zero and all **assets** and **liabilities** are carried forward.*

Second year depreciation

Income	Expenditure Depreciation expenses £20,000
Assets Fixed assets £60,000	**Liabilities** Depreciation provision £40,000

Third year depreciation

Income	Expenditure Depreciation expenses £20,000
Assets Fixed assets £60,000	**Liabilities** Depreciation provision £60,000

Maelstrom

Cost	Deprec. per year	No. of years	Cum. deprec.	Net book value	Selling price	Profit (loss)
12,000	3,000	5	12,000	0	0	0
13,000	3,250	4	13,000	0	250	£250
14,000	3,500	3	10,500	3,500	4,000	£500
16,000	4,000	2	8,000	8,000	4,000	(£4,000)
25,000	5,000	1	5,000	20,000	10,000	(£10,000)

Large losses can be incurred when **fixed assets** are disposed of before the end of their useful life. This is particularly the case for motor vehicles and computers. Because of this, investing in **fixed assets** is a source of risk. Hiring or leasing equipment is one way of reducing this risk.

Jazz Club

	Sales	Purchases	Expenses	Fixtures & furniture	Stock	Cash	Capital	Creditors	Depreciation
Capital						50,000	50,000		
Fixed assets				150,000		−150,000			
Cash sales	1,223,795					1,223,795			
Credit purchases		645,000						645,000	
Cash paid						−551,274		−551,274	
Expenses			434,796			−434,796			
Drawings						−12,000	−12,000		
YEA									
Stock		−12,344			12,344				
Depreciation			30,000						30,000
Total	1,223,795	632,656	464,796	150,000	12,344	125,725	38,000	93,726	30,000
Profit			126,343				126,343		
							164,343		

The Jazz Club has made a profit of £126,343 during the first year. As a result the owner's capital has increased from the original £50,000 to £164,343 allowing for the £12,000 already drawn out by the owner.

5 Trading and profit and loss account and balance sheet

This chapter explains the P&L account and the balance sheet and shows how they can be prepared.

Objectives

- Preparing P&L and BS from trial balance;
- Preparing P&L and BS from spreadsheets;
- Explaining P&L and BS.

Introduction

Importance of the subject

The P&L account and balance sheet summarise the financial position of a company at the end of the financial year, both in terms of profits, capital and all the other types of assets and liabilities. In a larger business, with established accounting systems, they will be prepared from a trial balance. In a new business situation they can be prepared from the spreadsheet format of the accounting framework.

Activities and outcomes

In this chapter you will bring different types of skills into action. The emphasis will be on the visual presentation of the figures. The formats for P&L account and balance sheet are important; follow them exactly and work to a high standard of presentation. There are two in-chapter exercises, which you should follow up by attempting the questions laid out at the end of the chapter. When they have been completed you should be able to understand and explain the financial information presented in the P&L account and balance sheet.

'Sales', 'turnover', 'revenue', 'operating revenue', 'income' and 'operating income' can all mean exactly the same thing, the value of the goods sold to customers during the year. In other words, 'Sales'.

Formats

Here is an example of a pro forma P&L account and balance sheet.

Mr. H. Bean Winesellers

Trading and Profit and Loss Account
Year Ended 28th February 20X1

	£	£
Sales		
Cost of sales		
Opening stock		
Add: purchases		
Less: closing stock		
Gross profit		
Less: expenses		
Wages		
Rent		
Insurance		
Marketing		
Depreciation		
Net profit		

Mr. H. Bean Winesellers

Balance Sheet
As at 28th February 20X1

	Cost	Accumulated depreciation	Net book value
Fixed assets			
Van			
Cash register			
Current assets			
Stock			
Debtors			
Cash			
Current liabilities			
Creditors			
Net current assets			
Total net assets			
Financed by:			
Opening capital			
Add: profit			
Less: drawings			
Loan			

The balance sheet is sometimes referred to as the statement of sources and uses of funds. The 'financed by' section details the sources of funds, while the fixed assets and current assets represent the uses of funds.

Presentation points

Communication is the most important skill in business. The P&L account and balance sheet communicate the accounting framework, allowing managers to measure the **profits** and monitor the sources and uses of funds. To be accessible, they have to be presented to a high standard. To achieve this, follow these points:

- Use a full heading with company name and period.
- Underline the heading.
- Identify £'s, £ thousands or £ millions.
- Use indenting for subheadings and keep subheadings in line.
- Underline to show an addition or subtraction.
- Double underline at the end of the calculation.
- Keep columns straight.
- Always start on a fresh page.
- Write clearly and neatly.
- Rough workings on a separate sheet.

The columns on the P&L account and balance sheet often cause managers confusion. The columns are purely for presentation: they do not represent income, expenditure, asset or liability. Nor do they represent debits or credits. The two columns in the P&L account, for example, are purely to have a separate column (the left-hand column) in which to show the detail of expenses and cost of sales, while the total of expenses and cost of sales is shown in the right-hand column. Numbers that are added or subtracted are always shown directly underneath each other. Take a careful look at the formats of the pro forma P&L account and balance sheet.

Although the spreadsheet format is used for the detail of the accounting framework and calculations, the results are best presented using word processing, e.g. Microsoft Word. The *Table* facility (see the top menu bar) is useful in this regard. When working with *Tables*, always align the figures to the right, while the text should be aligned to the left (see the *Format* command). Double underlining can be achieved by *Format~Font~Underline~Double*. Tables look better when centred. To achieve this try *Table~Height & Width~Centre*. It is possible to do addition and subtraction within a table. Use the command *Table~Formula*. Alternatively, figures calculated on a spreadsheet can be cut and pasted into another document.

The trading account

This is the top part of the trading and profit and loss account. In a retail or wholesale company it shows the gross profit generated from the buying and selling of goods (see Figure 5.1).

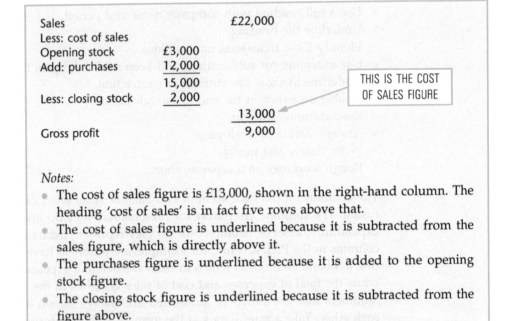

Sales		£22,000
Less: cost of sales		
Opening stock	£3,000	
Add: purchases	12,000	
	15,000	
Less: closing stock	2,000	
		13,000
Gross profit		9,000

THIS IS THE COST OF SALES FIGURE

Notes:
- The cost of sales figure is £13,000, shown in the right-hand column. The heading 'cost of sales' is in fact five rows above that.
- The cost of sales figure is underlined because it is subtracted from the sales figure, which is directly above it.
- The purchases figure is underlined because it is added to the opening stock figure.
- The closing stock figure is underlined because it is subtracted from the figure above.
- All of the stock and purchases figures are shown in the left-hand column so that the right-hand column contains only the totals.

Figure 5.1 The trading account

Short format

In some trading and profit and loss accounts the full details of the trading account and expenses are not given. This is called a short format trading and profit and loss account. The benefit of this format is that it gives competitors much less information about how a business works. For example, they cannot see how much stock is held.

Short Format P&L Account

Sales	£22,000
Less: cost of sales	13,000
Gross profit	9,000
Less: expenses	7,000
Net profit	£2,000

Service sector

In the service sector goods are not usually bought and sold at a profit. Consequently, there is no trading account in the profit and loss account. A service company such as an advertising agency, design consultancy or consulting engineers might have a format as follows:

Fees charged
Less: expenses
   Wages and salaries
   Motor and travel
   Insurance
   Interest and bank charges
   Discounts allowed
   Bad debts
   Printing and stationery
   Entertaining
   Advertising and promotions
   Accounting
   Training
   Rent and rates
   Sundries

Net profit before taxation

Manufacturing sector

The manufacturing sector is more complex because there are different types of stock, e.g. raw materials and finished goods, as well as work in progress. A manufacturing company might lay out its results as follows:

Sales or turnover
Less: factory costs
   Direct labour
   Direct materials
   Factory overheads
Gross profit
Less: expenses
   Distribution
   Marketing and promotion
   Personnel
   Finance
   Administration
   Interest

Net profit before taxation

Trial balance, P&L account and balance sheet

The trial balance links the accounting framework with the P&L account and balance sheet. Recall from Chapter 3 that the trial balance displays the totals for the year for sales, purchases, expenses, assets and liabilities, etc. From the trial balance there are just five steps to completing the P&L account and BS:

1. Stock adjustment.
2. Depreciation adjustment.
3. Preparing trading and profit and loss account.
4. Transfer of profit to capital.
5. Preparing the balance sheet.

Here is an example of these five steps.

Stanley Lineker

Stanley Lineker has used family connections to establish a sports equipment business supplying football clubs in the UK. The trial balance for the last accounting year has been extracted from the computerised accounting system as follows (all in £'s):

Stanley Lineker

Trial Balance
As at 30th September 200X

	Debit	Credit
Sales		250,000
Stock at the start of the year	31,000	
Purchases	190,000	
Printing and stationery	10,000	
Wages	12,000	
Electricity and insurance	3,500	
Freehold property	78,000	
Computers	12,000	
Provision for depreciation		3,000
Debtors	30,000	
Bank	500	
Creditors		12,000
Owner's capital		124,000
Drawings	22,000	
Total	**389,000**	**389,000**

Year end adjustments, not allowed for in the trial balance above, are:

- The year end stock count revealed the closing stock was worth £25,000.
- The computers are depreciated over four years, 25% per year.
- Freehold property is not presently depreciated.

This is all the information needed to prepare the P&L account and balance sheet. Every figure on the P&L account can be linked back to the trial balance or to a YEA.

Stanley Lineker

Trading and Profit and Loss Account
Year Ended 30th September 200X

	£	£
Sales		250,000
Less: cost of sales		
Opening stock	31,000	
Add: purchases	190,000	
	221,000	
Less: closing stock	25,000	
		196,000
Gross profit		54,000
Less: expenses		
Printing and stationery	10,000	
Wages	12,000	
Electricity and insurance	3,500	
Depreciation	3,000	
		28,500
Net profit		25,500

> THIS IS THE 'COST OF SALES' FIGURE

The company has earned a net profit of £25,500 during the year. A gross profit of £54,000 has been earned from trading, but expenses of £28,500 have also been incurred. The largest expense is wages, £12,000.

Make sure you are clear about every figure before you carry on.

Stanley Lineker

Balance Sheet
As at 30th September 200X (all in £'s)

	Cost	Accumulated depreciation	Net book value
Fixed assets			
Freehold premises	78,000	0	78,000
Computers	12,000	6,000	6,000
	90,000	6,000	84,000
Current assets			
Stock		25,000	
Debtors		30,000	
Cash		500	
		55,500	
Current liabilities			
Creditors		12,000	
Working capital			43,500
Total net assets			127,500
Financed by:			
Opening capital			124,000
Add: net profit		25,500	
Less: drawings		22,000	
			3,500
Closing capital			127,500

By the end of the year the company has only £500 in cash. Customers owe £30,000 to the company and £25,000 is held in stock. The total of the current assets is, therefore, £55,500, which compares favourably with current liabilities of £12,000. The main fixed asset is freehold premises, which have not been depreciated. The value of fixed assets, after allowing for depreciation, is £84,000, which gives a total net assets figure of £127,500. During the year the capital employed in the company rose from £124,000 to £127,500. This increase is small because the owner drew most of the profits (£25,500) out of the business (£22,000).

Make sure that you understand every figure, as well as the commentary, before you carry on. Note that depreciation is £3000 every year. The trial balance shows a provision for depreciation of £3000, relating to the previous year. The cumulative depreciation is, therefore, now £6000.

P&L account using the spreadsheet format

In the example above we prepared a P&L account from a trial balance. Established businesses do this at the end of every financial year, usually using a computerised trial balance. A different approach is needed in a business start up situation. New businesses use spreadsheets to prepare a forecast P&L account and forecast balance sheet, as part of their 'business plan'. In the Chapter 4 'Cassocks' example you saw how a spreadsheet could be used to provide a framework for all the years' transactions. The finished result looked like this:

Type	Income		Expenditure		Assets				Liabilities		
	Sales	Other	Purchases	Expenses	Equip.	Stock	Debt.	Cash	Capital	Credit.	Depreciation
Start up								10,000	10,000		
Cash sales	450,000							450,000			
Cash purchases			375,000					−375,000			
Wages				20,000				−20,000			
Computer					1,500			−1,500			
Drawings								−15,000	−15,000		
Stock			−25,000			25,000					
Depreciation				500							500
Total	450,000	0	350,000	20,500	1,500	25,000	0	48,500	−5,000		500
Profit	79,500								79,500		
									74,500		

These figures can be used to prepare a P&L account and balance sheet.

Cassocks

Cassocks

Trading and Profit and Loss Account
Year Ended 31st December 200X

	£	£
Sales		450,000
Cost of sales		
Opening stock	0	
Add: purchases	375,000	
	375,000	
Less: closing stock	25,000	
		350,000
Gross profit		100,000
Less: expenses		
Wages	20,000	
Depreciation	500	
		20,500
Net profit		79,500

The company has earned a net profit of £79,500 during the year. A gross profit of £100,000 is earned from trading, but expenses of £20,500 were also incurred. The largest expense is wages, £20,000.

Cassocks

Balance Sheet
As at 31st December 200X (all in £'s)

	Cost	Accumulated depreciation	Net book value
Fixed assets			
Computer	1,500	500	1,000
Current assets			
Stock		25,000	
Debtors		0	
Cash		48,500	
		73,500	
Current liabilities			
Creditors		0	
Net current assets			73,500
Total net asset			74,500
Financed by:			
Opening capital			10,000
Add: profit		79,500	
Less: drawings		15,000	
			64,500
Closing capital			74,500

By the end of the year the company has accumulated £48,500 in cash and £25,000 in stock. The total of the current assets is, therefore, £73,500. The value of fixed assets, after allowing for depreciation, is only £1000, which gives a total net assets figure of £74,500. During the year the capital employed in the company rose from £10,000 to £74,500 because only £15,000 of the £79,500 net profit was drawn out of the business.

You should be able to trace every figure from the spreadsheet format onto the P&L account or balance sheet. Check back to make sure you are clear about every figure. Notice the high standard of presentation.

Frequently asked questions

1. **Why does the balance sheet balance?**
   At the end of the financial year, income and expenditure net off to give the profit figure. Profit is a liability. At the year end everything is, therefore, either an asset or a liability. The total value of assets is equal to the total value of liabilities at the end of the year because all transactions have two aspects.
2. **Why is closing stock subtracted in the cost of sales calculation?**
   Closing stock is the value of goods bought during the year but not yet sold. Profit cannot be earned on goods, which have not been sold. Closing stock is, therefore, subtracted from purchases in the trading account.
3. **Why does the P&L account show gross profit as well as net profit?**
   So that the profit on trading is displayed, as well as the profit left after taking into account the expenses, e.g. wages.
4. **What is the 'financed by' section of the balance sheet?**
   It shows all your long-term sources of finance: capital, profits and loans.
5. **What is depreciation?**
   A measure of the using up of a fixed asset over its useful life.
6. **Why is depreciation on the balance sheet different to that on the P&L account?**
   All balance sheet items, assets and liabilities, are cumulative. All P&L account items, income and expenditure, relate to one year. Depreciation on the balance sheet is, therefore, cumulative while depreciation on the P&L account is a one-year figure.
7. **What is the difference between debtors and creditors?**
   Debtors are customers while creditors are suppliers.
8. **Why not put all the assets at the top of the balance sheet and all the liabilities under 'financed by'?**
   This would make it simpler to understand, but creditors are not a long-term source of finance, so they could not go under 'financed by'. Also, the Companies Act does not allow it.
9. **Why is the balance sheet made up of three columns?**
   To allow separate columns for totalling up cost, accumulated depreciation and net book value of fixed assets.
10. **What is the purpose of preparing the P&L account and balance sheet?**
    To show the profit earned and the sources and uses of funds.

11. **What is the difference between the P&L account and balance sheet?**
   The balance sheet displays the sources and uses of funds at the end of the year, while the P&L account shows the profit earned during the year.
12. **Why is capital a liability?**
   Because it is owed by the business to the owner.
13. **Why is profit a liability?**
   Because it is owed by the business to the owner.
14. **What is net current assets?**
   The difference between current assets and current liabilities, sometimes referred to as working capital.
15. **Why are drawings subtracted from capital?**
   Because they reduce the amount that the business owes the owner.

Conclusions

This chapter develops a new set of skills: the presentation of financial information and the short commentaries that accompany them. To practise these skills, attempt the questions provided. If you find it difficult to start, have a quick look at the answer before you begin. If you are stuck halfway through, have another look at the answer. If you don't want to look at the answers, check your progress against the in-chapter examples. Do each question two or three times, until you do not need to look at the answer at all.

After practising these questions you should be able to see how individual transactions percolate into the P&L account and balance sheet. Here are the stages within the process:

- Set up the accounting framework.
- Put in the balances brought forward from the previous year (if any).
- Reverse the year end stock adjustment (if any).
- Put all the transactions for the year into the accounting framework.
- Trial balance summarises the year.
- Count stock.
- Calculate depreciation.
- Prepare a P&L account.
- Add the profit to capital.
- Prepare a balance sheet.

Red Western Cedar Co.

Red Western Cedar Co. has been trading as a specialist timber merchant for many years. The company specialises in ecological hardwood. The latest trial balance shows the following:

Red Western Cedar Co.

Trial Balance
As at 30th September 200X

Capital		£75,000
Stock at start of year	£25,000	
Freehold property at cost	120,000	
Fixtures and fittings at cost	20,000	
Motor vehicles at cost	24,000	
Provision for depreciation at start of year		
Fixtures and fittings		9,000
Motor vehicles		12,000
Sales		250,000
Purchases	140,000	
Wages	35,000	
Rates and insurance	5,000	
Light and heat	3,000	
Motor vehicle expenses	6,000	
Loan interest paid	6,000	
Miscellaneous expenses	500	
Debtors	16,500	
Creditors		16,000
Cash	6,000	
Loans		60,000
Drawings	15,000	
	£422,000	£422,000

Year end adjustments (which have not yet been reflected in the figures above):

- Stock at 30th September 200X, £30,000.
- Depreciation is to be calculated: fixtures and fittings, 15% of cost per annum; motor vehicles, 25% of cost per annum. Freehold property is not depreciated.

Your task

Prepare a trading and profit and loss account for the year ended 30th September 200X for Red Western Cedar Co. and a balance sheet for the year ended on that date. Write a short commentary explaining the company's results.

Sion Corn

Sion Corn is a sole trader in the wholesale sweets and confectionery business. He has engaged your services to produce a trading and profit and loss account for the year ended 31st October 2004 and a balance sheet as at that date. The computerised accounting system (i.e. the accounting framework) has produced the following trial balance (all in £'s):

Sion Corn

Trial Balance
As at 31st October 2004

	Debit	Credit
Capital		60,000
Stock at 1st November 2003	25,000	
Freehold property at cost	100,000	
Fixtures and fittings at cost	20,000	
Motor vehicles at cost	24,000	
Provision for depreciation at		
1st November 2003		
Fixtures and fittings		6,000
Motor vehicles		12,000
Sales		190,000
Purchases	110,000	
Wages	25,000	
Rates and insurance	5,000	
Light and heat	2,000	
Motor vehicle expenses	5,000	
Loan interest paid	10,000	
Miscellaneous expenses	1,000	
Drawings	18,000	
Debtors	15,000	
Creditors		16,000
Bank balance	3,000	
Bank loan		79,000
Total	**363,000**	**363,000**

Year end adjustments (not yet reflected in the figures above):

- Stock at 31st October 2004 is valued at £30,000.
- Depreciation is to be calculated as follows: fixtures and fittings at 15%, motor vehicles at 25%. Freehold property is not depreciated.

Your task

Prepare a trading and profit and loss account for the year ended 31st October 2004 and a balance sheet as at that date.

Rollicks

Chad Timpson is the sole proprietor of a boat yard buying and selling traditional clinker built rowing boats. The business trades under the name 'Rollicks' and is based in freehold premises in Salcombe. Chad inherited these premises four years ago. At that time they had a market value of £70,000. Chad originally borrowed £10,000 from the bank, using the premises as security. This gave him the working capital to start the business, which has now been in operation for four years. Unfortunately, Chad has only generated modest profits. The following trial balance has been extracted from his accounting records (all in £'s):

Rollicks

Trial Balance
Year Ended 30th September 2004

	Debit	Credit
Sales	0	139,400
Purchases	98,400	0
Electricity	990	0
Rates and insurance	5,400	0
Staff costs	7,659	0
Motor vehicle expenses	2,100	0
Stationery and postage	500	0
Varnish, sandpaper, brushes, etc.	3,250	0
Advertising and promotions	3,300	0
Loan interest and bank charges	750	0
Freehold property at cost	70,000	0
Motor vehicle at cost	6,000	0
Office machinery at cost	4,000	0
Depreciation provision at		
1st October 2003	0	0
Motor vehicles	0	3,000
Office machinery	0	2,000
Stock at 1st October 2003	10,600	0
Debtors	8,950	0
Creditors	0	5,949
Cash at bank	50	0
Owner's capital	0	78,000
Loan	0	6,000
Drawings	12,400	0
Total	234,349	234,349

Year end adjustments (not reflected in the above):

- Stock at 30th September 2004 is valued at £10,000.
- Depreciation has been calculated as £1000 on office machinery and £1000 on motor vehicles.

Your task

Prepare a trading and profit and loss account for the year ended 30th September 2004, and a balance sheet as at 30th September 2004. Also, prepare a brief commentary explaining the company's results for the year.

Mr. H. Bean Winesellers

The first year

After the first full year of trading, Mr. H. Bean has summarised his financial position as follows (all in £'s):

Summary at the end of the first year of trading

Sales on credit	55,000
Sales for cash	45,000
Purchases on credit	84,800
Purchases for cash	200
Wages (paid in cash)	6,000
Rent (paid in cash)	4,000
Insurance (paid in cash)	500
Cash register (paid in cash)	1,200
Second-hand van (paid in cash)	4,000
Cash received from debtors	51,000
Cash paid to creditors	65,000
Drawings (paid in cash)	250
Capital	5,000

Year end adjustments:

- Depreciation on the van is to be calculated at 25% (four years) and the cash register 20% (five years).
- Stock at the end of the year has been valued at £5000.

The company's financial year ends in February.

Your task

1. Set up the accounting framework using the spreadsheet format. See the pro forma layout in Figure 5.2.
2. Enter all the transactions detailed above into the appropriate columns, each transaction having two sides.
3. Enter the year end stock adjustment.
4. Calculate depreciation.
5. Enter the year end depreciation adjustment.
6. Prepare a trading and profit and loss account using the standard formats.
7. Prepare a balance sheet.
8. Write a brief commentary.

	Sales	Purchases	Expenses	Van	Cash register	Stock	Debtor	Cash	Capital	Creditor	Depreciation van	Depreciation register
Start up												
Cash sales												
Credit sales												
Cash purchases												
Credit purchases												
Wages												
Rent												
Insurance												
Fixed asset												
Fixed asset												
Cash from debtors												
Cash to creditors												
Drawings												
YEAs												
Stock												
Depreciation van												
Depreciation register												
Total												
Profit												

Figure 5.2 Mr. Bean's first year: accounting framework pro forma

The second year

After the second full year of trading, Mr. Bean has summarised his financial position as follows (all in £'s):

Transactions during the second year of trading

Sales on credit	85,000
Sales for cash	45,000
Purchases on credit	98,500
Purchases for cash	500
Wages (paid in cash)	12,000
Rent (paid in cash)	4,000
Insurance (paid in cash)	1,000
Marketing (paid in cash)	10,000
Cash received from debtors	71,000
Cash paid to creditors	95,000
Drawings (paid in cash)	15,000

Note: The above does not include any assets or liabilities brought forward from the first year.

Year end adjustments:

- Depreciation on the van is to be calculated at 25% (four years) and the cash register 20% (five years).
- Stock at the end of the second year has been valued at £10,000.

Your task

As for the first year, see the eight points above. Take care to bring forward all the assets and liabilities from the first year. Also, remember to eliminate the opening stock by reversing the previous year's stock adjustment. See the pro forma layout in Figure 5.3.

Celtic Rugs

Rhiannon sells Celtic-style wall hangings and rugs. Looking at last year's accounts, the following fixed assets, stock, cash and capital were brought forward (all in £'s):

Capital	57,815
Stock	22,162
Cash at bank and in hand	2,453
Shop fittings at cost	30,000
Motor vehicles at cost	8,000
Office equipment at cost	4,000
Provision for depreciation	
Motor vehicles	4,000
Office equipment	1,800
Shop fittings	3,000

	Sales	Purchases	Expenses	Van	Cash register	Stock	Debtor	Cash	Capital	Creditor	Depreciation van	Depreciation register
Balances B/F												
Reverse stock												
Cash sales												
Credit sales												
Cash purchases												
Credit purchases												
Wages												
Rent												
Insurance												
Marketing												
Cash from debtors												
Cash to creditors												
Drawings												
YEAs												
Stock												
Depreciation van												
Depreciation register												
Total												
Profit												

Figure 5.3 Mr. Bean's second year: accounting framework pro forma

The books for this year show the following:

	£
Cash sales	221,506
Credit sales (still waiting for the cash)	34,500
Purchases	164,537
Wages	25,000
Rent and rates	12,600
Motor expenses	2,887
Advertising and promotions	9,870
Light, heat and power	3,000
Shop repairs	172
Insurance	509
Telephone and postage	939
Tea, coffee and lunch, etc.	770
Sundries	704
Drawings	12,000

All transactions are in cash apart from credit sales. Year end adjustments are as follows:

- Rhiannon undertook a detailed stock count at the end of the year. The total value of stock was £21,485.
- Depreciation is to be calculated as follows: motor vehicles 25%, office equipment 15%, shop fittings 10%.
- The financial year of the business ends on 31st December.

Your task

Using the spreadsheet format of the accounting framework, prepare a trading and profit and loss account for the financial year and a balance sheet at the end of the financial year.

Solutions

Red Western Cedar Co.

Trading and Profit and Loss Account
Year Ended 30th September 200X

Sales		£250,000
Less: cost of sales		
Opening stock	£25,000	
Add: purchases	140,000	
	165,000	
Less: closing stock	30,000	
		135,000
Gross profit		115,000
Less: expenses		
Wages	35,000	
Rates and insurance	5,000	
Light and heat	3,000	
Motor vehicle expenses	6,000	
Loan interest	6,000	
Miscellaneous	500	
Depreciation	9,000	
		64,500
Net profit		£50,500

During the year the company sold £250,000 worth of goods and generated a gross profit of £115,000. Expenses for the year totalled £64,500 and, as a result, the net profit for the year was £50,500. The largest single expense incurred by the business was wages, £35,000. Depreciation amounted to £9000.

Red Western Cedar Co.

Balance Sheet
As at 30th September 200X

	Cost	Depreciation provision	Net book value
Fixed assets			
Freehold property	£120,000	0	£120,000
Fixtures and fittings	20,000	12,000	8,000
Motor vehicles	24,000	18,000	6,000
	164,000	30,000	134,000
Current assets			
Stock		30,000	
Debtors		16,500	
Cash		6,000	
		52,500	
Current liabilities			
Creditors		16,000	
Working capital			36,500
Total net assets			£170,500
Financed by:			
Opening capital			£75,000
Add: net profit		50,500	
Less: drawings		15,000	
			35,500
Closing capital			110,500
Add: loan			60,000
			£170,500

The company is financed by a mixture of owner's capital and loans. The owner's capital at the start of the year was £75,000. Of the £50,500 profit earned during the year, £35,500 was reinvested in the business, rather than being drawn out of the business. Consequently, the closing owner's capital was £110,500. The bank loan stood at £60,000 at the end of the year.

The total net assets of the company stood at £170,500 at the end of the year. This was made up of fixed assets (after depreciation) of £134,000 and net current assets of £36,500. At the end of the year the company had cash of £6000.

Sion Corn

Trading and Profit and Loss Account
Year Ended 31st October 2004

Sales		£190,000
Less: cost of sales		
Opening stock	£25,000	
Add: purchases	110,000	
	135,000	
Less: closing stock	30,000	
		105,000
Gross profit		85,000
Less: expenses		
Wages	25,000	
Rates and insurance	5,000	
Light and heat	2,000	
Motor vehicle expenses	5,000	
Loan interest	10,000	
Miscellaneous	1,000	
Depreciation fixtures	3,000	
Depreciation motor	6,000	
		57,000
Net profit		28,000

The company made sales worth £190,000 during the year, which generated a gross profit of £85,000. Expenses totalled £57,000 and, as a result, the net profit was £28,000.

Sion Corn

Balance Sheet
As at 31st October 2004

	Cost	Accumulated depreciation	Net book value
Fixed assets			
Freehold property	£100,000	0	£100,000
Fixtures and fittings	20,000	9,000	11,000
Motor vehicles	24,000	18,000	6,000
	144,000	27,000	117,000
Current assets			
Stock		30,000	
Debtors		15,000	
Cash		3,000	
		48,000	
Current liabilities			
Creditors		16,000	
Working capital			32,000
Total net assets			£149,000
Financed by:			
Owner's capital			60,000
Net profit		28,000	
Less: drawings		18,000	
			10,000
			70,000
Loan			79,000
			£149,000

The company is financed by a mixture of owner's capital and long-term loans. At the start of the year the owner's capital stood at £60,000. During the year profit of £28,000 was earned, of which £10,000 was retained in the business. Consequently, owner's capital grew to £70,000 by the end of the year. The loans at the end of the year stood at £79,000. As a result, loans play a greater part in company finances than owner's capital.

During the year the company paid £10,000 in interest, the second largest expense item. If the company could reduce the loans, the loan interest would be reduced and a higher profit would eventually be earned.

Chad Timpson: Trading as 'Rollicks'

Trading and Profit and Loss Account
Year Ended 30th September 2004

Sales		£139,400
Less: cost of sales		
Opening stock	£10,600	
Add: purchases	98,400	
	109,000	
Less: closing stock	10,000	
		99,000
Gross profit		40,400
Less: expenses		
Staff costs	7,659	
Rates and insurance	5,400	
Advertising	3,300	
Varnish and consumables	3,250	
Motor vehicle expenses	2,100	
Electricity	990	
Stationery and postage	500	
Loan interest	750	
Depreciation	2,000	
		25,949
Net profit		£14,451

The company earned a net profit of £14,451 during the year. The gross profit from trading was £40,400 and the total expenses for the year were £25,949. Staff costs were the largest single expense, £7659.

Chad Timpson: Trading as 'Rollicks'

Balance Sheet
As at 30th September 2004

	Cost	Depreciation provision	Net book value
Fixed assets			
Freehold property	£70,000	0	£70,000
Motor vehicles	6,000	4,000	2,000
Office machinery	4,000	3,000	1,000
	80,000	7,000	73,000
Current assets			
Stock		10,000	
Debtors		8,950	
Cash		50	
		19,000	
Current liabilities			
Creditors		5,949	
Working capital			13,051
Total net assets			86,051
Financed by:			
Owner's capital			78,000
Net profit		14,451	
Less: drawings		12,400	
			2,051
			80,051
Loan			6,000
			£86,051

The company has cash balances of only £50 and owes suppliers £5949. Customers owe £8950, which is more than enough to pay the current liabilities. The company has substantial fixed assets of £73,000 after depreciation. The total net assets are £86,051.

The company is financed by owner's capital and a small bank loan. Owner's capital stood at £78,000 at the start of the year. Most of the profit earned during the year (£14,451) has been drawn out of the company and, consequently, the closing capital is £80,051. At the end of the year the bank loan stood at £6000.

Mr. H. Bean Winesellers THE FIRST YEAR

Trading and Profit and Loss Account
Year Ended 28th February 20X1

	£	£
Sales		100,000
Cost of sales		
Opening stock	0	
Add: purchases	85,000	
	85,000	
Less: closing stock	5,000	
		80,000
Gross profit		20,000
Less: expenses		
Wages	6,000	
Rent	4,000	
Insurance	500	
Depreciation	1,240	
		11,740
Net profit		8,260

In its first year the company has earned a gross profit of £20,000 from sales of £100,000. Expenses amount to £11,740, leaving a net profit of £8260.

Mr. H. Bean Winesellers

Balance Sheet
As at 28th February 20X1

	Cost	Accumulated depreciation	Net book value
Fixed assets			
Van	4,000	1,000	3,000
Cash register	1,200	240	960
	5,200	1,240	3,960
Current assets			
Stock		5,000	
Debtors		4,000	
Cash		19,850	
		28,850	
Current liabilities			
Creditors		19,800	
Net current assets			9,050
Total net assets			13,010
Financed by:			
Capital			5,000
Add: profit		8,260	
Less: drawings		250	8,010
			13,010

Mr. Bean's First Year

Accounting Framework

	Sales	Purchases	Expenses	Van	Cash register	Stock	Debtor	Cash	Capital	Creditor	Depreciation van	Depreciation register
Start up								5,000	5,000			
Cash sales	45,000							45,000				
Credit sales	55,000						55,000					
Cash purchases		200						−200				
Credit purchases		84,800								84,800		
Wages			6,000					−6,000				
Rent			4,000					−4,000				
Insurance			500					−500				
Fixed asset					1,200			−1,200				
Fixed asset				4,000				−4,000				
Cash from debtors							−51,000	+51,000				
Cash to creditors								−65,000		−65,000		
Drawings								−250	−250			
YEAs												
Stock		−5,000				+5,000						
Depreciation van			1,000								1,000	
Depreciation register			240									240
Total	100,000	80,000	11,740	4,000	1,200	5,000	4,000	19,850	4,750	19,800	1,000	240
Profit			8,260						8,260			

During the first year the company accumulated substantial cash reserves of £19,850, but it owes suppliers £19,800. The company holds small stocks worth £5000 and customers owe £4000. As a result, the current assets are £9050 greater than current liabilities. Owner's capital has grown from £5000 to £13,010.

Mr. H. Bean Winesellers THE SECOND YEAR

Trading and Profit and Loss Account
Year Ended 28th February 20X2

	£	£
Sales		130,000
Cost of sales		
Opening stock	5,000	
Add: purchases	99,000	
	104,000	
Less: closing stock	10,000	
		94,000
Gross profit		36,000
Less: expenses		
Wages	12,000	
Rent	4,000	
Marketing	10,000	
Insurance	1,000	
Depreciation	1,240	
		28,240
Net profit		7,760

Mr. H. Bean Winesellers

Balance Sheet
As at 28th February 20X2

	Cost	Accumulated depreciation	Net book value
Fixed assets			
Van	4,000	2,000	2,000
Cash register	1,200	480	720
	5,200	2,480	2,720
Current assets			
Stock		10,000	
Debtors		18,000	
Cash		−1,650	
		26,350	
Current liabilities			
Creditors		23,300	
Net current assets			3,050
Total net assets			5,770
Financed by:			
Capital			13,010
Add: profit		7,760	
Less: drawings		15,000	−7,240
			5,770

During the year the company has made a small profit of £7760, but the owner has drawn a substantial amount of money out of the business, £15,000. As a result, owner's capital has fallen from £13,010 to £5770. The drawings have also had the effect of wiping out cash reserves, to the extent that the company is overdrawn at the bank £1650. Fortunately current assets are still greater than current liabilities, but only by £3050.

Mr. Bean's Second Year

Accounting Framework

	Sales	Purchases	Expenses	Van	Cash register	Stock	Debtor	Cash	Capital	Creditor	Depreciation van	Depreciation register
Balances B/F	0	0	0	4,000	1,200	5,000	4,000	19,850	13,010	19,800	1,000	240
Reverse stock		+5,000				−5,000						
Cash sales	45,000							+45,000				
Credit sales	85,000						85,000					
Cash purchases		500						−500				
Credit purchases		98,500								98,500		
Wages			12,000					−12,000				
Rent			4,000					−4,000				
Insurance			1,000					−1,000				
Marketing			10,000					−10,000				
Cash from debtors							−71,000	+71,000				
Cash to creditors								−95,000		−95,000		
Drawings								−15,000	−15,000			
YEAs												
Stock		−10,000				+10,000						
Depreciation van			1,000								1,000	
Depreciation register			240									240
Total	130,000	94,000	28,240	4,000	1,200	10,000	18,000	−1,650	−1,990	23,300	2,000	480
Profit			7,760						7,760			

Celtic Rugs

Trading and Profit and Loss Account
Year Ended 31st December 200X

Sales		£256,006
Less: cost of sales		
Opening stock	22,162	
Add: purchases	164,537	
	186,699	
Less: closing stock	21,485	
		165,214
Gross profit		90,792
Less: expenses		
Wages	25,000	
Rent and rates	12,600	
Motor expenses	2,887	
Advertising and promotion	9,870	
Light and heat	3,000	
Shop repairs	172	
Insurance	509	
Telephone and postage	939	
Canteen	770	
Sundries	704	
Depreciation	5,600	
		62,051
Net profit		£28,741

During the year the business made sales of £256,006, generating a gross profit of £90,792. Expenses totalled £62,051 and, consequently, a net profit of £28,741 was earned. The largest single expense was wages, £25,000. Rent and rates amounted to £12,600.

Celtic Rugs

Balance Sheet
As at 31st December 200X (all in £'s)

	Cost	Accumulated depreciation	Net book value
Fixed assets			
Shop fittings	30,000	6,000	24,000
Motor vehicles	8,000	6,000	2,000
Office equipment	4,000	2,400	1,600
	42,000	14,400	27,600
Current assets			
Stock		21,485	
Debtors		34,500	
Cash		−9,029	
		46,956	
Current liabilities			
Creditors		0	
Working capital			46,956
Total net assets			74,556
Financed by:			
Owner's capital			57,815
Net profit		28,741	
Less: drawings		12,000	
			16,741
			74,556
Loan			0
			74,556

This business is financed entirely from owner's capital, and has no long-term loans; however, £9029 is owed to the bank. The business holds substantial stock of £21,485 and customers owe £34,500. As a result, the company does have the means to settle the amount owed to the bank.

The company also has fixed assets of an original cost of £42,000 which, after accumulated depreciation of £14,400, have a net book value of £27,600. The total net assets amount to £74,556. Of the £28,741 profit earned during the year, £16,741 was retained in the business. Consequently, owner's capital grew from £57,815 to £74,556.

Celtic Rugs

Accounting Framework

	Sales	Purchases	Expenses	Shop fittings	Motor vehicle	Office equipment	Stock	Debtors	Cash	Capital	Deprec. shop	Deprec. motor	Deprec. office
Balances B/F	0	0	0	30,000	8,000	4,000	22,162	0	2,453	57,815	3,000	4,000	1,800
Reverse stock		+22,162					−22,162						
Cash sales	221,506								+221,506				
Credit sales	34,500							34,500					
Cash purchases		164,537							−164,537				
Credit purchases			0										
Wages			25,000						−25,000				
Rent and rates			12,600						−12,600				
Motor expenses			2,887						−2,887				
Advertising and promotion			9,870						−9,870				
Light, heat and power			3,000						−3,000				
Shop repairs			172						−172				
Insurance			509						−509				
Telephone and post			939						−939				
Tea, coffee, etc.			770						−770				
Sundry expenses			704						−704				
Drawings									−12,000	−12,000			
YEAs													
Stock		−21,485					+21,485						
Depreciation motor			2,000									2,000	
Depreciation office			600										600
Depreciation shop			3,000								3,000		
Total	256,006	165,214	62,051	30,000	8,000	4,000	21,485	34,500	−9,029	45,815	6,000	6,000	2,400
Profit			28,741							28,741			

Cash flow forecasting

This chapter is about measuring the amount of cash flowing into and out of a business.

- Preparing a cash flow forecast;
- Explaining a cash flow forecast;
- Start up costs.

Introduction

*Importance of
the subject*

A company without cash cannot buy the people, materials or equipment it needs and, without these, a profit cannot be earned. Consequently, cash needs to be carefully monitored. A cash flow forecast (see Figure 6.1) shows the quantities of money flowing into and out of a business and the cumulative cash position. If more money is coming into a company than going out, there is no cash flow problem. If more money is going out than coming in, however, a cash flow problem exists. The company may not have enough money to pay for the resources it needs.

*Activities and
outcomes*

This chapter includes some new terminology, in-chapter exercises and a step-by-step guide. When you have completed the chapter, attempt the multiple choice questions before going on to the end of chapter questions. Having completed these you will be in a position to confidently prepare and explain a cash flow forecast.

Key cash flow terms

There are five key definitions you need to learn and understand. These are also the five main headings in a cash flow forecast.

Receipts	Cash received by the business. This is distinct from sales because of debtors.
Payments	Everything the company has to pay for, including expenses, purchases, fixed assets and drawings.

Net cash flow   Difference between total receipts and total payments.

Balance B/F   The amount of cash the company has in the bank on the very first day of the period. In the case of a business start up this may be nil.

Balance C/F   The amount of cash the company has at the end of the period.

If all sales are cash sales, then receipts are equivalent to sales. Most businesses, however, operate on credit sales and, therefore, have debtors. Consider this example. During a year a company has credit sales of £425,000. At the end of the year, debtors owe £15,000. All other credit sales have been received in cash. In the space provided write down the total receipts for the year.

The total receipts for the year were £410,000 (£425,000 − £15,000). Notice that the receipts are different from the sales.

For a New Business

Cash Flow Forecast
Year Ended 31st December 2004

	Jan	Feb	Mar	Apr	May	Jun	Jul	Aug	Sep	Oct	Nov	Dec	Total
Receipts													
Sales													
Other													
Total													
Payments													
Purchases													
Expenses													
Interest													
Fixed assets													
Drawings													
Total													
Net cash flow													
Balance B/F													
Balance C/F													

Figure 6.1 Cash Flow Forecast

Some of the cash received this year may relate to credit sales made last year. For instance, a company might make £10,000 of credit sales every month, but may have to wait two months to receive the cash. Credit sales made in December result in receipts in February. Credit sales in January result in receipts in March, etc.

As well as receipts being different from credit sales, payments are different from credit purchases. For example, during a year a company purchases on credit £720,000 of goods. At the end of the year £50,000 is owed to creditors and all the rest of the credit purchases are paid for. In the space provided, write down the total payments in the year.

The total payments in the year were £670,000 (£720,000 − £50,000). Notice that the payments figure is different from purchases.

Payments do not just include cash for purchases. Payments include everything the business pays for which results in cash flowing out of the business:

- Purchases
- Expenses
- Equipment
- Drawings
- Taxation

Net cash flow

Net cash flow is the difference between receipts and payments. If receipts are greater than payments there is no cash flow problem. If payments are greater than receipts there is a cash flow problem. Net cash flow indicates the existence and extent of cash flow problems.

If net cash flow is negative, more **cash** is going out of the business than coming in. If net cash flow is positive, more **cash** is coming in than going out. Look carefully at the following three months:

	Receipts	Payments	Net cash flow
Month 1	10,000	7,800	2,200
Month 2	11,000	12,300	−1,300
Month 3	12,000	14,600	−2,600

In the space provided write a short paragraph explaining why month 2 is a problem month.

In month 2 there *is* more money going out than coming in: £12,300 went out and only £11,000 came in. This is what you could have written:

> 'During month 2 total payments amounted to £12,300 and receipts only £11,000. As a result, more cash went out of the business than came in. This could be a problem for the business because, if the cash runs out, they will be unable to buy the materials, people and equipment they need.'

Assuming there is no cash in the bank at the start of month 1, the cumulative cash balance at the end of month 3 is −£1700. Check this on your calculator now. This is how the figure should be calculated:

Total receipts	£33,000
Total payments	£34,700
Total net cash flow	−£1,700

Preparing a cash flow forecast: step by step

Always follow these steps when preparing a cash flow forecast.

1. Determine the period for which a cash flow forecast is required, e.g. six months or one year.
2. Give a proper heading for the forecast including the name of the company, the period it covers and the date at which it was prepared.
3. Head up a column for each month in the period and, on the far right, leave space for a total column.
4. Find out if sales are cash sales or credit sales and when the cash will be received.
5. Find the purchases and the relevant dates of payment for purchases.
6. Identify all expenses including loan or overdraft interest and ascertain the date of payment for expenses.
7. Identify proposed fixed asset investments and dates of payment.
8. Identify proposed drawings or dividends and dates of payment.
9. Calculate the total of payments and of receipts in each month (use your calculator).
10. Calculate the net cash flow each month (receipts less payments).
11. Find the opening cash balance, which may be zero in a new business.
12. Calculate the balance C/F at the end of every month.

To check your work, add up the cash flow horizontally, completing the total column as you go. The total net cash flow plus the opening balance should give the closing balance. If not, there is a mistake somewhere. Using your calculator, check through all the figures again. Refer to the cash flow forecast in Figure 6.1 to see how it should be presented.

Cash flow forecast in action

Consider a cash flow forecast for a business start up situation. Nathalie has an idea for Sparkles Cleaning Services, a contract cleaning company. You have a detailed discussion with Nathalie, after which you make the following notes about her ideas:

1. Nathalie intends to pay £30.00 per day to employees and charge £50.00 per day to customers.
2. On the basis of five days per week and four weeks per month, every employee costs £600 per month and is charged to customers at £1000 per month.
3. All sales are cash sales paid in the month, so there is no time delay on the cash flow.
4. All wages are to be paid in the month, so there is no time delay on the cash flow.
5. Nathalie hopes to get one person out working in September, five in October, ten in November and ten in December.
6. Nathalie will incur a phone bill of £100 per month starting from July. This is paid quarterly, so £300 paid in September and £300 paid in December. Connecting a new business telephone line costs £50, paid in July.
7. A new computer and software costs £1200, paid in July.
8. Nathalie will advertise in August to attract cleaning staff, spending £1000, paid in July.
9. Nathalie will run the business from home, saving on rent, rates, electricity, insurance, etc.
10. Stationery costs are £50, paid in August.
11. There will be no drawings in the first six months.
12. Start up capital £2500 will be paid into a business bank account in July.

The cash flow forecast in Figure 6.2 has been prepared on the basis of the information above. Go through every figure carefully, linking it back to the information Nathalie gave.

On the basis of these figures the company is generating a cash surplus of £10,000; however, the cash flow may be rather over-optimistic. It assumes customers pay immediately (cash sales). It does not include insurance costs, e.g. employer's liability, and zero drawings mean that Nathalie takes nothing out of the business for six months. These shortcomings can easily be corrected.

Consider changing the sales from cash sales to credit sales. It will make a difference to the cash surplus generated in the period. Recalculate the net cash flow on the assumption that customers pay in the month following, e.g. September work received in October. Write your answer in the space provided below.

Sparkles Cleaning Services

Projected Cash Flow

	Jul	Aug	Sep	Oct	Nov	Dec	Total
Receipts							
Sales	0	0	1,000	5,000	10,000	10,000	26,000
Other	2,500						2,500
Total	2,500	0	1,000	5,000	10,000	10,000	28,500
Payments							
Wages			600	3,000	6,000	6,000	15,600
Telephone	50		300			300	650
Computer	1,200						1,200
Stationery		50					50
Advertising	1,000						1,000
Total	2,250	50	900	3,000	6,000	6,300	18,500
Net cash flow	**250**	**−50**	**100**	**2,000**	**4,000**	**3,700**	**10,000**
Balance B/F	0	250	200	300	2,300	6,300	0
Balance C/F	250	200	300	2,300	6,300	10,000	10,000

> THIS IS A NEW BUSINESS, SO IT HAS A ZERO STARTING BALANCE

> NOTE THAT THE B/F FIGURE IN AUGUST IS THE SAME AS THE C/F FIGURE IN JULY. THIS RULE APPLIES IN EVERY MONTH

> IF THESE TWO NUMBERS ARE NOT THE SAME, THERE IS AN ERROR IN THE CALCULATIONS

Notes:

- Receipts from sales start in September because this is when the first cleaning contract starts.
- The start up capital is only just enough to cover the cost of the computer, advertising and telephone line connection.
- The net cash flow is only negative in August.
- The balance B/F is zero because this is a new business, so there are no opening balances.
- The total of the net cash flow is equal to the cumulative balance because this is a new business.

Figure 6.2 Cash Flow in Action

Do not change any of the payments figures. With receipts, simply move the sales figures one month forward. The September sales will not be received in cash until October. The October sales will not be received in cash until November, and the November sales will not be received until December. The key point is December sales will not be received until January. As a result, there will be £10,000 less cash received in the period to December. The answer is, therefore, zero net cash flow in the six-month period. Exactly the same amount of cash is coming in as going out. This makes the business proposition look less attractive.

Key points in cash flows

There are some common errors, which regularly occur in cash flows:

- Depreciation is not a cash transaction; therefore, it does not appear on a cash flow.
- Where monthly payments are greater than receipts, the cash flow is negative. Do not forget the minus sign.
- When successive months have negative cash flows, the balance C/F may be negative. Do not forget the minus sign.
- Take care when using a calculator.
- Always check your work.

Differences between cash flow and P&L account

Net cash flow and profits are related concepts, but they are not the same. There are several differences between the two:

- Cash flow includes receipts rather than sales.
- Cash flow includes payments rather than purchases.
- Cash flow has no stock adjustment, unlike the P&L account.
- Cash flow has no depreciation, unlike the P&L account.
- Cash flow includes drawings, unlike the P&L account.
- Cash flow includes the payments for new fixed assets, unlike the P&L account.

Total net cash flow in any year will not be the same as profit for the year, for the reasons given above.

Start up costs

One of the most common applications of cash flow forecasting is in a business start up situation. In this context, cash flow identifies the amount of cash and capital needed to start a new venture. A common error is the omission of some of the costs of starting a new business, which can lead to negative net cash flow.

Every new business will need equipment and an initial stock of materials and components. Additionally, there are also start up expenses, which have to be paid before trading can begin. Here is a list of items to consider.

Legal:

- Limited company formation (see Chapter 11).
- Contracts of employment reviewed by a solicitor.

- Terms of business reviewed by a solicitor.
- Lease agreements reviewed by a specialist.
- Insurance agreements.

Marketing:

- Designing the company logo and image.
- Launch advertising.
- Special promotional events, e.g. launch party.
- Promotional offers.
- Web site design.
- Stationery.

Financing:

- Organising finance.
- Overdraft costs (interest and charges).

People costs:

- Recruitment costs, e.g. advertising or agency fees.
- Training costs.
- Travel expenses.

Start up costs can amount to several thousand pounds, even more if accountants and solicitors are involved, because they tend to charge out their time at premium rates, e.g. £25 per 15 minutes. These costs are in addition to equipment and initial stock. Entrepreneurs should ensure they have enough capital before launching a new business. The amount of capital needed does represent a serious barrier to setting up a new business. The lack of sufficient capital is one reason why many new businesses fail.

Conclusions

Negative net cash flow reduces the amount of cash in the bank account. After several successive months of negative net cash flow, cash in the bank may be reduced to zero and the company may become overdrawn. An overdraft is an example of a liability because the business owes money to the bank. This would be shown under current liabilities, as follows:

Current liabilities	
Creditors	2416
Overdraft	1579
	3995

One problem with an overdraft is that the rate of interest and other charges is often high. These increase expenses and reduce net profit. An overdraft often has to be repaid on demand and, as a result, it does not provide a foundation on which to build a business.

Use the questions attached to practise the art of preparing a cash flow forecast. Remember to work to a high standard of presentation and be alert for situations where net cash flow is negative. If a company runs out of cash it will effectively cease to exist, because it will not be able to buy materials and people. Running out of cash is, therefore, a major risk factor in business. Regular cash flow forecasting helps deal with the problem. Later, in Chapter 12, the techniques for maximising net cash flow will be explored.

Statistics vary, but broadly half of all new ventures fail within the first five years. Some people look upon these failures in a positive light. They can be viewed as an essential learning experience. A web site called startupfailures.com allows entrepreneurs to record and share their experiences of failure and success. Many of the contributors emphasise the importance of cash flow forecasting.

Multiple choice questions

Tick the box next to your answer.

1. Which of the following is not a receipt?
   - [ ] Cash received from customers
   - [ ] Interest received from the bank
   - [ ] Start up capital received from the owner
   - [ ] Cash paid to suppliers
   - [ ] Cash received when selling a fixed asset

2. Which of the following is not a payment?
   - [ ] Cash paid for purchases
   - [ ] Purchases bought on credit and not yet paid for
   - [ ] Cash paid for expenses
   - [ ] Cash paid for fixed assets
   - [ ] Cash drawn out by the owner

3. What is net cash flow?
   - [ ] The difference between assets and liabilities
   - [ ] The difference between cash and credit
   - [ ] The total money paid out in a year
   - [ ] The money held at the start of the year
   - [ ] The difference between receipts and payments

4. Receipts = £149 million, payments = £137 million, net cash flow = ?
   - [ ] +£2 million
   - [ ] −£12 million
   - [ ] −£149 million
   - [ ] +£12 million
   - [ ] +£12,000

5. Cash flow is negative when?
   - [ ] A new business starts
   - [ ] Money going out is greater than money coming in
   - [ ] New equipment is bought for cash
   - [ ] The starting balance is negative
   - [ ] Receipts are greater than payments

6. Why are receipts different from sales?
  ☐ Because sales includes VAT
  ☐ Receipts are always the same as cash
  ☐ Because the P&L account is for a year not a month
  ☐ Because cost of sales is subtracted from sales
  ☐ Because not all sales have been received in cash, i.e. debtors

7. Why is depreciation not included in cash flow?
  ☐ Because it is not a cash transaction
  ☐ Because fixed assets are used for more than one year
  ☐ Because fixed assets are not always paid for
  ☐ Because depreciation is an expense
  ☐ Because it is an estimate

8. Balance B/F is the cumulative balance
  ☐ At the start of the year
  ☐ On net cash flow
  ☐ At the middle of the year
  ☐ Of payments
  ☐ At the end of the year

9. Balance B/F = $1 million, NCF = $12 million, balance C/F = ?
  ☐ $1 million
  ☐ $13 million
  ☐ $11,000,000
  ☐ $12
  ☐ $12 million

10. Why is negative net cash flow bad?
  ☐ It increases staff motivation
  ☐ It increases the tax bill
  ☐ It increases drawings
  ☐ It increases interest received
  ☐ It reduces the money available for buying materials and equipment, etc.

Multiple choice answers

	Correct answer	Comment
1	Cash paid to suppliers	This is cash going out, all of the others are examples of cash coming in.
2	Purchases bought on credit	Credit purchases are different from cash purchases.
3	The difference between receipts and payments	The definition of net cash flow.
4	+£12 million	Subtract payments from receipts (£149m − £137m).
5	The money going out is more than the money coming in	Which is the same as payments being greater than receipts.
6	Because not all sales have been received in cash	Because of debtors (money customers owe to the business).

7	Because it is not a cash transaction	Depreciation spreads the impact of buying equipment that has already been paid for.
8	At the start of the year	Balance B/F always means the start of the period, e.g. month, week or year.
9	$13 million	Balance B/F + NCF = balance C/F ($1m + $12m = $13m).
10	It reduces the money available	It may also mean the business is making a loss.

Swizzels

Katie Price wants to start a business importing sweets into Europe from Hong Kong, trading under the name Swizzels. Katie intends to put £17,400 into a business bank account on 1st January 2004. Based on market research, the budgeted sales and purchases for the first six months are as follows:

	Sales	Purchases
January	2000	3200
February	4000	3350
March	6200	4185
April	7000	5500
May	8200	5700
June	8400	5900

- Katie has arranged two months' credit from suppliers for all purchases.
- She expects 25% of sales will be cash sales, the remainder credit sales.
- Credit sales will be on the basis of two months' credit.
- Wages are expected to be £800 per month, paid for in the month, e.g. January wages are paid in January.
- Office machinery will be acquired in January, £2500, and in April, £3500, and paid for in the following month.
- Rent for the warehouse £3000 per year, payable in monthly instalments.
- General office costs £1000 per month, payable every month.
- Katie has negotiated a loan of £4000, the cash to be received by the business in May. Repayments do not start until July.

Your task

Prepare a cash flow forecast for the first six months of the proposed new business. Interpret the cash flow and make a recommendation appropriate to the situation.

Ronnie Rosenthal

Ronnie has been preparing a business plan for a new venture. In relation to cash flow he has provided the following information:

1. Opening cash balance (balance B/F) zero, because this is a new venture.
2. Forecast sales and purchases:

	Sales	Purchases
April	34,000	26,000
May	36,000	27,000
June	40,000	30,000
July	44,000	31,000
August	42,000	32,000
September	39,000	29,000

Debtors pay in the month following the date of sale, so April sales are received in May. Creditors are paid in the month following the date of purchase, so April purchases are paid for in May.

Unusually, Ronnie has negotiated credit from the start of the business. No cash is actually paid or received in April.

3. Starting capital introduced in May, £3000.
4. Expenses are as follows (all in £'s):

May	4000
June	3000
July	5000
August	2000
September	6000
October	4000

Expenses are payable in the month in which they arise.

5. The firm buys new equipment during the year payable in May, £9000, and August, £5000.
6. Drawings by Rosenthal are £900 per month starting in May.

Rent of £2500 is payable in March, June, September and December.

Your task

Prepare a cash flow forecast for the six months up to 31st October 200X.

Macy Rae

Macy Rae has just started a new job but she is concerned about the state of her finances. She is sharing a flat and she has a small car. She has consulted her bank manager who has advised that most payments be made by monthly standing order, and has requested completion of a cash flow forecast for the 12 months to December 200X. So far, Macy has compiled the following information:

Salary

Macy earns £1500 per month with a 10% increase from 1st September 200X. She also expects a £500 bonus in December.

Monthly payments

Rent	400
Pension	200
Electricity	40
Petrol	120
Clothes	200
Groceries	150
Entertainment	150
Lunches	45
Mobile phone	40
Total	**1345**

Quarterly payments

Every March, June, September and December Macy pays bank charges of £15.

Annual payments

Macy expects to buy £300 of Christmas presents in November, £500 motor insurance and £120 road tax in February.

She expects to take a break at Easter costing £500 (payable in March) and one in September costing £1000, including spending money, all payable in August.

Opening balance

Macy has £150 in the bank on 1st January 200X.

Your task

1. Prepare a cash flow forecast suitable for submission to the bank manager.
2. Identify the month with the worst net cash flow.
3. Identify the month with the worst overdraft.
4. Make proposals for eliminating the need for an overdraft.

Katie Price: Trading as 'Swizzels'

Cash Flow Forecast
Six Months to 30th June 2004

	Jan	Feb	Mar	Apr	May	Jun	Total
Receipts							
Cash sales	500	1,000	1,550	1,750	2,050	2,100	8,950
Credit sales	0	0	1,500	3,000	4,650	5,250	14,400
Capital	17,400						17,400
Loan					4,000		4,000
Total	17,900	1,000	3,050	4,750	10,700	7,350	44,750
Payments							
Purchases	0	0	3,200	3,350	4,185	5,500	16,235
Wages	800	800	800	800	800	800	4,800
Rent	250	250	250	250	250	250	1,500
General	1,000	1,000	1,000	1,000	1,000	1,000	6,000
Office machine	0	2,500	0	0	3,500	0	6,000
Drawings	0	0	0	0	0	0	0
Total	2,050	4,550	5,250	5,400	9,735	7,550	34,535
Net cash flow	**15,850**	**−3,550**	**−2,200**	**−650**	**965**	**−200**	**10,215**
Balance B/F	0	15,850	12,300	10,100	9,450	10,415	0
Balance C/F	15,850	12,300	10,100	9,450	10,415	10,215	10,215

> THIS IS A NEW BUSINESS IDEA, SO IT STARTS FROM ZERO CASH BROUGHT FORWARD

In the first six months, the business will generate a positive net cash flow of £10,215. Although there is negative net cash flow in February, March and April, overall the initial capital of £17,400 is sufficient to start the business. The loan of £4000 is not necessary. The company might consider negotiating an overdraft facility rather than taking out a loan. Notice there are no **drawings**; Katie has decided not to take an income from the company during the first six months.

Ronnie Rosenthal

Cash Flow Forecast
Six Months to 31st October 200X

	May	Jun	Jul	Aug	Sep	Oct	Total
Receipts							
Sales	34,000	36,000	40,000	44,000	42,000	39,000	235,000
Other	3,000						3,000
Total	37,000	36,000	40,000	44,000	42,000	39,000	238,000
Payments							
Purchases	26,000	27,000	30,000	31,000	32,000	29,000	175,000
Expenses	4,000	3,000	5,000	2,000	6,000	4,000	24,000
Rent	0	2,500	0	0	2,500	0	5,000
Equipment	9,000	0	0	5,000	0	0	14,000
Drawings	900	900	900	900	900	900	5,400
Total	39,900	33,400	35,900	38,900	41,400	33,900	223,400
Net cash flow	**−2,900**	**2,600**	**4,100**	**5,100**	**600**	**5,100**	**14,600**
Balance B/F	0	−2,900	−300	3,800	8,900	9,500	0
Balance C/F	−2,900	−300	3,800	8,900	9,500	14,600	14,600

NEW BUSINESSES START
WITH ZERO CASH BALANCE
BROUGHT FORWARD

The company has generated a cash balance of £14,600 during the six-month period. May was the only month with a negative net cash flow. This was because of the purchase of equipment (£9000).

Macy Rae

Cash Flow Forecast
Year to 31st December 200X

	Jan	Feb	Mar	Apr	May	Jun	Jul	Aug	Sep	Oct	Nov	Dec	Total
Receipts													
Salary	1,500	1,500	1,500	1,500	1,500	1,500	1,500	1,500	1,650	1,650	1,650	1,650	18,600
Bonus	0	0	0	0	0	0	0	0	0	0	0	500	500
Total	1,500	1,500	1,500	1,500	1,500	1,500	1,500	1,500	1,650	1,650	1,650	2,150	19,100
Payments													
Monthly	1,345	1,345	1,345	1,345	1,345	1,345	1,345	1,345	1,345	1,345	1,345	1,345	16,140
Quarterly	0	0	15	0	0	15	0	0	15	0	0	15	60
Annual	0	620	500	0	0	0	0	1,000	0	0	300	0	2,420
Total	1,345	1,965	1,860	1,345	1,345	1,360	1,345	2,345	1,360	1,345	1,645	1,360	18,620
Net cash flow	155	−465	−360	155	155	140	155	−845	290	305	5	790	480
Balance B/F	150	305	−160	−520	−365	−210	−70	85	−760	−470	−165	−160	150
Balance C/F	305	−160	−520	−365	−210	−70	85	−760	−470	−165	−160	630	630

The month with the worst net cash flow and the worst overdraft is August.
Proposal: Pay monthly for insurance, e.g. £50 per month for 10 months. It may also
be possible to spread the cost of the Easter holiday.

7 Bad debt, discounts and adjustments

This chapter focuses on bad debts, an important risk factor in business, as well as discounts, other write offs and accounting adjustments.

Objectives	
	• Bad debts;
	• Liquidation and bankruptcy;
	• Discounts;
	• Writing off stock and equipment;
	• Accruals;
	• Prepayments.

Introduction

Importance of the subject

This chapter explores some special problems and situations, which have an impact on net profit and capital. Bad debt is one of the most serious risks a business is exposed to. This is examined in detail here, along with 'writing off' other assets such as stock. The impact of granting discounts to customers, together with accruals and prepayments, is also examined. The accounting framework, in the box, spreadsheet and trial balance format, is used to explain the effect of these transactions.

Writing off can be defined as reducing the value of an asset such as stock debtors or fixed assets.

Activities and outcomes

Your knowledge of the accounting framework will be broadened and deepened by studying the wide range of business situations covered in this chapter. The conclusions contain a summary of definitions, which you may find useful while working through the chapter. Use the multiple choice questions to check your understanding before attempting the end of chapter questions.

Bad debts

It is a common business practice to offer credit to customers (credit sales). Most businesses, therefore, have debtors and are exposed to the risk that customers may not pay for the goods they have bought. In some circumstances it may be difficult to recover the money owed because the customer may have gone into liquidation. Consequently, the debtor may have to be written off, because the money is irrecoverable. This situation is termed a bad debt.

In certain situations the impact of a bad debt may be sufficient to bankrupt a business, e.g. the losses caused by a bad debt may be greater than the profit earned during the whole year. If all sales are cash sales, there are no debtors and, therefore, there is no risk of bad debt. Bad debt is part of the risk of making credit sales.

The issue of bad debts can be broken down into four special transactions:

- Bad debt write off;
- Specific bad debt provision;
- General bad debt provision;
- Bad debt recovered.

If a customer refuses to accept goods that have been supplied because they are not happy with the quality or the wrong goods have been delivered, a credit note must be raised. Credit notes cancel out the original sale. A bad debt is different; it arises when a company refuses to pay or cannot pay for goods even though there was nothing wrong with them.

Bad debt write off

This is the situation where a debtor has been declared bankrupt, refuses to pay or simply cannot be traced and it becomes impossible to recover the money or goods. Part of the asset called debtors has to be reduced. The amount the bankrupt customer owes is written down to zero. The accounting framework shows both sides of a bad debt write off:

Debtors decrease and expenses called bad debt increase.

The box diagram shows a situation where debtors reduce by £1000 and expenses increase by £1000, to reflect both aspects of the bad debt:

Income	Expenditure
	Expenses (bad debt) +£1000
Asset	**Liability**
Debtors −£1000	

As a result of a £1000 bad debt, net profit will be £1000 lower and debtors are also £1000 lower. Gross profit is not affected, because neither sales nor cost of sales change.

If the bad debt amounted to £1,000,000 (one million pounds), the impact would be as follows:

Income	Expenditure
	Expenses (bad debt) +£1,000,000
Asset	**Liability**
Debtors −£1,000,000	

As a result of a £1,000,000 bad debt, net profit will be £1,000,000 lower, which may change a profitable year into a loss-making one.

Specific bad debt provision

If a business becomes aware that a customer is experiencing financial difficulties, it can anticipate that it is about to incur a loss. The term 'provision' means an estimated loss or liability. A specific bad debt provision is an anticipation of a bad debt:

A liability called specific bad debt provision increases and expenses bad debt increases.

Income	Expenditure
	Expenses (bad debt) +£2000
Asset	**Liability**
	Specific provision (bad debt) +£2000

As a result of a £2000 specific bad debt provision, net profit will be £2000 lower. Gross profit is not affected. Debtors are not reduced because the customer has not yet gone into liquidation. A liability has been created to cover the expected loss. If the provision were for £2,000,000, net profit would be £2,000,000 lower.

Often, not long after making a specific bad debt provision, the customer does indeed go into liquidation. The amount of money the customer owes becomes a bad debt, not just a provision. Having already made a provision, the impact of the bad debt has been anticipated. Consequently, there is no further impact on net profit:

A liability called specific bad debt provision decreases and an asset called debtors decreases.

The debtor figure is reduced, but there is no additional effect on net profit.

General bad debt provision

Bad debts are a normal part of business risk. Nearly every business experiences bad debt at some time, so it is prudent to anticipate some exposure. Then, when bad debts occur, the effect on net profit and capital is already allowed for. A general bad debts provision is an anticipation of bad debts in general:

A liability called general bad debt provision increases, expenses called bad debt increases.

Income	Expenditure
	Expenses (bad debt) +£3000
Asset	Liability
	General provision (bad debt) +£3000

As a result of a £3000 general bad debt provision, net profit will be £3000 lower. Gross profit is not affected. If the general provision were for £3,000,000, net profit would be £3,000,000 lower.

In the event of a bad debt occurring, the impact on net profit has been anticipated. A transfer can be made, out of the general bad debts provision, as follows:

A liability called general bad debts provision decreases, an asset called debtors decreases.

Bad debt recovered

When a customer goes into liquidation most companies write off the whole amount the customer owed. After due legal process, which can take some years, it is possible to recover some of the money, e.g. one penny for every pound of debtors. If the original bad debt was £100, the business might get £1 back. If the original bad debt was £1,000,000, the business might get £10,000 back. In this situation, the first step is to reinstate part of the debt originally written off:

An asset debtors increases by £1, expenses called bad debt decreases by £1.

This reinstates part of the original debtor. The second step is as follows:

An asset called cash increases by £1, an asset called debtors decreases by £1.

This accounts for the £1 received in cash and reduces the debtor to zero. The impact of a bad debt recovered is to reduce expenses and increase net profit and cash. Expenses are reduced because the impact of the bad debt has been reduced. If £10,000 were recovered from a £1,000,000 bad debt write off, net profit would increase £10,000.

Bad debts in the spreadsheet format

This is how the bad debt transactions fit into the spreadsheet format:

	Expend	Asset	Asset	Liability	Liability	Liability
	Expenses	Debtors	Cash	Creditors	Specific provision	General provision
Bad debt write off	+10,000	−10,000				
Specific provision	+100				+100	
General provision	+100					+100
Reinstate	−1	+1				
Cash received		−1	+1			

Bad debts and the provisions increase expenses, so they reduce net profits.

Put these three transactions in the spreadsheet format:

- Bad debt write off = £2500.
- Specific bad debt provision = £500.
- General bad debt provision = £1250.

	Expend	Asset	Liability	Liability
	Expenses	Debtors	Specific provision	General provision
Bad debt write off				
Specific provision				
General provision				
Total				

Make sure you attempt the question, before you look at my answer:

	Expend	Asset	Liability	Liability
	Expenses	Debtors	Specific provision	General provision
Bad debt write off	+£2500	−£2500		
Specific provision	+£500		+£500	
General provision	+£1250			+£1250
Total	+£4250			

The total impact of these transactions on expenses is £4250. As a result, net profit will be £4250 lower.

Bad debt and risk

Bad debts impact future cash flow, as well as net profit, because less money will flow into the business. Receipts will be lower and net cash flow may become negative. The effect of bad debt on net profit can be devastating. The company does not just lose the net profit on the sale, the whole value of the sale is lost. For example, if a company sells computers for £1000 each, making £100 net profit margin on each one, the whole £1000 is lost, not just the £100. In order to make up that £1000 loss, a further £10,000 of sales will have to be made.

Big businesses can withstand the impact of bad debt because they have larger profits and cash reserves. A small business is more exposed. This is particularly the case if a small business has a few customers, rather than many customers. Consider a small business, which has ten customers. If one of those customers becomes a bad debt the impact may be great enough to bankrupt the business. A small business with 100 customers is more likely to be able to survive.

New businesses are keen to attract new customers. They often offer favourable credit terms in order to win a new contract or customer. Credit should only be offered to customers with a good credit record. Many new businesses fail because they have offered too much credit and, as a result, they run out of cash.

Every business needs to monitor the level of risk posed by bad debts. The level of debtors should be monitored, and the types of customers offered credit needs to be controlled. The timely receipt of monies owed by customers should be reviewed daily. These are all procedures that can be used to prevent a situation arising where bad debt bankrupts the company.

Unfortunately, some firms buy goods on credit without any intention of paying for them. They often take advantage of new businesses that may not have established credit control procedures. The problem affects the e-business sector even more than traditional sectors. For more on this refer to Evan Schwartz, Digital Darwinism, Penguin, 1999, p. 62.

Liquidation and bankruptcy

Many businesses incur a trading loss at some time. There may be a quiet month during the year or a difficult year in the industry in general. If losses continue, however, the situation may become more serious. If losses accumulate over two or three years (less in a smaller company) they may threaten the existence of the business. The company may become insolvent, leading to liquidation or bankruptcy.

Bankruptcy is imminent when there is insufficient cash to pay liabilities. Liabilities represent what the company owes. They might be:

- Creditors
- Bank loans
- Overdrafts
- Taxes (such as sales tax and payroll tax)

If a company does not have enough cash to meet its liabilities as they fall due, the company no longer has 'liquidity'. Any of these liabilities, the bank or the creditors, can apply for the company to be wound up. If this happens to a limited company it is termed a 'liquidation'. If this happens to an individual it is termed a 'bankruptcy' (although the terms liquidation and bankruptcy are often used interchangeably). A legal official, called a liquidator or an insolvency administrator, is appointed to sell all of the company's assets and share out the cash between the liabilities.

The government often has first claim on any money the liquidator generates (sales taxes and payroll taxes, etc.). After the government, secured creditors are paid (bank loans, etc.). After that, if there is anything left, trade creditors are paid. Secured creditors have a claim on a particular asset, e.g. a building, and the proceeds of selling that asset go directly to the secured creditors.

Consider a small business in financial difficulties. The balance sheet may appear as:

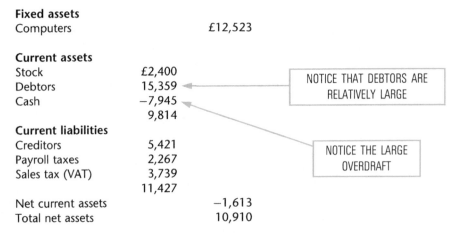

Fixed assets
Computers   £12,523

Current assets
Stock   £2,400
Debtors   15,359   NOTICE THAT DEBTORS ARE
Cash   −7,945   RELATIVELY LARGE
                          9,814

Current liabilities
Creditors   5,421
Payroll taxes   2,267   NOTICE THE LARGE
Sales tax (VAT)   3,739   OVERDRAFT
                         11,427

Net current assets   −1,613
Total net assets   10,910

In addition, there are other circumstances relevant to the financial position. The bank has set the overdraft limit at £7000 and will not permit any further payments out of the bank account. The payroll and sales taxes are more than two months overdue and the tax inspector has asked for an urgent meeting. Creditors have lost patience and have sent solicitors' letters regarding the amounts owed to them (£5421). Debtors include £12,451 due from a company that cannot be traced (bad debt). As a result, the true debtors figure is £2908. The net current assets are, therefore, negative (−£14,084).

This company is no longer solvent. It cannot meet liabilities as they fall due because the bank refuses to make any further payments. It does not have enough assets to meet its liabilities. It is only a matter of days before the bank, the tax authorities or the creditors start liquidation proceedings. When the assets are sold they may generate funds as follows:

Computers   £3500
Debtors   £2000
Stock   £2000
Total   £7500

This is enough to pay the taxes in full, but there is not enough left over to pay the creditors and bank in full.

Discounts allowed

Some firms allow customers a discount if they pay quickly, e.g. 2% off if they pay within one week. This is treated as an expense:

An expense called discounts allowed increases, an asset called debtors decreases.

Discounts received

Discounts received are the opposite of discounts allowed. They happen when a supplier grants a firm a discount for prompt payment:

An income called discounts received increases, a liability called creditors decreases.

In the P&L account, the best form of presentation is to subtract discounts received from discounts allowed. The P&L account, therefore, displays a reduced 'discounts allowed' figure under expenses.

Discounts in the spreadsheet format

This is how discounts fit into the spreadsheet format:

	Expend	Asset	Liability
	Expenses	Debtors	Creditors
Discounts received	−100		−100
Discounts allowed	+100	−100	

Place the following two transactions in the spreadsheet format:

- Discount received = £500.
- Discount allowed = £2250.

	Expend	Asset	Liability
	Expenses	Debtors	Creditors
Discounts received			
Discounts allowed			

Attempt it yourself, before you look at the answer below:

	Expend	Asset	Liability
	Expenses	Debtors	Creditors
Discounts received	−£500	−£500	
Discounts allowed	+£2250		−£2250

The total impact of discounts on expenses is £1750. As a result, net profit will reduce by £1750.

Other write offs

Business is a fast changing environment and **assets**, which at one time may have been valuable, can quickly lose their value. IT equipment is a good example. New IT innovations are constantly being introduced. A company could spend £250,000 on a new network or system expecting to use it for five years. If better technology is introduced and competitors quickly adopt it, the company faces a difficult choice. Either retain the existing system, which may put the company at a competitive disadvantage, or scrap the system and buy the new technology, which will require a substantial investment.

Often, companies feel they have no choice but to scrap the existing system and invest in new technology. This means writing off a substantial fixed asset. In the example above, £250,000 of equipment was expected to last five years. Depreciation, therefore, would be £50,000 per year:

		Cost £250,000		
Year 1	Year 2	Year 3	Year 4	Year 5
£50,000	£50,000	£50,000	£50,000	£50,000

The net book value at the end of year 1 would be £200,000, at the end of year 2 £150,000 and at the end of year 3 £100,000. If the equipment had to be written off after three years, a net book value of £100,000 would, therefore, have to be written off. The impact of the write off would be to reduce fixed assets by £100,000 and increase expenses by £100,000; see the diagram below:

Income	Expenditure
	Expenses (write offs) +£100,000
Asset	Liability
Fixed asset −£100,000	

As a result, net profit would reduce by £100,000.

Changing consumer preferences can lead to writing off stock. Marketing managers know that all products eventually decline and disappear (the product life cycle). When this happens, stocks of that product have to be written off because there is no longer a consumer demand for them. An asset called stock decreases and expenses increase. Consider writing off £25,000 of stock because customers no longer want the product; see the diagram below:

Income	Expenditure
	Expenses (write offs) +£25,000
Asset	**Liability**
Fixed asset −£25,000	

As a result of expenses increasing by £25,000, net profit decreases by £25,000.

On the P&L account the impact of these write offs would be shown as follows:

Less: expenses
Office costs
Marketing costs
Personnel costs
Equipment write offs ◄— THESE ARE SOMETIMES REFERRED TO AS 'EXCEPTIONAL' ITEMS BECAUSE THEY ARE NOT REGULAR OCCURRENCES
Stock write offs

The impact of write offs on net profit can be considerable. As a result, all assets carry some risks. This risk can be avoided by leasing equipment and minimising stock.

> A recent internal government investigation revealed that personal computers assigned a value of £192,000,000 were in fact worth less than £2,000,000 (www.nao.gov.uk).

Other accounting adjustments

There are instances where a company has to pay in advance for certain services. Insurance, for example, sometimes has to be paid for at the start of the year. IT support and maintenance contracts are another example. These contracts are important because systems failures can undermine the operation of a company.

Consider a two-year computer service agreement costing £10,000, which has to be paid for at the start of the agreement. At the end of the first year an adjustment is needed to reflect the fact that the business is still owed £5000 of maintenance work (half the period of the contract). This is an asset, referred to as a 'prepayment'. The full impact of the adjustment is as follows – expenses computer maintenance decreases by £5000, asset prepayment increases by £5000:

Income	Expenditure
	Expenses (maintenance) −£5000
Asset	**Liability**
Prepayment +£5000	

On the balance sheet prepayments may be disclosed as follows:

Current assets
Stock
Debtors
Prepayments
Cash

A prepayment is similar to debtors because they both represent amounts owed to the company. Debtors are customers that owe money and prepayments are suppliers that have been paid in advance for a service of some sort. Other types of contract, which often have to be paid for in advance, include licences and rental agreements. Paying in advance for any service is bad for cash flow.

There are also instances where, rather than paying in advance for a service, a company pays in arrears. Electricity is often paid for three months in arrears. At the end of a financial year, an adjustment may be necessary to reflect the fact that one, two or three months of electricity has not been invoiced or paid for. This is referred to as an accrual. The full impact of the adjustment is as follows: expenses electricity increase and liabilities accruals increase.

Consider a call centre where the phone bill is around £5000 per week, paid three months in arrears. At the end of the financial year there might be a few weeks not yet billed by the telephone company. If there were three weeks not billed, the required adjustment would be expenses telephone increase £15,000, liabilities accruals increase £15,000; see diagram below:

Income	Expenditure
	Expenses (write offs) +£15,000
Asset	**Liability**
	Accruals +£15,000

If there were five weeks unbilled the adjustment would be expenses telephone increase £25,000 and liabilities accruals increase £25,000; see below:

Income	Expenditure
	Expenses (write offs) +£25,000
Asset	**Liability**
	Accruals +£25,000

Accruals increase expenses and reduce net profit; however, payment in arrears benefits cash flow. On the balance sheet the accrual may be disclosed as follows:

Current liabilities
Creditors
Accruals
Sales tax (VAT)
Other taxes
Overdraft

Accruals are rather like creditors, in as much as they represent money that is owed to suppliers but which has not yet been invoiced. Other examples of accruals are sales commission paid to the sales team a month late, e.g. December sales commission paid in January, or interest costs charged monthly or quarterly in arrears. In summary, prepayments reduce expenses and increase net profit while accruals increase expenses and reduce net profit.

Trial balance format

The trial balance format shows the total of all the different types of asset, liability, income and expenditure. It will, therefore, show the total bad debts written off and the total bad debt provision. It shows the total discounts and the total accruals and prepayments.

Consider this example below:

	£ Debit	£ Credit
Sales		255,000
Purchases	64,000	
Opening stock	5,000	
General expenses	105,500	
Bad debts	2,000	
Stock written off	2,500	
Discounts allowed	4,000	
Discounts received		1,400
Fixed assets at cost	250,000	
Accumulated depreciation		56,000
Debtors	5,000	
Prepayments	1,000	
Bank overdraft		2,000
Creditors		4,850
Accrual		750
Bank loan		19,000
General bad debt provision		1,000
Drawings	31,000	
Capital		130,000
Total	**470,000**	**470,000**

Year end adjustments:

- Year end stock is valued at £3500 (not yet included above).
- This year's depreciation has been calculated at £25,000 (not yet included above).
- The adjustments for accruals and prepayments have already been allowed for above.

Trace these figures through to the P&L account below:

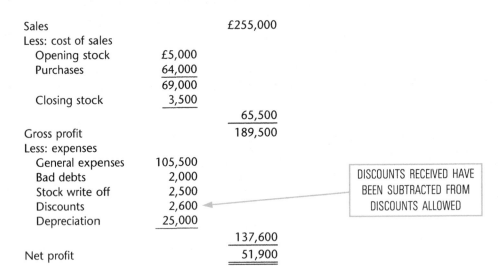

Sales		£255,000
Less: cost of sales		
Opening stock	£5,000	
Purchases	64,000	
	69,000	
Closing stock	3,500	
		65,500
Gross profit		189,500
Less: expenses		
General expenses	105,500	
Bad debts	2,000	
Stock write off	2,500	
Discounts	2,600	
Depreciation	25,000	
		137,600
Net profit		51,900

DISCOUNTS RECEIVED HAVE BEEN SUBTRACTED FROM DISCOUNTS ALLOWED

Make sure you can trace every figure from the trial balance on to the P&L account.

Conclusions

The impact of bad debts on net profits is severe. The whole value of the goods is lost, not just the profit element. Because of the risk of bad debts, some companies make provisions, which smooth out the effect of bad debts. Many people managing their own business understand the dangers of relying on a few large customers. If a small company relies on two or three large customers, a bad debt will almost certainly bankrupt the business. In Chapter 12 the procedures for minimising the risk of bad debt will be outlined.

Other types of asset may also have to be written off. This reduces net profits, as do discounts allowed and accruals. Discounts received, prepayments and bad debts recovered increase net profit.

Keywords

Bad debt	A customer who will not pay or cannot pay for goods or services they have received.
Credit note	A negative sales invoice. If a customer refuses to accept the goods, a credit note is raised reversing the original sale.
Specific provision	An anticipation of a particular bad debt.
General provision	An anticipation of bad debts in general.
Liquidation	If a company cannot meet its liabilities a liquidator will be appointed to realise (sell) the assets of the company and share the money amongst the different creditors. Bankruptcy is the equivalent for an individual. Strictly speaking a company cannot be bankrupt, only an individual can be bankrupt. The term 'liquidate' means to turn an asset into cash.
Discount received	A discount received by a business from a supplier. Reduces expenses and increases net profits.
Discount allowed	A discount granted by a business to a customer. Tends to increase expenses and reduce net profit.
Prepayments	A year end adjustment reflecting payment in advance for a service, e.g. insurance, rates, rent, service agreements, etc. It reduces expenses and increases assets.
Accrual	A year end adjustment reflecting amounts owed but not yet invoiced, e.g. electricity, gas, telephone, etc. It increases expenses and increases liabilities.

Multiple choice questions

Tick the box next to your answer.

1. Bad debt write off leads to an increase in?
   ☐ Profits
   ☐ Cash
   ☐ Fixed assets
   ☐ Debtors
   ☐ Expenses

2. Why do bad debts reduce cash?
   ☐ More money going out of the business
   ☐ More money coming in to the business
   ☐ Net cash flow stays the same
   ☐ Less money coming in to the business in the future
   ☐ Increases in balance brought forward

3. Specific bad debt provision is made against?
   - [ ] Debtors in general
   - [ ] A specific customer
   - [ ] A specific supplier
   - [ ] A fixed asset
   - [ ] Owner of the business

4. When cash is unexpectedly received from a bad debt already written off
   - [ ] Debtors stay the same
   - [ ] Expenses increase
   - [ ] Cash remains the same
   - [ ] Depreciation increases

5. Which of these situations increases net profit the most?
   - [ ] An increase in discounts allowed
   - [ ] A proportional increase in both discounts allowed and received
   - [ ] A decrease in discounts allowed and an increase in discounts received
   - [ ] An increase in discounts received
   - [ ] A decrease in discounts received

6. Which of these is not a liability?
   - [ ] Creditors
   - [ ] Sales tax
   - [ ] Corporation tax
   - [ ] Stock
   - [ ] Overdraft

7. Negative net current assets means?
   - [ ] More assets than liabilities
   - [ ] More current assets than current liabilities
   - [ ] Fewer assets than liabilities
   - [ ] Fewer current assets than current liabilities
   - [ ] More capital than loans

8. Which of these does not increase the risk of bad debt?
   - [ ] Trying to attract new customers with generous credit terms
   - [ ] Concentrating on two or three big customers, rather than many small customers
   - [ ] Increasing credit terms from 60 to 90 days
   - [ ] Asking customers to pay cash up front
   - [ ] Ignoring the retail market and concentrating on wholesale

9. Current assets are £24,410 and current liabilities are £32,220, therefore
   - [ ] Net current assets = +£8810
   - [ ] Net current assets = +£56,630
   - [ ] Net current assets = +£7810
   - [ ] Net current assets = −£7810
   - [ ] Net current assets = £0

10. Which of these is paid out last in a company liquidation?
    - [ ] Sales tax
    - [ ] Corporation tax
    - [ ] Secured bank loan
    - [ ] Secured overdraft
    - [ ] Creditors

11. Which of these is not a reason for writing off a fixed asset?
    - ☐ Computer system out of date
    - ☐ Delivery vans do not meet new pollution regulations
    - ☐ Factory roof declared unsafe by local building inspectors
    - ☐ Chief executive's car involved in a road traffic accident
    - ☐ Property values have increased recently

12. Sales commission paid a month late leads to?
    - ☐ A prepayment
    - ☐ An accrual
    - ☐ A stock write off
    - ☐ A fixed asset reduction
    - ☐ An increase in cash

13. January rent of £2500 paid in advance on 29th December leads to a December prepayment of?
    - ☐ £0
    - ☐ £500
    - ☐ £2000
    - ☐ £2500
    - ☐ £5000

14. Insurance for the whole year paid in advance during June is £1000. The December (end of financial year) prepayment should be
    - ☐ £0
    - ☐ £100
    - ☐ £500
    - ☐ £1000
    - ☐ £2000

15. A company's telephone bill is about £100 per week, paid in arrears. Four weeks need to be accrued at the end of December. Total amount accrued at the end of December?
    - ☐ £100
    - ☐ £400
    - ☐ £0
    - ☐ £4000
    - ☐ £32

Multiple choice answers

	Correct answer	Comment
1	Expenses	Bad debts are treated as an expense, not a reduction in sales (turnover).
2	Less money coming in to the business in the future	If a customer cannot pay, this means the business will receive less money. It also means the business has effectively given the goods away for nothing.
3	A specific customer	There must be a good reason to suspect that the customer is in financial difficulties, e.g. they have recently lost an important contract.

4	Debtors stay the same	The debtor has already been written off, so the money received reduces the bad debt expense.
5	A decrease in discounts allowed and an increase in discounts received	The money received from customers goes up and the money paid to suppliers goes down. The business gains in both cases.
6	Stock	An easy one.
7	Fewer current assets than current liabilities	More money going out than coming in. This suggests the company is not a 'going concern'.
8	Asking for cash up front	This removes the possibility of incurring a bad debt.
9	Net current assets = −£7810	A negative net current assets figure. The company may not be able to meet its liabilities as they fall due.
10	Creditors	They often receive nothing in a liquidation.
11	Property values have increased	This option suggests an increase in the value of fixed assets rather than a reduction.
12	Accrual	This is money the company owes to the sales team.
13	£2500	The £2500 paid in December relates to January so it is a payment in advance.
14	£500	By the end of December half the year's insurance was still owed to the company.
15	£400	Four weeks at £100 per week. Quite a simple one.

The Unlucky Company

Muncorn has been very unlucky in the first year of his new business. In order to attract customers, he has offered generous credit terms. Unscrupulous customers have taken advantage of his lack of experience. Two customers have refused to pay, even though there was nothing wrong with the goods delivered. Muncorn has recently heard that another customer is in financial difficulties.

Muncorn has already prepared his financial statements for the first year of the new business (see below), but he has not yet incorporated the difficulties he has had with debtors. He wants to write off the bad debts, which have a value of £12,000, and **also** make a specific provision with a value of £8000. Muncorn also allowed a customer a discount of £3500, which is not recognised in the figures below.

The Unlucky Company

Summary Trading and Profit and Loss Account
Year Ended 31st December 200X

Sales	£183,745
Less: cost of sales	122,495
Gross profit	61,250
Less: expenses	38,725
Net profit	£22,525

The Unlucky Company

Balance Sheet
As at 31st December 200X

Fixed assets		£0
Current assets		
Stock	£55,435	
Debtors	42,328	
Cash	250	
	98,013	
Current liabilities		
Creditors	3,567	
		94,446

The debtors figure above has not yet been adjusted for bad debt write off or specific bad debt provision or discount allowed. Muncorn has leased all his fixed assets, to reduce the capital needed to start the business. He started the business with an original capital of £75,000 and has taken drawings of just £3079 in the first year.

Your task

Redraft the trading and profit and loss account and balance sheet making the necessary adjustments for bad debts write off, specific bad debt provision and discounts allowed.

Oki Doki

The company accountant has summarised the results for the last financial year as follows (all in £000's).

Oki Doki

Summary Trading and Profit and Loss Account
Year Ended 31st December 200X

Sales	152
Less: cost of sales	94
Gross profit	58
Less: expenses	32
Net profit	26

Oki Doki

Balance Sheet
As at 31st December 200X

Fixed assets (net book value)	255
Current assets	
Stock	13
Debtors	36
Cash	3
	52
Current liabilities	
Creditors	4
Net current assets	48
Total assets less current liabilities	303
Financed by:	
Capital	277
Add: profit	26
	303

The company has found out that £17,000 of the £36,000 debtors is a bad debt. The company also wants to make a specific provision against another debtor of £3000. In addition, the company has scrapped five personal computers with a total net book value of £4000. Recalculate the net profit and the total net assets.

Mr. Robert Billington: Trading as 'Warriors'

Robert Billington runs a security company in London employing young people from Australia and New Zealand. The business has been established for three years and normally makes between £30,000 and £50,000 **net profit** per year. The company's up to date financial position is as follows:

Mr. Robert Billington: Trading as 'Warriors'

Balance Sheet
As at 31st December 2004

Fixed assets

Van		£3,799
Office equipment		599
		4,398

Current assets

Stock	£500	
Debtors	29,331	
Petty cash	52	
	29,883	

Current liabilities

Creditors	3,421	
Overdraft	945	
Sales tax	1,267	
Company tax	2,739	
	8,372	
Net current assets		21,511
Total net assets		25,909

The bank has set the overdraft limit at £1000. Robert has just heard that a major customer has gone into liquidation, owing him £19,478. There is little chance he will recover anything. The rest of the debtors will pay up within the next week and the creditors are not due for another month.

Your task

Redraft the balance sheet to take account of the impact of the bad debt and determine from the figures if the bad debt is serious enough to make the company insolvent.

Year end adjustments

Calculate the accruals and prepayments needed in the situation set out below and show the impact of these by completing the spreadsheet format.

Paid in arrears:

- The sales team is owed £450 of sales commission.
- The bank is owed £329 of interest.
- The company owes £75 for parking fines.
- The company has not received a bill for telephone calls for two weeks. The bill is normally about £100 per week.

Paid in advance:

- The company has paid £300 in advance for a year's membership of a trade association. Only half the year has elapsed.
- The company has paid in advance for staff health insurance £10,000 but only a quarter of the year has elapsed.

	Expenses	Liability	Asset
		Accruals	Prepayments
Sales commission			
Bank interest			
Parking fines			
Telephone calls			
Subscription			
Health insurance			
Total			

Attempt it yourself, before you look at the answer below.

Solutions

The Unlucky Company

Revised Trading and Profit and Loss Account
Year Ended 31st December 200X

Sales		£183,745
Less: cost of sales		122,495
Gross profit		61,250
Less: expenses		
General	£38,725	
Bad debt write off	12,000	
Bad debt provision	8,000	
Discounts allowed	3,500	
		62,225
Net profit (loss)		(975)

The P&L account now shows a loss (£975). The gross profit (£61,250) is unchanged because bad debts are an expense item and, as such, do not affect cost of sales.

The Unlucky Company

Balance Sheet
As at 31st December 200X

Fixed assets		£0
Current assets		
Stock	£55,435	
Debtors	26,828	
Cash	250	
	82,513	
Current liabilities		
Creditors	3,567	
Specific provision	8,000	
	11,567	
Total net assets		70,946
Financed by:		
Original capital		75,000
Add: net profit (loss)	(975)	
Less: drawings	3,079	
		(4,054)
		70,946

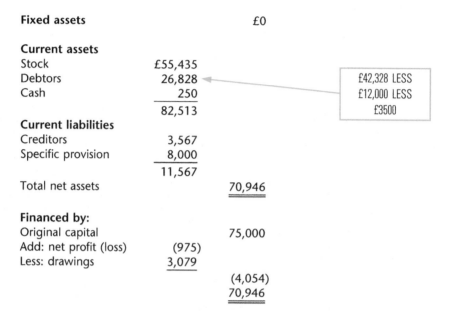

£42,328 LESS
£12,000 LESS
£3500

The specific provision is under the heading 'current liabilities'. Also, the owner's capital is now lower than starting capital because of the effect of the loss and the drawings.

Oki Doki

Revised Trading and Profit and Loss Account
Year Ended 31st December 200X (£000's)

Sales		152
Less: cost of sales		94
Gross profit		58
Less: expenses		
General	32	
Bad debt write off	17	
Bad debt provision	3	
PCs written off	4	
		56
Net profit		2

The company is still making a small net profit of £2000.

Oki Doki

Revised Balance Sheet
As at 31st December 200X (£000's)

Fixed assets (net book value)		251
Current assets		
Stock	13	
Debtors	19	
Cash	3	
	35	
Current liabilities		
Creditors	4	
Bad debt provision	3	
Net current assets		28
Total assets less current liabilities		279
Financed by:		
Capital		277
Add: profit		2
		279

The net assets of the company have fallen by £24,000, reflecting a reduction in debtors of £17,000, a bad debt provision of £3000 and a write off of computer equipment of £4000. The company has sufficient current assets to meet current liabilities as they fall due.

Mr. Robert Billington: Trading as 'Warriors'

After the bad debt write off the balance sheet will look as follows:

Fixed assets		
Van		3,799
Office equipment		599
		4,398
Current assets		
Stock	500	
Debtors	9,853	
Petty cash	52	
	10,405	
Current liabilities		
Creditors	3,421	
Overdraft	945	
Sales tax	1,267	
Company	2,739	
	8,372	
Net current assets		2,033
Total net assets		6,431

The bad debt will reduce net profit but the impact is not sufficient to bankrupt the business. The current assets are £10,405, which is more than the current liabilities, £8372. Most of the debtors will pay Robert in the next few days, so there will be enough cash in the business to pay all the liabilities. If debtors do not pay on time, however, the situation could become more serious.

Year end adjustments

	Expenses	Liability	Asset
		Accruals	Prepayments
Sales commission	450	450	
Bank interest	329	329	
Parking fines	75	75	
Telephone calls	200	200	
Subscription	−150		150
Health insurance	−7500		7500
Total	−6596	1054	7650

The total impact of these adjustments is to reduce expenses by £6596 and, therefore, increase net profit by £6596. The single biggest adjustment is for staff health insurance. Without this adjustment, the net profit may have been significantly understated. Current assets on the balance sheet will be £7650 higher and current liabilities will be £1054 higher. As a result, the net current assets will be £6596 higher, which strengthens the balance sheet.

8 Budgeting

This chapter is about business planning and measuring performance.

Objectives	• Product life cycle; • Measuring performance against budget; • Preparing a budget using spreadsheets.

Introduction

The 'circuit of capital' (see Chapter 1) shows that business works in four stages:

- Put money into the business;
- Buy the people, materials and equipment needed;
- Make the product or provide the service;
- Sell the product for *more* than it cost to make.

Importance of the subject

These activities have to be co-ordinated and typically businesses have different departments responsible for each activity. The purchasing department obtains the materials and equipment needed. The personnel department recruits people with the right knowledge and skills. The production department makes goods to the correct specifications and the sales team sells those goods at the right price. If one of these departments fails, the whole process may stop and no profit will be earned. Budgeting is a way of co-ordinating the work of all the different departments in a business.

A budget is a plan using figures, rather than just words. Say a company plans to introduce a new product in six months' time. The budget shows how many units of the product they hope to sell and how much they will sell it for. It shows how much it costs to make the product and how much will be spent on the product launch. The budget shows the *detail* of the company's plans.

Every department has its own budget. The sales budget, for instance, shows the amount of each type of product the company hopes to sell and the month it hopes to sell them in. The production budget shows how many units of product the company hopes to make and when. The purchasing budget shows which types of materials are needed and when they will be delivered. These sub-budgets are brought together in the budgeted trading and profit and loss account (P&L) and the budgeted balance sheet.

As well as planning and co-ordinating, another benefit of a budget is that it gives a benchmark against which to measure performance. If the budgeted sales for a year are £800,000 and by month 6 the sales are £250,000, this suggests there is a problem, because the sales are not on target. Experienced managers compare actual results to budget on a monthly basis. This highlights areas in which targets are not being achieved. Once problems are highlighted and quantified they can be fully investigated and corrective action can be taken. Budgeting is a tool that provides the information needed to help managers run a business effectively and profitably.

This chapter explores in detail the process of budgeting and the factors and influences that need to be considered. There are two in-chapter examples, one for a new business and another for a continuing one, both of which make use of the accounting framework in the spreadsheet format. Use the multiple choice questions to check your understanding before attempting the end of chapter questions. After completing these you will be able to prepare, explain and employ a budget in a range of business situations including e-business.

> A number of contributors to startupfailures.com cite lack of co-ordination and communication as major causes of company failure. Particular examples include a marketing department not knowing what customers want, a production department not communicating with the marketing department and a sales team not liaising with production. Another factor cited is concentrating too much on one or two large customers.

Definition of a budget

A budget can be defined as follows:

- A quantitative plan of action;
- Prepared in advance of a predetermined period, e.g. the next financial year;
- For the purpose of achieving an objective;
- With detail as appropriate to the organisation.

In a budget, sales refers to forecasted or predicted sales for the next financial quarter, half year or year. Wages refers to the wages that will be paid in the next predetermined period, rather than the amount already paid in the current period. The budgeted profit is the profit a company *hopes* to earn next year (half year, quarter, etc.).

The starting point for a budget is an objective, such as making £1,000,000 profit, or increasing market share by 20% or introducing two new products to the product range. Different companies have different objectives, so their budgets will be distinct. Large organisations have large budgets – over 100 pages of figures covering every department in every month of their year. Small companies may just produce a budgeted P&L account, budgeted balance sheet and cash flow forecast for each quarter.

The budgeting process

New companies are characterised by a small, committed management team and a limited product range. Management processes, such as recruitment and budgeting, are usually informal. Over a period of five to ten years, companies usually evolve a more formal management structure. In this situation the process of preparing a budget often proceeds as follows:

- Sales budget – how many units of product can be sold, which types of product and when?
- Production budget – how many units of product have to be made to meet the demand forecasted in the sales budget? Which particular types of product and when?
- Purchasing budget – what components and materials are needed to meet the production budget? When do these need to be delivered?
- Personnel budget – how many permanent employees are needed and how many on more flexible contracts? How many in the sales team and how many in production?
- Expenses – what types of services will be needed to support production and sales, e.g. insurance?
- Fixed assets – what new equipment will be needed, not just in production but also in administration?
- Cash – is a fresh injection of cash required, e.g. to buy new IT equipment or recruit more staff?
- Prepare budgeted P&L account, for different subsidiaries and in total.
- Prepare budgeted balance sheet.

As a company grows, it may add further departments such as market research, product development and distribution. It may also develop subsidiaries or joint ventures in different countries. All this adds to the complexity of preparing a budget. Often, work on a budget for a particular financial year commences more than 12 months before the start of that year. For example, work on the budget for the financial year 2005 may start at the end of 2003.

Product life cycle

The product life cycle is important when forecasting or budgeting sales. Products do not last forever because consumers tire of them or advances in technology make them obsolete. Marketing managers have identified four stages in the life of a product:

- Launch
- Growth
- Maturity
- Decline

This is termed the product life cycle (see Figure 8.1).

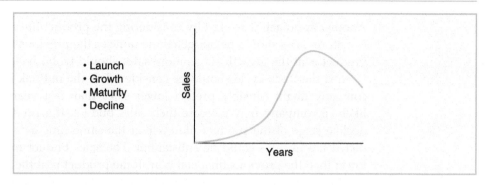

- Launch
- Growth
- Maturity
- Decline

Figure 8.1 Product life cycle

At the launch stage the company concentrates on attracting the attention of consumers, encouraging them to try the product. Sales are low. During the growth stage, more and more consumers are turned on to the product. It begins to become widely accepted and sales grow quickly. The maturity stage is when the product is widely accepted by a large number of consumers. Innovative consumers, however, are the first to become tired of the product, and eventually more and more consumers move on to something new. Sales are then in decline.

For some products the life cycle can take many years. The motor car, for instance, is now a mature product showing the first signs of decline, owing to environmental concerns. Electric and gas powered cars are set to replace the internal combustion engine. Bars and nightclubs are at the other end of the spectrum. Typically, a bar opens, after an expensive refit, with a new theme, e.g. 'Cuban Bar'. It becomes the 'in' place to be and everyone flocks to the venue; however, it quickly becomes passé and people move on to somewhere new. The whole cycle may be completed in 18 months. If a product is moving into the decline phase, it is unwise to forecast an increase in sales.

Another type of cycle that can influence sales is the trade cycle. This is the pattern of boom and bust that the world economy works through every ten years or so. The years of recession were around 1971, 1981, 1991 and 2001. The years of boom 1978, 1988, 1998, etc. Some firms do well in a recession, but on average sales and profits fall in recession years. Equally, some firms will do badly during a boom, but on average sales and profits will rise. If the world economy is moving into recession, it is unwise to forecast an increase in sales.

Factors in setting the sales budget

The sales budget is, in most companies, the starting point for the budgeting process. Forecasting sales is difficult. Some companies take a simple approach – they look at last year's sales and add 10%:

Last year's actual sales	£1,000,000
Add	10%
Next year's budgeted sales	£1,100,000

Another approach is to start by considering the product life cycle. If the product is mature, sales should be budgeted the same as the previous financial year. If the product is at the growth stage, more sales should be budgeted than last year.

Next the trade cycle should be considered. If the outlook is for a recession, a company might sensibly predict lower sales than last year. If a boom seems likely, a company may increase their sales budget. If a product moves into the decline stage of the product life cycle at the same time as a recession, the predicted fall in sales could be substantial. The sales budget may have to be 20% lower than the previous financial year. If the product is at the growth stage when a boom is imminent, the sales budget may be 20% higher than the last financial year.

Also inflation and interest rates should be taken into account. If inflation is expected to be around 5%, a firm might sensibly increase the sales budget by 5%. If inflation is expected to be low, e.g. 2%, budgeted sales may be the same as last year. Interest rates also have an impact on consumer spending. If an increase in interest rates is likely, firms should consider reducing sales budgets.

Finally, when predicting sales, competition is a significant factor. If competitors are launching new products or conducting intensive advertising campaigns, the potential impact should be taken into account in sales budgets. If all the right factors are considered, the sales budget will be more accurate.

Measuring performance against budget

Once a budget has been set, it provides a basis for measuring the performance of a business or department or section. Business is a fast changing environment and, as a result, it is perfectly normal for there to be a difference between what was budgeted and what actually happened. The difference between budgeted figures and actual figures is termed a budget 'variance'. This is calculated by subtracting the actual figure from the budgeted figure. Consider the variances set out below:

	Budget	Actual	Variance	Per cent	Favourable
Sales	400,000	300,000	100,000	25.00%	No
Cost of sales	300,000	200,000	100,000	33.33%	Yes
Gross profit	100,000	100,000	0	0.00%	Yes
Expenses	40,000	45,000	−5,000	(12.50%)	No
Net profit	60,000	55,000	−5,000	(8.33%)	No

The sales variance is £100,000, the difference between the budgeted sales (£400,0000) and the actual sales (£300,000). The variance percentage is calculated as follows:

$$(\text{Variance}/\text{budget}) \times 100$$

The sales variance percentage is (£100,000/£400,000) × 100 = 25%. The favourable column indicates whether the variance is favourable to profit or not favourable to profit. If sales are less then expected, profits are normally less than expected. The 25% sales variance in the table above is, therefore, unfavourable to profit.

Sales and cost of sales are closely related. In order to sell more a company must first buy more, and vice versa. The variances above show that the actual sales are lower than budgeted and, as expected, the cost of sales figure is also lower than budgeted. However, look at the percentages in the table. The sales are 25% less than budgeted, whilst the cost of sales is 33.33% less than budgeted. This indicates that during the year cost of sales was reduced by more than could be explained by the reduction in sales alone. The company may have found a cheaper supplier or may have negotiated a lower price with an existing supplier.

Whenever actual is greater than budget, a negative variance arises. A negative sales variance is good because it indicates that sales were higher than expected. A negative expense variance, on the other hand, is bad for profit, because it indicates that spending was higher than expected.

Look back at the variances above, and then:

Write a paragraph explaining why net profit is 8.33% less than budgeted.

You may find it helpful to think of this task in four parts, as follows:

- What has happened to sales compared to budget?
- What impact has this had on gross profit?
- What has happened to expenses compared to budget?
- What impact has this had on net profit?

Take it step by step. Sales are 25% less than budgeted, which is bad for profit. Cost of sales is also less than budgeted, which is good, because the business has spent less than expected. Cost of sales is, in fact, 33.33% less than forecasted. Because of this disproportionately large decrease in cost of sales, the gross profit is as expected. The variance on gross profit is, therefore, zero. Look back at the table now. Can you see the zero variance on gross profit? Don't go on until you are happy with the zero variance.

Expenses were more than budgeted, which is unfavourable for profit. As a result of the expenses being overspent by £5000, net profit was less than expected by £5000. The £5000 shortfall in percentage terms is 8.33% of the original budgeted net profit. Check my percentage calculation on your calculator now.

The solution to the task set can be summarised succinctly as follows:

Sales were lower than expected, which tends to reduce profits, but a considerable saving was made on cost of sales, which counterbalanced the disappointing sales. As a result, gross profit was on budget. Expenses were higher than expected by £5000 and net profits, therefore, were £5000 lower than expected. This represents an 8.33% shortfall on budgeted net profit.

Functions of a budget

Budgets play a number of different roles in the management of a business:

- Planning – a budget helps managers plan ahead.
- Co-ordinating – a budget helps departments in a business co-ordinate their activities, e.g. production and sales.
- Communication – a budget provides a framework for communication in many different directions (upwards, downwards and across).
- Motivation – a budget is a target, which can be a good way of motivating staff.
- Control – once a budget has been set, it can be used to monitor progress through the year. Variances can act as signals for management action.

These benefits will only be achieved if the budgeting process is properly carried out. If the original budget is inaccurate, or if regular comparison of budget to actual is not made, budgeting is ineffective.

Limiting factors

One way to increase profits is to increase sales; however, additional sales have to be won from competitors, and this is always difficult. As a result, the main factor constraining the growth of most businesses is that they cannot easily increase their share of the market. Because most firms are constrained by the amount they can sell, the starting point for the budgeting process should be the sales budget or sales forecast. If you look back at the budgeting process section, you will see that it starts with a sales budget.

Some organisations work under different constraints and, consequently, they need to adopt a different starting point. A small firm in a specialist market may be able to sell *everything* it produces. The constraint may be that they are unable to produce enough because they are already at full capacity on existing machines. The limiting factor in this case is production capacity. The budgeting process should, therefore, start from the production budget.

Another possible limiting factor is cash. Many small firms start with insufficient funds and, as a result, they operate at, or near, the overdraft limit. In this case, budgeting should start from the cash flow forecast. Where unusual materials are used in production, a shortage of materials can be the limiting factor. In this case, the budgeting process should start from the purchasing budget. Many firms are constrained by a shortage of skilled and experienced staff. In this case, the training and recruitment budget should be the starting point. In summary, as well as having different objectives, businesses also have different constraints.

Over the life of a business, the limiting factor changes. In a business start up situation cash is often the main constraint. After a few years the business becomes established and looks for ways to expand. At this stage problems in recruiting skilled people can hold the business back. After five or ten years the company may have a substantial market share, but may find it difficult to grow further. Sales are, therefore, the limiting factor. As a business matures, different approaches to budgeting have to be adopted.

Problems with budgeting

Budgeting can be a solution to many business problems, but certain difficulties can be encountered within the budgeting process:

- Responsibility for variances is often shared, so variances cannot be linked directly to one department. For example, if sales are less than budgeted, responsibility may lie partly with production for making faulty goods and partly with distribution for not delivering the goods on time.
- Sales teams often underestimate the potential market, to make it easier to achieve targets. For example, if a sales team think they can sell goods worth £36,000,000, they may forecast sales at £30,000,000 to reduce pressure and make the target easier to achieve.
- Annual budgets can quickly become irrelevant because of changes in the market place. For example, early in the financial year it may become obvious that new software is urgently needed, or a new competitor may enter the market. Consequently, the budget is out of date.
- Unrealistic targets demotivate employees. If there is no chance of achieving target, staff may give up trying altogether. For example, if sales of £10,000 per week have been targeted but only £4500 per week achieved, the sales team may become demotivated.
- Budgeting can lead to an exclusive focus on figures, rather than managing broader issues such as customer service and quality of product. For example, if a business has been set a target of £1,000,000 profit, managers will strive to increase sales to achieve target, regardless of, for instance, customers' credit-worthiness. They may not think strategically about the long-term future of the company.

Budgeting in action

To understand how budgeting works in practice, follow this case study carefully.

Ali Chat has been working in a guitar shop for six years; he is 25 years old. He has accumulated a considerable amount of knowledge about the products and he is enthusiastic. Ali has always wanted his own shop, selling a new range of guitars. In the course of the last two years, Ali has received £5000 in bonuses, which he has placed in a high-interest bank account. Ali is considering the possibility of setting up a business on the Internet.

You are an experienced financial consultant. Ali has asked you to find the cost of setting up an Internet guitar shop and what the likely profit would be. You have not yet carried out any market research, but you have had a series of meetings with Ali and, as a result, you have the following figures.

Forecast monthly sales units

January	1
February	2
March	5
April	10
May	15
June	20
July	20
August	20
September	20
October	20
November	20
December	20
Total	**173**

The pattern of purchases is slightly different to that of sales. Ali needs to purchase 10 guitars in January. After that, the same number of guitars is purchased as are sold, e.g. two guitars purchased in February.

Purchases are paid for during the month for the first six months, and after that one month in arrears.

For each guitar

Selling price	£250
Purchase price	£170
Cost of delivery to customer	£10

The cost of delivery is paid for in cash by Ali every month.

Start up costs

Web page design	£2000
Internet connection	£200
Advertising	£1000
Stationery	£1000
Insurance	£400

All the start up costs are paid for in cash in January.

Monthly expenses

Internet subscription	£50
Telephone	£100
Computer leasing	£100
Bank charges	£50
Sundry	£100

All the monthly expenses are paid in cash every month. Note that computer equipment is leased, not bought. The cost of purchasing such equipment would be around £5000.

Other expenses

Accounting (not paid until the second year)	£500
Advertising in October (paid in November)	£1000

Note that the accounting charges will be a creditor at the end of the first year.

This is all the information needed to calculate sales, purchases, expenses, capital, cash, stock and creditors, etc. The first step is to calculate all these figures.

Ali Chat: Trading as 'Internet Guitar Shop'

Budget Calculations

	Calculations	**Result**
Sales	173 guitars at £250	£43,250
Purchases	182 guitars at £170	£30,940
Cash purchases	62 × £170	£10,540
Credit purchases	120 × £170	£20,400
Credit purchases paid	100 × £170	£17,000
Start up expenses		£4,600
Monthly expenses		
Internet subscription	£50 × 12	£600
Telephone	£100 × 12	£1,200
Computer leasing	£100 × 12	£1,200
Bank charges	£50 × 12	£600
Others	£100 × 12	£1,200
Delivery costs	173 × £10	£1,730
Other expenses	Accounting (not yet paid)	£500
	Advertising (paid in November)	£1,000
Stock	(182 − 173) × £170	£1,530
Debtors	Zero, all sales are cash sales	0
Cash	See cash flow	
Capital	from Ali's savings	£5,000
Fixed assets	None, all equipment is leased	0

The stock was calculated in four steps as follows:

Step 1	Units sold	173 units
Step 2	Units purchased (10 units in January, then the same as sales)	182 units
Step 3	Units left in stock (182 − 173)	9 units
Step 4	Valued at £170 each	£1530

The next step is to use the accounting framework to organise all the figures.

Ali Chat: Trading as 'Internet Guitar Shop'

Budgeted Accounting Framework

	Sales	Purch.	Exp.	Stock	Debtor	Cash	Capital	Creditor
Start capital						5,000	5,000	
Sales	43,250					43,250		
Cash purchases		10,540				−10,540		
Credit purchases		20,400						20,400
Cash paid						−17,000		−17,000
Delivery			1,730			−1,730		
Start up costs			4,600			−4,600		
Subscription			600			−600		
Telephone			1,200			−1,200		
Leasing			1,200			−1,200		
Bank charges			600			−600		
Sundry			1,200			−1,200		
Accounting			500					500
Advertising			1,000			−1,000		
Stock		−1,530		1,530				
Total	**43,250**	**29,410**	**12,630**	**1,530**	**0**	**8,580**	**5,000**	**3,900**
Profit	1,210						1,210	
Closing capital							6,210	

This shows the net profit earned in the first year is expected to be £1210 and the company expects to accumulate £8580 of cash by the end of the year. From here it will be quite a simple matter to do the budgeted P&L account. Check back over every figure on the accounting framework before you move on.

Ali Chat: Trading as 'Internet Guitar Shop'

Budgeted Trading and Profit and Loss Account
Year Ended 31st December 200X

	£	£
Sales		43,250
Cost of sales		
Opening stock	0	
Add: purchases	30,940	
	30,940	
Less: closing stock	1,530	
		29,410
Gross profit		13,840
Less: expenses		
Start up costs	4,600	
Delivery	1,730	
Subscription	600	
Telephone	1,200	
Leasing	1,200	
Bank charges	600	
Sundry	1,200	
Accounting	500	
Advertising	1,000	
		12,630
Net profit		1,210

During the first year of trading the business hopes to make sales of £43,250 and generate a gross profit of £13,840. Total expenses in the first year are expected to be £12,630. This includes start up costs of £4600, some of which would not be incurred in year 2. As a result, expenses in year 2 of the business could be less.

The business plan is based on leasing equipment, rather than buying it. As a result, there is no depreciation needed in the P&L account. Only a small profit is being earned, which is to be expected in the first year of a new business.

Make sure you are happy with every figure before you go on to look at the balance sheet.

Ali Chat: Trading as 'Internet Guitar Shop'

Budgeted Balance Sheet
As at 31st December 200X

	Cost	Accumulated depreciation	Net book value
	£0	£0	£0
Fixed assets	£0	£0	£0
Current assets			
Stock		1,530	
Debtors		0	
Cash		8,580	
		10,110	
Current liabilities			
Creditors		3,900	
Net current assets			6,210
Total net assets			6,210
Financed by:			
Opening capital			5,000
Add: profit		1,210	
Less: drawings		0	
			1,210
Closing capital			6,210

By the end of the first year the company will have accumulated cash of £8580 and have stock valued at £1530. The company, however, will owe suppliers £3900 and, as a result, will have net current assets of £6210. Because there are no fixed assets, total net assets are also £6210.

The company will be financed entirely from owner's capital. The net profit earned during the year will be £1210 and the owner intends to draw no money out of the company. Consequently, the original capital of £5000 will grow to £6210.

Link every figure back to the accounting framework before you carry on.

Ali Chat: Trading as 'Internet Guitar Shop'

Cash Flow Forecast

	Jan	Feb	Mar	Apr	May	Jun	Jul	Aug	Sep	Oct	Nov	Dec	Total
Receipts													
Sales	250	500	1,250	2,500	3,750	5,000	5,000	5,000	5,000	5,000	5,000	5,000	43,250
Other	5,000												5,000
Total	5,250	500	1,250	2,500	3,750	5,000	5,000	5,000	5,000	5,000	5,000	5,000	48,250
Payments													
Purchases	1,700	340	850	1,700	2,550	3,400		3,400	3,400	3,400	3,400	3,400	27,540
Expenses	400	400	400	400	400	400	400	400	400	400	400	400	4,800
Start up	4,600												4,600
Delivery	10	20	50	100	150	200	200	200	200	200	200	200	1,730
Advertising											1,000		1,000
Drawings	0	0	0	0	0	0	0	0	0	0	0	0	0
Total	6,710	760	1,300	2,200	3,100	4,000	600	4,000	4,000	4,000	5,000	4,000	39,670
Net cash flow	−1,460	−260	−50	300	650	1,000	4,400	1,000	1,000	1,000	0	1,000	8,580
Balance B/F	0	−1,460	−1,720	−1,770	−1,470	−820	180	4,580	5,580	6,580	7,580	7,580	0
Balance C/F	−1,460	−1,720	−1,770	−1,470	−820	180	4,580	5,580	6,580	7,580	7,580	8,580	8,580

Net cash flow is negative only in the first three months of the life of the proposed business. The forecast suggests that over the year as a whole the business will generate £8580. Because the opening balance of cash is zero, £8580 is also the closing cash balance. The fact that there is negative cash flow in the first three months suggests that £5000 is not adequate capital to start the business. The figures indicate that an overdraft facility or short-term loan will be needed. The fact that drawings are zero raises the issue of what Ali is going to live on during the first year of the business. These points suggest that £10,000 starting capital is needed to properly finance the business.

Budgeting in an established business

Ali Chat is a business start up situation. In an existing business, budgeting is slightly more complex because the assets and liabilities are brought forward from the previous financial year, e.g. the cash column starts with the cash brought forward from the end of the previous year. Here is an example of budgeting in an established business.

In January 2001, Anita Rodreguez opened The Coffee Canal, a small coffee shop near the Business School at Manchester University. The first few months of the new business were really exciting, but Anita is disappointed that, after all her hard work, she made a loss in the first year. She has had problems recruiting the right staff and problems with security. The bank has raised concerns about her overdraft.

Anita originally invested £10,000 of her own money and also borrowed £5000 from the bank. This is being repaid at the rate of £100 per month and the interest is £25 per month. The profit margin on the product is substantial. Every cup of coffee sells for £1.50. The freshly ground coffee that goes into making it costs approximately 20p. The milk, cocoa powder and sugar, etc. cost less than 5p per cup. Anita is keen to plan the second year more carefully to ensure an adequate profit.

Anita has collected the following data relating to her plans for 2002.

The assets and liabilities at the end of 2001 are as follows:

	Assets	Liabilities
Owner's capital		7,080
Padua coffee machine	5,250	
Fixtures and fittings	6,580	
Computer and till	2,575	
Depreciation		
Padua coffee machine		1,000
Fixtures and fittings		1,000
Till and computer		500
Stock	1,647	
Loan		4,800
Creditors		900
Overdraft		772
Total	**16,052**	**16,052**

During 2002 the following costs are expected:

Monthly wages	1200
Monthly running costs	300
Monthly interest	25
Monthly loan repayments	100
Monthly drawings	700
Closing stock at end 2002	1000
Quarterly rent	1260

Monthly costs are paid for in the month in which they are incurred. Rent is paid on the first day of the quarter to which it relates. First quarter rent is payable on 1st January 2002.

During 2002 the following sales (in cups) and purchases (in £) are expected:

	Cups of coffee sold	Purchases of coffee	Other purchases (sugar, milk, etc.)
January	4,000	800	200
February	4,000	800	200
March	4,000	800	200
April	2,500	500	125
May	2,500	500	125
June	2,000	400	100
July	2,000	400	100
August	0	0	0
September	4,000	800	200
October	4,500	900	225
November	5,000	1,000	250
December	4,000	800	200
Total	**38,500**	**£7,700**	**£1,925**

Every cup of coffee is sold for £1.50. Customers always pay cash and Anita has negotiated one month of credit from suppliers. January purchases (£1000 in total) are paid in February. As a result, there are creditors at the end of 2002, but no debtors.

Café Rodreguez

Budget 2002 Calculations

	Calculations	**Result**
Sales	38,500 × £1.50	£57,750
Purchases	£7700 + £1925	£9,625
Cash purchases	All on credit	0
Credit purchases		£9,625
Credit purchases paid	£900 + £9625 − £1000	£9,525
Monthly payments		
Wages	£1200 × 12	£14,400
Running costs	£300 × 12	£3,600
Interest	£25 × 12	£300
Loan repayment	£100 × 12	£1,200
Drawings	£700 × 12	£8,400
Quarterly rent	£1260 × 4	£5,040
Stock		£1,000
Debtors	All sales are cash sales	0
Cash	See accounting framework	

Café Rodreguez

Budget 2002 Accounting Framework

	Sales	Purchases	Expenses	Coffee machine	Fixtures	Computer	Stock	Cash	Capital	Creditors	Loan	Coffee machine	Fixtures	Computer
Opening	0	0	0	5,250	6,580	2,575	1,647	-772	7,080	900	4,800	1,000	1,000	500
Reverse		1,647					-1,647							
Cash sales	57,750							57,750						
Credit purchases		9,625								9,625				
Cash paid								-9,525		-9,525				
Wages			14,400					-14,400						
Running costs			3,600					-3,600						
Interest			300					-300						
Rent			5,040					-5,040						
Loan repayment								-1,200			-1,200			
Drawings								-8,400	-8,400					
Depreciation			1,000									1,000		
Depreciation			1,000										1,000	
Depreciation			500											500
Stock		-1,000					1,000							
Total	**57,750**	**10,272**	**25,840**	**5,250**	**6,580**	**2,575**	**1,000**	**14,513**	**-1,320**	**1,000**	**3,600**	**2,000**	**2,000**	**1,000**
Profit		21,638	21,638						21,638					
									20,318					

Café Rodreguez

Budgeted Trading and Profit and Loss Account
Year Ended 31st December 2002

	£	£
Sales		57,750
Cost of sales		
Opening stock	1,647	
Add: purchases	9,625	
	11,272	
Less: closing stock	1,000	
		10,272
Gross profit		47,478
Less: expense		
Wages	14,400	
Rent	5,040	
Running costs	3,600	
Interest	300	
Depreciation	2,500	
		25,840
		21,638

During the second year of trading, Anita hopes to make sales of £57,750 and generate a gross profit of £47,478. Total expenses are expected to be £25,840. The largest expense is wages, £14,400. The business expects to generate a net profit of £21,638 in the second year, which is a great improvement on the first year.

Make sure you are clear about every figure before you go on to look at the balance sheet.

Café Rodreguez

Budgeted Balance Sheet
As at 31st December 2002

	Cost	Accumulated depreciation	Net book value
Fixed assets			
Padua coffee maker	£5,250	£2,000	£3,250
Fixtures and fittings	6,580	2,000	4,580
Till and computer	2,575	1,000	1,575
	14,405	5,000	9,405
Current assets			
Stock		1,000	
Debtors		0	
Cash		14,513	
		15,513	
Current liabilities			
Creditors		1,000	
Net current assets			14,513
Total net assets			23,918
Financed by:			
Opening capital			7,080
Add: profit		21,638	
Less: drawings		8,400	
			13,238
Closing capital			20,318
Loans			3,600
			23,918

By the end of the second year the company will have accumulated cash of £14,513 and will have stock valued at £1000. However, the company will owe suppliers £1000 and, consequently, will have net current assets of £14,513. The net book value of fixed assets will be £9405 and, as a result, the total net assets are expected to be £23,918. These assets are mainly financed by owner's capital of £20,318, but the company also has a loan of £3600.

Conclusions

Budgeting is common sense. Before the start of a new financial year, the management team should start to think about what can be achieved in the coming year. This will help clarify the company's objectives for the year. Next, the management team should plan in detail the role of every department in achieving these objectives. This will include specifying the exact numbers of products that will have to be made and sold, etc. The budgeted P&L account and balance sheet summarise these detailed plans. Every month, progress should be monitored by comparing budget to actual and calculating variances. If targets are not being met, the underlying causes and problems should be identified and then corrective action taken.

Another contributor to startupfailures.com put it succinctly:
Make sure you have a plan.

Multiple choice questions

Tick the box next to your answer.

1. What is a variance?
   - ☐ Difference between budget and actual
   - ☐ Actual plus budget
   - ☐ A plan set out in money terms
   - ☐ Something with a changing value
   - ☐ Difference between gross profit and net profit

2. If actual sales are more than budgeted
   - ☐ Profit margins must be higher than anticipated
   - ☐ Cash decreases
   - ☐ Expenses decreases
   - ☐ Customers have bought more than was planned
   - ☐ Fixed assets reduce

3. Why is opening stock zero in a new business?
   - ☐ New businesses do not need stock
   - ☐ New businesses cannot afford stock
   - ☐ There is no previous year from which to bring forward stock
   - ☐ Assets are set back to zero at the end of every financial year
   - ☐ It is fully depreciated

4. A new business expects to buy 15,000 units in the first year and sell 12,000 units; therefore, the number of units left in stock at the end of the year is expected to be
   - ☐ 15,000 units
   - ☐ 18,000 units
   - ☐ 12,000 units
   - ☐ 9000 units
   - ☐ 3000 units

5. Why do new businesses have to pay cash for materials and equipment?
   - ☐ They receive cash from customers
   - ☐ Because it improves cash flow
   - ☐ They have plenty of cash received from the owner
   - ☐ To increase drawings
   - ☐ They have no credit history or trading record with which to obtain credit

6. If actual expenses are greater than budgeted
   - ☐ Actual net profit is reduced
   - ☐ Actual cost of sales increases
   - ☐ Actual net profit is increased
   - ☐ Actual drawings increases
   - ☐ Actual net profit is unaffected

7. Budgeted sales £742,456, actual sales £724,546
   - ☐ Unfavourable sales variance
   - ☐ Sales variance 57% favourable
   - ☐ Zero sales variance
   - ☐ Sales variance 2% favourable
   - ☐ Favourable sales variance

8. Budget = £10,000, actual = £15,000, variance % = ?
   - [ ] 150%
   - [ ] 100%
   - [ ] 75%
   - [ ] 50%
   - [ ] 0%

9. What is the most likely constraint on a new Internet business started by one individual with limited savings and no other sources of finance?
   - [ ] Cash
   - [ ] Office space
   - [ ] Availability of web designers
   - [ ] Advertising space
   - [ ] Improvements in technology

10. What is the difference between budgeted net cash flow and actual net cash flow?
    - [ ] Actual comes before the budget
    - [ ] Actual cash flow is monthly, the budgeted is quarterly
    - [ ] Actual cash flow is negative, the budgeted is positive
    - [ ] Actual is what was predicted or forecast would happen
    - [ ] Budgeted is what was planned, actual is what happened

11. Which of these is not a valid objective for a business?
    - [ ] Expand market share
    - [ ] Expand the product range
    - [ ] Increase profit by 20%
    - [ ] Launch a web site for customers
    - [ ] Reduce market share and profits

12. Which of the following does the production department not liaise with when preparing its budget?
    - [ ] Marketing department
    - [ ] Purchasing department
    - [ ] Product development team
    - [ ] Sales team
    - [ ] Competitors

13. Which of the following is the most urgent problem to address?
    - [ ] Zero variance on net profit
    - [ ] 50% unfavourable variance on sales
    - [ ] 1% unfavourable variance on expenses
    - [ ] 5% favourable variance on cost of sales
    - [ ] Zero variance everywhere

Multiple choice answers

	Correct answer	Comment
1	Difference between budget and actual	If you were not sure of this answer, go back over the whole chapter again.
2	Customers have bought more than planned or expected	This should lead to a net profit higher than budgeted. But, if expenses or cost of sales move disproportionately, this may not be the case.
3	There is no previous period from which to bring forward stock	This is the first year of the business; therefore, there is no previous year.
4	3000 units	These units should be valued; e.g. if they cost £5.00 each, stock has a value of £15,000.
5	New businesses have no credit history	Credit checks are usually based on previous financial history.
6	Net profit is reduced	Higher expenses always reduce net profit.
7	Unfavourable sales variance	Because the sales are lower than budgeted, which tends to reduce profit.
8	Variance 50%	$(£5000/£10,000) \times 100$.
9	Cash	Lack of cash can prevent smaller businesses taking advantage of opportunities that arise.
10	Budgeted is what was planned, actual is what happened	What actually happens often bears little relation to what was expected. This is part of the risk of being in business.
11	Reduce market share and profits	Reducing profit can never be a valid objective.
12	Competitors	One of the objectives of budgeting is to take market share away from competitors; therefore, they are unlikely to provide the production department with useful information.
13	50% unfavourable sales variance	This means that sales are 50% less than budgeted. Gross profit will also probably be 50% less than budgeted; therefore, it is unfavourable to profit.

Take your time with multiple choice questions.

Stratosphere

Stratosphere are preparing budgeted accounts for the year to 31st October 2003 (all figures in £000's). The assets and liabilities at 1st November 2002 (the first day of the financial year) were as follows:

	Assets	Liabilities
Stock	32	
Freehold property	100	
Motor vehicles at cost	24	
Fixtures and fittings at cost	20	
Depreciation provision		
Motor vehicles		12
Fixtures and fittings		6
Owner's capital		121
Loan		24
Overdraft		13
Debtors	0	
Creditors		0
Total	**176**	**176**

The following items are forecast for the year ended 31st October 2003:

	Total	Cash paid or received during the year	Amounts owing or owed at year end
Sales	£335	£316	£19
Purchases	201	177	24
Expenses	98	82	16
Loan interest	2	2	0
Loan repayment	4	4	0
New computer	8	8	0
Drawings	32	32	0

Year end adjustments:

- Stock on 31st October 2003, £38.
- Depreciation is to be calculated as follows:

Motor vehicles	25%
Fixtures and fittings	15%
Computer	25%

The company does not depreciate freehold property.

Your task

Prepare a budgeted trading and profit and loss account for the year ended 31st October 2003 and a budgeted balance sheet as at 31st October 2003.

Romany Trading

Romany Trading have collected the following information in order to prepare their budget for the year to 31st December 2003. All figures are in £000's. The assets and liabilities at the start of the year (1st January 2003) are as follows:

	Assets	Liabilities
Owner's capital		234
Freehold property at cost	200	
Fixtures and fittings at cost	20	
Motor vehicles at cost	28	
Depreciation		
Fixtures and fittings		9
Motor vehicles		7
Debtors	29	
Stock	15	
Creditors		27
Bank overdraft		15
Total	**292**	**292**

The following figures (all in £000's) are forecast for the year:

1. In April 2003 loan capital of £25 will be received.
2. In May 2003 a new computer system will be bought and paid for, costing £30.
3. Repayment of the loan capital will be at the rate of £0.5 per month starting in May 2003.
4. Loan interest will be £0.25 per month starting in May 2003.
5. Drawings will be £2 per month throughout the year.
6. Other amounts as follows:

		Sales	Purchases	Expenses
November	2002	25	12	7
December	2002	29	15	6
January	2003	16	8	5
February	2003	15	9	4
March	2003	18	8	5
April	2003	26	10	6
May	2003	28	13	7
June	2003	26	14	8
July	2003	25	15	6
August	2003	24	13	7
September	2003	21	14	6
October	2003	23	12	5
November	2003	26	15	7
December	2003	35	20	9
Total		**337**	**178**	**88**

Note: Debtors pay in the month following the date of sale. Purchases are paid for two months after the date of purchase. Expenses are paid for in the month in which they are incurred.

7. Stock as at 31st December 2003 is budgeted at £23.

8. Depreciation is to be calculated as follows:

Fixtures and fittings	15%
Motor vehicles	25%
Computer	20%

The company does not depreciate freehold property.

Your task

(a) Prepare a cash flow forecast for the year ending 31st December 2003.
(b) Prepare a budgeted trading and profit and loss account for the year ended 31st December 2003.
(c) Prepare a budgeted balance sheet as at 31st December 2003.

Solutions

Stratosphere

Budgeted Trading and Profit and Loss Account
Year Ended 31st October 2003

	£000's	£000's
Sales		335
Cost of sales		
Opening stock	32	
Add: purchases	201	
	233	
Less: closing stock	38	
		195
Gross profit		140
Less: expenses		
General expenses	98	
Interest	2	
Depreciation (6+3+2)	11	
		111
Net profit		29

During the financial year ending October 2003 the company is planing to make sales of £335,000 and generate a gross profit of £140,000. Expenses are expected to be £111,000 and, as a result, the company expects to earn a net profit of £29,000.

Stratosphere

Budgeted Balance Sheet
As at 31st October 2003

All in £000's	Cost	Accumulated depreciation	Net book value
Fixed assets			
Freehold property	100	0	100
Motor vehicles	24	18	6
Fixtures	20	9	11
Computer	8	2	6
	152	29	123
Current assets			
Stock		38	
Debtors		19	
Cash		(2)	
		55	
Current liabilities			
Creditors		40	
Net current assets			15
Total net assets			138
Financed by:			
Opening capital			121
Add: profit		29	
Less: drawings		32	
			(3)
Closing capital			118
Loan			20
			138

By the end of October 2003 the company expects to be overdrawn at the bank by £2000 and expects to owe £20,000 on long-term loans. Creditors are expected to be £40,000. The overdraft is a matter for concern. During the year a new computer system will be acquired for £8000 and drawings of £32,000 are expected. In light of the predicted overdraft, the company should reconsider these substantial cash outflows. The company does have substantial fixed assets, some of which (in an emergency) could be sold to generate working capital.

Stratosphere

Budgeted Accounting Framework (£000's)

	Sales	Purchases	Expenses	Freehold	Motor	Fixtures	Compute	Stock	Debtor	Cash	Creditor	Loan	Capital	Deprec. motor	Deprec. fixtures	Deprec. computer
Balances brought forward				100	24	20		32	0	-13	0	24	121	12	6	0
Reverse stock		32						-32								
Sales	335								335							
Purchases		201									201					
Expenses			98								98					
Loan interest			2							-2						
Loan repayment										-4		-4				
Cash received from debtor									-316	+316						
Cash paid to creditors										-177	-177					
Cash paid to expenses										-82	-82					
New computer							8			-8						
Drawings										-32			-32			
Stock		-38						38								
Depreciation motor			6											6		
Depreciation fixtures			3												3	
Depreciation computer			2													2
Total	335	195	111	100	24	20	8	38	19	-2	40	20	89	18	9	2
Profit			29										29			
Closing capital													118			

Romany Trading

Budgeted Trading and Profit and Loss Account
Year Ended 31st December 2003

	£000's	£000's
Sales		283
Cost of sales		
Opening stock	15	
Add: purchases	151	
	166	
Less: closing stock	23	
		143
Gross profit		140
Less: expenses		
General expenses	75	
Interest	2	
Depreciation motor	7	
Depreciation fixtures	3	
Depreciation computer	6	
		93
Net profit		47

During 2003 the company is expecting to make sales of £283,000 and generate gross profit of £140,000. Expenses are expected to be £93,000, including £16,000 for depreciation. The expected net profit is £47,000.

Romany Trading

Budgeted Balance Sheet
As at 31st December 2003

All in £000's	Cost	Accumulated depreciation	Net book value
Fixed assets			
Freehold property	200	0	200
Fixtures	20	12	8
Motor vehicles	28	14	14
Computers	30	6	24
	278	32	246
Current assets			
Stock		23	
Debtors		35	
Cash		9	
		67	
Current liabilities			
Creditors		35	
Net current assets			32
Total net assets			278
Financed by:			
Opening capital			234
Add: profit		47	
Less: drawings		24	
			23
Closing capital			257
Loan			21
			278

The company is financed mainly by owner's capital accompanied by a small loan (£21,000). By the end of the year the company expects to have accumulated £9000 in cash. The company also expects to have substantial fixed assets, as well as stock and debtors. The budgeted drawings of £24,000 are reasonable in the light of an expected profit of £47,000. The company expects to be in good financial shape by the end of the financial year.

Romany Trading

Cash Flow Forecast
Year Ended 31st December 2003 (£000's)

	Jan	Feb	Mar	Apr	May	Jun	Jul	Aug	Sep	Oct	Nov	Dec	Total
Receipts													
Sales	29	16	15	18	26	28	26	25	24	21	23	26	277
Loan				25									25
Total	29	16	15	43	26	28	26	25	24	21	23	26	302
Payments													
Purchases	12	15	8	9	8	10	13	14	15	13	14	12	143
Expenses	5	4	5	6	7	8	6	7	6	5	7	9	75
Interest	0	0	0	0	0.25	0.25	0.25	0.25	0.25	0.25	0.25	0.25	2
Repayment	0	0	0	0	0.5	0.5	0.5	0.5	0.5	0.5	0.5	0.5	4
Computer					30								30
Drawings	2	2	2	2	2	2	2	2	2	2	2	2	24
Total	19	21	15	17	47.75	20.75	21.75	23.75	23.75	20.75	23.75	23.75	278
Net cash flow	10	−5	0	26	−21.75	7.25	4.25	1.25	0.25	0.25	−0.75	2.25	24
Balance B/F	−15	−5	−10	−10	16.00	−5.75	1.50	5.75	7.00	7.25	7.50	6.75	−15
Balance C/F	−5	−10	−10	16	−5.75	1.50	5.75	7.00	7.25	7.50	6.75	9.00	9

The company will start the year with an overdraft of £15,000. It is expected that during the year most months will show a positive net cash flow. Taking the year as a whole, the net cash flow is £24,000, which means that £24,000 more cash is coming in than going out. As a result, the company will accumulate a cash balance of £9000 by the end of the year. During the year the company expects to spend £30,000 on new computer equipment. A loan will be negotiated to help finance the new equipment. The amount of the loan is £25,000, which is £5000 less than the cost of the equipment.

Romany Trading

Budgeted Accounting Framework 2003 (£000's)

	Sales	Purchases	Expenses	Freehold	Motor	Fixtures	Compute	Stock	Debtor	Cash	Creditor	Loan	Capital	Acc. deprec. motor	Acc. deprec. fixtures	Acc. deprec. computer
Balances brought forward	0	0	0	200	28	20	0	15	29	-15	27	0	234	7	9	
Reverse stock		+15						-15								
Credit sales	283								283							
Purchases		151									151					
Expenses			75							-75						
Loan interest			2							-2						
Loan										25		25				
Loan repayment										-4		-4				
Cash received from debtor									-277	277						
Cash paid to creditors										-143	-143					
New computer							30			-30						
Drawings										-24			-24			
Stock		-23						23								
Depreciation motor			7											7		
Depreciation fixtures			3												3	
Depreciation computer			6													6
Total	283	143	93	200	28	20	30	23	35	9	35	21	210	14	12	6
Profit			47										47			
Closing capital													257			

9 Budget interpretation

This chapter is about understanding and interpreting complex business problems.

Objectives	
	• Interpreting business problems;
	• Recommending action to solve problems;
	• Report writing.

Introduction

Importance of the subject

Variances help identify problem areas in a business. Once identified, the causes can be investigated and action taken by the management team. Some business problems are relatively easy to analyse, e.g. a particular product may be moving into the decline stage of the product life cycle. Many business problems, however, are more complex because they involve a mixture of different factors. For instance, a company might be facing a situation in which its products and production processes are outdated, global competition is increasing, staff motivation is low and the bank is concerned about the overdraft. Multifaceted situations like this require careful interpretation and analysis. In particular, the problems need to be prioritised and the relationships between problems need to be understood.

Earlier chapters concentrated on explaining the P&L account and balance sheet using short written commentaries. Interpretation of the figures is more complex. It means bringing together different types of information and understanding how they are connected. Typically, in a budgeting context, variances relating to a particular company are interpreted, in report format, to show how they reflect facts about the business. Combining facts and figures in this way enables managers to identify, interpret and prioritise business problems, draw conclusions and make detailed recommendations.

Activities and outcomes

This chapter reviews report writing and common causes of variances before moving on to a case study incorporating facts and figures in a report format. Use the multiple choice questions to check your progress, before moving on to the final case study in which you will prepare a report. By the end of this chapter you will be able to interpret a complex business situation blending together facts and figures in a structured report.

Variance analysis and interpretation

Every business situation, scenario or case study represents a unique combination of circumstances. There are no readymade interpretations or solutions to business problems; however, to help develop interpretation skills, it is useful to explore a number of common problems. One of the most common business problems is falling sales. Interpretation involves examining the extent of the reduction in sales and its exact cause. There are some common causes of sales variances, and also some common remedies, which are detailed below.

Sales variances

Cause	Action
Downturn in the market as a whole because of the trade cycle	Look for export markets or diversify
Prices too high	Special offers
Moving into the decline stage of the product life cycle	Market research to identify changing customer preferences
Promotions not effective	Improve marketing strategy
Lack of experienced sales staff	Recruitment campaign
Distribution problems in the supply chain	Consider 'contracting out'

A common cause of falling sales is that customers, in general, buy less because of a recession. There is little an individual company can do about global economic conditions. One possible strategy is to attempt to find markets unaffected by the downturn or to diversify the product range.

Another cause of falling sales is charging a price that is too high. A simple remedy might be to cut all selling prices, but an alternative approach is to develop some 'special offers'. If these are ineffective, consider cutting the prices of some goods. Other causes of falling sales are distribution problems in the supply chain and changing customer preferences pushing the product into the decline stage of the life cycle. If the cause of a problem can be identified it is easier to recommend a solution, enabling managers to take effective action. This is the importance of interpretation.

There are many other types of variances, such as purchase variances and expense variances. The causes of these, and possible remedies, are summarised below.

Purchase variances

Cause	Action
Buying in bulk	Check there is sufficient cash and storage space
High wastage of materials	Introduce 'right first time' and better planning
Poor quality materials	Look for alternative suppliers
Long 'lead times' for special components	Consider making components 'in house', or agree a 'long-term contract'
Incorrect reorder levels	Review stock control systems and retrain staff

An unfavourable purchase variance indicates a business has spent more than budgeted on purchases. Many companies have a dedicated purchasing department, ensuring that the goods and components acquired are the right quality and quantity and are ordered on time. Smaller companies may not have a specialist purchasing department, making it more difficult to identify causes of variances.

Suppliers often offer a lower price if large orders are placed. This is sometimes referred to as a 'bulk discount'. Bulk discounts are beneficial if a company has enough cash to fund a large order. Unfortunately, many companies do not have sufficient cash reserves to buy in bulk. Another disadvantage of bulk discounts is the materials have to be stored safely, while they are waiting to be used. They can easily be damaged or deteriorate in storage.

Materials that are wasted have to be replaced. For instance, a company buying fresh food ingredients may have to dispose of them if they are not used quickly. Consequently, wastage can be one cause of a purchase variance. Waste can be reduced by introducing better planning and a 'right first time' policy.

Another reason why actual purchases may be more than forecast is that poor quality material has been bought. When a company recognises this problem, it usually has to buy replacement materials. Some components have to be made to order, which may take a number of weeks. This is referred to as long 'lead time'. Where companies face long lead times for components, they often buy many more than they need, to ensure they do not run out, causing a purchase variance. The proper solution in this case is to plan ahead more carefully, or find a supplier with low lead times. An unfavourable purchase variance has a negative impact on cash flow.

There are many different types of expenses, or 'overheads' as they are often called. An unfavourable expense variance indicates overheads are too high. Some of the reasons why expenses may be higher than forecast are detailed below.

Expense variances

Cause	Action
Rent reviews	Reduce the space needed
Pay rises	Reduce overtime or bonuses and review staff levels
Insurance premiums increased	Review insurance cover
Loss on disposal of fixed asset	Try to find alternative uses for the fixed assets in the business
Bad debts	Try factoring, or tighten up credit control procedures (see Chapter 12)
Increases in interest rates	Reduce borrowings, e.g. by sale of fixed assets
Excessive overtime worked by staff	Increase the flexibility of the work force, e.g. annualised hours
Unexpected building or machinery repairs and maintenance	Replace the machinery or the property causing the problem
Legal costs	Take out insurance to cover legal costs

As well as variances arising on the P&L account, variances also arise on assets and liabilities. Cash is one of the assets essential to the survival of a business; therefore, variances on cash are particularly significant. Specific causes of cash variances are detailed below.

Cash variances

Cause	Action
Customers slow paying	Improve credit control and review terms of business (see Chapter 12)
Paying suppliers too fast	Monitor cheque runs more closely
Interest charges high	Restructure borrowing, or raise share capital
Drawings too high	Reduce personal expenses
Big customer goes bankrupt	Try to broaden the customer base and credit check every new customer

Report writing

There are a number of factors to consider when analysing the causes of variances and interpreting complicated business problems. The complexity of the relationships between these factors, and the unique nature of every business, necessitate the presentation of all the facts and figures in a report. A business report should be structured as follows:

- Introduction
- Methodology
- Results
- Conclusions
- Recommendations

In the introductory section the people or person to whom the report is addressed should be clearly stated and the main themes identified. If the key issue dealt with in the report is disappointing sales, the prevailing economic situation should be summarised. If the readers are unaware of the nature of the business, its products, people and processes should be explained. If the report is about e-business, background on the potential of the Internet and examples of successful e-businesses should be outlined. These points provide a context for the report and orientate the reader towards key issues. Often the key issues only emerge once the results and conclusions are known and, consequently, the introduction should be written after analysing the facts and figures.

The methodology section explains and justifies the particular approach adopted in the report, forewarning the reader about what is contained in the results and conclusions sections. In the context of a budgeting report, the first step is comparing actual to budget and the calculation of variances. Next, the variances are interpreted using facts about the business. If a member of the management team prepares the report, he or she will already be familiar with many of the facts about the business. If the writer is an external consultant, however, it will be necessary to carry out interviews, collect facts and opinions. The specific methods used to collect these facts should be detailed in the methodology section.

The results section should include a table of variances and a detailed explanation of their causes using facts relating to the business. The conclusions summarise and prioritise the problems facing the business. The recommendations section should explain ways of correcting the problems identified in the conclusions section. Both financial and non-financial recommendations should be included. For example, recommendations may include raising more cash (financial), as well as expanding the product ranges (non-financial).

To achieve a high standard of presentation in reports:

- Use double line spacing (*format~paragraph~line spacing*).
- Two inch margin on the left (*view~margin*).
- Write in the third person: 'It is recommended' rather than 'I recommend'.
- Page numbers (*insert~page numbers*).
- Contents page at the front.
- Bibliography at the back, giving full details of sources.

A clear structure, combined with a high standard of presentation, will result in a good quality report.

Interpretation and report writing in action

Read the following case study carefully and then examine the two sets of figures.

'Franks' video and DVD store

Background

Frank Quentin graduated in Film Studies three years ago. After leaving college he had a variety of jobs and, because he lived at home rent-free, he was able to save his money. When he had accumulated £12,000 he was able to fulfil his ambition and start his own video and DVD store.

He found some suitable premises, in quite a nice area, and not as expensive as he had imagined. A friend prepared a business plan, including a budgeted P&L account and balance sheet for the first year (see Figure 9.1). Within three weeks he was trading. It was the most exciting time of his life.

Current situation

The first year has not worked out as well as Frank had hoped. In fact, the P&L account shows a loss (see Figure 9.2). The shop window has been broken three times and the door has been forced. Frank replaced the door and bought an alarm system. Some of the 'new release' DVDs have been stolen, or at least not returned. When Frank has tried to contact the people involved, they could not be found at the address they had given.

Frank has not asked all new members to supply full ID, e.g. utility bills, driving licence, bank statement, etc. He has not imposed fines for late returns. Frank has encountered more competition in the area than he expected. A nearby wine store has a small video section and, although more than a mile away, there is a national video and DVD store, with secure parking facilities, which opened seven months ago. Frank has a few very loyal customers who listen carefully to his recommendations. In fact these people can often be seen chatting to Frank in the early evenings. These customers rent the more artistic European and foreign language videos, rather than mainstream Hollywood productions.

There is a good profit margin on these European and specialist videos, which have a loyal following. Some customers have expressed an interest in buying rather than just renting. Some postgraduate students at the Film Studies Department have mentioned to Frank the possibility that he could become a 'preferred supplier' to the University. This contract could generate about £40,000 of sales every year.

Frank has found it hard to recruit enthusiastic staff to help out in the shop. He has had to work long hours and has been too tired to think about special promotions, developing the product range, introducing ice cream and popcorn, etc. These are all aspects of the job he had been particularly looking forward to.

'Franks' Video Shop

Extract from the Business Plan
Budgeted Trading and Profit and Loss Account
Year Ended 30th November 2003

	£	£
Sales		100,000
Less: cost of sales		75,000
Gross profit		25,000
Less: expenses		
Rent	5,000	
Wages	4,000	
Advertising and promotions	5,000	
Travel	1,000	
Depreciation	1,800	
Insurance	500	
		17,300
Net loss		7,700

'Franks' Video Shop

Extract from the Business Plan
Budgeted Balance Sheet
As at 30th November 2003

	Cost	Accumulated depreciation	Net book value
Fixed assets			
Lease premium	4,000	400	3,600
Fixtures and fittings	4,000	1,000	3,000
Computer and till	2,000	400	1,600
	10,000	1,800	8,200
Current assets			
Debtors		0	
Bank		14,000	
		14,000	
Current liabilities			
Creditors		2,500	
Working capital			11,500
Total net assets			19,700
Financed by:			
Owner's capital			12,000
Add: net profit		7,700	
Less: drawings		0	
			7,700
			19,700

Figure 9.1 Budgeted Figures

'Franks' Video Shop

Actual Trading and Profit and Loss Account
Year Ended 31st November 2003

	£	£
Sales		97,500
Less: cost of sales		83,000
Gross profit		14,500
Less: expenses		
Rent and rates	6,000	
Wages	2,000	
Advertising and promotions	4,000	
Travel expenses	500	
Insurance	500	
Bank charges and interest	750	
Repairs	1,500	
Accounting	500	
Depreciation	2,200	
		17,950
Net loss		(3,450)

'Franks' Video Shop

Actual Balance Sheet
As at 30th November 2003

	Cost	Accumulated depreciation	Net book value
Fixed assets			
Lease premium	4,000	400	3,600
Fixtures and fittings	4,000	1,000	3,000
Computer and till	2,000	400	1,600
Alarm	2,000	400	1,600
	12,000	2,200	9,800
Current assets			
Debtors		500	
Bank		0	
		500	
Current liabilities			
Creditors	2,000		
Bank overdraft	2,750		
		4,750	
Working capital			(4,250)
Total net assets			5,550
Financed by:			
Owner's capital			12,000
Add: net profit		(3,450)	
Less: drawings		3,000	
			(6,450)
			5,550

Figure 9.2 Actual Figures

Frank has become overdrawn at the bank and the interest charges are high. He has also incurred bank charges. One problem with the location is that it is quiet at weekends, when Frank had expected it to be busy. Frank has been feeling depressed for a few weeks. He has started to open up the shop late and sometimes shuts early. Friends have commented privately that he is not as lively and enthusiastic as he used to be. They are worried about him.

Frank has asked a professional firm of accountants to prepare a P&L account and balance sheet for the first year. These are presented in Figure 9.2. Depreciation has been calculated on the following basis:

- Lease premium 10%
- Fixtures and fittings 25%
- All others 20%

Sales refer to the income generated from renting out videos. Cost of sales refers to videos purchased during the year. Because of theft, Frank has had to buy about £7000 of extra videos.

This case study is about a new business. It poses the question 'What has gone wrong in the first year and how can it be put right?' There are a lot of facts and figures, so it is a complex situation. To answer the question comprehensively, a report format will be needed. The challenge is to prepare a report which:

- Compares the budgeted results to actual for the first year of the business;
- Calculates variances;
- Interprets the variances using facts from the case study;
- Identifies the main problems;
- Makes reasoned recommendations for action.

The first step is to calculate the variances.

'Franks' Video Shop

Variance Analysis

	Budgeted	Actual	Variance	%	Favour?
Sales	100,000	97,500	2,500	2.5%	No
Cost of sales	75,000	83,000	8,000	11%	No
Gross profit	25,000	14,500	10,500	42%	No
Less: expenses					
Rent and rates	5,000	6,000	1,000	20%	No
Wages	4,000	2,000	2,000	50%	Yes
Advertising and promotions	5,000	4,000	1,000	20%	Yes
Travel	1,000	500	500	50%	Yes
Depreciation	1,800	2,200	400	22%	No
Insurance	500	500	0	0%	No
Bank charges and interest	0	750	750	NA	No
Repairs	0	1,500	1,500	NA	No
Accounting	0	500	500	NA	No
Total	17,300	17,950	650	4%	No
Net profit	7,700	−3,450	11,150	144%	No
Fixed assets (net book value)	8,200	9,800	−1,600	20%	Yes
Debtors	0	500	−500	NA	Yes
Cash	14,000	−2,750	16,750	120%	No
Creditors	2,500	2,000	500	20%	Yes
Working capital	11,500	−4,250	15,750	137%	No
Total net assets	19,700	5,550	14,150	71.8%	No
Capital	12,000	12,000	0	NA	Yes
Add: profit (loss)	7,700	3,450	11,150	145%	No
Less: drawings	0	3,000	3,000	NA	No
	19,700	5,550	14,150	71.8%	No

The table shows the expected net profit (£7700) turned out to be a loss (£3450). The net profit variance is £11,150. Most of this can be attributed to the gross profit variance £10,500, while the variance on total expenses is only £650. The sales variance was unfavourable, but of a low magnitude. In fact sales were only 2.5% under budget, which is a creditable performance. The main problems arose not in sales, but in cost of sales. The next step is to link the variances to the facts about the business.

'Franks' Video Shop

Causes of the Variances

Variance	Value	Cause
Sales	£2500 unfavourable	Only just under budget. An encouraging figure in the first year of the business. There are prospects for higher sales next year.
Cost of sales	£8000 unfavourable	This is the single biggest cause of the net profit variance. The theft of videos cost the business £7000, which accounts for most of this variance.
Gross profit	£10,500 unfavourable	There are two causes of this variance. Cost of sales was increased by the theft of videos and, in addition, the effect of a small shortfall in sales.
Expenses	£650 unfavourable	A very mixed picture. Some of the overspend is the result of forgetting to budget for accounting and rates. Other overspends reflect the problems the business had with security. Some of the expense items are underspent. For instance, wages are underspent because of the difficulties in recruiting staff. Travel and advertising are underspent because Frank did not have time to pursue these aspects of the business.
Net profit	£11,150 unfavourable	See above.
Fixed assets	£1600 favourable	New alarm system.
Debtors	£500 favourable	Not a significant variance in the light of £11,500 net profit variance.
Cash	£16,750 unfavourable	This is because of the extra money spent on videos (£7000), equipment (£1600), expenses (£650), drawings (£3000) and less money coming in from sales.
Creditors	£500 favourable	Not a significant variance in the light of £11,150 net profit variance.
Drawings	£3000 unfavourable	These were omitted from the original business plan, which was a mistake; however, Frank has done well to keep drawings to a minimum. He may have been too busy to spend money on himself.

The case study suggests a business with many problems; however, the variance analysis gives a different picture. The variances indicate one issue, the theft of videos, is causing most of the problems. Certainly, there are other problems (sales and expenses, etc.), but they are of a lower magnitude.

At this stage some initial conclusions can be drawn and recommendations made which are best recorded in note form before drafting the final report:

- Sales are encouraging and could improve further.
- The main problem identified is the theft of videos (£7000).
- A number of smaller problems exist on expenses, but they are largely dealt with.
- The premises are cheap and although they are quiet at weekends, sales are relatively healthy.
- Frank has only drawn £3000 out of the business, which is good for cash flow.
- The overdraft is a cause for concern.
- Frank may have to work long hours for some time yet, but he should continue to look for additional staff.
- If the issue concerning the theft of videos could be dealt with, the business could be profit making.
- Many new businesses make a loss in their first year. There are genuine reasons why Frank should be optimistic.

On the basis of these initial conclusions, the following recommendations would be appropriate:

- The specialist market (European and foreign language videos and DVDs) has a higher profit margin than the mass market. It also complements the extra quality of service offered by Frank. He should consider focusing on the specialist market, rather than the mass market.
- Pursue the idea of selling specialist videos in addition to renting them.
- Follow up the possibility of a 'preferred supplier' contract with the University.
- Insist on formal proof of identity for all new members.
- Fines should be levied on late returns.
- Formulate a marketing strategy in order to attract consumers with special interests who will be willing to travel further to visit the shop.
- Contact the Film Studies Department and advertise for a member of staff. It should be possible to attract someone passionate about film.
- Find out where local customers are going at the weekend – it could be a sales opportunity.
- Get a mobile phone with a text facility and e-mail, so customers can keep in regular contact. To an extent Frank could be able to work from home.
- Persuade a student at the University to design a web site for the business.
- Consider offering a delivery service at the weekend – it might stimulate the market.
- Think of ways of stimulating the specialist market, e.g. a 'European Film Club' or promotions such as 'Leon' night or 'Once Were Warriors' weekend.
- Contact the bank, explain the problems and let them know the new strategy.
- Continue to keep drawings under control.

All the ingredients needed to write a report are now present. Here is an outline of the report, showing how to integrate the facts and figures into a coherent argument.

Introduction

This is a report to the owner of the business, so there is no need to give background on the products, people and processes. The theme in this case study is the problems affecting a new business. It would be appropriate to make the point that the first year of a new business is always difficult. Next it would make sense to argue that the positive achievements of the first year outweigh the disappointments.

Methodology

Explain about calculating variances and interpreting the situation by using the facts from the case study to explain the variances.

Results

Show the variances in a table, as shown above, and the causes of the variances.

Conclusions

The main conclusions are listed in note form above. Use these to develop a fuller explanation of the conclusions drawn.

Recommendations

The recommendations are listed in note form above. Again, use these to develop a full set of recommendations for the business.

Conclusions

The skill being developed in this chapter is the ability to explain complex business problems using both facts and figures. A report is a convenient vehicle for organising the material. This skill has applications extending beyond budgeting. If you can interpret a complex budget variance, you will be more able to interpret any complex business situation. If you can write a report on variances, you will be better able to write a report on any business problem. The ability to analyse and interpret a complex situation and prepare a report, which makes reasoned recommendations, is an essential skill for a manager.

Multiple choice questions

Tick the box next to your answer.

1. Which of these causes a reduction in sales (an unfavourable sales variance)?
   - [ ] Increase in selling price
   - [ ] General economic boom
   - [ ] Reduction in interest rates
   - [ ] Successful advertising campaign
   - [ ] Reduction in selling price

2. Which of these causes a favourable sales variance?
   - [ ] Launch of a successful new product line
   - [ ] General economic recession
   - [ ] Increase in interest rates
   - [ ] Increase in selling price
   - [ ] Competitor reduces selling price

3. Which of these causes an unfavourable wages expense variance?
   - [ ] Staff leaving the company and not replaced
   - [ ] Fall in overtime hours
   - [ ] Unexpected increase in wages and salaries
   - [ ] Reduction in the number of temporary workers
   - [ ] Reduction in training costs

4. Which of these does **not** cause an expense variance?
   - [ ] A large bad debt
   - [ ] An increase in depreciation
   - [ ] Scrapping a fixed asset half way through its useful life
   - [ ] An increase in purchases
   - [ ] A large pay rise for all employees

5. Taking out a new bank loan will
   - [ ] Reduce cash in the bank
   - [ ] Reduce interest payments to the bank
   - [ ] Increase interest payments to the bank
   - [ ] Increase income
   - [ ] Reduce liabilities

6. If sales variance is 10% favourable, what would you expect to happen to debtors and cash?
   - [ ] No impact on debtors
   - [ ] Debtors higher than budgeted and cash lower than budgeted
   - [ ] Both lower than budgeted
   - [ ] Both higher than budgeted by about 10%
   - [ ] Both 50% higher than budgeted

7. Which of these causes an unfavourable cash variance?
   - [ ] Acquisition of a fixed asset for cash
   - [ ] Scrapping a fixed asset
   - [ ] Increase in the useful life of fixed assets
   - [ ] Borrowing money from the bank
   - [ ] Negotiating a higher overdraft limit

8. If a company has a large overdraft, an increase in interest rates will cause
   - [ ] An increase in interest received
   - [ ] A reduction in purchases
   - [ ] A reduction in depreciation
   - [ ] Increases in interest paid
   - [ ] Reductions in interest paid

9. If the owner of a business increases drawings
   - [ ] Sales increase
   - [ ] Net profit falls
   - [ ] Expenses rise
   - [ ] Cash falls
   - [ ] Fixed assets fall

10. In a report to the 'Board of Directors' about the potential of e-business, which of the following should be explained?
    - [ ] The recent history of the company
    - [ ] Products manufactured and services provided by the company
    - [ ] The management structure of the company
    - [ ] The impact of the Internet on the company
    - [ ] The importance of making a profit

Multiple choice answers

	Correct answer	Comment
1	Increase in selling price	An increase in selling price encourages customers to go to competitors; however, in a niche market, e.g. 'Franks' Video Shop, the situation could be different.
2	Launch of a successful new product line	If customers like the new product, sales will increase.
3	Unexpected increase in wages and salaries	Increases in wages increase the total 'Wages' expense. All the other options reduce the 'Wages' expense.
4	An increase in purchases	Purchases are not the same as expenses.
5	Increase interest payments to the bank	The more a company owes the bank, the more interest it pays.
6	Both higher than budgeted by about 10%	If sales increase, both debtors and stock increase.
7	Acquisition of a fixed asset for cash	If a fixed asset is acquired for cash, a large amount of cash goes out of the business.
8	Increases in interest paid	The more the company borrows, the greater the risk posed by high interest rates.
9	Cash falls	Drawings are not an expense, so net profit is unaffected. The other element changing is capital.
10	The impact of the Internet on the company	The Board of Directors are already aware of the other areas. In a report to the bank about e-business, for instance, the other information might be useful because the bank does not know the company as well as the Board.

Mei Lin Chiang

Background

Mei Lin has been in the business of wholesale supply of children's clothing for more than eight years. She started the business when her father left her some commercial property in a run down part of Hong Kong. Mei Lin has made a success of the business. Many customers originally came to her because they had known her father. As it turned out, Mei Lin had a flair for buying the right clothes and selling them to retailers.

As the business has grown, Mei Lin has had to take on a more managerial role. This has meant getting involved with stock control, distribution and finance, etc. Mei Lin prefers buying and selling, which she excels at. When she started the business she was single, childless and a workaholic. She now has to make room for a husband, child and large family house. She used to enjoy trips to New York and Milan. Now they disturb the domestic routine.

Mei Lin supplies shops throughout the Hong Kong area and she is now starting to acquire customers further afield. The company does not yet sell on the Internet, but Mei Lin sometimes uses it to look at new collections of clothes. The clothes supplied by Mei Lin are expensive and exclusive – it is not a mass market business.

Fifteen months ago Mei Lin introduced an integrated accounting and stock control system. After a few initial problems, the system started to work smoothly and the full benefits are reflected in the results for 200X (see below). Mei Lin has not invested in upgrading the freehold property and as a result it is now in a poor condition.

Mei Lin's father was a great believer in budgeting and Mei Lin keeps up the family tradition, but she does not compare budget to actual on a monthly basis. She waits until the end of the year before comparing budget to actual. The company's financial year ends in February.

Current situation

Mei Lin has just received the P&L account and balance sheet for 200X. She is trying to understand the variances from the budget set out at the start of the year. Just before the start of 200X Mei Lin made some important decisions, which she knows will have affected the business:

- She stopped travelling abroad to buy clothes. She now uses her existing contacts to help her make buying decisions. She also looks at products on the Internet, where possible.
- She decided to spend less time managing the company and concentrate instead on buying and selling. As a result, the company has many new customers as well as retaining existing ones. Many of the new customers are further afield.
- At the start of the accounting year Mei Lin introduced a new range of clothing, the 'Little Emperor' collection, which has been popular with customers and sold well. Some customers, however, have started to complain about slow delivery. At the same time some competitors are starting to offer same-day delivery.

Unfortunately, both the delivery manager and the warehouse manager (stock controller) left during 200X. The bookkeeper and the credit controller have not been able to cope without Mei Lin's help. Delivery costs and times are increasing because some of the vans are old and need replacing.

During 200X the broader economic climate deteriorated. Because of currency speculation, the government increased interest rates during the year. This has reduced consumer spending considerably, especially on luxury items.

See the budgeted and actual P&L account and balance sheet. The figures have been converted into £ sterling.

Your task

Using the method established in the in-chapter case study, write a report that analyses the company's results for the year and makes recommendations for future action. Check your progress against the outline answer step by step. The projected and actual P&L account and balance sheet are presented below:

Mei Lin Chiang

Projected Trading and Profit and Loss Account
Year Ended 28th February 200X

Sales		3,127,000
Less: cost of sales		
Opening stock	327,000	
Add: purchases	2,454,000	
	2,781,000	
Less: closing stock	347,000	
		2,434,000
Gross profit		693,000
Less: expenses		
Staff costs	342,000	
Advertising and promotions	63,000	
Light, heat and insurance	12,000	
Delivery costs	35,000	
Travel expenses	83,000	
Office and accounting costs	23,000	
Interest	25,000	
Other expenses	7,000	
Building maintenance	1,000	
Depreciation	27,000	
		618,000
Net profit		75,000

Mei Lin Chiang

Projected Balance Sheet
As at 28th February 200X

	Cost	Accumulated depreciation	Net book value
Fixed assets			
Freehold premises	100,000	25,000	75,000
Delivery vehicles	80,000	60,000	20,000
Warehouse fixtures	40,000	18,000	22,000
IT equipment	25,000	10,000	15,000
	245,000	113,000	132,000
Current assets			
Stock		347,000	
Debtors		308,000	
Bank and cash		89,000	
		744,000	
Current liabilities			
Creditors		323,000	
Working capital			421,000
Total net assets			553,000
Financed by:			
Owner's capital			343,000
Add: net profit		75,000	
Less: drawings		40,000	
			35,000
			378,000
Loan			175,000
			553,000

Mei Lin Chiang

Actual Trading and Profit and Loss Account
Year Ended 28th February 200X

Sales		3,545,000
Less: cost of sales		
Opening stock	327,000	
Add: purchases	2,908,000	
	3,235,000	
Less: closing stock	453,000	
		2,782,000
Gross profit		763,000
Less: expenses		
Staff costs	338,000	
Advertising and promotions	69,000	
Light, heat and insurance	14,000	
Delivery costs	44,000	
Travel expenses	54,000	
Office and accounting costs	24,000	
Interest	32,000	
Other expenses	8,000	
Building maintenance	9,000	
Depreciation	27,000	
		619,000
Net profit		144,000

Mei Lin Chiang

Actual Balance Sheet
As at 28th February 200X

	Cost	Accumulated depreciation	Net book value
Fixed assets			
Freehold premises	100,000	25,000	75,000
Delivery vehicles	80,000	60,000	20,000
Warehouse fixtures	40,000	18,000	22,000
IT equipment	25,000	10,000	15,000
	245,000	113,000	132,000
Current assets			
Stock		453,000	
Debtors		371,000	
Bank and cash		−27,000	
		797,000	
Current liabilities			
Creditors		332,000	
Working capital			465,000
Total net assets			597,000
Financed by:			
Owner's capital			343,000
Add: net profit		144,000	
Less: drawings		67,000	
			77,000
			420,000
Loan			177,000
			597,000

Solution

Mei Lin Chiang

Variance Analysis
Year Ending 28th February 200X

All figures in £000's	Budget	Actual	Variance	%	Favour?
Sales	3,127	3,545	418	13.4%	Yes
Less: cost of sales	2,434	2,782	(348)	14.3%	No
Gross profit	693	763	70	10.1%	Yes
Less: expenses					
Staff costs	342	338	4	1.2%	Yes
Advertising and promotions	63	69	(6)	9.5%	No
Light, heat and insurance	12	14	(2)	16.6%	No
Delivery costs	35	44	(9)	25.7%	No
Travel expenses	83	54	29	34.9%	Yes
Office and accounting costs	23	24	(1)	4%	No
Interest	25	32	(7)	28%	No
Other	7	8	(1)	14.2%	No
Building maintenance	1	9	(8)	800%	No
Depreciation	27	27	0	0%	Yes
Total	618	619	(1)	0.10%	No
Net profit	75	144	69	92%	Yes
Fixed assets (net book value)	132	132	0	0%	Yes
Stock	347	453	106	30.5%	Yes
Debtors	308	371	63	20.4%	Yes
Cash	89	−27	116	130%	No
Creditors	323	332	9	2.8%	No
Net current assets	421	480	59	14%	Yes
Total net assets	553	597	44	8%	Yes
Capital	343	343	0	0%	Yes
Add: profit	75	144	69	92%	Yes
Less: drawings	40	67	27	67.5%	No
	378	420	42	11.1%	Yes
Loans	175	177	2	1%	No
	553	597	44	8%	Yes

Mei Lin Chiang

Interpretation of Variances
Year Ended 28th February 200X

Variance	Value (£000's)	Cause
Sales	£418 favourable	Mei Lin has concentrated on selling and has introduced a new collection, which has sold well. The increase in interest rates and slow deliveries have had no noticeable effect.
Cost of sales	£348 unfavourable	Has risen broadly in line with sales.
Gross profit	£70 favourable	Has risen in line with sales.
Staff costs	£4 favourable	Have increased because of more deliveries, but reduced because two managers left during the year.
Advertising and promotions	£6 unfavourable	Extra money spent on promoting the new 'Little Emperor' collection.
Light, heat and insurance	£2 unfavourable	No obvious explanation for this small variance. It is not material when compared to a budgeted net profit of £75,000.
Delivery costs	£9 unfavourable	Increased because the vans are getting old and because there are more deliveries, some of which are further afield.
Travel expenses	£29 favourable	Reduced because Mei Lin is not travelling abroad as much, which does not seem to be affecting the business.
Office and accounting	£1 unfavourable	Not material to net profit.
Interest	£7 unfavourable	Increased because interest rates have increased during the year.
Other	£1 unfavourable	Not material to net profit.
Building maintenance	£8 unfavourable	The building is old, so it needs constant maintenance. This should have been budgeted for.
Depreciation	£0 favourable	No variance here.
Total expenses	£1 unfavourable	A mixed picture, with some big overspends and some big underspends. Total expenses are surprisingly close to budget.

Net profit	£69 favourable	Increased because sales have increased; however, the cash is not coming in quickly enough— see balance sheet variances below.
Stock	£106 favourable (but bad impact on cash)	Mei Lin is concentrating on buying and selling; she is not focused on stock control. During the year the stock controller left. As a result, this area of the business has been neglected. Too much stock has been bought, resulting in more money than necessary being paid out. This has turned a cash balance into an overdraft.
Debtors	£63 unfavourable (but bad impact on cash)	Mei Lin has not been getting involved on the financial side of the business. The credit controller has not been able to cope on her own. Debtors have not been contacted regularly and as a result cash receipts have fallen.
Cash	£116 unfavourable	Money has been spent on unnecessary stock and increased drawings while debtors have been allowed to increase.
Creditors	£9 favourable	Not a material variance (2%).
Drawings	£27 unfavourable	Increased because of personal commitments. This exacerbated the overdraft. This should be budgeted more accurately.

In summary, the P&L account shows a favourable net profit variance, but the liquidity position is not favourable. The management of stock, debtors and cash has been neglected. The 'circuit of capital' (Chapter 1) shows profit is not secure until cash is received.

Results and findings

From the analysis above, the following results and findings are apparent:

- Sales are buoyant.
- Gross profit is 10% higher than expected.
- Disappointingly, some overheads have increased, but overall expenses are in line with budget.
- Not travelling abroad has reduced expenses, with no adverse impact on sales.
- Net profit is above budget.
- The balance sheet reveals some liquidity issues.
- Stock is 30% over budget, suggesting the company is spending money unnecessarily.
- Debtors are 20% over budget, suggesting lax credit control.
- The increase in stock and debtors has a cumulative impact on cash.
- The increase in drawings has further exacerbated the cash situation.
- A positive cash balance has become an overdraft.

Conclusions

- Many of these problems could have been foreseen.
- Action should have been taken during the year.
- Increasing sales is key, but other areas of the business must not be neglected.
- Mei Lin must consider the whole business.

Recommendations

- Mei Lin should continue to concentrate on buying and selling – this seems to have worked well.
- Mei Lin should continue not to travel abroad – this helped reduce expenses.
- Appoint a general manager for the business as a whole, reporting to Mei Lin.
- Strengthen credit control in order to chase debtors effectively.
- Replace the stock control manager as a matter of urgency because stocks need to be reduced to more sensible levels.
- Prepare a cash flow forecast for the bank, so they do not get alarmed at the overdraft.
- Monitor cash flow on a weekly basis until the overdraft is eliminated.
- Perform only emergency building maintenance in the coming year.
- Once the overdraft is eliminated, think about replacing the delivery vans.
- Budget more accurately – some items were underestimated or omitted, e.g. drawings and building maintenance.
- Investigate the possibility of moving to a new building. It does not make sense to have all the latest computer software in an inefficient old building. A new, purpose built, facility will help the business achieve same-day delivery.
- A web site would be useful, particularly for achieving same-day delivery.
- Compare budget to actual on a monthly basis and take early action.
- Monitor balance sheet as much as P&L account.
- Identify objectives for the business, and structure the budget around achieving those objectives. The immediate objective is to eliminate the overdraft. The long-term objective is to put in place a management structure allowing Mei Lin to buy and sell while making sure that other areas of the business are not neglected.
- In light of the fact that the vans need replacing and the building is in poor condition, it might be worth considering a fresh injection of capital into the business. A partner capable of acting as a general manager, as well as injecting new capital, would be ideal.

All the ingredients needed to write a report are now present. Consider what needs to be included in the introduction and methodology sections. In the introduction the theme of the report should be established. The theme of this case study is the fact that as a business grows, management becomes more complex and important. Mei Lin does not want to manage the business because she enjoys specialising in selling and buying. The fact that she does not want to manage the business is the main theme. In the introduction put this point in diplomatic language, as follows:

This report has been prepared for Mei Lin Chiang. It evaluates the progress of the business over the last year. During this period a new computer system and product range were introduced, both of which represent major achievements. As the business grows, new challenges will emerge, right across the managerial spectrum. It will become increasingly difficult to co-ordinate buying, stock control, selling, distribution and credit control. All of these areas of the business have to run smoothly if the business is to be successful.

This would be appropriate in the methodology section:

For the purposes of preparing this report the actual and budgeted figures relating to the company have been made available. The company has been visited and the proprietor (Mei Lin Chiang) and other members of the management team have been interviewed.

In order to judge the progress made during the year, the budgeted results have been compared to actual on both the profit and loss account and the balance sheet. Variances for all the major items have been calculated. These variances have been interpreted in light of the issues and problems facing the company, as well as in light of the major achievements the company can point to.

This interpretation allows conclusions to be drawn about successes and failures experienced by the company over the last year. Where failures have occurred, recommendations are offered for making further improvements to the business.

Now complete the conclusions and recommendations sections.

10 Accounting ratios

This chapter shows how ratios can help identify business issues and problems.

Objectives	
	• Calculate and explain ratios;
	• Ratio interpretation;
	• Porter's Five Forces.

Introduction

Importance of the subject

Ratios help identify business issues and problems by highlighting the relationship between different figures. They are calculated by comparing one figure from the P&L account or balance sheet to another. Calculating ratios also helps develop a deeper understanding of these financial statements and improves interpretative skills.

Structure of this chapter

There are many ratios that can be useful in business and this chapter focuses on ten *key* ratios. For each of these ten ratios we will consider:

• The formula for calculating the ratio;
• The interpretation of the ratio.

Once you have mastered the calculation and interpretation of the ten key ratios, you will be able to apply the technique to a range of business situations and relationships. Porter's Five Forces model is also introduced in this chapter to complement and develop the analysis of ratios.

To calculate a ratio one figure is divided by another, e.g. gross profit divided by sales. When dividing one figure by another, the first figure is expressed per unit of the second figure. For example, consider the following:

Net profit *divided by* total number of employees

Numerator and denominator

The first figure, net profit, is expressed per unit of the second figure, total number of employees. The result will be net profit per employee. If sales are divided by the total number of employees:

Sales *divided by* total number of employees

The first figure, sales, is expressed per unit of the second figure, total number of employees. The result is sales per employee. The first figure is referred to as the numerator and the second as the denominator.

Consider this situation. Many large retail companies aim to have an outlet in every major city and town. As a result, they have a large number of stores. The directors of such a company will consider a range of ratios, one of which will involve this calculation:

Sales *divided by* total number of shops

The denominator in this case is the total number of shops. The unit of measurement is the number of shops or stores. In the space below, write a short sentence explaining what this ratio means.

Did you try? If not, go back. The answer is 'sales per shop'. This indicates the average value of sales from a single store, giving a benchmark to measure the performance of other stores. It will help identify stores that are below average, as well as those that are above average.

Activities and outcomes

This chapter contains a substantial case study exercise. Use the multiple choice questions at the end of the chapter to measure your progress and understanding before attempting the other end of chapter questions. After completing these you will be able to calculate and explain accounting ratios as well as interpret them within Porter's Five Forces model.

Accounting ratio formulas

The formulas for the ten *key* ratios are set out below:
1. Gross profit % = (gross profit/sales) × 100
2. Net profit % = (net profit/sales) × 100
3. Expenses % = (expenses/sales) × 100
4. Stock turnover = cost of sales/average stock
   Average stock = (opening stock + closing stock)/2
5. Current ratio = current assets/current liabilities
6. Acid test = (debtors + cash)/current liabilities
7. Debtor days = (debtors/credit sales) × 365
8. Creditor days = (creditors/credit purchases) × 365
9. Return on capital employed % = (net profit/total net assets) × 100
10. Gearing % = (loans/total net assets) × 100

Ratios in action

The easiest way to understand ratios is to practise calculating them. Consider the example set out below.

BOMBASTIC

BOMBASTIC is a small company that deals in, restores and copies vinyl records to CD and digital audio tape (DAT). The latest results are as follows:

BOMBASTIC

Trading and Profit and Loss Account
Year Ended 31st December 200X

Sales		£200,000
Less: cost of sales		
Opening stock	£20,000	
Purchases	125,000	
	145,000	
Less: closing stock	25,000	
		120,000
Gross profit		80,000
Less: expenses		
Wages	24,750	
Rent and rates	11,250	
Cleaning materials	2,270	
Advertising and web site	14,230	
Legal advice	2,500	
General administration	5,000	
		60,000
Net profit		£20,000

The company has been in existence for three years. Losses were made in the first two years, but this year a net profit of £20,000 has been earned. The main customers are specialist retail outlets and DJs. Customers can order and buy on line using the web site, but this facility has not been popular because most customers need advice before buying. All sales are credit sales.

At the moment, there are no other companies providing this comprehensive service. As a result, BOMBASTIC recently increased prices and now insists on speedy payment from debtors. The overdraft has been falling in recent months. The company does not realise, however, that a group of DJs is thinking of starting their own company.

BOMBASTIC

Balance Sheet
As at 31st December 200X

	Cost	Accumulated depreciation	Net book value
Fixed assets			
Mixing desk	£2,000	£1,200	£800
Computer and editing software	2,250	1,350	900
Turntables	800	440	360
CD multicopier	2,200	660	1,540
Fixtures	1,750	350	1,400
	9,000	4,000	5,000
Current assets			
Stock		20,000	
Debtors		14,000	
		34,000	
Current liabilities			
Creditors	9,320		
Overdraft	6,470		
		15,790	
Working capital			18,210
Total net assets			23,210
Financed by:			
Share capital			1,000
Profit			20,000
			21,000
Loans			2,210
			23,210

Your task

Using the P&L account and balance sheet calculate the ten key ratios.

BOMBASTIC: Solution

The ten key ratios are presented below. Look carefully at every figure and work out the answer on your calculator.

Gross profit percentage	$(80,000/200,000) \times 100 = 40\%$
Net profit percentage	$(20,000/200,000) \times 100 = 10\%$
Expense percentage	$(60,000/200,000) \times 100 = 30\%$
Stock turnover	$(20,000 + 25,000)/2 = £22,500$ $120,000/22,500 = 5.33$ times per year
Current ratio	$34,000/15,790 = £2.15$
Acid test	$14,000/15,790 = £0.88$

Debtor days	$(14,000/200,000) \times 365 = 26$ days
Creditor days	$(9320/125,000) \times 365 = 27$ days
Return on capital employed %	$(20,000/23,210) \times 100 = 86.17\%$
Gearing %	$(2210/23,210) \times 100 = 9.5\%$

Trace every figure above back to the P&L account and balance sheet.

Interpreting accounting ratios

As well as calculating ratios it is important to understand their meaning and usefulness. Here is an explanation of what the ten key ratios mean.

1. Gross profit %

The formula shows that the denominator is sales. The ratio, therefore, calculates the gross profit per £ of sales, i.e. the amount of gross profit, on average, earned from every £ of sales. If the gross profit % is 20%, then on average there is 20p gross profit in every £1 worth of sales. If the gross profit % is 50%, there is 50p worth of gross profit, on average, in every £1 worth of sales.

Most companies have a range of different products. Each one may have a different profit margin. The gross profit % relates to the company as a whole and may hide considerable variation within the product range. Some products may have a large profit margin, others a small profit margin. Some products may be being sold at a loss. The gross profit % is sometimes referred to as 'profit margin' or 'mark up'.

Businesses want gross profit % to be as high as possible.

2. Net profit %

The formula shows that the denominator is, again, sales. This ratio, therefore, calculates the net profit per £ of sales, i.e. the amount of net profit, on average, earned from every £ of sales. If net profit % is 5%, then on average there is 5p worth of net profit in every £1 worth of sales. If net profit % is 10%, then on average there is 10p worth of net profit in every £1 of sales.

Businesses want net profit % to be as high as possible.

3. Expense %

The formula shows that the denominator is, again, sales. This ratio therefore calculates expenses per £ of sales. This can be interpreted as the extent to which sales revenue is spent on expenses. More specifically, on average, how much of every £1 worth of sales is spent on expenses. If expense % is 15% then, on average, 15p of every £1 worth of sales is spent on expenses. If expense % is 30% then, on average, 30p of every £1 of sales is spent on expenses.

As a company grows, expenses or 'overheads' often grow more quickly than sales. Figure 10.1 shows a situation where the rate of growth of expenses is greater than that of sales.

One of the reasons expenses have to be monitored is because of their impact on net profit. Every £1 spent on expenses reduces net profit by £1. If expenses increase by £10,000, net profit falls by £10,000. If expenses increase by £15,000, net profit falls by £15,000. Consequently, it is vital that a growing business controls overheads.

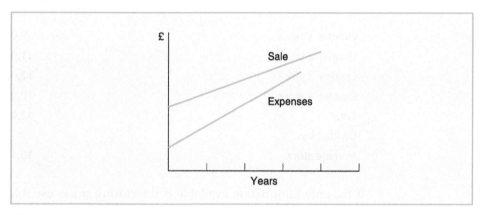

Figure 10.1 Expense %

Expense % can also be calculated for individual items of expenses. For instance, wages expense % indicates the extent to which sales revenue is spent on wages and other payroll-related costs. An interest expense % indicates the extent to which sales revenue is spent on interest costs.

Businesses want expense % to be as low as possible.

4. Stock turnover

Every company should utilise stock quickly and efficiently. The speed of using up stock is termed stock turnover. A high stock turnover reflects efficient use of stock. A low stock turnover indicates a long delay between purchase and use. The problem with having too much stock is that it has to be paid for, draining cash. It can also get damaged or deteriorate, causing an expense.

Stock turnover shows the number of times stock is used up in a year. A stock turnover of 4 indicates stock is used up four times a year, i.e. on average, stock is three months old. A stock turnover of 12 indicates stock is used up 12 times a year, so it is usually a month old. A stock turnover of 6 indicates stock is used up six times a year, so it is usually two months old. If stock turnover is 365, it means stock is used up every day, e.g. a fresh food retailer.

Businesses want stock turnover as high as posible

Most companies have an opening and a closing stock figure, in which case an average stock can be calculated as follows:

Opening stock	23,437
Closing stock	19,423
Total	42,860
Divided by	2
Average stock	21,430

Some companies count stock at the end of every quarter, in which case an average of the four quarterly stock figures can be calculated as follows:

Quarter 1 stock	9,000
Quarter 2 stock	11,000
Quarter 3 stock	12,000
Quarter 4 stock	10,000
Total	42,000
Divided by	4
Average stock	10,500

If the only information available is the closing stock, use this figure to calculate stock turnover.

On some occasions, stock turnover is required in days rather than in times per year. To do this, take the stock turnover and divide it into 365. If stock turnover is 6 times per year, in terms of days:

$$365/6 = 61 \text{ days}$$

If stock turnover is 12 times per year:

$$365/12 = 30 \text{ days}$$

If stock turnover is expressed in times per year, it should be as high as possible. If expressed in days, it should be as low as possible. Unless specifically requested otherwise, always give the answer in times per year.

5. Current ratio

The current ratio measures liquidity, the flows of cash in and out of a company in the short term, i.e. weeks or months. Current assets are composed of three elements: stock, debtors and cash. Stock is the materials that are waiting to be sold to turn into cash. Debtors are the goods that have already been sold, but the company is still waiting for the cash. Cash is the total amount of cash, in the bank and in petty cash, the company already has in its possession. Current assets, therefore, represent different stages in the process of accumulating cash.

While current assets represents the amount of cash that the company has or is hoping to receive in the short term, current liabilities represents the opposite, the amount of cash the company will have to pay out in the short term. The ratio of current assets to current liabilities is, therefore, the ratio of cash coming in to cash going out. This is a similar concept to net cash flow.

A current ratio of £2 indicates that for every £1 paid out, £2 is received. A current ratio of £3 indicates that for every £1 paid out, £3 is received. A current ratio of £1 indicates that for every £1 paid out, £1 is received. A current ratio of £0.75 indicates that for every £1 paid out, only 75p is received, suggesting negative net cash flow. Prolonged negative net cash flow can lead to the bankruptcy of the company. To provide a margin of safety and a profit margin, current ratio should ideally be greater than £2 (although many successful businesses survive on less).

Businesses want current ratio to be as high as possible.

6. Acid test

This ratio is similar to the current ratio, but omits stock. The reason for the omission is that stock often takes a long time to turn into cash. If stock is slow turning into cash, it is questionable whether current assets represents cash you are about to receive. The acid test omits stock and as a result for companies with slow stock turnover it is a more reliable guide to liquidity. Companies with a fast stock turnover do not need to calculate acid test.

An acid test of £2.5 indicates that, excluding stock, £2.5 is received for every £1 paid out. An acid test of £1.25 indicates that, excluding stock, £1.25 is received for every £1 paid out. A high acid test indicates that there is more money flowing into the business than flowing out.

Businesses want an acid test as high as possible.

7. Debtor days

The formula shows that this ratio is in two parts. Firstly, debtors are divided by sales and secondly, they are multiplied by 365. This ratio indicates the average number of days' sales tied up in debtors. In a company making an average of £5000 sales per day, debtors of £50,000 represents 10 days' sales. If debtors fell to £20,000, this would represent 4 days' sales. If debtor days is 30 days, on average debtors take 30 days (one month) to settle their debts. If debtor days is 60 days, on average customers take 60 days (two months) to settle their debts.

Debtor days gives an average across all customers. Some customers may pay immediately, others may not pay at all (bad debts; see Chapter 7). As a result, debtor days can mask great variation in the speed with which customers settle their accounts. The higher the debtor days, the slower customers are, on average, in settling debts. High debtor days means cash is received slowly.

Businesses want debtor days to be as low as possible.

8. Creditor days

The formula shows that this ratio is, again, in two parts. Firstly, creditors are divided by purchases and secondly, they are multiplied by 365. The ratio indicates the average number of days' purchases in creditors. If average purchases are about £2000 per day, creditors of £16,000 represents 8 days' purchases. Creditors of £20,000 would represent 10 days' purchases.

Creditor days indicates the average number of days it takes the company to pay suppliers. If creditor days is 30, on average it takes the company 30 days (one month) to pay suppliers. If creditor days is 60, on average the company takes 60 days (two months) to pay suppliers.

The lower the creditor days the quicker suppliers get paid. Paying suppliers quickly means cash flows out of the business quickly, reducing the cash balance. If cost of sales is given, instead of purchases, use it to calculate creditor days. You may be able to calculate purchases from the cost of sales figure, by adjusting for stock.

Businesses want creditor days to be as high as possible.

9. Return on capital employed % (ROCE)

The formula shows that the denominator is total net assets, which is also the total amount of capital invested in the business. This ratio indicates the net profit per £ of capital invested in the business. A 10% return on capital indicates, on average, every £1 invested in the business yields 10p net profit every year. A 20% return on capital indicates 20p of net profit for every £1 invested. If the return on capital employed is low compared to other industries or countries, an investor might consider moving capital to more profitable areas.

A higher than average return on capital can often be earned in a risky business sector. The promise of an above average return encourages investors to take on extra risk. Oil exploration is an example of a high-risk business because the costs of exploration are considerable and there is a possibility oil will not be found. A low-risk business, e.g. a water utility where the demand for the product is certain, often earns a lower than average return on capital (see Figure 10.2).

Over time the return on capital will tend towards an average figure. Where a high return on capital is being earned, new companies will tend to be attracted into the market. This will increase competition in the market, which, in turn,

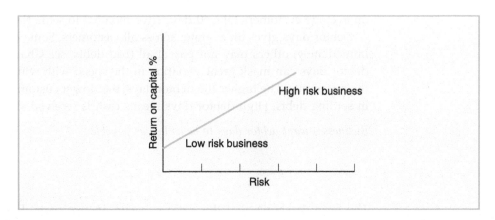

Figure 10.2 ROCE

tends to reduce the return on capital. If a low return on capital is being earned, companies will tend to leave the sector. This reduces competition, which increases the return on capital. It is difficult to quote a 'normal range' for the return on capital because it depends on the risks involved, the trade cycle, geographical location and industry sector.

Businesses want return on capital employed to be as high as possible.

10. Gearing %

The formula shows that the denominator is, again, total net assets. This ratio gives borrowings or loans as a percentage of total net assets. A gearing % of 50% indicates half a company's net assets are financed by borrowing. A gearing % of 15% indicates 15% of a company's net assets are financed by borrowing.

Borrowing money is a source of risk because the repayments have to be made every month. A company may not have the cash available to make a regular monthly payment. Gearing % is, therefore, an indicator of risk and to minimise the risk, gearing should be kept low, e.g. less than 25%. Some entrepreneurs and managers enjoy taking a risk and can tolerate higher levels of gearing.

Businesses should keep gearing % as low as possible.

The ten key ratios are not isolated from each other, rather they are closely connected:

- An increase in gross profit % will also tend to increase net profit %.
- An increase in expense % will decrease net profit %.
- An increase in stock turnover may reduce expense % by reducing overdraft interest and reducing the costs of storing and looking after the stock.
- An increase in debtor days will increase expense % by increasing overdraft interest and increasing bad debt.

The ratios that were calculated for BOMBASTIC can be interpreted as follows:

BOMBASTIC

Gross profit %	40%	On average there is 40p of gross profit in every £1 of sales. There may be different rates of gross profit on restoration work compared to, say, copying work.
Net profit %	10%	On average there is 10p worth of net profit in every £1 of sales.
Expense %	30%	On average 30p out of every £1 of sales is spent on expenses.
Stock turnover	5.33 times per year	This is a slow stock turnover. On average stock is more than two months old. If the vinyl records are stored properly they will not deteriorate; however, excess stock has an adverse effect on cash and may help explain the overdraft.

Current ratio	£2.15	For every £1 paid out £2.15 is received, a healthy liquidity or 'net cash flow' position.
Acid test	£0.88	Excluding stock, which is slow turning over, for every £1 paid out of the business, only 88p is received. This is a worrying figure, which needs to be monitored. The overdraft, however, has been falling in recent weeks, so the situation may not be serious.
Debtor days	26 days	Customers settle their bills after 26 days, on average. This means cash is coming in quickly.
Creditor days	27 days	Suppliers are paid after 27 days. This is slightly more than debtor days, helping cash flow.
Return on capital %	86.17%	This is a very high rate of return. It compensates for losses incurred in previous years. The high return on capital, however, will attract new competition into the market, e.g. the DJs' new company.
Gearing %	9.5%	This is a low gearing level, indicating the company is not dependent on borrowing. The company is not exposed to the risk of having to make regular monthly repayments, but it is exposed to other risks, e.g. more competition in the market.

> One of the most successful applications of the Internet has been in the highly competitive bookselling market. In recent times a well-known Internet bookseller has been enjoying a gross profit % of 22%, which suggests that on average there is 22p of gross profit in every £1 of turnover.

Uses of accounting ratios

Companies have different ways of using ratios, adapting them to their own particular situations. In competitive industries, gross profit % is important, because it monitors the effect of competition on profits. In a recession, focus may shift towards net cash flow, current ratio, debtor days and gearing %.

There are broadly two ways of using ratios. They can be used to compare the results of different companies in the same year (a cross-section) or to review the results of the same company over a number of years (a time series). A cross-section of gross profit % shows the profit margins earned by all the companies in a particular market. It can be used to identify the company with the highest profit margin. A gross profit % time series tracks the profit margin of a single company over a number of years. This may reveal a downward or upward trend in profit margins.

In principle, there are two ways of making a large gross profit:

- High volume of sales with a low gross profit %.
- Low volume of sales with a high gross profit %.

The first of these is referred to as a mass market and the second a niche market. Cross-section analysis can reveal which competitors fall into which categories.

A cross-section analysis of expense % reveals which companies are run efficiently and which are spending too much on overheads. Time series analysis of expense % can reveal a slow but steady increase in overheads, which characterises many growing businesses. Similarly, a cross-section analysis of stock turnover reveals which companies are the most efficient in managing stock. Time series data may reveal a trend towards more efficient or less efficient use of stock.

> Stock turnover at a well-known Internet bookseller is around 5 times per year, meaning that books are held in stock for about ten weeks on average.

Porter's Five Forces model

Ratios can identify important business issues requiring management attention. Another way of analysing business problems is Porter's Five Forces model (Michael Porter Competitive Strategy, Free Press, 1980). This model suggests there are five key factors, which influence the state of a market or industry:

- Buyer power
- Supplier power
- Barriers to entry
- Substitution
- Rivalry

Combining ratios with Porter's Five Forces model (see Figure 10.3) combines quantitative data and a qualitative framework or model, making a powerful tool for strategic management.

Buyer power means a business has two or three big customers who influence decision making. A company cannot afford to lose a big customer and, consequently, the buyers (customers) may dictate price and quality. A company with many smaller customers does not suffer from buyer power. Losing one small customer will not affect the business significantly. It is preferable to have a large number of smaller customers, rather than a small number of larger customers. The worst situation is being dependent on one large customer.

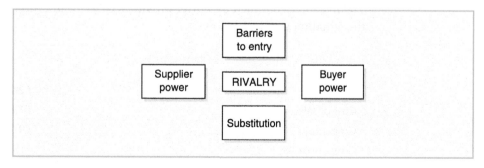

Figure 10.3 Porter's Five Forces

Supplier power means the business has two or three dominant suppliers who dictate terms of business (price, quality, delivery times, etc.). These suppliers may often increase their prices knowing that customers cannot take their business elsewhere. A business with a large number of small suppliers can dictate terms of business to them. For example, it can demand a discount and threaten to remove their custom. It is preferable to have a large number of small suppliers, rather than a small number of large suppliers. The worst situation is being dependent on one large supplier.

Barriers to entry prevent competitors accessing a market. Some markets are easy and cheap to enter, e.g. retailing, and others require a huge investment, e.g. aviation, or specialist knowledge, e.g. pharmaceuticals. If a company earns a high return on capital, competitors will be encouraged to enter the market. If it is simple and cheap to enter the market, many companies will be attracted in. As a result, profits will fall. If there are barriers to entry, however, it may be impossible for others to enter the market and profits can stay high.

Substitution is the extent to which alternative products exist, which customers can easily switch into. For instance, if holiday accommodation is of poor quality in Greece, customers can easily switch to Spain or Portugal. If the price of petrol increases, some customers may switch to rail travel. Where customers can switch, any overcharging or quality problems will result in a rapid reduction in sales. In any industry in which it is easy to switch, it will be difficult to raise prices and, therefore, net profits.

Rivalry is the extent to which firms compete. This will depend on several factors, such as the number of firms in the market and the extent of collusion between the firms. Where there is rivalry, prices will be held down and quality improved, benefiting customers. If there is no rivalry or competition, customers will probably be affected by rising prices.

In summary, if a business is in a situation where there are a few powerful buyers and a few powerful suppliers, it is unlikely to make a substantial profit and it may experience falling gross profit %. If the industry is one that is easy to enter or has many substitutes, these factors will also constrain profits. Finally, if many firms are actively competing in the market, profits and gross profit % will tend to be reduced.

Ratios and Porter's Five Forces model

The five forces outlined by Porter provide a basis for interpreting ratios. Consider the situation outlined below:

Company A (all figures in £ million)

Sales	£2.20
Cost of sales	£1.87
Gross profit	£0.33
Gross profit %	15%
Market share	9%

Total market

Total market size	£25 million
Number of firms in the market	12 firms in total

Company A is making sales of £2,200,000 and generating a gross profit of £330,000. Check the gross profit % calculation on your calculator. This suggests on average every £1 of sales generates 33p of gross profit. The total market is worth £25,000,000 and there are a total of 12 firms chasing these customers. The market share calculation is £2.2 million/£25 million.

If buyer power increased, prices would tend to fall and, as a result, the sales, gross profit and gross profit % of all the 12 companies in the market would fall. The value of the market as a whole would also be reduced. The more powerful buyers become, the more gross profit % falls.

An increase in supplier power will tend to increase the amount paid out for purchases, which in turn reduces gross profit. Consequently, if suppliers get more powerful, gross profit % will tend to fall. If buyer power and supplier power both increase at the same time, the reduction in gross profit and gross profit % could be drastic.

If there is a lot of rivalry between the 12 firms, they will try to win market share from one another. This may be by differentiating their products or by cutting selling price. As a result, rivalry tends to reduce the sales and gross profit of all the companies in the market. This may impact gross profit %.

Companies are always looking for opportunities to increase prices. Higher prices mean higher profits, but this can attract new companies into the market. If barriers to entry exist, new firms cannot easily enter the market. As a result, barriers to entry allow firms to increase gross profit and gross profit % without attracting new companies into the market.

> Porter's Five Forces model suggests that takeovers and mergers are important determinants of profits because they can be used to reduce buyer and supplier power and reduce rivalry. One of the largest ever mergers was between America On Line and Time Warner.

Conclusions

Businesses often face both short-term (operational) and long-term (strategic) problems. Ratios assist in the analysis of both types of problems. The courses of action which management take to improve ratios are the same as those given in the budgeting section (Chapter 9). An improvement in gross profit %, for example, can be achieved by increasing selling price or reducing the prices paid to suppliers. Porter's model suggests that in the long term, strategic variables impact ratios. For instance, a long-term improvement in gross profit % can be achieved by taking over suppliers to reduce supplier power or merging with competitors to reduce rivalry. Investing in barriers to entry such as patents, trade marks and brands can prevent competitors entering the market, helping to maintain the return on capital.

The foundation of interpretation and analysis is understanding the relationship between the quantitative data (figures) and qualitative considerations (people, markets, processes, technology, etc.). Ratios highlight the interconnections between figures, enriching the data available in the P&L account and balance sheet. Porter's Five Forces model provides a structure for understanding the wide range of qualitative factors that impact profitability, and provides a method for identifying long-term strategic variables. A business strategy should coherently integrate both theoretical models and quantitative data.

> Ben and Jerry's, the ice cream people, noticed the tendency for overheads to rise in line with sales. Every time they managed to increase sales, expenses also increased and wiped out all the extra profit. To find out how they solved the problem, consult Ben Cohen and Jerry Greenfield, Ben and Jerry's Double-Dip, Simon and Schuster, 1997, p. 22.

Multiple choice questions

Tick the box next to your answer.

1. Which ratio gives the average amount of gross profit per £ of sales?
   - ☐ Net profit %
   - ☐ Expense %
   - ☐ Current ratio
   - ☐ ROCE
   - ☐ Gross profit %

2. Which of the following increases the gross profit %?
   - ☐ Increase in the volume of sales
   - ☐ Reduction in expenses
   - ☐ Giving longer credit to customers
   - ☐ Increasing the selling price
   - ☐ Increase in the price paid to suppliers

3. If sales fall, but expenses stay the same
   - ☐ Net profit % increases
   - ☐ Expense % increases
   - ☐ Gross profit % stays the same
   - ☐ Net profit % stays the same
   - ☐ Expense % falls

4. For every £1 paid out £2 is received
   - ☐ Current ratio = 2
   - ☐ Current ratio = 0.5
   - ☐ Current ratio = 1
   - ☐ Current ratio = 0
   - ☐ Current ratio = 10

5. If debtor days = 90 days
   - ☐ On average debtors take one month to pay
   - ☐ On average debtors take two months to pay
   - ☐ On average debtors take three months to pay
   - ☐ Debtors are zero
   - ☐ All sales must be cash sales

6. An increase in selling price
   - ☐ Increases gross profit %
   - ☐ Reduces gross profit %
   - ☐ Increases the volume of sales
   - ☐ Is connected to supplier power
   - ☐ Has no effect on net profit

7. Company A has four suppliers, but two merge and all the suppliers increase their prices. The impact on company A?
   - ☐ Cost of sales stays the same
   - ☐ Sales increase
   - ☐ Cost of sales increases
   - ☐ Gross profit stays the same
   - ☐ Cost of sales falls

8. An increase in the number of companies competing for market share leads to?
   - ☐ An increase in rivalry in the market
   - ☐ An increase in the price consumers pay
   - ☐ An increase in substitution
   - ☐ A reduction in supplier power
   - ☐ A reduction in barriers to entry

9. If debtor days is greater than creditor days
   - ☐ Money is received faster than it is paid out
   - ☐ Current ratio = 2
   - ☐ Money is paid out faster than it is received
   - ☐ Cash balance must stay the same
   - ☐ Stock turnover increases

10. A rapid increase in return on capital
    - ☐ Increases barrier to entry
    - ☐ Encourages firms to leave the market
    - ☐ Increases gross profit %
    - ☐ Encourages firms to enter the market
    - ☐ Increases interest rates

Multiple choice answers

	Correct answer	Comment
1	Gross profit %	Review the interpretation of ratios again if you are unsure.
2	Increasing the selling price	An increase in the volume of sales will increase gross profit but it will not increase gross profit %.
3	Expense % increases	The denominator, sales, falls while the numerator, expenses, stays the same.
4	2	Suggesting no liquidity problems.
5	Three months	Debtors need to be contacted immediately. Three months is too long to wait to receive the cash.

6	Increases gross profit %	The business charges customers more and pays suppliers the same amount.
7	Cost of sales increases	The business pays more to suppliers.
8	An increase in rivalry in the market	Less chance of collusion. More chance one competitor will reduce prices and others will follow.
9	Money is paid out faster than it is received	For example, debtors wait 60 days to settle, but suppliers are after 30 days.
10	Encourages firms to enter the market	To take advantage of the good return on capital available. Barrier to entry may stop them coming into the market.

VIVID Limited

The latest results from this small trading company, supplying high street fashion wear, are as follows (all in £'s):

VIVID Limited

Trading and Profit and Loss Account
Year Ended 31st December 200X

Sales		150,000
Less: cost of sales		
Opening stock	10,000	
Purchases	66,000	
	76,000	
Less: closing stock	16,000	
		60,000
Gross profit		90,000
Less: expenses		
Wages	60,000	
Advertising	15,000	
Sundry	5,000	
		80,000
Net profit		10,000

VIVID Limited

Balance Sheet
As at 31st December 200X

	Cost	Depreciation	Net book value
Fixed assets			
Freehold property	80,000	8,000	72,000
Fixtures and fittings	40,000	20,000	20,000
Motor vehicles	10,000	2,000	8,000
	130,000	30,000	100,000
Current assets			
Stock		16,000	
Debtors		22,500	
		38,500	
Current liabilities			
Creditors	11,000		
Overdraft	24,500		
		35,500	
Working capital			3,000
Total net assets			103,000
Financed by:			
Share capital			93,000
Profit			10,000
			103,000

Your task

Calculate and interpret ten ratios using the data provided.

VIVID Limited

Gross profit percentage	
Net profit percentage	
Expense percentage	
Stock turnover	
Current ratio	
Acid test	
Debtor days	
Creditor days	
Return on capital %	
Gearing %	

Catalonian Goats Cheese

Catalonian Goats Cheese import goats cheese from Spain and distribute it, using a team of bearded cycle couriers, throughout the Highgate area of North London. The cheese has to be paid for in euros. Sterling has been rising against the euro, making it cheaper to buy the goats cheese. A 10% increase in the value of sterling reduces the company's cost of sales by 10% and vice versa.

The Managing Director has prepared the budgets for the coming year – see below (all in £'s).

Catalonian Goats Cheese

Budgeted Trading and Profit and Loss Account
Year Ended 30th November 202X

	£000	£000
Sales		220
Less: cost of sales		110
Gross profit		110
Less: expenses		
Wages	60	
Office costs	18	
Depreciation	6	
Interest	12	
Insurance	2	
Other	1	
		99
Net profit		11

Catalonian Goats Cheese

Budgeted Balance Sheet
As at 30th November 202X (£000's)

	Cost	Accumulated depreciation	Net book value
Fixed assets			
Freehold premises	200	0	200
Motor vehicles	48	25	23
Delivery vans	85	1	84
	333	26	307
Current assets			
Stock		30	
Debtors		80	
Bank		20	
		130	
Current liabilities			
Creditors		60	
Working capital			70
Total net assets			377
Financed by:			
Owner's capital			300
Add: net profit		11	
Less: drawings		1	
			10
			310
Bank loan			67
			377

Your task

Calculate ten ratios for the figures above. Write a short paragraph of interpretation for each.

eXUBERANT

eXUBERANT operates a strict budgeting system. Managers are asked to account for budget variances on a monthly basis. They are also often asked to explain the discrepancy between budgeted ratios and actual ratios. All figures in £000's.

eXUBERANT

Trading and Profit and Loss Account
Year Ended 31st December 200X

	Budget	Actual
Sales	120	100
Less: cost of sales	72	60
Gross profit	48	40
Less: expenses	35	35
Net profit	13	5

eXUBERANT

Balance Sheet
As at 31st December 200X

	Budget	Actual
Fixed assets	70	70
Current assets		
Stock	9	8.5
Debtors	12	10
Bank	1	0
	22	18.5
Current liabilities		
Creditors	9	7.5
VAT	2	2
Overdraft	0	2.6
	11	12.1
Net current assets	11	6.4
Total net assets	81	76.4
Share capital	50	50
Profit	31	26.4
	81	76.4

Your task

1. Calculate ten ratios from both the budgeted and the actual figures.
2. Using columns, display your ten ratios and the variances between them.

217

3. For each variance, identify if it is favourable or unfavourable to the business.
4. Prepare a one-page interpretation of the company's financial position.

eXUBERANT

Ratio Variances

	Budgeted	Actual	Variance	Favourable?
Gross profit %				
Net profit %				
Expense %				
Stock turnover				
Current ratio				
Acid test				
Debtor days				
Creditor days				
Return on capital %				
Gearing %				

Solutions

VIVID

Gross profit percentage	$(90,000/150,000) \times 100 = 60\%$
Net profit percentage	$(10,000/150,000) \times 100 = 6.66\%$
Expense percentage	$(80,000/150,000) \times 100 = 53.33\%$
Stock turnover	$(10,000 + 16,000)/2 = £13,000$ $60,000/13,000 = 4.62$ times per year
Current ratio	$38,500/35,500 = 1.08$
Acid test	$22,500/35,500 = 0.63$
Debtor days	$(22,500/150,000) \times 365 = 55$ days
Creditor days	$(11,000/66,000) \times 365 = 61$ days
Return on capital	$(10,000/103,000) \times 100 = 9.71\%$
Gearing	$(0/103,000) \times 100 = 0\%$

Look carefully at every figure above and link it back to the P&L account and balance sheet. Then attempt to interpret the situation. Glance at my interpretation of the situation, below, before you start.

VIVID: Interpretation

During the year the company made a net profit of only £10,000 on sales of £150,000. As well as having low profits, the company also has a large overdraft of £24,500. The company enjoys a high gross profit % of 60%, generating gross profit of £90,000. The expense %, however, is very high, 53.33%, suggesting 53p in every pound of sales is spent on overheads. As a result, expenses drain a healthy gross profit. The company should review expenses immediately, paying particular attention to wages.

There is an urgent issue relating to stock, as well as the overdraft. The stock turnover is 4.6 times per year so, on average, stock is just less than three months old. This indicates stock management is inefficient and needs to be improved. Any improvement in this area would have a positive impact on cash flow, reducing the overdraft.

Debtors could be pursued more effectively because they are taking on average 55 days to settle. Pleasingly, creditor days are more than debtor days. If it were possible to reduce debtor days to 30, the overdraft could be significantly reduced, but this might be difficult to achieve without upsetting customers.

The current ratio illustrates the need to improve the cash position. 1.08 indicates more is coming in than going out, but only just. Only 8p more is coming in than going out, and this includes stock, which is moving slowly. The company could do with an injection of cash, possibly from the sale of freehold property or from a loan secured on the property. The return on capital is low, only 9.71%.

In summary, it is recommended that:

- An immediate review of the expenses is undertaken, to find ways of reducing overheads.
- Improvements in stock control procedures are introduced.
- The company should consider finding new sources of cash.

eXUBERANT

	Budgeted	Actual	Variance	Favourable?
Gross profit %	40%	40%	0%	Yes
Net profit %	10.83%	5%	5.83%	No
Expense %	29.17%	35%	5.83%	No
Stock turnover	8 times	7.06 times	0.94 times	No
Current ratio	2	1.53	0.47	No
Acid test	1.18	0.83	0.35	No
Debtor days	36 days	36 days	0 days	Yes
Creditor days	46 days	46 days	0 days	Yes
Return on capital	16%	6.5%	9.5%	No
Gearing	0%	0%	0%	NA

The company originally budgeted for a net profit of £13,000 for the year and a cash balance of £1000. This target, although modest, was not achieved. Actual net profits were only £5000, a shortfall of £8000 (61%), and the year end cash position was an overdraft of £2600, a £3600 shortfall.

The sales achieved in the year were £20,000 (16.66%) less than budgeted, just £100,000. The gross profit % was stable and, as a result, the gross profit was reduced in proportion to sales. Despite the fact that sales fell, expenses were not reduced in line with sales. Consequently, expense % increased to 35% from a budget of 29.17%. Net profit fell dramatically below budget because of the failure to reduce expenses – only £5000 net profit was earned against a target of £13,000. Management needs to find out why sales were below budget, and why expenses were not curtailed in line with sales. If the company introduced a monthly review of actual results against budget, problems could have been identified sooner and appropriate action taken.

Stock control was not as effective as it might have been. The budgeted stock turnover was 8 times per year, and only 7 times was achieved. This failure has exacerbated the cash flow difficulties. Management needs to find out what caused the stock control problems and to take corrective action.

The difficulties described above combine to produce a serious cash flow problem. Current ratio is 1.53 against a budget of 2, meaning for every £1 paid out £1.53 is received. This includes stock, however, which as shown above is turning over slowly. The acid test shows 0.83. There is, therefore, no room for complacency regarding the cash flow position. Happily, debtors and creditors days were in line with budget.

Catalonian Goats Cheese

Gross profit %	$(110/220) \times 100$ On average there is 50p worth of gross profit in every £ of sales This is a good profit margin, which has been helped by the strength of the £	50%
Net profit %	$(11/220) \times 100$ On average there is 5p worth of net profit in every £ of sales This is a low net profit margin	5%
Expense %	$(99/220) \times 100$ On average 45p of every £1 of sales goes to pay expenses Expenses are too high compared to sales. They must be reduced. Wages should be carefully reviewed	45%
Stock turnover	110/30 Slow stock turnover. Stock is more than three months old, on average The company should control stock more effectively, particularly as the product is cheese	3.66 times
Current ratio	130/60 For every £1 paid out of the company £2.17 is received. So the liquidity position is healthy	£2.17

Acid test	100/60 Stock is very slow moving, so it is dangerous to include it in current ratio. Excluding stock, there is £1.66 received for every £1 paid out	£1.66
Debtor days	$(80/220) \times 365$ On average debtors are taking 132 days to settle their accounts. This is far too long and requires urgent management attention	132 days
Creditor days	$(60/110) \times 365$ This is a very long credit period. On average the company is taking 199 days to pay suppliers. This is good for cash flow, but needs investigating	199 days
Return on capital	$(11/377) \times 100$ A low return on capital employed. Management should consider diversification into more lucrative ventures	2.9%
Gearing	$(67/377) \times 100$ A moderate gearing figure showing only 17% of net assets are financed by borrowing	17.7%

11 Limited liability and the stock market

This chapter is about the impact of limited liability on business.

Objectives	• Limited liability and risk; • Classifying businesses; • plc formats; • Stock markets and investment ratios; • Groups.

Introduction

Importance of the subject

The concept of limited liability is an important one in modern business. Many new businesses are limited companies and most large businesses are public limited companies (plc's). Limited company status does not lead to higher profits, or a higher return on capital. Rather, limited liability reduces the risk associated with being in business.

All businesses are exposed to the risk of making a loss. If losses accumulate over a number of years, a company can become insolvent (see Chapter 7). Limited liability protects shareholders in the event of insolvency. In the event of a limited company becoming insolvent, the assets belonging to the company can be sold for the benefit of creditors. Assets belonging to the shareholders cannot be sold. The shareholders' liability is limited to the money they originally invested in the business.

The position with a sole trader or partnership is quite different. In the event of a sole trader becoming insolvent both the assets belonging to the business and the assets belonging to the owner(s) can be sold for the benefit of the creditors. Consequently, in the event of insolvency, a sole trader can lose all his or her personal possessions, e.g. family house, motor car, jewellery, etc. Anyone conducting business as a sole trader or partnership is exposed to greater risk than a business with limited liability status.

The reason shareholders are offered the protection of limited liability is that it encourages them to invest in business. Some businesses can be started with small amounts of capital, others need many millions of pounds. Consider organising the Olympic Games. This venture would need enough capital to pay for stadiums, transport, accommodation, security, insurance, etc. The total cost might be, say, $1,000,000,000 (one billion dollars).

Spreading risk

It would be difficult to raise this much capital. A lot of wealthy people willing to contribute their money would have to be found, e.g. 1000 people willing to contribute $1,000,000 each or, more likely, 10,000 people willing to contribute $100,000, spreading the risk among more investors. The importance of limited liability is that it allows wealthy individuals to invest in business ventures without risking their entire fortune. A wealthy person would not invest if all their personal assets were at risk. Wealthy individuals, however, can be persuaded to invest if their liability is limited to the money invested in the business. Without limited liability it would be impossible to fund large projects such as airports, railways, new factories, research projects, oil exploration, property development, e-business, etc.

Structure of this chapter

As well as developing the concepts of limited liability and risk, this chapter examines the varieties of business enterprise and the difficulty in classifying businesses. The workings of the stock market and the use of investment ratios are explored. The P&L and balance sheet formats used by plc's are examined in detail, including the concept of consolidated accounts. All of these issues come to bear on stock market investment decisions.

Activities and outcomes

This chapter emphasises knowledge and understanding more than numerical and technical subjects. Many new terms are introduced which are summarised in the conclusions section. Make sure you understand all the concepts and terms before tackling the end of chapter questions. By the end of this chapter you will understand the importance of stock markets, the format of consolidated P&L accounts and the interpretation of stock market ratios.

> The total market value of the shares listed on the New York Stock Exchange at the end of year 2000 was $12,372,304,000,000.
> *Source: NYSE.com*

Risk

Before exploring the implications of limited liability further, consider first the nature of business risk. Risk is the chance of making a loss rather than a profit. It reflects the possibility that capital and net assets will be reduced rather than increased. It includes the possibility of the company becoming insolvent, in which case all the capital invested in the business and the assets of the business may be lost.

Part of the role of a manager is to minimise the possibility of losses and bankruptcy. Many factors causing losses are, however, outside the influence of managers, in particular competitors' strategies. Even though some factors are beyond the control of managers, they can still predict or anticipate their impact. Part of a manager's role is to take account of what might happen in the future.

Risk is difficult to measure because it is based on uncertainty. One method of measuring risk is to calculate the difference between the best outcome and the worst outcome (possible bankruptcy) in a particular instance. Consider this situation. A wealthy individual is evaluating the possibility of launching a company developing web sites for small and medium-sized enterprises (SMEs). Start up capital of £4,000,000 would be required. Ten web site designers and an experienced management team would be hired.

A business proposition such as this might have a best/worst profile as follows:

Best outcome after 5 years	£6,000,000 profit
Worst outcome after 5 years	£4,000,000 loss

An entrepreneur who has already amassed a fortune of £4,000,000 would be unwise to risk it just for the chance of increasing it to £6,000,000. The best outcome suggests a 50% return on the original investment over five years, equivalent to an average of 10% annualised rate of return on capital. The worst outcome is a massive loss of £4,000,000. The 10% annual return on capital seems modest in light of the possible losses. It is not sufficient to justify the risk associated with the investment.

If the net profits could be increased to £12,000,000 over the first five years, the rate of return would be more attractive. Another approach might be to find ten individuals willing to invest £400,000 each. This would spread the risk among ten people, making the potential annual return slightly more appealing. There are other methods of measuring risk, including breakeven analysis and standard deviation, which will be explored later.

Types of business

There are an infinite variety of types of business, both in terms of size and sector. Consequently, businesses are notoriously difficult to classify. The size of a business can be measured in a number of ways, including:

- Sales
- Net profit
- Total net assets
- Number of employees
- Market value of shares

Sometimes businesses with large sales do not have large net profits. Businesses with many millions of pounds worth of net assets may have few employees. Consequently, it is impossible to state exactly the size of a business. Many attempts have been made to derive a scale of measurement, such as below:

Micro firm	0–9 employees
Small firm	10–49 employees
Medium firm	50–249 employees
Large firm	250+ employees

To illustrate the problem with this approach, consider a small stockbroking firm with five experienced traders and analysts. They may have many millions of pounds worth of capital to invest and may make huge profits when the stock market is doing well. But according to the scale above they are a micro firm, because they only have five employees. Firms classified as small or medium sized may in reality be large enterprises.

There are a number of ways of classifying sectors of the economy, e.g. agriculture, manufacturing, etc. Governments operate a standard industry classification (SIC), which is detailed. A more accessible classification can be found in the financial press. The Financial Times London Share Service shows classifications such as banks, transport, utilities, media, etc.

Many large companies are diversified into a number of sectors. For instance, a company may be involved in such diverse activities as tobacco and financial services. Sectors experiencing steady growth in recent years include leisure, entertainment and healthcare. The definition of a sector, however, is not always clear. Modern retailing could be viewed as a form of entertainment because retailers aim to make it a 'fun' experience. Classifying business by sector can be problematic.

It is possible to classify businesses by legal status. The types of legal status available include partnership, sole trader, limited company, company limited by guarantee, public limited company and registered charity. The legal status of a company, however, does not convey much information about its activities and products.

In summary, the best approach to classifying business is to give the main sectors and legal status as well as a range of measurement variables in the following manner:

Guadalope is a clothing retailer and a plc company quoted on the London Stock Exchange. The company has a turnover of around £360 million and pre-tax profits of around £3 million. The company operates mainly in the UK, owning many retail outlets. The company employs 200 people and the total net assets are around £350 million.

This conveys a balanced picture of the company.

Starting a limited company

Any two individuals can join together and form a limited company. For less than £150 in legal costs, two people can start a limited company with 100 shares with a nominal value of £1 each. The total nominal share capital would amount to £100. The nominal value of a share is simply its starting value when the company is formed. Nominal values of £1, 10p, 1p or £10 are common.

If 100 shares with a nominal value of £1 each are issued, share capital of £100 will be raised for the business. If 1,000,000 shares with a nominal value of £1 each are issued, share capital of £1,000,000 will be raised. If 1,000,000 shares with a nominal value of 10p each are issued, share capital of £100,000 will be raised.

A share with a nominal value of £1 may be sold for, say, £1.50 or £2.00. If 1,000,000 shares with a nominal value of £1 each are issued and sold for £1.50, share capital of £1,500,000 will be raised. This will be made up of the nominal value £1,000,000 plus a premium of £500,000. The share premium is the amount above the nominal value.

If 1,000,000 shares with a nominal value of 10p each are issued and sold for 20p, £200,000 share capital would be raised. This is made up of nominal value £100,000 and share premium £100,000. The share premium shows that shareholders were willing to pay above the nominal value for the shares. If 1,000,000 shares with a nominal value of £1 each were issued and sold for £2.20 the money raised would be as follows:

Nominal value	£1,000,000
Share premium	£1,200,000
Total share capital	£2,200,000

A total of £2.2 million would be raised to start a business. The nominal value of the shares is £1 million and the share premium is £1.2 million. The size of the share premium indicates the confidence of the shareholders in the prospects of the new business.

Returning to a simpler situation, if two individuals issue 100 shares with a nominal value of £1 each and sell them for £1 each, the impact on company finances would be as follows:

	Asset	Liability	Liability
	Cash	Share capital	Share premium
100 shares £1 each	100	100	0

This raises £100 capital for the business.

If those shares were sold for £1.20 the situation would be as follows:

	Asset	Liability	Liability
	Cash	Share capital	Share premium
100 shares £1 each sold for £1.20	120	100	20

This raises more capital for the business (£120), so there is more money available to buy the equipment, materials and people required.

If 1,000,000 shares with a nominal value of £1 were issued at par (i.e. for £1):

	Asset	Liability	Liability
	Cash	Share capital	Share premium
1,000,000 shares of £1 each issued at par	1,000,000	1,000,000	0

This raises £1,000,000 capital for the business.

If 10,000,000 shares with a nominal value of 10p were issued at par (i.e. for 10p):

	Asset	Liability	Liability
	Cash	Share capital	Share premium
10,000,000 shares of 10p each issued at par	1,000,000	1,000,000	0

This raises £1,000,000 capital for the business.

If 10,000,000 shares with a nominal value of 10p were issued at 12p:

	Asset	Liability	Liability
	Cash	Share capital	Share premium
10,000,000 shares of 10p each sold for 12p	1,200,000	1,000,000	200,000

This raises £1,200,000 capital for the business.

The long-term value of a share is determined by the success of the company. If a company is successful the value of the shares will rise above nominal value, e.g. a share with a nominal value of £1 may be sold for, say, £2.40. If the company is not successful a share with a nominal value of £1 may be traded for, say, 60p.

> The top five companies on NYSE measured by market value at the end of 2000 were as follows: General Electric, Exxon Mobil Corp., Merck and Co., Citigroup Inc. and Wal-Mart Stores.
> *Source: NYSE.com*

Taxation, dividends and reserves

The term 'share' refers to a share of profits. If a person owns 1 out of 100 shares, this represents 1% of the company and 1% of the profits. It also confers the right to cast one vote at the annual general meeting (see later). If a person owns 25 out of 100 shares, this represents 25% of the company, 25% of the profits and 25% of the voting rights. A company cannot afford to pay all its profits to shareholders every year. Some profit has to be kept back in reserve to be reinvested in the business. A common policy is to pay around 30–40% of the net profit back to the shareholders. The rest is kept to pay tax and reinvest in the business. Growing businesses retain more profit for investment, mature businesses less.

The amount a company pays to its shareholders is termed the dividend. Every shareholder should receive the same dividend, e.g. 10p dividend for every share they own. If a person owns ten shares they will receive a total dividend of £1. If a person own 1,000,000 shares they will receive a total dividend of £100,000. Dividends may only be paid from profits, which have already been earned. If a company makes a loss, it may not pay a dividend in that year. If a company makes a substantial profit it can pay a bigger dividend, or with a small profit a smaller dividend.

The rules relating to the taxation of limited companies are distinct from those relating to individuals. Before shareholders can receive a dividend, taxation must be paid. Dividends are, therefore, only paid from 'profit after tax'. Corporation tax may not have to be paid until the following financial year. The tax at the end of a company's financial year is, therefore, an estimate or provision, referred to as a 'corporation tax provision'.

Because dividends can only be paid from profit after tax, the P&L account of a limited company will show the following:

Profit before taxation	£1,200,000
Less: corporation tax	300,000
Profit after tax	900,000
Less: dividends	400,000
Retained profit	500,000

This company estimates it will have to pay £300,000 tax on its £1,200,000 net profits (profit before taxation). This leaves a profit after tax of £900,000. The Board of Directors have decided to pay a total dividend of £400,000. This leaves £500,000 retained in the company for investment in people, equipment and materials, etc.

Because companies retain some profit every year, the amount retained accumulates. For instance, if a company retained £500,000 for the last three years, the cumulative retained profit would be £1,500,000. When the current year's retained profit is added it will increase again. This is how the situation would be disclosed at the bottom of the P&L account:

Retained profit brought forward	£1,500,000
Add: current year's retained profit	500,000
Retained profit carried forward	2,000,000

By the end of the current year the company has retained £2,000,000 profit. This is often referred to as 'reserves' or 'retained profit'. One of the benefits of a company accumulating reserves is that it will have funds available in the event of a loss being incurred. If a company has accumulated reserves, it can still pay a dividend, even in the event of a loss. Retained profits, therefore, increase the chance that shareholders will receive a dividend every year.

Many people rely on dividends for their pensions. It is, therefore, important that a stable dividend is paid, irrespective of the types of risk the company is exposed to. The shareholders' desire for a stable dividend sometimes conflicts with the Board of Directors' wish to invest for the long term. At the annual general meeting (AGM), shareholders appoint the Board of Directors to run the company. Shareholders, therefore, own and ultimately control the company, but the day-to-day running of the company is not a matter for shareholders.

Setting the dividend is the responsibility of the Board of Directors. It is sometimes the case that the Board wants to reduce the dividend in order to increase the funds available for investment, while the shareholders want to increase the dividend. If the shareholders are displeased with the Board of Directors they can vote them out of office at the next AGM. They can also sell their shares, which is a quicker and simpler way to signal shareholder discontent.

Types of shares

All shareholders should receive the same dividend per share. A company can, however, have different classes of shareholder. Some shareholders are willing to take a higher risk in order to enjoy a higher return, whilst other shareholders want lower risk and return. In recognition of the different types of shareholder, some companies create different classes of share carrying different levels of risk. For example, a company may have ordinary shares (sometimes referred to as equity shares) and at the same time have preference shares.

Preference shares are designed for shareholders wanting lower risk. They receive the same dividend every year. This dividend is often quoted as a percentage, e.g. 5% Preference Shares meaning that every year preference shareholders receive 5p dividend per share. In profitable or loss-making years, if there are sufficient reserves, they still receive 5p dividend per share.

Preference shareholders receive a dividend before ordinary shareholders. If the preference share dividend exhausts cash reserves, ordinary shareholders receive nothing. If there is a substantial profit after taxation, ordinary shareholders may receive an increased dividend. If there is a small profit they may get a low or zero dividend. Ordinary shares are, therefore, more risky than preference shares.

Some preference shares are cumulative. If the company makes a loss and cannot pay a dividend to preference shareholders, they have the right to receive dividends in arrears. If preference shares are cumulative, it may make it less likely that ordinary shares receive a dividend, since the preference arrears have to be paid first. Some preference shares are non-voting shares and others are redeemable, which means that the company agrees to buy them back at a future date. Cumulative redeemable preference shares carry a lower risk than normal preference shares and, as a result, they receive a lower dividend. A company might issue 7.5% preference shares, 5% cumulative redeemable preference shares and ordinary shares. Investors can choose the level of risk and return which suits their investment aim.

Formats for plc's

The format of the P&L account and balance sheet relating to limited companies is laid down in law. Consider the formats presented below.

Specimen plc

Trading and Profit and Loss Account

Turnover
Less: cost of sales
Gross profit
Less: expenses
  Administration
  Distribution
Operating profit
  Less: interest paid
Profit before taxation
  Less: corporation tax
Profit after taxation
  Less: dividends
Retained profit
Reserves brought forward
Reserves carried forward

Specimen plc

Balance Sheet

Fixed assets

Current assets
Stock
Debtors
Cash

Creditors: amounts falling due within one year

Net current assets

Creditors: amounts falling due in more than one year

Total net assets

Financed by:
Share capital
  Ordinary shares
  Preference shares
Share premium account
Reserves carried forward

Notice the following special features of these formats:

- Sales is referred to as turnover.
- Expenses are split two ways: 'administration' and 'distribution'. Interest is presented separately lower down.
- Taxation and dividends are disclosed on the P&L account.
- Reserves retained in the current financial year are added to the reserves brought forward to show the reserves carried forward at the base of the P&L. The figure is also shown at the bottom of the balance sheet.
- Current liabilities are referred to as 'creditors: amounts falling due within one year'.

- Because of the importance of showing the share capital, long-term loans are shown in the top section of the balance sheet.
- Long-term loans are referred to as 'creditors: amounts falling due in more than one year'.
- The 'financed by' section is devoted to shareholders only.
- Different types of shares are shown in the 'financed by' section.
- Reserves carried forward appear at the foot of the balance sheet.

In principle the P&L account and balance sheet of a limited company are similar to that of any other enterprise. In practice, however, they appear rather different because of specialist terminology and more detailed formats. The main difference is that the 'financed by' section is more complex and the loans are now referred to as 'creditors: amounts falling due in more than one year'.

The P&L account and balance sheet of a limited company or plc are subject to an independent audit. This ensures the appropriate formats are used and the figures are correct. Auditors test a company's accounting system to ensure it is accurate and evaluate any judgements or assumptions the Board of Directors have made. They formally express an opinion on the accuracy of the financial statements, which usually confirms they show a true and fair view of the financial affairs of the company. Sometimes auditors are not satisfied with some aspect of the accounts and they present a qualified opinion in which they highlight their concerns. In recent years questions have been raised about the effectiveness of audits and audit firms in particular.

Formats in action

The accounts of Guadalope plc, a company operating in the high street fashion sector, are presented below.

Guadalope plc

Consolidated Trading and Profit and Loss Account
Year Ended 31st December 2003 (£ million)

Turnover	111
Cost of sales	55
Gross profit	56
Distribution costs	38
Administrative expenses	7
Operating profit	11
Interest receivable	1
Interest payable	0
Profit before taxation	12
Taxation	4
Profit after taxation	8
Dividend	4
Retained profit for the period	4
Reserves brought forward	20
Reserves carried forward	24

The company has made £8 million profit after tax on a turnover of £111 million. Of this, £4 million has been paid out in dividends and £4 million retained in reserve. By the end of the year the company has accumulated reserves of £24 million.

Guadalope plc

Consolidated Balance Sheet
Year Ended 31st December 2003 (£ million)

Fixed assets	
Tangible	1
Intangible	21
	22
Current assets	
Stock	15
Debtors	5
Cash	5
	25
Creditors: amounts falling due in **less** than one year	17
Net current assets	8
Total assets less current liabilities	30
Creditors: amounts falling due in **more** than one year	1
Total net assets	29
Capital and reserves	
Share capital	5
P&L account reserves	24
	29

The company has substantial intangible fixed assets of £21 million. Current assets of £25 million are set against creditors due in less than one year of £17 million. The company has little long-term borrowing. The total value of the net assets is £29 million. The company is, therefore, in a strong financial position.

Using the figures from the P&L account and balance sheet above and the formulas from Chapter 10, calculate the following key ratios:

Gross profit %	
Expense %	
Net profit %	
Current ratio	
Acid test	
Stock turnover days	
Debtor days	
Creditor days	
Return on capital %	
Gearing %	

The answers are as follows:

Ratio	Working	Answer
Gross profit %	(56/111) × 100	50.45%
Expense %	(45/111) × 100	40.54%
Net profit %	(12/111) × 100	10.81%
Current ratio	25/17	1.47
Acid test	10/17	0.58
Stock turnover days	55/15	3.6 times per year
Debtor days	Not applicable	
Creditor days	(17/55) × 365	112 days
Return on capital %	(12/29) × 100	41.3%
Gearing %	(1/29) × 100	3.4%

The company is earning on average 50p gross profit on every £1 of sales, but 40p is spent on expenses, leaving 10p of profit before taxation. Stock turnover seems slow for a company engaged in the fashion business. Creditor days are high, but this may reflect the fact that creditors due in more than one year includes accruals and unpaid tax. The company enjoys an excellent rate of return on capital of 41%, possibly reflecting the risks involved in predicting high street fashions. Half of the profits after taxation are paid to shareholders in the form of dividends.

Stock markets

A private limited company is formed when a small number of people join together to start a new venture. A public limited company (plc) is formed when a large number of people, investing large sums, buy shares in a company that is a member of a recognised stock market, e.g. London Stock Exchange. Most plc's have many millions of shares. A stock market is an electronic market in the shares of member companies. In this market, shares in member companies are bought and sold 24 hours a day. The value placed on the shares of member companies depends on the balance between buyers and sellers (demand and supply). A member company reporting increasing profits will attract the attention of buyers and the share price will tend to rise. A member company reporting lower profits will prompt shareholders to consider the risks affecting the company, particularly the risk of reduced dividend. In this case there may be more sellers than buyers and the price will tend to fall.

One of the benefits to shareholders of investing in a plc is that they have access to a ready market in which to sell their shares. Consequently, capital invested in the shares of a plc can be released at any time. The shareholders will receive the market price for their shares at the time they sell them. The ability to release the capital invested in a plc further reduces the risk investors take on. The existence of an efficient stock market greatly increases the flow of funds into new investment opportunities and, therefore, promotes economic growth, new technology and globalisation.

The main buyers in stock markets are pension funds, insurance companies, unit trusts, banks and wealthy private investors. There are also a significant number of private investors taking responsibility for their own savings and pension arrangements. Some people also look upon stock market investment as a dangerous but amusing hobby. In contrast, large financial institutions employ analysts, specialising in particular sectors, to carry out detailed research into the relative risks and returns associated with the shares of member companies. These analysts make regular buy and sell recommendations influencing share prices.

Gaining membership of a recognised stock market is an expensive and lengthy process. Membership of the New York Stock Exchange costs in the region of $1,000,000. Only companies with an established record of making profits are admitted. There are smaller markets with less onerous membership criteria. These are suitable for smaller, more risky companies, e.g. NASDAQ in New York or the Alternative Investment Market (AIM) in London. Companies that are successful on the junior markets can in due course apply for membership of the senior market.

Stock market ratios

Ratios play a key role in the day-to-day workings of the stock market. The three key stock market ratios are:

- Earnings per share (EPS)
- Price to earnings ratio
- Dividend yield

The main factor affecting the price of a share is fluctuation in profits after taxation. This includes the level of profit in the current year compared to the previous financial year, the potential for growth in profits in future years and the volatility or risk attached to the profits.

The term 'share' refers to a share in the profits. The first stock market ratio calculates the profit per share as follows:

Profit after taxation *divided by* number of ordinary shares

The denominator is the number of shares the company has issued, which may be many millions. The ratio, therefore, yields the profit per share in a year. In many countries profit is referred to as 'income' or 'earnings' and the P&L account is often referred to as the 'income statement' or the 'earnings statement'. Consequently, this ratio is referred to as 'earnings per share'. If earnings per share is 10p, this is the equivalent of 10p profit per share in that particular year.

Guadalope's £5 million share capital is made up of 50,000,000 ordinary shares of 10p each. The earnings per share, therefore, is given by:

$$£8,000,000/50,000,000 = 16p$$

A share in Guadalope plc is the equivalent of 16p profit. The dividend will not be 16p, because only a fraction of profit after tax is paid in dividend in any one year. Over five to ten years, however, the whole of the 16p will be paid out to shareholders.

The price to earnings ratio, sometimes referred to as the PE ratio or PER, involves the EPS and the share price. It is calculated as follows:

Price per share *divided by* earnings per share

EPS, the denominator, is equivalent to the profit per share in a year. Consequently, this ratio expresses the price of a share in terms of a number of years' profit. If the price of a share is £2 and the earnings per share is 10p, the price of the share is 20 times greater than profits. This suggests that at the current rate of profit the price of the share represents 20 years' profit. In other words, at the current rate of profits, it will take 20 years to earn the price of the share. Waiting 20 years does not seem like a good bargain.

Consider the following examples:

	Price per share (pence)	Earnings per share (pence)	PE ratio
Utility company	500	50	10
Technology company	1500	20	75

The utility company might be one involved in water or electricity supply. The technology company could be involved in designing web sites or installing optical cabling. Shares in the technology company cost £15 and each share is the equivalent of 20p of profits in a year. The £15 share price is, therefore, the equivalent of 75 years' profit. An individual buying the share would have to wait 75 years, at the present rate of profits, to earn that money back. At first glance, this does not seem like good value for money. There is always the possibility, however, that profits in the technology sector will increase sharply in the future.

The shares of the utility company can be bought for £5 each and each share is the equivalent of a 50p share of profit. The £5 share price represents 10 years' worth of profit. This does sound like good value for money, because the price of the share is earned back in 10 years. It is unlikely profits will rise in the future because of the nature of the sector (water, electricity, etc.); in fact, they may decline.

The average PER in recent years is around 20, suggesting 20 years' worth of profits are anticipated in average share prices. This is a high figure, which may reflect the market's view that profits will continue to grow in future years, possibly because of inflation. It also suggests, on average, the markets do not consider ordinary shares to be a high risk. In view of the fact that stock markets around the world have crashed on several occasions, e.g. 1929 and 1987, the average PE ratio seems too high.

> The share price of some of the most respected global companies has fallen significantly in recent years. For instance, General Electric's share price reached a peak of $60 in August 2000 before falling back to nearer $30. There was more than one cause of this trend, including low inflation expectations, trade cycle, accounting irregularities and terrorism. For more on this see the Economist, 4th May 2002, p. 69.

The third investment ratio is dividend yield. Money placed in a bank earns interest while money invested in shares earns a dividend. Investors need to be able to compare interest earned with dividends in order to determine which investment yields the best return. The dividend yield converts dividend into a figure, which can be compared to an interest rate. The ratio is calculated as follows:

$$(\text{Dividend per share } divided\ by \text{ price per share}) \times 100$$

The denominator is the price per share. The ratio expresses the dividend as a percentage of the price of a share. Consider buying a share for £2 paying a 25p dividend. The yield is 12% – see below:

$$(25p/200p) \times 100 = 12.5\%$$

Consider the dividend yield on these two companies:

	Dividend per share (pence)	Price per share (pence)	Dividend yield (%)
Utility company	45	500	9
Technology company	12	1500	0.8

The yield on the utility company is a high one. Money invested in the shares of the utility company may earn a higher return than money invested in a bank. On the other hand, money invested in the technology company earns a low return. This is because the profits of a technology company will be earned in the future. The average yield on the stock market is between 2% and 3%. On average an investor can get a better return at the bank. Money deposited in a bank, however, does not appreciate and is eroded by inflation. The value of shares can increase year on year, and usually increase in line with inflation.

Additional stock market ratios

Analysts use a range of other ratios to interpret company results, including 'interest cover' and 'dividend cover'. Together these monitor the balance between share capital and borrowings which is key to managing financial risk. These ratios measure how many times interest and dividend payments are covered by profits. For instance, if a company pays out 25% of profits as dividends, the dividends are covered four times. The ratios are calculated as follows:

$$\text{Interest cover} = \text{profit before interest and taxation } divided\ by \text{ interest payable}$$

$$\text{Dividend cover} = \text{profit after taxation } divided\ by \text{ dividends}$$

Notice the definition of profit in the two ratios differs. Interest is an allowable expense for the purposes of taxation; therefore, it is compared to profit before taxation. A dividend, however, can only be paid from profits after taxation, so is compared to profits after taxation.

Interest cover of 4 suggests profits are four times bigger than interest. Interest cover of 2 indicates profits are twice as much as interest. In this case a sharp increase in interest rates could wipe out most of the profits. Interest cover of 4 is, therefore, preferable to 2. Dividend cover of 3 suggests profits are three times bigger than dividends, suggesting dividends are well covered. Dividend cover of 1 indicates that all the profit is distributed to shareholders, leaving none for reinvestment.

High interest and dividend cover indicates a stable company. Low interest cover, e.g. 2, indicates high borrowings. Low dividend cover, e.g. 2, indicates dividends are too high.

Using the results presented below, calculate the interest and dividend cover for both years (all figures in £000's).

	2004	2003
Turnover	7595	5355
Less: cost of sales	5222	3823
Gross profit	2373	1532
Less: expenses		
Administration	381	301
Distribution	321	171
Operating profit	1671	1060
Less: interest payable	261	272
Profit before taxation	1410	788
Less: taxation	450	275
Profit after taxation	960	513
Less: dividends	360	120
Retained earnings	600	393
Reserves brought forward	1503	1110
Reserves carried forward	2103	1503
Earning per share (pence)	17p	10p

Interest cover = £1671/£261 and £1060/£272

Dividend cover = £960/£360 and £513/£120

Interest cover	6.4 times	3.9 times
Dividend cover	2.7 times	4.2 times

The company has increased profits after tax from £513,000 to £960,000 during the year. EPS has risen sharply to 17p per share and the dividend has also increased sharply. As a result, the dividend cover has fallen from 4.2 to 2.7. The increase in dividend is not fully justified by the profit earned during the year. The company does, however, have substantial reserves brought forward (£1,503,000). Interest payments fell during the year, possibly as a result of a fall in interest rates. Operating profit increased and, as a result, interest payments were covered more than six times. Company borrowings are, therefore, at safe levels.

Stock market ratios in action

Investors use stock market ratios, as well as the P&L account, balance sheet and ten key ratios, to identify suitable investments. As mentioned above, stock markets have an average PE ratio of around 20 and a dividend yield of around 3%. At first glance, this does not seem like a promising investment opportunity. The averages, however, conceal a wide range of different types of companies, both in terms of size, financing and sector. The problem is how to identify the companies delivering above average returns.

Investing in the stock market is risky. The potential gains are high, and so are the potential losses. It is possible to lose all the money invested in shares because of the risk of company bankruptcy. Consequently, only individuals with significant personal wealth should consider stock market investment. Attitudes to risk vary. Some people enjoy taking a risk, but these are a minority. Most people avoid risk and the guiding principle of their approach to stock market investment is the avoidance of risk.

Some sectors of the economy are more risky than others. Where products are at the launch stage in the product life cycle, e.g. new technology companies, there is no guarantee that a profitable product will ever emerge. High technology companies, therefore, are too risky for most investors. Companies with products that are mainly mature, but with some prospects for further growth, are less risky. Sectors such as healthcare, education, transport, leisure and entertainment have steady growth prospects.

Stock market investment should be orientated towards an aim that is appropriate to the individual concerned. Someone aged 25 years can take a much more long-term view than someone aged 65 years. A common aim is to accumulate a portfolio of shares, over a period of 15 years, which will supplement retirement income, or fill the gap between retirement and receiving a pension. The portfolio would need to pay total dividends of at least £5,000 per year. As the average yield on shares is quite low, a sum of around £200,000 would be required to produce adequate dividends. Hopefully, over the 15 years, dividends will grow.

The planning horizon for the investment aim is about 15 years. As a result, companies with a PE ratio of around 15 are appropriate. A PE of 15 indicates that the stock market values the company at 15 times its present level of profits. The market is confident that there are prospects for 15 years of profitability.

The investment aim specifies dividends in 15 years' time. If a company is stable and profitable it should already be paying a dividend. Consequently, companies with a lower than average yield, e.g. 1% or 2%, are suitable. These are companies that are ploughing back profits so they can pay a higher dividend in the future.

One of the most important risk factors in business is borrowing. Low gearing is a sign of patient and careful management and high gearing is often a sign of rapid growth and high risk. Companies with a low gearing ratio are preferred.

An ideal investment would have the following characteristics:

Sector	Healthcare
PE ratio	15
Dividend yield	2%
Gearing ratio	5%

This is a company with little borrowing, in a safe sector and paying a modest dividend. The market is confident of 15 years' profits.

Consider the situation below, which relates to a company in the retail sector with a good track record of profits over 10 years:

Share price	£2.00
Profit after taxation	£4,000,000
Number of ordinary shares (nominal value £1 each)	20,000,000
Number of preference shares	0
Long-term loans	£500,000
Dividend per share	£0.04
Cumulative retained profits (reserves)	£7,000,000
Total net assets	£27,000,000

From the information given calculate dividend yield, earnings per share, price to earnings ratio and gearing ratio and record your answers below:

Earnings per share	
PER	
Dividend yield	
Gearing ratio	

Did you try? If not go back before checking the answers below:

Earnings per share	20p
PER	10
Dividend yield	2%
Gearing ratio	2%

This company meets all the criteria, except the PE is rather low. The PE could reflect the fact that the stock market perceives low growth prospects for this company. Alternatively, it could mean the price is too low. This opportunity warrants further investigation using resources such as the Financial Times and Investors Chronicle as well as web sites such as Hemscott.com.

Groups, holding companies and subsidiaries

A group is defined as a holding company and its subsidiaries. A holding company is one that does not trade in its own right, but holds investments in other companies:

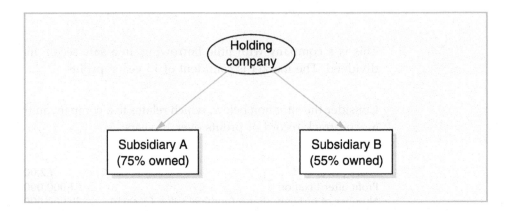

The only assets held by a holding company are the shares it owns in other companies and the cash balances it holds ready to pay dividends. The only profit a holding company makes is the dividend received from subsidiaries.

A company owned by another company is termed a subsidiary. Subsidiaries are often trading and manufacturing companies, which pass on their profits to a holding company for distribution to shareholders. A holding company only needs to hold 51% of the shares in another company in order to make it a subsidiary. This is because 51% of the votes will always carry a majority at the AGM.

There are many reasons to buy all, or a substantial number of, the shares in another company including:

- Buying up rivals and reducing competition in the market.
- Buying up suppliers and reducing supplier power.
- Diversifying to reduce the overall risk to the company.
- Buying a foreign company to access export markets.

A holding company and its subsidiaries can be considered as a single entity because the holding company controls all of the subsidiaries. The holding company together with its subsidiaries is termed a 'group'. When a group declares its results for a year, they are referred to as the 'consolidated income statement' and 'consolidated balance sheet'. These results are not just the holding company and not just the subsidiaries, but the whole group treated as one entity. Consolidated means all the subsidiaries and the holding company added together. Most of the companies quoted on major stock exchanges are holding companies, some with more than 100 subsidiaries.

The balance sheet of a holding company would appear as follows (all in $ millions):

Fixed assets	Notes		
Tangible			0
Investments	1		5237
			5237
Current assets			
Stock		0	
Debtors		0	
Cash	2	267	
			267
Creditors due in more than one year			0
Total net assets			5504
Financed by:			
Ordinary shares	3		5000
Share premium account	4		100
Reserves	5		404
			5504

THE TOTAL AMOUNT IT COST THE COMPANY TO BUY SHARES IN THE SUBSIDIARIES

The holding company does not have tangible fixed assets, stock or debtors because it is not a trading company. It does not make or sell products or services. It merely holds investments in subsidiary companies ($5237 million) and receives dividends from those subsidiaries, which it pays to shareholders. The notes on the balance sheet provide further details such as the identity of the subsidiaries.

If the holding company had two subsidiaries, the consolidated P&L account would be as follows (£m):

	Subsidiary A	Subsidiary B	Consolidated
Turnover	112	279	391
Cost of sales	35	196	231
Gross profit			160
Administration expenses	34	12	46
Distribution costs	59	6	65

Conclusions

This chapter has introduced many new terms, some of which are different ways of saying exactly the same thing. All of the following terms are equivalent:

Earnings statement	*same as*	P&L account or income statement
Turnover	*same as*	Sales or operating revenue or operating income
Equity share	*same as*	Ordinary share or common stock
Earnings per share	*same as*	Profit per share or income per share

The new terms are summarised below:

Share	The right to share in profits and vote at the AGM.
Shareholder	A person who owns a share. All shareholders are treated equally, so they are sometimes referred to as 'equities'.
AGM	A meeting of shareholders to determine the Board of Directors.
Limited liability	In the event of company insolvency, only the money invested by shareholders can be lost. Shareholders' personal assets are not at risk.
Nominal value	The starting value of a share, e.g. £1 or 10p.
Dividend	The amount of money paid to shareholders, e.g. 1p per share.
Preference share	A type of share suitable for a risk-averse shareholder. It pays the same dividend every year.
Reserves	The cumulative profit earned by the company and not paid in dividends.
Shareholders' capital	The original money invested by shareholders, e.g. 100 shares of £1 each.
Share premium account	The amount the original shareholders were willing to pay above the nominal value, e.g. pay £1.20 for a £1 share.
Group	Holding company and subsidiaries considered as one entity.
Consolidated income statement	Shows the profit earned by the whole group, i.e. the holding company and the subsidiaries.
Limited company	A company enjoying limited liability status.
plc	Public limited company shares are actively traded on a stock market.

One business term difficult to define is 'small business'. Many businesses may be small in terms of staff numbers but large in terms of profit or turnover. Many smaller limited companies are owner managed. The shareholders are exactly the same individuals as the Board of Directors. This does not, however, change the legal responsibilities attached to those roles. It could be argued the essence of small business is its character as an enterprise owned, financed and managed by the same people without bank or shareholder interference.

Limited liability status allows large amounts of capital to be raised. It allows a business to continue after the founder has died and allows companies to break free from family ties. Limited liability is, however, often abused by people who set up a company, buy goods on credit and then go into voluntary liquidation. These individuals often immediately set up another company, under a new name, and start applying for credit terms again. Used in this way, limited liability can be a means of defrauding suppliers. This is one reason great care is needed when selling on credit to new customers.

Although limited liability reduces the risk taken by shareholders, it does not alter the requirement that profit after tax has to be sufficient to justify the capital invested in the business and the inherent risks of being involved in business.

Multiple choice questions

Tick the box next to your answer.

1. Turnover is a different name for
   - ☐ Sales
   - ☐ Stock
   - ☐ Current assets
   - ☐ Taxation
   - ☐ Fixed assets

2. Rather than drawings, limited companies have
   - ☐ Closing capital
   - ☐ Overdrafts
   - ☐ Dividends
   - ☐ Cash
   - ☐ Profits

3. 'Creditors: amounts falling due in less than one year' is equivalent to
   - ☐ Debtors
   - ☐ Loans
   - ☐ Owner's capital
   - ☐ Fixed assets
   - ☐ Current liabilities

4. A dividend is
   - ☐ Money paid out to each share in a limited company, e.g. 25p per share
   - ☐ Money paid out to the bank
   - ☐ A person of limited intelligence
   - ☐ Money paid to company directors
   - ☐ Money paid to the auditors

5. Why are limited companies so popular in business?
   - ☐ They are **not** subject to taxation
   - ☐ They pay lower rates of taxation
   - ☐ Shares can be traded on the stock exchange
   - ☐ They cost nothing to set up
   - ☐ In the event of insolvency, personal assets are not at risk

6. What is 'return on capital employed'?
   - ☐ The amount of profit per pound (£) of net assets invested
   - ☐ The interest earned on cash at the bank
   - ☐ Dividends
   - ☐ The number of employees
   - ☐ The expected life of a fixed asset

7. What is risk?
   - ☐ Cash
   - ☐ The possibility of losing money
   - ☐ An increase in capital
   - ☐ Something certain to happen, e.g. Christmas
   - ☐ A profit

8. How can risk be measured?
   - ☐ The difference between the best and worst outcomes
   - ☐ The difference between assets and liabilities
   - ☐ The same as capital
   - ☐ The difference between capital and cash
   - ☐ Profit after tax

9. What is a holding company?
   - ☐ A company holding shares in other trading companies
   - ☐ A subsidiary
   - ☐ A dormant company
   - ☐ A bank
   - ☐ A trading company

10. What is a 'group'?
    - ☐ A modern musical ensemble, e.g. Beatles
    - ☐ A subsidiary
    - ☐ A holding company
    - ☐ A holding company plus its subsidiaries
    - ☐ An industry

11. Profit after tax = £1.5m, total net assets = £15m; therefore, return on capital employed = ?
    - ☐ 1%
    - ☐ 5%
    - ☐ 10%
    - ☐ 50%
    - ☐ 100%

12. Profit after tax = £2m, total number of shares issued = 20m; therefore, earnings per share (EPS) = ?
    - ☐ £0.001
    - ☐ £0.01
    - ☐ £0.10
    - ☐ £1.00
    - ☐ £10.00

13. Earnings per share (EPS) = £0.20, price of the shares = £3.00; therefore, price to earnings ratio (PER) = ?
    - ☐ 1
    - ☐ 5
    - ☐ 10
    - ☐ 12
    - ☐ 15

14. Price to earnings ratio (PER) = 20 suggests a company is
    - ☐ Making a loss
    - ☐ In a particularly risky sector
    - ☐ With high borrowings (gearing)
    - ☐ With inexperienced management
    - ☐ With average risk and returns

15. A company with no long-term borrowing or overdrafts has what gearing ratio %?
- ☐ 100%
- ☐ 90%
- ☐ 50%
- ☐ 25%
- ☐ 0%

Multiple choice answers

	Correct answer	Comment
1	Sales	Sales means exactly the same as turnover.
2	Dividends	Dividends are only paid if a profit has been earned.
3	Current liabilities	Usually due in weeks or months.
4	Money paid out to each share in a limited company	Every ordinary share will receive the same amount of dividend. This is why they are sometimes termed 'equities'.
5	In the event of insolvency, personal assets are not at risk	It enables entrepreneurs to sleep at night.
6	The amount of profit per £ of net assets invested	The higher the risks involved in a business, the higher the return needed to attract investors.
7	The possibility of losing money	Risk can come from many different sources
8	The difference between the best and worst outcomes	This is an unsophisticated measure of risk. Spreadsheets can be used to develop more complex models. Probability is also useful.
9	A company holding shares in other trading companies	The only income earned is a dividend from subsidiaries, and the only assets it holds are shares in subsidiaries and some cash.
10	A holding company plus its subsidiaries	The holding company is the parent, and the subsidiaries are the children.
11	10%	On average every £1 invested in the business earns 10p of profit every year.
12	£0.10	Every share is the equivalent of 10p of earnings (profits).
13	15	Share price is 15 times greater than profit.
14	With average risk and returns	In general, high PE means the stock market is confident about the company's prospects.
15	0%	Borrowing is the same as 'gearing'.

Messenger & Company

Mel Singer worked in the IT department of a large university and was particularly interested in digital photography. In his spare time he developed a process for enhancing high-resolution digital photographs. He has patented the process using his own money and now wants to raise about £5,000,000 to develop the commercial applications of the process.

He is considering creating a public limited company, Messenger & Co., with 10,000,000 shares of £1 each. He plans to issue 5,000,000 of these shares and sell them for £1.10. The other 5,000,000 shares will be kept back for future needs. Mel anticipates that more equipment will be needed in two or three years.

The company will need £3,000,000 for specialist equipment and £1,000,000 per year for running costs (sales team, technical support team, etc.). The equipment is unlikely to have any second-hand value because of its specialist nature. If the venture is successful the business could make a total profit of £12,000,000 over the next five years.

Your task

- Show the financial impact of issuing 5,000,000 shares of £1 for £1.10. Show what would happen if institutional investors were only willing to pay £1 for the shares.
- Show the best and worst outcome and describe the risks involved.

Portmadog Pottery

Calculate four stock market investment ratios on the basis of the figures given below and comment.

Share price	£2.50
Profit after taxation	£5,000,000
Number of ordinary shares (nominal value £1 each)	20,000,000
Number of preference shares	0
Long-term loans	£1,000,000
Dividend per share	£0.15
Cumulative retained profits (reserves)	£8,000,000
Total net assets	£28,000,000

The company produces household goods and has earned a profit in each of the last 15 years. Products are mature or in gentle decline and new product launches have not been successful. Many of the company's shares are still held by family members. A number of directors and the Chairman of the Board have family connections with the business.

Guadalope plc

Here is another set of results for Guadalope plc.

Guadalope plc

Trading and Profit and Loss Account
Year Ended 2004 (£ million)

Turnover	120
Cost of sales	66
Gross profit	54
Distribution costs	41
Administrative expenses	7
Operating profit	6
Interest receivable	2
Interest payable	0
Profit on ordinary activities before taxation	8
Taxation	2
Profit after taxation	6
Dividend	3
Retained profit for the period	3
Reserves brought forward	24
Reserves carried forward	27
Earning per share	12p

The share price is currently 144p and the dividend per share is 2p.

Guadalope plc

Consolidated Balance Sheet
Year Ended 31st December 2004 (£ million)

Fixed assets	
Intangible	0
Tangible	21
	21
Current assets	
Stock	22
Debtors	3
Cash	6
	31
Creditors: amounts falling due in **less** than one year	19
Net current assets	12
Total assets less current liabilities	33
Creditors: amounts falling due in **more** than one year	1
Total net assets	**32**
Capital and reserves	
Share capital	5
P&L account reserves	27
	32

Your task

On the basis of the information given calculate key ratios and, where possible, stock market ratios.

A railway company

On the basis of the information given, consider this company from the point of view of an investment opportunity.

Sector	Railways
PE ratio	11
Dividend yield	3%
Gearing ratio	45%

The company has increased profits every year for the last five years, but there have been three accidents in the last nine months and the costs of improving safety have caused an operating loss. This is the first time the company has made a loss. The share price has already fallen.

Solutions

Messenger and Co.

Selling 5,000,000 £1 shares for £1.10:

	Asset	Liability	Liability
	Cash	Share capital	Premium
5,000,000 shares of £1 sold for £1.10	5,500,000	5,000,000	500,000

Selling 5,000,000 £1 shares for £1:

	Asset	Liability	Liability
	Cash	Share capital	Premium
5,000,000 shares of £1 each at par	5,000,000	5,000,000	

The best outcome is £12m profit over five years; however, it is difficult to predict future profits in a high technology venture. It often takes many years before new technology finds profitable applications.

The company will require further capital to fund the business. The first round of financing will only fund the first two years. Mel should think carefully about the total amount of capital that is needed to properly fund the whole project, especially if profits are slow to emerge. It might be prudent to try to raise £8m, which would be sufficient to cover five years' running costs and equipment.

If 8,000,000 shares were issued Mel would no longer hold a majority of the shares. The majority shareholders could vote Mel off the Board of Directors. If the company is successful, however, this is unlikely. Mel should prepare a detailed business plan, including a cash flow statement, which will show exactly how much capital the venture needs.

Portmadog Pottery

Earnings per share	25p
PE ratio	10
Dividend yield	6%
Gearing ratio	3.5%

These shares pay a large dividend compared to the market average. The product range is mature and, consequently, the possibilities for growth are limited. In addition, much of the profit is paid out in dividend, so little is left over for investment. This share is suitable for an investor who is already retired or is close to retirement – it is not a long-term growth share.

Guadalope plc

The ratios are as follows:

Gross profit %	45%
Expense %	40%
Net profit % (operating profit %)	5%
Current ratio	1.63
Acid test	0.47
Stock turnover (times per year)	3
Debtor days	9 days
Creditor days	105 days
Return on capital %	25%
Gearing %	3%
Dividend cover	2
Interest cover	N/A
PE ratio	12
Dividend yield	1.4%

The company is profitable and has low borrowings. Stock turnover, however, is slow and the acid test reveals liquidity may be an issue. The company might consider reducing the dividends to increase cash reserves, as dividends are high in relation to profits.

Distribution costs are high and the company might investigate ways of reducing them, e.g. contracting out. Creditor days seem high because 'creditors: amounts due in more than one year' includes taxation liabilities as well as trade creditors. This detail can be found in the notes to the accounts.

A railway company

This is a sector usually considered low risk because the technology involved, as well as the customer base, is well established. Recent events, however, show there are considerable risks in the sector associated with safety. The gearing ratio is high, reflecting the fact that 45p of every £1 invested in the company is borrowed. Consequently, there are two clear risk factors associated with this company: losses and high borrowings.

The PE ratio is lower than average. This reflects the fact that the stock market now realises the additional risks associated with the company and has reduced the price of the shares accordingly. The dividend yield is average, but in the light of the losses and high interest payments there is a strong possibility that dividends will be reduced.

Neither of the risk factors can be eliminated quickly; therefore, avoid buying shares in this company.

12 Financial management

This chapter is about raising finance for business and working capital management.

- Raising finance;
- Managing stock;
- Managing debtors;
- Managing cash;
- Working capital cycle;
- Intangible fixed assets;
- Goodwill.

Introduction

Importance of the subject

This chapter explores in detail two issues essential to business success: the varied sources of finance available and the procedures for managing working capital. The importance of these topics lies in the fact that insufficient or inappropriate sources of finance and ineffective management of stock, debtors and cash will tend to lead to business failure.

Business context

Businesses are diverse and difficult to classify, incorporating many different legal forms, sectors and sizes (see Chapter 11). Different types of businesses have different capital requirements. Some businesses need long-term capital, others short term. Some need all the capital at inception, while others need regular injections of capital. Some are risky, others less so. Financial management involves matching up business needs with appropriate sources of finance and working capital procedures.

Return on capital employed

The return on capital employed (ROCE) is a better measure of business performance than profit alone because it balances profit against the amount of capital invested. As well as maximising the amount of profit earned, companies should minimise the amount of capital needed to earn that profit. Debtors and stock tend to rise as sales grow, but they should not be allowed to grow by more than is necessary to achieve sales growth. The benefits of holding stock and granting credit have to be carefully balanced against the costs and risks.

Fixed and current assets

The capital requirements of a business are composed of two elements. The fixed capital requirement, needed to buy equipment and premises, etc., and the working capital requirement for stock, debtors and cash. These correspond exactly to the terms 'fixed assets' and 'current assets'. Fixed assets, in turn, can be split into tangible and intangible. Examples of tangible fixed assets, freehold premises, delivery vehicles, etc., have already been examined in previous chapters. This chapter considers intangible fixed assets, e.g. licences, computer software, patents, trademarks, etc., which play an increasing role in modern business.

Structure of
this chapter

In summary, this chapter examines sources of finance, the management of stock, debtors and cash, and the different types of intangible fixed assets, which are important in modern business. These three topics should all be understood in the context of the overriding requirement to earn an adequate rate of return on capital. The conclusions section summarises the new terms introduced in this chapter and the multiple choice questions can be used to test your understanding before attempting the longer questions.

Sources of finance

In principle, there are only three sources of finance: reinvesting profits, owner's capital and borrowing. In practice, however, there are many variations on these three themes, including:

- Personal savings
- Family members
- Bank loans
- Bank overdrafts
- Retained profits
- Invoice factoring
- Creditors
- Debentures or corporate bonds
- Ordinary shares
- Preference shares
- Venture capital
- Business angels
- Leasing
- Government grants

This list, although extensive, is not quite complete. Every business is free to negotiate the best possible deal. Consequently, every financing deal is, to an extent, unique and new forms of finance are constantly being developed and negotiated.

A small business can be launched on the basis of personal savings, so long as the equipment and materials needed are not too expensive. Personal savings have the advantage of being simple and quick to access because there is no paperwork to complete. Another advantage is that an individual providing 100% of the finance for a business is normally entitled to 100% of the profits. Other sources of finance involve sharing profits with other parties, e.g. shareholders or a bank. Providing 100% of the capital, however, also means bearing

100% of the risk. The more risky the venture, the less appropriate are personal savings as a source of capital.

Once a small business has been successfully established for, say, one year, a bank can normally be persuaded to grant an overdraft facility and suppliers can be persuaded to grant credit. Early success can, therefore, open up new sources of finance to help the business grow. If a company does become overdrawn at the bank, there may be a monthly charge for the overdraft, in addition to interest incurred. These charges need to be monitored carefully using the expense % ratio. An overdraft normally has to be repaid on demand and, as a result, is not a long-term source of capital.

Many small businesses need substantial sums of capital from the outset, for example to buy a piece of equipment. Savings are often insufficient to meet these needs. Family members can be a useful source of additional capital. If the business is successful, it will not be difficult to pay the money back. If the business is not successful, the consequences of owing money to a family member are less serious, in legal terms, than owing money to a bank (the impact on personal relationships is a different matter). Family members, however, may want to share in the profits or wish to be consulted about decisions. They may even expect to be employed within the business. The involvement of family works best when they bring new skills to the business, as well as capital. In many cultures using family connections is an accepted method of establishing a new business.

> Business can be thought of as the art of spending other people's money; however, it is simpler and quicker to start a business with your own personal savings. For more on this, see the Alexander Dumas quote in Terry Smith, Accounting for Growth, Century, 1992, p. 169.

Where an expensive piece of equipment is needed, leasing can provide the solution. This has the advantage that the company does not have to spend a large sum of money to acquire the equipment. Rather, rental or leasing costs are paid every week or month for a fixed period, e.g. three years. Over the useful life of the equipment, leasing will cost more, because of the leasing company's profit margin. The extra expense over a few years, however, is justified by the initial cash flow advantage. Under certain taxation regimes, there may be a taxation advantage to leasing.

Entrepreneurs should read the small print of leasing agreements carefully. The agreement should have 'get out' clauses, such as an agreed period of notice to terminate the agreement. Without such a clause all the risks of obsolescence fall on the business rather than the leasing company. It should not involve giving a personal guarantee, because this will have the effect of negating limited liability. It may be worthwhile an entrepreneur obtaining a legal opinion before signing a leasing agreement. Not all equipment can be obtained under lease agreements and businesses need to invest in stock, advertising and recruitment as well as equipment. Leasing is, therefore, only a partial solution.

Sometimes governments make grants available to new businesses. It can be a long and slow process applying for this type of funding and it is often only available under certain conditions and in certain situations. If funds are available, however, it can be worth taking the time and trouble to access them. Often the knowledge and contacts developed during initial funding can make it easier to access future funds. Companies in receipt of government funding are well placed to bid for government contracts.

Bank loans are another major source of finance. They can cover different lengths of time, e.g. five years or ten years, and the cash can be used to buy whatever the business needs, e.g. equipment, stock, recruitment, etc. Consequently, loans can be tailored to the needs of a particular business. Also, in most taxation regimes, interest payments are an allowable deduction for the purposes of taxation. Company tax is calculated after interest has been deducted from profits. Consequently, interest payments tend to reduce the company tax bill. When borrowings and interest rates are high, the taxation advantage of borrowings are more pronounced.

The disadvantage of a bank loan is that repayment is inflexible. Companies are contracted to pay a definite amount on specified days, e.g. £1000 on the first day of every month. It is impossible to be certain a business will have a definite amount of cash in the bank on a particular day. A loan agreement can, therefore, be a dangerous commitment. Failure to make a repayment (known as 'default') is a serious matter, possibly leading to the insolvency of the business. Because of the rigidity of repayments, borrowings pose a risk to the survival of businesses. The level of company borrowings should be closely monitored using gearing ratio and interest cover.

Banks often insist on security before entering into a loan agreement. This means, in the event of default, the bank has the right to sell a particular asset on which the loan is secured in order to repay the amount outstanding. Freehold property and stocks are assets, which often provide such security for bank loans. Security can take the form of a fixed charge on a particular asset or a floating charge on company assets in general. Viewed from the perspective of risk, secured bank loans are particularly unattractive. In the event of default, the bank is entitled to seize certain assets and consequently, the bank is in a 'no lose' situation. The bank is not sharing any of the risk. Shareholders, on the other hand, share the profits and the risk.

Another disadvantage of bank loans is the volatility of interest rates. Companies with high borrowings, e.g. 50% gearing, will be particularly affected by an increase in interest rates, whereas companies raising funds from share-holders will not be. This disadvantage of bank loans is compounded by the fact that increases in interest rates often coincide with reductions in consumer demand. Consequently, a company with high borrowings can experience an increase in interest payments at the same time as a reduction in sales. This double impact could be sufficient to force the company into liquidation.

Venture capitalists work on behalf of institutions such as pension funds and insurance companies. They seek out growing businesses and offer them capital in return for a stake in the business, e.g. £5,000,000 investment in return for 20% of the shares. Venture capitalists are experienced and professional investors. They reject the majority of business plans they receive. Consequently, it is not a quick and simple route to raising finance. In recent years, Internet-based companies have made extensive use of venture capital and the subject is explored further in Chapter 17, along with business angels.

Companies requiring access to many millions of pounds or dollars of capital should consider stock markets (Chapter 11). These spread risk among a wide range of private and institutional investors, enabling large sums to be raised. The liability taken on by investors is limited and a ready market for shares exists if they should need to withdraw from the investment. One disadvantage is that stock markets are highly regulated. Complying with their rules and regulations is a time consuming and expensive procedure.

Floating on a stock exchange often results in the company founders relinquishing control of the company. If shareholders come into conflict with the founders, for instance about dividend policy, the founders can be voted off the Board of Directors. Companies floated on a stock exchange can be subject to takeover by competitors. In practice the decision to raise stock market finance changes the character of a company completely.

A debenture is a loan evidenced by a deed of trust. It is often divided into units similar to shares. Each unit pays a certain amount of interest on certain dates. Like preference shares (see Chapter 11), debentures, or corporate bonds as they are sometimes referred to, can be redeemable or irredeemable. They are also freely traded on stock markets in a similar manner to ordinary and preference shares. The risk borne by a debenture holder is less than that of shareholders because the interest payments are not connected with profits. The value of bonds, just like ordinary and preference shares, is determined by demand and supply. Additionally, interest rates also influence their value. If interest rates in general rise, the fixed rates of interest paid by debentures seem less attractive. If interest rates fall, the fixed interest paid by debentures seems more attractive.

Debenture holders are exposed to the risk that the value of the debentures will fall either because profits are falling or interest rates are rising. Should the company become insolvent, debentures can become worthless. Although debentures carry less risk than ordinary shares, they are still more risky than placing money in a bank deposit account. Some debentures are convertible into ordinary shares at a future date.

The single most important source of finance for business is retained profits. Every year most companies retain 30–40% of profit before tax for reinvestment in the business. This provides a simple and quick source of finance. It is not a source of finance appropriate to a start up situation, because profits have yet to be earned and in a growing business it can lead to slow growth. Without alternative sources of finance, opportunities for fast growth, e.g. by acquisition, may be missed. On the other hand, it is well known that rapid growth can increase the risk of bankruptcy. Every company should retain some profit for reinvestment, but it should not be the only source of finance.

Most businesses make credit sales and, consequently, have large amounts of money tied up in debtors. Debt factoring and invoice discounting are ways of releasing this money more quickly. Debt factoring involves subcontracting the whole of credit management, often termed the 'sales ledger' department, to a specialist company in return for a percentage of the sales. It allows the company to focus on core issues, such as customer service and quality, but it reduces profit margins and can give the impression that the company cannot manage its own finances. Invoice discounting involves receiving an advance on sales invoices from a factoring company. The advance may be around 75% of the value of a sales invoice. In this case the factoring company does not undertake sales ledger work and, consequently, the cost of invoice discounting is lower than debt factoring.

Another source of finance is making the best use of credit facilities offered by suppliers. When negotiating credit terms companies often try to extend the period of credit for as long as possible, e.g. 60 or 90 days. Once the credit period is agreed, it should be strictly observed. Late payment can result in interest being charged, jeopardise the continuing relationship with a supplier and tarnish the company's reputation.

In summary of the sources of finance, companies are best advised to use a range of sources of finance and not become dependent on one. Many finance deals are negotiable and companies should endeavour to negotiate the most favourable terms possible. The amount of capital required will, to an extent, determine which methods of raising capital are suitable. If $100,000,000 is needed, personal savings are unlikely to be appropriate. Entrepreneurs wishing to retain 100% ownership will favour long-term borrowing over stock market floatation.

In some circumstances speedy access to funds is essential, in which case stock market capital will not be appropriate. In other circumstances only short-term financing may be needed, in which case an overdraft could be ideal. In high taxation regimes, the tax treatment of different sources of finance can be key. This may make borrowing preferable to share capital. Figure 12.1 shows how sources of finance can be matched to a ten-year growth path for a new business.

Working capital management: stock control

Every business has its own approach to working capital management, taking into account organisational structure, size, industry sector, etc. Efficient management of stock, debtors, creditors and cash is crucial. There are some general principles, which can be adapted to a range of situations.

In a large company, specialist managers will be employed to manage stock levels. In a smaller company, this role will be performed by non-specialists who may encounter problems. There are three types of stock: materials, work in progress and finished goods, which correspond to different stages of the production process. The benefit of holding stock is that materials are always on hand if needed in production, and finished goods are on hand if needed by customers. If the right materials are not available, the whole production process may come to a halt. This is known as a 'stock out'. 'Stock outs' are expensive because they result in people and equipment standing idle. The most serious aspect of a 'stock out', however, is that potential customers will be disappointed and possibly lost to competitors. Once lost, customers can be difficult and expensive to recapture.

The main problem with holding stock is the impact on cash flow. If a company orders materials to be held in stock, those materials have to be paid for, reducing cash balances. There are other costs of holding stock, set out below:

- Storage
- Insurance

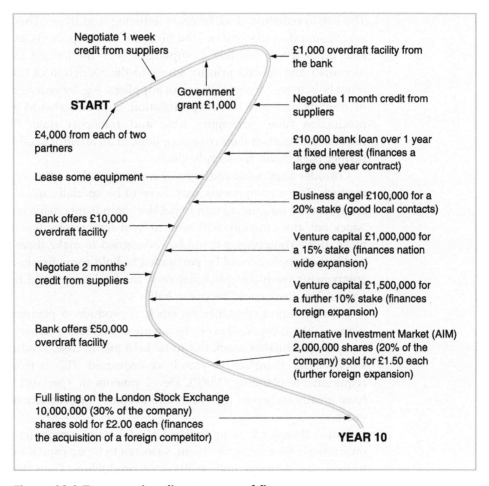

Figure 12.1 Ten year time line, sources of finance

- Obsolescence
- Damage or deterioration
- Management time
- Theft

The costs of holding stock should be balanced against the costs of 'stock out'. The difficulty in balancing these two aspects is determined by lead times. A lead time is the time which elapses from placing an order with a supplier to the day that the materials or components are delivered. This could be a few hours or a matter of months. Long lead times necessitate stock and short lead times eliminate the need for stock:

Lead time		Value of stock
Zero lead time (one hour)	**leads to**	Zero stock
Short lead time (one week)	**leads to**	Small stock
Long lead time (one month)	**leads to**	High stock

The key to reducing stock levels is reducing lead times. This can be achieved by asking suppliers to stipulate lead times for all components and negotiating lower lead times where possible. Components with the longest lead times should be identified and special priority given to the reduction of those times. This can often be achieved by working with suppliers, e.g. by redesigning the component or simplifying the technical specification. Suppliers should be asked to examine production time, packaging time and transport time. Suppliers could be requested to contact their own suppliers, in an attempt to eliminate inefficiencies further back down the supply chain.

Consider a specialist engineering company holding three types of components in stock. These components may have to be specially made by suppliers. As a result, it may take one month to get the components delivered. To guard against 'stock out' the company will need to hold four weeks' worth of stock, possibly more. If the components could be redesigned to make them more standardised and if the supplier could be persuaded to hold some finished or nearly finished components ready for quick delivery, the lead time could be cut to one or two weeks. The stock could be cut in half.

Another aspect of managing stock is production planning. If production is planned, the company knows in advance the stock needed. If a company does not plan production, stock has to be held just in case. Production planning and stock should, therefore, be closely co-ordinated. This is referred to as material requirements planning (MRP). Developments in specialist computer software have greatly increased the speed and accuracy of production planning in recent years.

Rather than stock piling finished goods, many companies manufacture goods only when customers order them, so as not to tie up capital unnecessarily. This is termed the 'demand pull' method of production. Consider again a specialist engineering company. Ideally production should be planned every day or week on the basis of goods which customers have already ordered. Once production is planned, it is easy to specify exactly the components and materials needed. If lead times are short, it may be possible to get the components delivered on the exact day they are required. Materials or components stock need not, therefore, be held. Once the goods are manufactured they can be delivered direct to the customer and finished goods stock need not be held. As a result, it is theoretically possible to operate a business without materials or finished goods stock. This is called the 'just in time' system. In practice, however, most firms do retain some stocks because of the possibility of 'stock out'.

The efficient management of stock is based upon an accurate system for recording stock levels. If the system suggests there are four items of a certain component in stock and, in fact, there are none in stock, there is an immediate danger of 'stock out'. It is essential, therefore, that stock control systems function accurately and all errors are investigated and eliminated immediately. One of the reasons firms build up excessive stock is that the stock control systems are inaccurate.

In summary, the management of stock should comprise:

- Regular review of stock turnover (see Chapter 10), identifying problem areas.
- Pursuit of lower lead times.

- Demand pull production.
- Production planning.
- Component ordering on the basis of production plans.
- Regular stock counts.
- Regular reconciliation of the stock count figures to the stock control system.
- Investigation of all discrepancies.

Companies should keep stock to the minimum while at the same time avoiding stock outs.

Managing debtors

In addition to stock, the other major component of working capital is debtors. Credit control, i.e. the management of debtors, is critical for cash flow. If debts are not collected speedily, cash receipts will tend to fall and, eventually, there may be insufficient cash for purchases, etc. Further, if debtors are not closely monitored and controlled, bad debts will increase (see Chapter 7), increasing expenses and reducing operating profit.

Credit control is composed of three activities:

- Granting credit to customers
- Administering credit
- Collecting overdue accounts

Problems with debtors start from granting credit to customers who are, or become, a bad risk. Every new customer should be allocated a credit limit, either as a monthly amount or a total. All accounts should be regularly monitored to ensure credit limits are not exceeded. If a customer has reached the set limit, no further sales should be authorised until a payment is received or there is justification for increasing the credit limit. Before setting credit limits, information about customers should be collected. This information can be gleaned from a range of sources, such as:

- Requesting trade references.
- Contacting trade associations.
- Viewing the company web site.
- Obtaining a copy of their audited accounts.
- Requesting company accounts from the registrar of companies.
- Buying a full credit report from a credit reference agency.
- Obtaining bankers' references.
- Talking to the sales team – they may know the customer already.
- Finding articles in the financial press about larger quoted companies.
- Obtaining analysts' reports on larger quoted companies.

Some companies applying for credit do not have sound finances. The following characteristics and signs can indicate a potential credit risk:

- High overdraft.
- Substantial borrowings and high gearing %, e.g. 50%.
- Low interest cover, e.g. 2.

- Low dividend cover, e.g. 1.
- Operating losses.
- Low current ratio, e.g. 1.5.
- Low acid test, e.g. 0.90.
- Low price to earnings ratio, e.g. 5.
- Low or reducing trend in gross profit %, e.g. 5%.
- Low rate of return on capital employed, e.g. 9%.
- Falling share price.
- Low or negative P&L reserves.
- New companies with no trading history.

The product life cycle and Porter's Five Forces model can also be used to identify risky customers, e.g. companies with declining products. As well as ensuring credit limits are not exceeded, credit limits should be regularly reviewed, e.g. requesting updated accounts and monitoring the financial press. In addition to setting a credit limit, terms of business need to be agreed in writing, including the length of credit, e.g. 30 or 60 days, etc.

The efficient administration of credit is the second aspect of credit control. Many companies have a separate suite of software for handling debtor balances. A typical sales ledger system works as follows:

- Invoices are raised every week (two copies) and sent out in the post.
- Incoming mail is opened every day.
- Cheques are listed and batched for input to screen.
- Cheques are banked every other day.
- Debtor balances are updated every week on the basis of copy invoices, credit notes and the cheque received lists.
- An 'aged debtor' analysis is produced every month.
- Follow-up calls are made on the basis of the aged listing.

The 'aged debtor' analysis usually has the following form:

D.E. McKenzie

Aged Debtor Analysis
31st December 2003 (all in £'s)

Customer	Total balance	30 Days	60 Days	90 Days	Over 90 days
BJO Plasterers	547	247	100	200	0
KG Electrical	1457	1000	200	200	57
JAM Plumbers	234	0	0	0	234
ASO Water Tanks	927	0	0	0	927
Total	**3165**	**1247**	**300**	**400**	**1218**

This format allows the overdue amounts to be identified quickly. In the example above, there are many unpaid sales invoices over 90 days (three months) old. The company seems to have a serious problem.

The system described above can be improved as follows:

- Sales invoices should be raised and despatched immediately.
- The credit period commences from the day the invoice is sent out.
- A summary statement showing the total amount owed by each customer and the agreed credit limit should be sent every month.
- Cheques should be banked every day.
- Debtor balances should be updated every day.
- Aged debtor analysis should be produced weekly.

With these improvements, it will be immediately apparent when a credit limit is exceeded. If the aged debtors list is prepared weekly, problems will be identified much earlier. Overdue collection procedures can come into action more quickly. One of the most common excuses for not paying an outstanding balance is the existence of unresolved issues or queries. Queries should be followed up as soon as possible. If the customer has a problem with an individual invoice, relating to some damaged goods, a credit note should be raised immediately, eliminating the customer's excuse for not settling the rest of the outstanding balance.

The collection of overdue accounts, the third aspect of credit control, should be a matter of routine. Customers failing to settle their balances on time should be contacted immediately by phone or e-mail. If this is not successful, standard letters should be sent as follows:

- Polite note
- Formal letter
- Inform the customer that all credit is withdrawn
- Final letter warning of impending legal action
- Solicitor's letter
- Solicitor's action

Credit control is an area in which staff training can be cost effective. Credit control should have a high priority within every organisation and the co-operation of other departments, especially the sales team, should be forthcoming.

Managing cash

Cash surplus to requirements should be paid to shareholders as a dividend. Consequently, companies should undertake regular cash flow forecasting (see Chapter 6) to calculate the cash balance to be retained within the company. In these forecasts allowances should be made for the many uncertainties and unknown factors which can unexpectedly affect a business. In addition, some cash should be held in reserve so that, in the event of a profitable opportunity arising, a quick decision can be made.

Businesses often hold a range of liquid and near liquid assets including, in order of liquidity, the following:

- Petty cash (liquid but no interest earned).
- Bank current account (liquid but little or no interest earned).

- Overnight deposit accounts (a short access restriction but earns interest).
- Restricted access deposit accounts, e.g. 30 days' notice required (not liquid but a higher interest rate).

This list shows 'liquidity' is a question of extent, depending on whether cash can be accessed immediately, the following day, the following week or the following month.

The final factor to take account of in the management of cash is interest rates. If interest rates are high, the company can earn significant sums on cash. If interest rates are low, there is little return on cash balances. Small companies rarely enjoy the luxury of excessive cash balances. On the other hand, holding companies regularly receive dividends from subsidiaries and have to manage cash carefully. This is termed 'treasury management'.

Working capital cycle

Working capital consists of stock, debtors and cash less creditors. One of the main influences on these four figures is waiting time. The longer suppliers' lead times the more stock is needed. The greater the debtor days the higher debtors will be. The higher the creditor days the higher creditors will be. These three periods of waiting can be combined into a total working capital cycle measured in days. The working capital cycle is the length of time elapsing between buying goods and receiving money from customers. It is made up of three components:

- Stock days
- Debtor days
- Creditor days

Review Chapter 9 to see how these are calculated.

Consider the example below:

Stock days	30
Add: debtor days	60
Less: creditor days	0
Total days	90

The company pays for purchases immediately (cash purchases). After goods are bought they are kept on average for 30 days before being sold to customers or used in production. Customers then wait on average 60 days before paying for the goods. As a result, the company has to wait in total 90 days, on average, from buying the goods to receiving money from customers.

Consider the same company if it had access to credit from suppliers. Say suppliers initially allowed five days' credit, i.e. the company pays suppliers at the end of the week:

Stock days	30
Add: debtor days	60
Less: creditor days	5
Total days	85

The working capital cycle takes 85 days, on average, because the company now pays out for the goods five days later. Consider the four companies below, which are all in different sectors:

Working capital cycle

Company	Stock days	Debtor days	Creditor days	Total days
Jeweller	120	0	60	60
Fashion retailer	30	0	60	−30
Architect	0	90	0	90
Manufacturer	30	60	60	30

Jewellers and fashion retailers make cash sales, so they have zero debtor days. Fashion is a fast moving industry, so stock turnover is only 30 days on average. In the jewellery sector, on the other hand, stock has a longer life. Stock turnover is 120 days on average. Jewellers and the fashion retailers both benefit from 60 days' credit (on average) from suppliers.

Because jewellers have so much money tied up in stock, the average working capital cycle takes 60 days (two months). Fashion retailers are in an enviable position. Because of the generosity of suppliers, the working capital cycle is negative. Money is received from customers before it is paid out to suppliers. As a result, little or no working capital is required once this type of business is established, but the risks in trying to predict fashion trends are great.

The architect's practice has to wait 90 days on average before receiving payment and, because it is a service business, there is little stock and few suppliers. The main costs are payroll costs and office costs. The working capital cycle is, therefore, 90 days on average.

Attempt the following questions, writing your answers in the spaces provided.

Which company has the longest working capital cycle?

Can you explain why fashion retailing has a negative working capital cycle?

Why does the architect's practice have little or no stock days or creditor days?

Why is a long working capital cycle bad for business?

How can the working capital cycle be reduced?

Make sure you attempt these questions before looking at the answers below.

Which company has the longest working capital cycle?	The architect's, because they have to pay out wages every month and customers (often building firms) are slow to pay.
Can you explain why fashion retailing has a negative working capital cycle?	Suppliers give generous credit and the product is sold quickly.
Why does the architect's practice have no stock days or creditor days?	It is a service business. It does not buy goods to sell at a profit, so it has no stock and few creditors.
Why is a long working capital cycle bad for business?	Because companies have to wait a long time before receiving cash. As a result, more working capital needs to be invested in the business, reducing the return on capital. Debtors and stock also carry certain risks, e.g. bad debt and theft.
How can the working capital cycle be reduced?	Follow the advice given above about managing stock and debtors. Negotiate long credit with suppliers.

Intangible fixed assets

The management of fixed assets is a different matter to current assets. Fixed assets benefit the company over many years rather than months. The risks associated with fixed assets stem from the possibility of obsolescence or malfunction. For example, developments in IT can quickly make new computer hardware obsolete.

Intangible fixed assets, e.g. computer software, play an increasing role in modern business. The term 'intangible fixed assets' covers a range of situations and contracts, such as:

- Software
- Patents and trademarks
- Brand names
- Leases
- Copyright
- Goodwill

A software licence represents the right to use software – it does not confer ownership of the software, which is retained by the development company. A patent represents the right to use a process or a device. Patents promote scientific discovery by allowing companies investing in research to retain rights over their discoveries. Copyright reserves legal rights over text, making it illegal to photocopy or scan the text. A trademark reserves legal rights over a business name or symbol, making it possible to build up brand identities known all over the world. A lease represents the right to use a property, rather than own it.

Intangible fixed assets should be depreciated just like tangible fixed assets. Many intangibles specify a period of time in the agreement, e.g. the right to use material requirement planning software for five years. Consider the case of a company acquiring the rights to a chemical process in return for paying the present patent holder £1,000,000 to use the process for ten years. Depreciation per year would be as follows:

$$£1,000,000/10 \text{ years} = £100,000 \text{ per year}$$

Buying shares gives rise to an intangible fixed asset called 'investments' (see Chapter 11 on holding companies), which is the only type of fixed asset not depreciated because, rather than being used in the business, it is an asset held for strategic reasons.

Goodwill arises when one business buys another. Imagine the case of a company paying £15m (termed the consideration) to acquire a company with net assets of £12m. In strict terms, £3m too much has been paid. This excess is called 'goodwill':

Consideration	£15m
Less: fair value of the net assets	£12m
Goodwill	£3m

The decision to buy another company is a strategic one with long-term implications. Goodwill can, therefore, be depreciated over long periods. If goodwill of £3m were depreciated over ten years, the depreciation would be as follows:

$$£3,000,000/10 \text{ years} = £300,000 \text{ per year}$$

Other firms might take the view that, in a fast changing business environment, ten years is too long for the depreciation of goodwill. Consequently, depreciation of goodwill could be as follows:

$$£3,000,000/5 \text{ years} = £600,000 \text{ per year}$$

On this basis depreciation per year will be doubled and operating profit would be £300,000 lower every year.

Consider a situation in which a large company with mature products buys a growing business, which recently launched some new products. The purchase price is £34,000,000 paid in shares and cash. The net assets of the growing company only amount to £14,000,000. The goodwill is calculated as follows:

Consideration	£34m
Less: value of the net assets	£14m
Goodwill	£20m

Depreciation per year over ten years would be as follows:

$$£20,000,000/10 \text{ years} = £2,000,000$$

The expenses of the larger company would increase by £2,000,000 every year for ten years. Companies that expand rapidly by acquiring other companies may build up substantial goodwill. The depreciation of goodwill can become a major expense item. In this situation, the choice of depreciation period would be key to determining operating profit. Sometimes, the depreciation of goodwill and other intangibles is referred to as 'amortisation'.

On a company's balance sheet, intangibles are shown as follows:

	Cost	Depreciation	Net book value
Fixed assets			
Software			
Patents			
Goodwill			

A consolidated balance sheet may have tangible fixed assets and intangible fixed assets, e.g. goodwill from acquiring subsidiaries and investments. In this complex case, notes to the balance sheet are needed to show the detail of the financial position – see the example below (£m):

	Note	2003	2002
Fixed assets			
Tangible	1	1.4	1.7
Intangible	2	0.9	1.0
Investments	3	0.2	0.2
		2.5	2.9

Conclusions

Here is a summary of the new terms introduced in this chapter:

Keywords

Lead time	Number of days between placing an order and taking delivery of components or materials.
Stock out	Running out of stock of finished goods or materials.
Just in time	Materials and components arrive just in time to be used and, as a result, stock is not needed.
Demand pull	Making goods that customers have already ordered, rather than making goods to go into stock. If customers order no goods, production will be zero.
Materials requirements planning	Co-ordinating production plans with purchases so the correct components arrive at the right time to produce specific units of output.
Aged debtors	A report showing the age of debtors' balances, e.g. more than 30 days old.
Working capital cycle	The number of days elapsing between buying stock and receiving money from customers.

Intangibles	Assets which are not physical but confer rights and benefits useful to the business.
Goodwill	The difference between the fair value of the separable net assets and the total consideration paid for the company acquired.
Amortisation	Depreciation of goodwill and other intangibles.

Adequate and appropriate sources of capital provide the foundation of a thriving business. Day-to-day management of stock ensures appropriate quantities of cash are tied up in stock, balancing the costs against the benefits of stock holding. Day-to-day management of debtors ensures the speedy transfer of debtors back into cash, completing the circuit of capital. The regular circulation of cash provides the foundation of a regular payment of dividends to shareholders.

Companies that are well managed win the support and confidence of stock markets. As a result, they find it easier to raise new funds to finance organic growth or takeover activity. Some companies seek slow and steady growth financed by reinvesting profits, but they can easily be taken over by more aggressive companies enjoying stock market backing.

Multiple choice questions

Tick the box next to your answer.

1. Which of these sources of finance is not affected by interest rates?
   - ☐ Bank overdraft
   - ☐ Bank loans over 5 years
   - ☐ The price of debentures or bonds
   - ☐ Reinvesting profits
   - ☐ Bank loans over 10 years

2. Which of these reduces the founder's share of a business?
   - ☐ A bank loan
   - ☐ Reinvesting profits
   - ☐ Government grants
   - ☐ Unsecured overdraft
   - ☐ Issuing shares to the public

3. Are creditors a free source of finance?
   - ☐ Yes, they are the same as a 0% overdraft
   - ☐ Yes, suppliers are charitable institutions
   - ☐ No, suppliers owe the business money
   - ☐ No, the costs of giving credit is probably reflected in prices
   - ☐ No, it is always better to pay cash up front

4. Which of these is *not* a benefit of reinvesting profits?
   - ☐ Quick and simple to access
   - ☐ Does not dilute the founder's share of the business
   - ☐ Encourages organic and steady growth
   - ☐ No interest has to be paid
   - ☐ Enables rapid growth by acquisition

5. Why can't a small retail business be floated on a major stock exchange?
   - [ ] The costs of floatation are too high, e.g. £1,000,000
   - [ ] The retail sector is not popular with institutional investors
   - [ ] Only firms based in the USA are floated on major stock exchanges
   - [ ] Major stock markets cannot raise sufficient funds
   - [ ] Institutional investors like taking big risks

6. What is a secured loan?
   - [ ] A loan to a security firm
   - [ ] A loan with a low interest rate
   - [ ] An overdraft
   - [ ] A loan agreement allowing the bank to sell certain company assets in the event of default
   - [ ] Extra security at branches of high street banks

7. Stock days 30, debtor days 60 and creditor days 15 – working capital cycle?
   - [ ] WCC = 30 days
   - [ ] WCC = 60 weeks
   - [ ] WCC = 90 days
   - [ ] WCC = 105 years
   - [ ] WCC = 75 days

8. Which of these is *not* a way of reducing the working capital cycle?
   - [ ] Reduce debtor days
   - [ ] Reduce stock turnover
   - [ ] Increase creditor days
   - [ ] Increase debtor days
   - [ ] Reduce debtor days and stock turnover

9. A company with total net assets of £5m bought for consideration of £6m results in goodwill of?
   - [ ] Zero
   - [ ] £5m
   - [ ] £6m
   - [ ] £1m
   - [ ] £11m

10. Which of these is a way of reducing lead times?
   - [ ] Ask the supplier not to hold finished goods stock
   - [ ] Make the manufacturing process more complex and time consuming
   - [ ] Redesign the product to make it simpler and quicker to make
   - [ ] Find a supplier with an old fashioned and slow distribution network
   - [ ] Find a supplier without e-mail, fax or a web site

11. Which of these is *not* a cost of holding stock?
   - [ ] Damage
   - [ ] Theft
   - [ ] Obsolescence
   - [ ] Deterioration
   - [ ] Prevents stock outs

12. Demand pull production means?
   - [ ] Manufacturing goods to go straight into stock
   - [ ] Customers are pulled in off the street, often against their will
   - [ ] Goods are made only when customers order them
   - [ ] Goods are subject to demanding quality checks
   - [ ] Demand and supply determine the price of goods

13. Why should credit notes be issued quickly to customers?
    - ☐ Credit notes increase sales
    - ☐ Credit notes increase bad debts
    - ☐ Outstanding queries prevent prompt payment
    - ☐ Credit notes increase the sales team's commission
    - ☐ Credit notes are good for operating profit

14. Aged debtor analysis
    - ☐ Identifies slow paying customers
    - ☐ Shows customer's birthdays
    - ☐ Shows the amount of money owed to suppliers
    - ☐ Is a list of suppliers
    - ☐ Is the same as debtor days ratio

15. Which of these is not a way of reducing bad debt?
    - ☐ Perform credit checks on all new customers
    - ☐ Set a credit limit for all customers
    - ☐ Review aged debt analysis regularly
    - ☐ Wait patiently for customers to pay and do not hassle them if they are slow
    - ☐ Send out statements every month

Multiple choice answers

	Correct answer	Comment
1	Reinvesting profits	One of the simplest and quickest sources of finance.
2	Issuing shares to the public	The founder should try to retain 51% of the shares in the business, in order to retain control of the business.
3	No, the cost of credit is probably reflected in the price	Often suppliers will offer a lower price if goods are paid for in advance or on delivery.
4	Enables rapid growth by acquisition	Borrowing money or venture capital often finances rapid growth.
5	The costs are too high	The costs of floatation would be greater than the profit earned by a small retail business.
6	A loan agreement allowing the bank to sell certain company assets in the event of default	Assets subject to security are sometimes referred to as 'collateral'.
7	75 days	60 days + 30 days − 15 days.
8	Increase debtor days	Increasing debtor days reduces net cash flow.
9	£1m	The difference between consideration and total net assets.
10	Redesign the product to make it simpler and quicker to make	This will result in faster production and delivery.

11	Prevents stock outs	This is a benefit of holding stock, not a cost of holding it.
12	Goods are made only when customers order them	Customer demand 'pulls' goods through the production process.
13	Outstanding queries prevent prompt payment	Prompt issuing of credit notes ensures customers have no excuse not to settle their balances.
14	Identifies slow paying customers	These are the customers most likely to cause a bad debt.
15	Wait patiently for customers to pay and do not hassle them if they are slow	This would quickly result in increased debtor days.

Financing diversification

Carnaby & Co. has been operating as a high street retailer for ten years. Customers are fashion conscious consumers in the 15–26 age group. The company's strategy is to diversify the product range in order to reduce the level of volatility and risk the company is exposed to. Two years ago the company raised finance on a junior stock market and plans, in the next five to ten years, to join a senior market. The company owns some freehold property, which has not yet been used to secure any borrowings, and also has many leased properties. The founders are still the major shareholders in the business.

Stock market analysts understand that competition is increasing in the sector. They perceive a need for management to be able to respond quickly to new trends and source goods of a reasonable quality from all over the world. Analysts are confident in the Carnaby & Co. management team's ability in these areas. Analysts also believe interest rates will increase in the near future and product life cycles are becoming shorter. They are also concerned about increasing high street rents on leasehold properties. They favour the development of 'out of town' locations.

Carnaby & Co. are considering raising finance of $10,000,000, probably by means of a bank loan, to acquire a company in a more stable retail sector.

Your task

Identify and explain four points in favour of financing diversification by bank loan as opposed to other forms of financing, e.g. a share issue. Additionally, identify four points against this proposal and four key negotiating points relating to bank borrowing. If possible, suggest an alternative financing (or indeed corporate) strategy the management team might consider.

Darling Inc.

Darling Inc. is a retail company operating in the luxury goods market, selling well-known luxury brands. Shares are quoted in New York and London. The company has been suffering a gradually reducing gross profit % because of rivalry and competition in the market place. The company is considering acquiring a competitor, which owns prime retail property in locations such as London, Cape Town, Hong Kong and Sydney. The total net assets of a suitable target company are as follows:

All in $m

Fixed assets	
Freehold property	1234
Other	345
	1579
Current assets	250
Creditors due in more than one year	40
Net current assets	210
Total net assets	1789

Darling Inc. is offering to buy the company for $2 billion ($2,000,000,000). The money is to be raised by selling 5% debentures, convertible into ordinary shares in five years' time. The purpose of the takeover is that, with less competition and prime retail sites, gross profit % can be increased sharply.

Your task

Calculate the goodwill created by the acquisition and describe the impact of the deal on Darling Inc.'s finances. Also, explain why the company would consider paying more than the fair value of the total net assets to acquire a competitor.

Spontaneous Human Combustion

SHC design and manufacture denim jeans in Cape Town, South Africa. The company's results are as follows (000's rand):

Turnover		10,000
Less: cost of sales		2,500
Gross profit		7,500
Less: expenses		
Administration	3,000	
Distribution	2,000	
		5,000
Profit before taxation		2,500

Extracts from the balance sheet and notes are as follows:

Average stock	0.417 million
Debtors	1.644 million
Creditors	0.21 million

Your task

Calculate the following ratios:

- Gross profit %
- Expense %
- Net profit %
- Stock turnover
- Debtor days
- Creditor days
- Working capital cycle

Also, comment on the financial position of the company.

The Kowloon Trading Company

The company's balance sheet is presented below:

	Notes	£ Million	£ Million
Fixed assets			
Tangible			8.4
Investments			5.0
			13.4
Current assets			
Stock		6.1	
Debtors		4.4	
Cash		7.6	
		18.1	
Creditors: amounts due in one year		4.6	
Net current assets			13.5
Creditors: amounts due in more than one year			1.1
(unitised loans)			
Total net assets			25.8
Financed by:			
Share capital			
Ordinary £1 shares			2
6% preference shares			1
5% cumulative preference shares			1
Share premium			3
Reserves			18.8
			25.8

Your task

List the sources of finance that the company have used and comment.

Credit risk assessment

Two companies have recently contacted you requesting credit facilities. They have supplied their audited accounts and you have scanned the financial press looking for the latest news about the companies. The sales team is aware of company A's excellent reputation, while company B is not well known. Last month, company A made a cautiously optimistic press release, but there seems to be no comment at all on company B. Company A has an informative web site, but company B appears to have no web site.

Risk indicators relating to both companies are as follows:

	Company A	Company B
Current ratio	2.5	1.2
Acid test	1.8	0.7
Gearing ratio	20%	56%
Overdraft	0	£0.43m
PE ratio	15	4
Net profit %	22%	19%
Operating profit	£1.5m	£0.96m

Your task

Determine which of these companies is the greater credit risk. Suggest ways of minimising the risk.

Solutions

Financing diversification

Points in favour of borrowing:

- Freehold properties are available to provide security, so it might be possible to negotiate a low cost loan from the bank.
- A long-term bank loan complements the long-term strategy.
- A bank loan allows the company to raise the finance confidentially and have the cash available for when a suitable acquisition opportunity arises. The publicity surrounding a share issue, on the other hand, alerts competitors to the company's intentions.
- Compared to a share issue, a bank loan is relatively simple and quick to arrange.
- The money could be spent in different ways, e.g. rather than buying a company, build up a new division organically. Another alternative might be a joint venture or a web-based division.

Points against the loan:

- Interest rates may rise, increasing the repayments.
- Repayments are not flexible.
- Giving the bank security over certain assets might make the company insolvent if the security is exercised.
- Bank loans often carry restrictive covenants, e.g. no further borrowing allowed. This might jeopardise the company's plans to join the senior market.
- Loans increase the stock market's perception of risk, rather than reduce it. As a result, the financing strategy could defeat the aim of reducing risk.

Negotiation points:

- Aim for a low interest rate.
- Agree a fixed period for the interest rates to prevent surprise increases.

- Security should be granted on non-crucial assets only.
- No restrictive covenants.
- Ability to repay the loan in full at short notice.

Other strategic issues which are relevant:

- Diversifying into new areas can be risky. Many firms have failed in their attempts to do it. The stock market may perceive more risk in diversification rather than less. Talk to analysts and research the possibilities further.
- Instead of diversifying, use additional finance to acquire freehold premises and develop 'out of town' retail sites. These both reduce risk without the dangers inherent in diversification.

Darling Inc.

The goodwill arising on this deal will be as follows:

Consideration	$2000m
Less: value of the net assets	$1789m
Goodwill	$211m

The financial impact on Darling Inc. of this takeover deal will be as follows:

- Fixed asset investments will increase by $2 billion on the holding company balance sheet.
- The goodwill created will increase the intangible fixed assets on the new group's consolidated balance sheet by $11 million.
- Expenses will be increased both because of interest payments to debenture holders and goodwill amortisation.
- The company hopes selling prices will be increased.
- Sales and gross profits should rise.
- Customers, however, may react adversely to the increase in prices.

The company is willing to pay $2 billion for the competitor because it hopes the resulting reduction in competition will allow profit margins to be restored. Profits earned in the core business as well as the newly acquired businesses should increase. This increase in profits may, over a number of years, exceed the goodwill paid.

One of the risk factors is that sales of luxury goods are more volatile than ordinary goods. If the takeover coincided with a recession, sales of luxury goods could easily fall, in which case the $2 billion investment would not pay off. Also, new competitors may enter the market, which may further increase the level of competition and reduce selling prices. The risks are, therefore, considerable.

Spontaneous Human Combustion

All in rand

Gross profit %	7.5 million/10 million	75%
Expense %	5 million/10 million	50%
Net profit %	2500/10,000	25%
Stock turnover times per year	2500/417	6 times
Stock turnover days	365 days/6 times per year	61 days
Debtor days	(1.644 million/10 million) × 365	60 days
Creditor days	(0.21 million/2.5 million) × 365	31 days
Working capital cycle	61 days + 60 days – 31 days	90 days

The company enjoys a high average gross profit % (75%) and, even though expense % is also high (50%), the net profit % of 25% is still a relatively high figure.

Stock turns over on average every two months (61 days). Debtor days are longer, on average, than creditor days, which is not good for cash flow. As a result, the company has a long working capital cycle of 90 days. This will tend to reduce the rate of return on capital employed (ROCE).

The company might consider closer monitoring of debtors to reduce debtor days and the negotiation of longer credit terms from suppliers, e.g. 60 days. These would both reduce the working capital cycle.

The Kowloon Trading Company

	£ Million	£ Million
Long-term finances		
Ordinary shares (including premium)		5
6% preference shares		1
5% cumulative preference shares		1
Reserves		18.8
Total shareholders' funds		25.8
Unitised loans		1.1
		26.9
Short-term finance		
Creditors	4.6	
Overdraft	0	
		4.6
		31.5
Employed in:		
Fixed assets		13.4
Current assets		18.1
Total assets		31.5

The single most important source of finance is accumulated P&L reserves of £18.80 million, representing 60% of the £31.5 million capital invested in the business. This is characteristic of a company experiencing steady growth. Most of the shareholders are ordinary shareholders. Preference shares only account for £2 million, or 6%, of the money invested in the company. Borrowing is an even smaller proportion of the company's finances.

The company is not exposed to the risk of increased interest rates or the need to make regular large loan repayments because borrowing is a small proportion of total financing.

Credit risk assessment

All the indicators show company B is the greater risk. It has lower liquidity, higher gearing, lower profitability and the stock market values the shares at only four times current EPS. Other significant factors are that company B is unknown to the sales team and has no web site.

At first glance it may seem that outright rejection of company B is the only course of action. This would, however, probably result in zero sales being made to the company. The purpose of credit is to attract customers, not repel them.

Company B is trading profitably and therefore a very low credit limit could be set, which could be increased as cash is received. Alternatively, a very short credit period could be set, which again could be increased. This would ensure exposure to risk is minimised without alienating a potential customer.

13 Breakeven and margin of safety

This chapter explores the concept of breakeven and its uses in a range of business situations.

Objectives	
	• Fixed and variable costs;
	• Breakeven and margin of safety;
	• Breakeven graph;
	• Interpreting breakeven and margin of safety;
	• Fixed cost and risk;
	• Uses and limitations of breakeven.

Introduction

Importance of the subject

Breakeven means the sales revenue flowing into a business in a particular period is exactly equal to the costs incurred. It means no profit and no loss: an exact balance between income and expenditure. The concept of break-even is one managers and entrepreneurs find useful in a range of situations, many of which are explored below. The importance of the concept lies in the fact that it combines both profit and risk. Once a firm reaches breakeven, the risk of making a loss has been averted and managerial attention can switch to maximising profits.

Business context

In this chapter the focus is mainly on the manufacturing sector rather than retailing. The distinctive feature of manufacturing is that, instead of just buying and selling, manufacturers buy components and raw materials, make a product and then sell the finished product at a profit. Instead of splitting expenditure into purchases and expenses, expenditure will now be split into fixed and variable costs.

Structure of this chapter

The distinction between fixed and variable costs is the foundation of break-even analysis and the first topic dealt with in this chapter. Next, the calculation and interpretation of both breakeven and margin of safety % is examined. The graphical presentation of breakeven, its implications for business risk and the limitations of the concept are also explored.

Activities and outcomes

In this chapter several management accounting issues emerge which are explored in more detail in the following chapter. Here the main emphasis is on single product companies, while in the next chapter multi-product companies are considered. After completing this chapter you will be able to calculate, explain and apply the concept of breakeven, as well as understanding the limitations of the technique. Use the questions at the end of this chapter to check your progress and develop your understanding.

Fixed and variable costs

In a manufacturing process some costs vary with the level of output and sales. These are termed variable costs. The main variable costs are raw materials, components and labour going directly into making a product. The costs of powering equipment and packaging and delivering goods also vary with production and sales. If output doubles, variable costs double. If output halves, variable costs halve. If output increases by 10%, variable costs increase by 10%. In short, variable costs are the expenditures that increase and decrease as output and sales increase or decrease.

The behaviour of variable costs can be presented in the form of a graph, as seen in Figure 13.1. The graph shows that increases in the number of units of output cause proportional increases in variable costs. When the number of units of output falls to zero, variable costs are also zero.

If a cost is not a variable cost, it must be classified as a fixed cost. Fixed costs are not related to output. They include office administration, insurance, rent, the cost of running the personnel department, e.g. salaries and training, and the costs of running the production planning department, e.g. computers and travel expenses. If output doubles, fixed costs are unaffected. If output halves, fixed costs are, again, unaffected.

The behaviour of fixed costs can be presented in the form of a graph, as in Figure 13.2. Changes in the number of units of output have no impact on fixed costs. When output falls to zero, fixed costs are unaffected because, even if no goods are produced, fixed costs still have to be paid.

Fixed costs are always related to a period of time. A factory rent agreement might be for five years. A loan, and the associated interest payments, might be for a period of ten years. Insurance might be for one year. Salaries might be on the basis of three months' notice. Fixed costs are fixed for different periods and, after

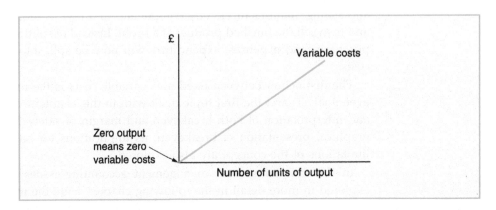

Figure 13.1 Variable costs

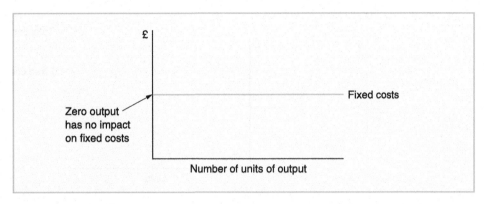

Figure 13.2 Fixed costs

that time has elapsed, they change. Like expenses, there are many different types of fixed cost.

Consider a company making mobile phones in a large factory incorporating a highly automated production line as well as a buying department, a personnel department and a marketing department. The components, including the memory chip, display screen and case, which are assembled in the production process, are the main variable costs. Because the production process is highly automated, labour costs, on the other hand, tend to be fixed in nature. If production increases, only a slight increase in labour costs will result. The costs of running the factory and all the service departments in it (buying department, etc.) are all fixed costs.

Fixed costs, variable costs and total costs can be represented on one graph as seen in Figure 13.3. When output falls to zero, variable costs are zero and fixed costs are unaffected.

Some companies have high fixed costs and low variable costs. This case is presented in Figure 13.4. The variable cost line has been omitted because the variable costs are part of the total costs shown in Figure 13.3.

This can be compared to firms with low fixed costs and high variable costs, as presented in Figure 13.5. The gradient of the total cost line reflects the high cost of producing each additional unit of output, i.e. high variable cost per unit.

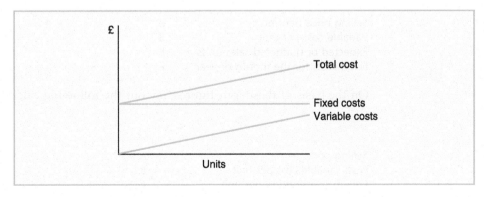

Figure 13.3 Total costs

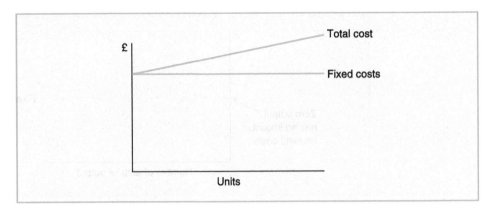

Figure 13.4 High fixed costs

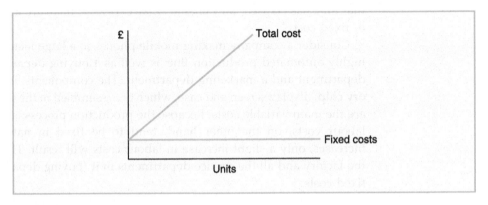

Figure 13.5 Low fixed costs

Calculating breakeven and margin of safety

The calculation of breakeven and margin of safety % can be carried out in five steps described in detail below. Before carrying out the five-step procedure, four *key* figures should be identified.

Key figures

Selling price per unit	A
Variable cost per unit	B
Expected or budgeted sales units	E
Fixed costs for the month or year	F

On the basis of these four figures, lay out the following calculations:

Working 1

Selling price	=	A
Less: variable cost per unit	=	B
Equals: contribution per unit	=	C

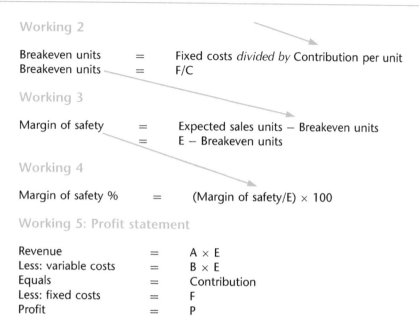

Working 2

Breakeven units	=	Fixed costs *divided by* Contribution per unit
Breakeven units	=	F/C

Working 3

Margin of safety	=	Expected sales units − Breakeven units
	=	E − Breakeven units

Working 4

Margin of safety %	=	(Margin of safety/E) × 100

Working 5: Profit statement

Revenue	=	A × E
Less: variable costs	=	B × E
Equals	=	Contribution
Less: fixed costs	=	F
Profit	=	P

Follow the five-step format when attempting a breakeven question. Notice the term 'revenue' is used above, rather than sales, to distinguish the fact that selling price is multiplied by the number of units sold.

Breakeven in action

Here is an example of the five-step approach to breakeven.

The Internet Furniture Company, based in Brighton, sells handmade chairs, mainly to customers in Central London. The selling price of the chairs is £2600 each. The company does not have retail premises, just a small workshop. Orders are taken over the phone or through the web site. Wood and textiles are the only variable costs, and amount to £600 per chair. The only fixed asset is a second-hand delivery van.

Output is approximately one chair per week. The expected output for the coming year is 30 chairs. The chairs are delivered to customers on a Saturday morning.

Expected fixed costs for the coming year

Lease on workshop	£5,000
Staff costs	8,000
Hire of computer and printer	2,100
Internet service provider	288
Telephone	220
Bank charges	193
Web site updates and advertising	4,500
Insurance	199
Van maintenance, petrol and depreciation	3,500
Total	**£24,000**

Key figures

A = Selling price	£2,600
B = Variable cost per unit	£600
E = Expected sales units	30 chairs
F = Fixed costs for the year	£24,000

Working 1: Contribution per unit

Selling price	£2,600
Less: variable cost per unit	£600
Contribution per unit	£2,000

Working 2: Breakeven units

Fixed costs	£24,000
Contribution per unit (see above)	£2,000
Breakeven units	12 chairs

Working 3: Margin of safety

Expected sales units	30
Breakeven sales units	12
Margin of safety	18

Working 4: Margin of safety %

Margin of safety	18
Expected sales units	30
Margin of safety %	60%

Working 5: Profit statement (£'s)

Revenue (£2600 × 30)	78,000
Less: variable costs (£600 × 30)	18,000
Contribution per unit	60,000
Less: fixed costs	24,000
Profit	36,000

Breakeven graph

Pictures and graphs play an important role in business analysis. Breakeven and margin of safety % are well suited to graphical presentation. The relationship between revenue and number of units sold is a simple one: the more units of product sold, the greater the sales revenue. For instance, if the number of units sold increases by 10%, sales revenue increases by 10%. This relationship is presented in Figure 13.6. An increase in sales units leads to a proportional increase in revenue. If sales units fall to zero, revenue is also zero. If the selling price falls (see dotted line), the revenue line becomes less steep.

The revenue line can be combined with the cost lines to give a breakeven graph as presented in Figure 13.7. The breakeven point is where revenue meets the total cost line. The ten steps involved in preparing a breakeven graph are presented below.

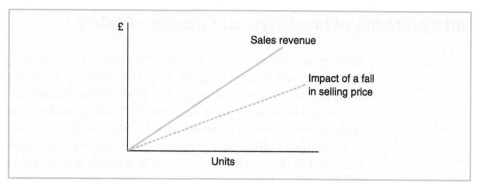

Figure 13.6 Sales revenue

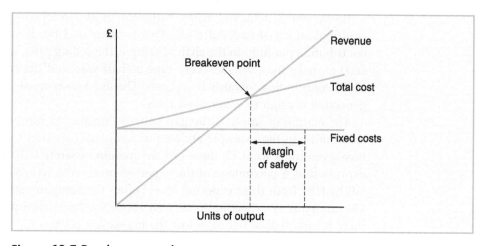

Figure 13.7 Breakeven graph

Breakeven graph: step by step

1. Draw the upright axis from zero to the revenue figure (A × E). This is the Y axis.
2. Draw the bottom axis from zero to E, the expected sales units. This is the X axis.
3. Find F, the fixed costs, on the Y axis and draw a line straight across. This is the fixed cost line.
4. Find the point where revenue meets E, the expected sales, which should be up in the top right-hand corner.
5. Mark the point.
6. Draw a line from the point through the origin. This is the revenue line.
7. From the profit statement, add the fixed costs to the variable costs to give the total cost.
8. Find the point where total cost meets E, the expected sales. This should be in the top right-hand corner, but underneath the revenue line. Mark the point.
9. Draw a line from the point to F, the fixed costs, on the Y axis. This is the total cost line.
10. Identify the breakeven point on the graph and also identify the margin of safety.

Interpretation of breakeven and margin of safety

Having understood how to calculate breakeven, attention can now turn to explaining and interpreting its meaning. When a unit of output is sold, the company receives the selling price – £2600 in the example above. The company, however, has already paid the variable costs of making the chair (£600). The company has, therefore, earned £2000, which can be used to cover the fixed costs.

If a business sells a unit of output for £10.00, and the variable cost of making it is £6.00, a £4.00 contribution towards fixed costs has been earned. If a unit is sold for $110.00 and its variable cost is $40.00, a contribution of $70.00 has been earned. When sufficient contribution has been earned to cover all fixed costs, the business can then make a profit.

Breakeven is achieved when sufficient units have been sold to generate a contribution equal to fixed costs. This is calculated by dividing fixed costs by contribution per unit. In the chairs example, the selling price was £2600 but it cost £600 to make the chair, so every time a chair was sold the company received a £2000 contribution towards fixed costs. The fixed costs were £24,000, so 12 chairs generated enough to cover fixed costs.

The margin of safety is the gap between breakeven sales units and expected sales units. In the example above, the company expected to sell 30 chairs and breakeven units were 12; therefore, the margin of safety is 18 chairs. This can be expressed as a percentage of the expected units: 60% [(18/30) × 100]. Sales can fall by 60% from their expected level before the company starts to make a loss. The company is expecting to be well above the breakeven point; consequently, there is little risk of falling below the breakeven point.

Another example

Consider a motor manufacturer selling cars for £10,000 each. The variable cost of each car, including materials, components, labour and overheads, is £2000. The total fixed cost of running the factory, services and administration is expected to be £200,000,000 for the coming year. The company is confident it can sell 30,000 cars during the year.

Key figure summary

A = Selling price	£10,000
B = Variable cost per unit	£2,000
E = Expected sales units	30,000
F = Fixed costs	£200 million

Working 1: Contribution per unit

Selling price	£10,000
Variable cost per unit	£2,000
Contribution per unit	£8,000

Every sale earns an £8000 contribution to covering fixed costs. Once fixed costs are covered, every sale is the equivalent of £8000 net profit.

Working 2: Breakeven units

Fixed costs	£200,000,000
Contribution per unit (see above)	£8,000
Breakeven units	25,000 cars

Selling 25,000 cars generates enough revenue to cover all fixed and variable costs. Selling fewer cars will result in a loss and selling more a profit.

Working 3: Margin of safety

Expected sales units	30,000 cars
Breakeven sales units	25,000 cars
Margin of safety	5,000 cars

The company hopes to sell 5000 more cars than are needed to break even.

Working 4: Margin of safety %

Margin of safety	5,000 cars
Expected sales units	30,000 cars
Margin of safety %	16.66%

The margin of safety represents 16.66% of expected sales. Sales can fall by up to 16.66% of their expected level before the company is in danger of making a loss.

Working 5: Profit statement (£m)

Revenue	300
Less: variable costs	60
Contribution per unit	240
Less: fixed costs	200
Profit	40

If the company sells 25,000 cars in the coming year it will exactly break even. Any more and it will make a profit and any less a loss. The company expects to sell 30,000 cars next year, which suggests a margin of safety of 5000 cars, or 16.66%. If sales fall by more than 16.66% from their expected level, a loss will be incurred. At the expected sales level the company will make a profit of £40,000,000.

> Breakeven can be useful in the e-business context. Many of the best web resources are only available on subscription. The costs of maintaining and updating a web site are fixed in nature and additional subscribers cause no (or very little) extra costs. Breakeven analysis helps identify the number of subscribers required to break even. For more on this consult Evan Schwartz, Digital Darwinism, Penguin, 1999, p. 98.

Fixed costs and risk

Margin of safety % measures the risk of making a loss, but it is not the only measure of risk. Risk assessment should incorporate consideration of a worst case scenario (see Chapter 10). For instance, consider the possibility of a company making zero sales. This is, admittedly, unlikely, but it is part of risk assessment. A company making zero sales will make a loss equal to fixed costs. This is because zero sales leads to zero variable costs and the only remaining cost is fixed costs. Say fixed costs are £1,000,000 per month. If the company makes zero sales, the loss for the month will be £1,000,000. If sales are zero, a company still has to pay the fixed costs, at least until they can renegotiate some element of fixed costs, e.g. salaries.

Consider zero sales combined with fixed costs of £5,000,000 per year. The loss incurred will be as follows:

Profit statement for the year (£000's)

Revenue	Zero
Less: variable costs	Zero
Contribution	Zero
Less: fixed costs	5000
Loss	5000

The worst case scenario for any company is making a loss equal to the fixed costs. The higher a company's fixed costs, the bigger the worst case loss. A company with zero fixed costs has a zero worst case loss. A company with low fixed costs has a low worst case loss. A company with high fixed costs has a high worst case loss. Fixed costs are, therefore, an indicator of risk. This can be presented on a graph as seen in Figure 13.8.

An example of a sector with high fixed costs is airlines. The fixed costs include the cost of aircraft, flight crew, ground crew, landing charges, etc. In this sector breakeven analysis can be used to calculate the number of passengers required to break even. Because variable costs are low, it is common practice in the airline sector to discount the price of tickets. For more on this consult Evan Schwartz, Digital Darwinism, Penguin, 1999, p. 50.

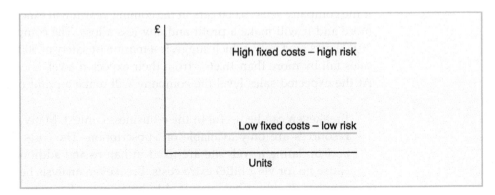

Figure 13.8 Risk and fixed costs

One of the most interesting developments in business in recent years has been low cost air travel. The business model can be characterised as follows:

- Short flights,
- Quick turnaround at airports,
- Secondary airports,
- No frills service,
- Single aircraft,
- Selling on the Internet,
- Minimum leg room.

Multi-product companies

In the case of a company with more than one product, breakeven becomes more complex. In a multi-product environment each product has a different contribution per unit. The simplest way to achieve breakeven is to sell as much as possible of the product with the highest contribution per unit and as little as possible of the product with the lowest contribution. Consider the two-product situation below:

	Product A	Product B
Selling price	10	12
Variable cost per unit	6	7
Contribution per unit	4	5
Expected sales per month	24,000	11,000

Fixed costs for the month are £50,000. Every unit of B contributes £5, compared to £4 for A. Selling 10,000 units of B will result in breakeven. Selling 12,500 units of A will also break even. Additionally, selling 5000 of B combined with 6250 of A will also break even. In multi-product companies there are multiple breakeven points. This tends to reduce the effectiveness of breakeven as a target, because there are many ways of achieving the target, which causes confusion.

A two-product company should calculate the profit earned on each product. This entails preparing two P&L accounts. A five-product company has to prepare five P&L accounts. These multi-product P&L accounts might be set out as follows.

Multi-product profit statement

	Product A	Product B	Total
Revenue			
Variable cost			
Materials			
Labour			
Overheads			
Contribution			
Fixed costs			
Purchasing			
Marketing			
Personnel			
Administration			
Profit			

The practical problems posed by the need to split all costs and revenues by product are considerable. In the case above, two sales figures have to be maintained, rather than just one. Similarly, two materials figures and two labour figures are required. Now consider the situation if there were five products: problems are magnified by a factor of five.

Another issue in multi-product environments is the link between certain overheads and products. Take the purchasing department as an example. They purchase components and materials for both products A and B. To prepare an accurate multi-product P&L account the purchasing department would need to differentiate the work relating to product A from product B. This is difficult and time consuming. The problem is exacerbated by the fact that some materials purchased are common to products A and B. Chapter 14 explores this problem and its implications in more detail.

Fixed costs in the long run

Different types of fixed costs are fixed for different periods of time. Consequently, it is impossible to achieve an immediate reduction in fixed costs. Salaries can be reduced by issuing a period of notice to employees, e.g. three months. Insurance agreements terminate after one year. Leasing or licensing agreements may be for two to five years. In the medium to long term it is possible to achieve step by step reductions in fixed costs.

On the other hand, growing companies can experience step increases in fixed costs. Consider a company that has experienced steady growth for five years and now wants to expand the marketing department and then open a research and development department (Figure 13.9). The costs of marketing and research and development tend to be fixed costs. As a result, fixed costs and breakeven increase, as shown in Figure 13.10.

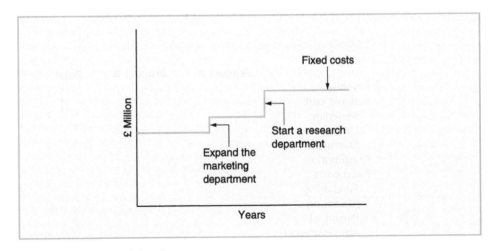

Figure 13.9 Stepped fixed costs

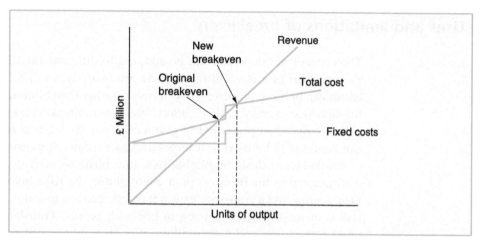

Figure 13.10 Impact of stepped fixed costs

Linear relationships

The relationship between sales units and selling price can be more complex than allowed for above. In the analysis above, selling price remained constant as sales units increased. This yielded a straight (linear) revenue line. Increases in the number of units sold can often only be achieved by reducing the selling price. In other words, the relationship between units and selling price may not be linear. Consider the non-linear sales revenue line in Figure 13.11.

As the number of units increases, the revenue line gradually becomes less steep and finally turns downwards. This reflects the fact that, in order to sell more goods, the selling price has to fall. As well as the revenue line being non-linear, the variable cost per unit may also be subject to the influence of the number of units sold. For instance, as the level of production increases, suppliers' discounts may increase, which reduces the costs of materials and components.

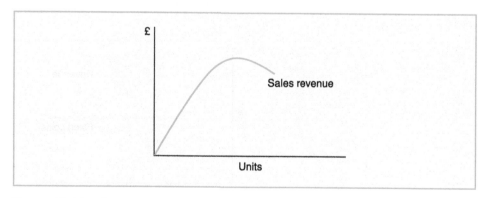

Figure 13.11 Sales revenue curve

Uses and limitations of breakeven

The concept of breakeven can be adapted to different situations and sectors. In the first year of a new business, there are many types of set up costs, and revenues can be slow to increase. As a result, rather than aiming to make a profit in the first year, a more realistic aim is breakeven. Breakeven is easily understood, particularly when presented in graphical form. As a business grows, breakeven can continue to be used as a target and as a means of motivating staff.

Breakeven analysis highlights risk. In a business start up situation it can be incorporated in the business plan, highlighting the risks involved in a proposed new venture. As a company grows it can be used to monitor the extent to which risk is increasing or decreasing in line with profits. Translating fixed costs into breakeven targets and graphs allows management to emphasise to staff the need to keep overheads down. The graphs illustrate clearly that increases in fixed costs make breakeven harder to achieve.

The application of breakeven is not limited to the manufacturing sector. Services, transport and distribution sectors can also use breakeven analysis. Take a company running a shuttle bus between a major airport and a city centre (see Figure 13.12). The costs involved include the wages of the driver, fuel, hire of the bus, insurance and the licence to run the service. None of these costs vary as the number of passengers varies. All the costs are, therefore, fixed costs, suggesting a high level of risk. Breakeven analysis will reveal the number of passengers required to cover all the fixed costs and the maximum losses that may be incurred if the service is not successful.

The limitations of breakeven analysis are considerable. Most companies have a range of products. As a result there are many different ways of achieving breakeven. Fixed costs are constantly being renegotiated to achieve better value for money or to allow the company to grow. Every change in fixed costs leads to a new breakeven target, which tends to reduce the credibility of breakeven as a target. The relationship between selling price and sales volume can be complex, making it difficult to identify breakeven.

Breakeven is more robust when viewed over a two or three-month time horizon, rather than say one or two years. In the short term, fixed costs cannot change and the relationship between price and volume can be specified with

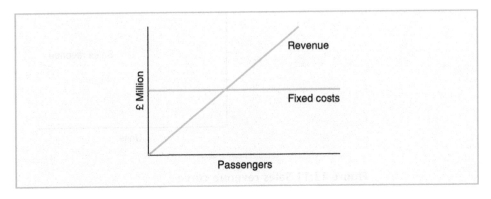

Figure 13.12 Shuttle bus

greater certainty. Difficulties tend to come into play over a longer run period. As a result, breakeven may be better suited to short run thinking, e.g. the first six months of a new business.

Conclusions

It is important to master the terminology needed in breakeven calculations.

Keywords

Breakeven	A situation where a company has revenue exactly equal to costs. No profit and no loss.
Units of output	The goods the company produces.
Variable costs	Those costs varying in direct proportion to the number of units of output.
Variable cost per unit	Total variable cost *divided by* number of units of output. The variable cost of making one unit of output.
Fixed costs	Costs remaining constant over a wide range of units of output.
Fixed cost per unit	Total fixed costs *divided by* number of units of output. The fixed cost of making one unit of output.
Total cost	Variable cost + fixed cost.
Revenue	Number of units of output × selling price.
Profit or loss	Revenue − total cost.
Contribution	Revenue − variable cost.
Contribution per unit	Selling price − variable cost per unit.
Breakeven units	Fixed costs *divided by* contribution per unit.
Margin of safety	Number of units of output − breakeven units.
Margin of safety %	(Margin of safety *divided by* number of output units) × 100.

Breakeven combines the concepts of risk and profit, both of which are fundamental to business analysis. There are, however, difficulties in operationalising breakeven analysis, which tend to limit its application. Crucially, breakeven analysis omits consideration of the rate of return on capital employed (ROCE). Consequently, breakeven should be used in conjunction with P&L account, balance sheet and key ratios.

Multiple choice questions

Tick the box next to your answer.

1. Selling price £100, variable cost per unit £75; contribution per unit?
   - [ ] £175 per unit
   - [ ] £100 per unit
   - [ ] £75 per unit
   - [ ] £1 per unit
   - [ ] £25 per unit

2. Fixed costs £100,000, contribution per unit £25; breakeven units?
   - [ ] 4 units
   - [ ] 25%
   - [ ] £25,000
   - [ ] 2 units
   - [ ] 4000 units

3. What is the breakeven point?
   - [ ] Revenue = variable costs
   - [ ] Revenue = total costs
   - [ ] Revenue = zero
   - [ ] Revenue = margin of safety
   - [ ] Revenue = fixed costs

4. A high margin of safety % means?
   - [ ] No profit
   - [ ] Low risk
   - [ ] High breakeven
   - [ ] High risk
   - [ ] High fixed costs

5. If variable cost per unit is zero, selling price is the same as?
   - [ ] Fixed costs
   - [ ] Variable costs
   - [ ] Total costs
   - [ ] Contribution per unit
   - [ ] Margin of safety %

6. A reduction in fixed costs leads to?
   - [ ] Higher breakeven and no change to margin of safety %
   - [ ] Higher breakeven and lower margin of safety
   - [ ] Lower breakeven and higher margin of safety %
   - [ ] No change in breakeven
   - [ ] Lower breakeven and lower margin of safety %

7. Fixed costs £10m per month, contribution per unit £1000; breakeven units?
   - [ ] 10,000 units per year
   - [ ] 1000 units per year
   - [ ] 1,000,000 units per month
   - [ ] 10,000 units per month
   - [ ] 100 units per month

8. Selling price £1, variable cost per unit 20p; contribution per unit?
   - [ ] £1
   - [ ] 60p
   - [ ] 20p
   - [ ] 80p
   - [ ] £1.20

9. Which of these is best for a business?
   - ☐ High risk and high return on capital
   - ☐ High risk and low return on capital
   - ☐ No risk and no return on capital
   - ☐ Low risk and low return on capital
   - ☐ Low risk and high return on capital

10. High fixed costs indicate?
   - ☐ Low breakeven
   - ☐ The possibility of a large worst case loss
   - ☐ High profits
   - ☐ The possibility of a small worst case loss
   - ☐ Low risk

Multiple choice answers

	Correct answer	Comment
1	£25 per unit	Every unit sold represents a £25 contribution towards covering fixed costs.
2	4000 units	Note it is 4000 units of product, not £4000.
3	Revenue = total costs	Which is the same as zero profit and zero loss.
4	Low risk	Sales have to fall a long way before the loss-making zone is approached.
5	Contribution per unit	Breakeven would be given by fixed costs *divided by* selling price.
6	Lower breakeven and higher margin of safety %	Lower fixed costs are always welcome in business.
7	10,000 units per month	£10,000,000 *divided by* £1000. Take care with the number of zeros.
8	80p	Selling price less variable cost per unit.
9	Low risk and high return on capital	Eventually competitors will be attracted into the market, increasing competition and eventually reducing return on capital employed.
10	The possibility of a large worst case loss	The loss may be large enough to bankrupt the company.

Discussion questions

1. Explain in your own words how breakeven analysis (including the distinction between variable and fixed costs) combines the concepts of risk and profit.

2. Explain one business situation in which breakeven analysis would be useful and one where it would not be useful. Describe in each case the sector, the size of the company and the rate of growth as well as particular issues and constraints.

Consult the companion web site for answers to these questions.

The Rail Group

The Rail Group make solar powered trains (SPT) in a well-established manufacturing facility in Scotland. The Group's cost accountant has produced the following unit variable cost calculation for an SPT:

SPT unit variable cost	£'s
Materials	250,000
Labour	125,000
Variable overheads	25,000
Total	400,000

The fixed overheads for the year are £600,000. The selling price of an SPT is £500,000. The Group expects to make and sell 10 SPTs during the year.

Your task

1. Calculate the breakeven sales level for the year in units.
2. Calculate the margin of safety % for the year.
3. Calculate the profit the Group can expect to earn in the year.

Sweet 35

Mike and Judy had been working together for about three years making sunbeds, which they sold for £250 each. Mike was under the impression he was an equal partner in the business, but Judy looked upon him as a senior employee.

Mike is now looking at the possibility of starting up his own business, trading under the name Sweet 35. He has obtained the following quotations:

Variable cost of assembling a sunbed (£)

Frame	£50.00
Bulbs	100.00
Wiring	25.00
Total	**£175.00**

The fixed costs for a month are as follows (£):

Workshop rental	£1500
Heat, light and power	250
Distribution	250
Total	**£2000**

Mike intends to sell the sunbeds for £225 and in the first few months he would like to sell 50 sunbeds per month.

Summary

1. Selling price = £225.00 = A.
2. Variable cost per unit = £175.00 = B.
3. Expected sales units per month = 50 sunbeds = E.
4. Fixed costs per month = £2000 = F.

Your task

Using these figures calculate the following:

1. Breakeven units per month.
2. Margin of safety.
3. Margin of safety %.
4. Monthly profit statement.

Pen Y Bryn Motors

Pen Y Bryn Motors are the only motor bike manufacturers in Wales. A unique feature of the company is that it currently manufactures on site half the components making up the finished product. The other half are imported from abroad.

The company is planning to increase output to 20 bikes per month, but the owners are unsure if they have the capacity to make even more components on site. They are currently considering two options:

1. Borrow one million pounds (£1m) for a new factory and continue to buy in 50% of components.
2. Borrow one and a half million pounds (£1.5m) for a larger factory and use the extra space to make more components on site, reducing the proportion of bought in components.

The Managing Director wants to incorporate breakeven analysis into the decision-making process. She has identified the main variable cost to the business as being the bought in components and has provided the following information:

	Option 1	Option 2
Selling price per bike £000's	20	20
Number of bikes sold per month	20	20
Variable cost per bike £000's (bought in components)	5	3
Fixed costs per month £000's		
Staff	79	92
Machines	24	37
Factory	20	27
Distribution	20	20
Office	5	5
Interest	5	7

Note that many of the fixed costs are higher in option 2, but the variable costs (bought in components) are lower.

1. Calculate the profit expected in each of the two options, presenting your figures in the form of a profit statement.
2. Calculate the breakeven and margin of safety %.
3. Decide which option is best for the company and write a paragraph explaining three reasons for your choice.
4. Comment on the inclusion of staff costs in fixed costs.

Scandanavian Lights SA

Scandanavian Lights SA organise tours to visit Sweden's magnificent Northern Lights. Customers are usually between the age of 23 and 35, often in 'stag and hen' parties. The company charges €500 per person. Most customers come from the UK, Ireland and Germany.

The variable costs per person are as follows (euros):

Flight	105
Accommodation	112
Transfers	42
Drinks	60
Entertainment	55
Insurance (travel and medical)	26
Total	400

The company accountant has estimated the following fixed costs for the year ended 2004 (euros):

Customer information and reservations team	89,000
Accounting and finance team	31,000
Customer care team	33,000
Office costs	12,000
General management	35,000
Total	200,000

The company hopes to take 3000 people to see the Northern Lights during 2004. Business is spread evenly throughout the year.

Your task

Using these figures calculate:

1. Breakeven number of holidays.
2. Margin of safety.
3. Margin of safety %.
4. Profit statement for 2004.

Present your answers in euros.

Solutions

The Rail Group

The key figures

Selling price	500,000
Variable cost per unit	400,000
Fixed costs	600,000
Expected sales units	10 SPTs

Working 1: Contribution per unit

Selling price	500,000
Less: variable cost per unit	400,000
Contribution per unit	100,000

Every time a train is sold the company earns £100,000 contribution towards covering fixed costs.

Working 2: Breakeven units

Fixed costs	£600,000
Contribution per unit (see above)	£100,000
Breakeven units	6 SPTs

Six trains are enough to cover all the costs for the year. The seventh train will make a profit.

Working 3: Margin of safety

Expected sales units	10
Breakeven sales units	6
Margin of safety	4

Working 4: Margin of safety %

Margin of safety	4
Expected sales units	10
Margin of safety %	40%

Sales would have to fall by 40% before the company went into the loss-making zone. This is quite a safe position, with no immediate risk.

Working 5: Profit statement (£000's)

Revenue	5,000,000
Less: variable costs	4,000,000
Contribution per unit	1,000,000
Less: fixed costs	600,000
Profit	400,000

A profit of £400,000 will be earned if 10 trains are manufactured and sold.

Sweet 35

Working 1

Selling price	225.00
Less: variable cost per unit	175.00
Equals: contribution per unit	50.00

Each sunbed sold earns £50.00 contribution towards fixed costs.

Working 2

Fixed costs	£2000
Divided by: contribution per unit	£50.00
Equals: breakeven units	40 sunbeds

Selling 40 sunbeds covers all the costs for the year. The 41st sunbed yields a profit.

Working 3

Expected sales units	50 sunbeds
Less: breakeven sales units	40 sunbeds
Equals: margin of safety	10 sunbeds

Working 4

Margin of safety	10 sunbeds
Divided by: expected sales units	50 sunbeds
	0.20
Multiplied by:	100
Equals: margin of safety %	20%

Sales would have to fall 20% before the company was in the loss-making zone, so the company would be in quite a safe position.

Working 5: Monthly profit statement (£)

Revenue (A × E)	11,250
Less: variable cost (B × E)	8,750
Equals: contribution	2,500
Less: fixed costs per month (F)	2,000
Equals: profit per month	500

A very small profit per month: equivalent to £6000 profit per year.

Pen Y Bryn Motors

Working 1

	Option 1	Option 2
Selling price	20	20
Less: variable cost per unit	5	3
Equals: contribution per unit	15	17

Working 2

	Option 1	Option 2
Fixed cost per month	153	188
Divided by: contribution per unit	15	17
Equals: breakeven units per month	10 bikes	11 bikes

Working 3

	Option 1	Option 2
Expected sales units	20	20
Less: breakeven sales units	10	11
Equals: margin of safety	10	9

Working 4

	Option 1	Option 2
Margin of safety	10	9
Divided by: expected sales units	20	20
	0.5	0.45
Multiplied by:	100	100
Equals: margin of safety %	50%	45%

Working 5: Monthly profit statement (£)

	Option 1	Option 2
Revenue (A × E)	400,000	400,000
Less: variable cost (B × E)	100,000	60,000
Equals: contribution	300,000	340,000
Less: fixed costs per month (F)	153,000	188,000
Equals: profit per month	147,000	152,000

Interpretation

Option 2 earns £5000 more profit than option 1. The level of risk, however, is also higher in option 2 because the margin of safety is lower and the fixed costs are higher. It is, therefore, a choice between a higher risk with potentially higher profits, and a lower risk with lower profits. The risk and the profit have to be balanced against each other.

The increase in profit option 2 achieves is small, less than 5%. The increase in risk in terms of fixed costs is quite substantial, more than 20%, while the reduction in margin of safety is 5%. The additional risk posed by the increase in fixed costs does seem disproportionately large compared to a mere 5% rise in profits. This suggests option 1 may be preferred.

It is useful, however, to consider 'what if' analysis. Customers like the fact components are made in the factory because their perception is of a 'handmade', quality product. It is possible that option 2, by increasing this perception of quality and craftsmanship, could stimulate demand. It might be a sensible precaution to do some market research on this possibility and then rework the figures.

Scandanavian Lights SA

Working 1

Selling price	€500
Less: variable cost per holiday	400
Equals: contribution per holiday	100

Working 2

Fixed cost	€200,000
Divided by: contribution per holiday	100
Equals: breakeven number of holidays	2,000

Working 3

Expected number of holidays sold	3,000
Less: breakeven number of holidays	2,000
Equals: margin of safety	1,000

Working 4

Margin of safety	1,000
Divided by: expected sales units	3,000
	0.3333
Multiplied by:	100
Equals: margin of safety %	33.33%

Working 5: Monthly profit statement (€)

Revenue (A × E)	1,500,000
Less: variable cost (B × E)	1,200,000
Equals: contribution	300,000
Less: fixed costs (F)	200,000
Equals: profit	100,000

14 Costing

This chapter outlines a technique for calculating the cost of a single unit of product.

Objectives	
	• Production and service departments;
	• Allocation, apportionment and absorption;
	• Ten-step method.

Introduction

Importance of the subject

This chapter focuses on companies in the manufacturing sector making more than one type of product. Selling goods or products for more than it costs to make them generates profit. To make a profit, therefore, a company must know the cost of making a unit of product. This chapter examines the techniques used to calculate this.

Context

An established manufacturing company is normally organised around departments such as production, purchasing, personnel, marketing, etc. One of the key distinctions in costing is between production departments and service departments. Once this distinction is established, the allocation of costs between departments can take place and the apportionment of costs out of service departments can be considered. Finally, the amount of cost to be absorbed into each unit of product can be calculated using a ten-step method.

Structure of this chapter

The underlying question addressed in this chapter is, how much does it cost to make a unit of product? The difficulty arises from overheads rather than from direct costs. Most companies can easily ascertain the value of components, raw materials and labour, which go directly into making a product. Calculating the amount of overhead to add to the direct costs, however, can be problematic. Consider the data set out below:

Cost per unit

Direct labour	12.50
Direct materials	4.50
Prime cost	17.00
Overhead absorbed	?
Full cost	?

THIS IS THE FIGURE THAT HAS TO BE CALCULATED

The direct materials and labour costs of making a unit of product are already known (£17.00 in total). What is unknown is the amount of overhead.

Activities and outcomes

By the end of this chapter you will be able to calculate the full cost of making a unit of product using the ten-step method. Make sure you understand the logic of the ten-step method as well as practising worked examples. Use the multiple choice questions to test your understanding. The conclusions section contains a summary of key costing terms, which you may find useful to refer to while working through the chapter.

Production departments and service departments

In a manufacturing company some departments will be directly concerned with making products while others provide services supporting the production process. Production departments are responsible for making the product. In a motor manufacturing company, they would include the assembly line and paint shop. In a printing company, the production departments might include text preparation, printing and binding. A company making furniture might have production departments such as cutting, assembling and finishing.

All products normally pass through every production department. In a printing company both books and magazines pass through text preparation, printing and binding departments. All the different types of furniture (tables, chairs, etc.) pass through the cutting, assembling and finishing departments. Figure 14.1 shows a company with three production departments.

Service departments, on the other hand, do *not* make products. They ensure the correct raw materials, components, people and equipment are available to keep production running efficiently. Service activities include purchasing the materials needed in production, planning production schedules, maintaining machines used in production and staff recruitment. Although service departments do not manufacture goods, problems within service departments can disrupt production. For example, if the correct materials are not in stock, or if machines are not properly maintained, production cannot take place. Service departments exist purely to assist and facilitate production.

As a company grows the number of service departments often increases. A large manufacturing company might have many service departments, including:

- Purchasing
- Stock control

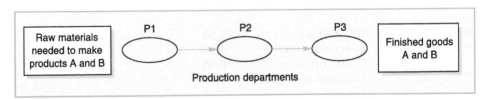

Figure 14.1 Production departments

- Personnel
- Production planning
- Equipment maintenance
- Distribution
- Market research
- Sales
- Research and development
- Accounting
- Administration

Smaller companies might have two or three service departments. Figure 14.2 shows a company with two service departments.

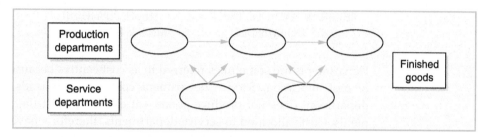

Figure 14.2 Production and service departments

Allocation

Management accounting systems

Every department employs staff, uses computers, occupies space and consumes materials and energy, etc. Most manufacturing companies organise financial information by allocating costs to the relevant department. For instance, in a furniture manufacturer, payroll costs of the wood cutters are allocated to the cutting department. The cost of the computers used in the purchasing area is allocated to the purchasing department. The cost of the stationery used in accounting is allocated to the accounts department.

Usually a coding system is used to allocate costs to the correct department. Production departments are allocated codes such as P1, P2, P3 and service departments are allocated codes such as S1 (purchasing department), S2 (maintenance department), etc. Staff costs might be allocated a code such as 001, raw materials 002, computer costs 003. These codes are used to allocate all costs to the correct department. Consequently, costs can be summarised as follows:

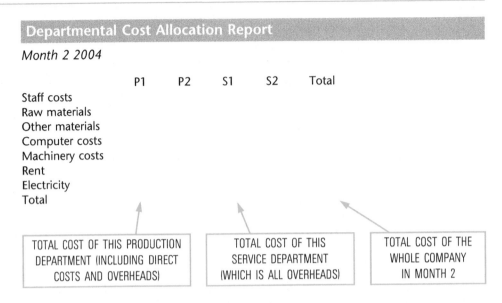

Departmental Cost Allocation Report

Month 2 2004

	P1	P2	S1	S2	Total
Staff costs					
Raw materials					
Other materials					
Computer costs					
Machinery costs					
Rent					
Electricity					
Total					

TOTAL COST OF THIS PRODUCTION DEPARTMENT (INCLUDING DIRECT COSTS AND OVERHEADS)

TOTAL COST OF THIS SERVICE DEPARTMENT (WHICH IS ALL OVERHEADS)

TOTAL COST OF THE WHOLE COMPANY IN MONTH 2

Departments are sometimes referred to as cost centres because of the importance of cost allocation. Service department costs are overheads because a service department does not produce goods – it exists to assist the production departments. Costs allocated to service departments, therefore, have to be apportioned among the production departments. This is the subject to which we now turn.

Apportionment

Service departments ensure production departments have the materials, people and equipment needed; therefore, they are closely linked. Take the example of an equipment maintenance department. During the course of a year the number of emergency and routine maintenance jobs undertaken might be as follows:

Equipment Maintenance Department

Job Analysis

	P1	P2	Total
Routine checks and servicing	157	48	205
Emergency repairs	12	143	155
Total	169	191	360
	47%	53%	

THE DEPARTMENT CARRIED OUT 360 SEPARATE JOBS DURING THE YEAR

Production department 2 needed a lot of emergency repairs, whereas P1 was more routine. The figures above suggest 47% of the work of the maintenance department related to P1 and the remaining 53% related to P2. As a result, the costs of the maintenance department can be apportioned to P1 and P2. If the departmental cost allocation report showed that the cost of the maintenance department was £97,524, £45,836 would be apportioned to P1 and £51,688 to P2.

Next, consider the apportionment of personnel department costs. If the number of employees in P1 is the same as P2, the costs of the personnel department can be shared equally between the two. Say the number of employees was as follows:

Staff Analysis Report

Month 1

	P1	P2	Total
Supervisors	19	25	44
Staff	201	237	438
Temporary staff	23	55	78
Total	243	317	560
	43%	57%	

The cost of the personnel department would be apportioned 43% to P1 and 57% to P2.

Using the data set out below, relating to month 2, calculate the relevant percentages and put your answer in the space provided.

Staff Analysis Report

Month 2

	P1	P2	Total
Supervisors	19	25	44
Staff	197	246	443
Temporary staff	8	65	73
Total	224	336	560
	?	?	

Apportionment should be on the basis of 40% to P1 and 60% to P2. Notice the total number of staff is the same as in month 1, but some people have been transferred from P1 into P2. Consequently, P2 will now attract a higher percentage of the personnel department cost.

Absorption

Absorption means calculating the amount of overhead absorbed into a single unit of output. This also means calculating the amount of overheads to be added to the prime costs (direct labour and materials) in order to find the full cost.

Cost per unit

Direct labour	12.50
Direct materials	4.50
Prime cost	17.00
Overhead absorbed	?
Full cost	?

THIS IS THE FIGURE THAT HAS TO BE CALCULATED

If a company manufactures one product only, the calculation of overhead per product is a simple one. Firstly, add up the overheads in all the different departments, and then divide by the number of units of output:

Overheads divided by units of output

Consider a company making one type of mobile phone. If output for the year is 1,500,000 phones and the total of all overheads is £30,000,000:

£30,000,000/1,500,000 phones = £20 per phone

The amount of overhead to be added to the prime cost is £20 per phone. If the direct costs amounted to £12, the full cost of making the phone would be £32 (see below).

Cost per mobile phone

Direct labour	2.00
Direct materials	10.00
Prime cost	12.00
Overhead absorbed	20.00
Full cost	32.00

This is termed the 'unit of output' method.

Most mobile phone companies make more than one type of phone. Consequently, they cannot use the unit of output method because this would mean different types of phones absorbing the same level of overhead. Some mobile phones are relatively simple and quick to manufacture, while others have special features such as Internet connection and photo messaging, etc. The standard phones are often much cheaper than the sophisticated phones. The level of overhead added to the sophisticated phones should reflect the extra work that goes into making them.

The method of absorption should reflect the fact that some products are quick and simple to make, while others are more complex and take longer to make. This can be achieved by calculating overhead per labour hour. Say the overhead per labour hour is £5. If a product takes one hour to make, £5 worth of overhead is added to the cost of the product. If a product is more complex and takes two hours to make, £10 is added to the cost. If the product is simple and only takes half an hour to make, £2.50 is added to the cost of making the product. Calculating overhead per hour gives the flexibility of adding more overheads to more complex products.

To calculate overhead per hour the total number of hours worked in each of the production departments is required. This can be obtained from the personnel department. Only direct labour hours should be included. Hours worked in service departments or spent on supervision should not be included:

Overheads *divided by* total direct labour hours

In some companies machine time is more important than labour time. In this case, overheads can be divided by the total machine hours. This is applicable to high technology factories where there is little labour input:

Overheads *divided by* total machine hours

Absorption: step by step

Allocation, apportionment and absorption can be combined in a ten-step procedure as follows.

Product costing: step by step

1. Set up a column for each of the production departments.
2. Place the overheads, which have been allocated to each production department, in the appropriate column. This information can be obtained from the departmental cost allocation report.
3. Perform apportionment calculations, splitting service department costs among the production departments using percentages.
4. Put the apportioned amount in the relevant column.
5. Add up the columns (both allocated and apportioned figures).
6. Divide the column totals by the total number of hours worked in each production department (this could be machine hours or labour hours depending on what is appropriate to the company).
7. The resulting figure is the overhead absorption rate, e.g. overheads per direct labour hour.
8. Identify how long it takes to make each unit of product in each production department (labour or machine time).
9. Multiply the length of time in each department by the overhead absorption rate for the department.
10. Add the result to the direct cost of making the product to achieve the absorption cost per unit (the full cost).

The ten-step calculations should be laid out as follows:

Product costing pro forma

Old Snow's Garden Sheds

Product Costing Calculation

Step		Cutting	Assembling
1			
2	Allocation		
	Apportionment		
3&4	Personnel		
	Administration		
	Maintenance		
5	Total overheads		
6	Total labour hours		
7	Overheads per hour		
8	Time taken		
9	Overhead absorbed		

		Cutting	Assembling	Total
10	Direct labour			
	Direct materials			
	Prime cost			
	Overhead absorbed			
	Total absorption cost			

Product costing in action

The ten-step method is best understood by example.

Old Snow's Garden Sheds

Old Snow's Garden Sheds have been in business since 1935. They have recently carried out a detailed review of costs and have found the cost of producing a shed, including a share of overheads, is £70.00. This leaves no room for profit, because the current selling price of a shed is around £70.00.

The Managing Director, Mrs. Snow, has been looking at cost savings in every department. She believes it must be possible to make a shed for less than £60.00 (including a share of overheads). You have met the company accountant and obtained the following information, which takes account of possible cost savings.

The company has two production departments (cutting and assembling) as well as four service departments (purchasing, maintenance, distribution and administration).

Fixed costs for a typical month are:

Cutting	8,000
Assembling	10,000
Purchasing	6,000
Maintenance	4,000
Distribution	4,000
Administration	2,000

The work of the service departments is split as follows:

	Cutting	Assembly
Purchasing	66.666%	33.333%
Maintenance	75%	25%
Distribution	50%	50%
Administration	50%	50%

For costing purposes the production departments absorb overheads on the basis of direct labour hours. The direct labour hours for a typical month are:

Cutting	1000 direct labour hours
Assembly	2000 direct labour hours

The direct costs of producing a shed are:

Cutting

Direct materials	£8
Direct labour (0.50 hrs at £10.00 per hr)	£5

Assembly

Direct materials	£5
Direct labour (2 hrs at £10.00 per hr)	£20

Prepare a product costing statement showing the total cost of making one shed using the ten-step method and write a paragraph comparing the total cost of making the shed to the target cost.

Old Snow's Garden Sheds: Solution

Step		Cutting	Assembling
1			
2	Allocation	8,000	10,000
	Apportionment		
3&4	Purchasing	4,000	2,000
	Maintenance	3,000	1,000
	Distribution	2,000	2,000
	Administration	1,000	1,000
5	Total overheads	18,000	16,000
6	Total labour hours	1,000	2,000
7	Overheads per labour hour	£18.00	£8.00
8	Time taken	0.5 hrs	2 hrs
9	Overhead absorbed	£9.00 per shed	£16.00 per shed

Product Costing Statement

		Cutting	Assembling	Total
10	Direct labour	5	20	25
	Direct materials	8	5	13
	Prime cost	13	25	38
	Overhead absorbed	9	16	25
	Total absorption cost	22	41	63

The full cost of making a garden shed is £63.00 – made up of direct costs £38 plus overheads of £25. Overheads have been absorbed on the basis of direct labour hours. If the sheds could be sold for £70.00 each, a profit of £7.00 per shed would be earned. The target set by the Managing Director was a cost of £60.00 per shed, and this target has not been met. The profit of £7.00 per shed, therefore, may not be sufficient. The company may need to look for further cost reductions, e.g. using cheaper timber.

Another example

Daiwong Telecoms Corporation

The Daiwong Telecoms Corporation (DTC) have established a large manufacturing facility outside Beijing, China. The world market for mobile phones is very competitive; as a result, it is important DTC can make a standard phone for less than £25.00 (all the figures in this question have already been converted into £ sterling).

The company has two production departments: circuiting and assembly. The circuiting department prepares the complex electronics and the assembling department fits the circuits into the casing and assembles the rest of the components. There are three service departments: purchasing, maintenance and testing.

The finance director has been collecting the information needed to calculate the cost per phone in the next financial year. The company absorbs overheads on the basis of direct labour hours.

The expected overheads (fixed costs) for the next year are:

Production departments (£'s)

Circuits	240,000
Assembly	140,000

Service departments (£'s)

Purchasing	160,000
Maintenance	80,000
Testing	40,000

The work of the service departments is split as follows:

	Circuits	Assembly
Purchasing	70%	30%
Maintenance	60%	40%
Testing	50%	50%

The direct labour hours in the next year are expected to be as follows:

Circuits   80,000 hrs
Assembly   20,000 hrs

The variable cost of producing a phone is (£'s):

Circuits
Direct materials   3
Direct labour (1 hr per phone)   6

Assembly
Direct materials   1
Direct labour (0.5 hrs per phone)   3

Using the ten-step method, prepare a product costing statement showing the cost of making a phone and compare your answer to the target cost of £25.00 per phone. State the profit per phone if the selling price is £30.00.

Step		Circuits	Assembly
1			
2	Allocation	240,000	140,000
	Apportionment		
3&4	Purchasing	112,000	48,000
	Maintenance	48,000	32,000
	Testing	20,000	20,000
5	Total overheads	420,000	240,000
6	Total labour hours	80,000 hrs	20,000 hrs
7	Overheads per labour hour	£5.25 per hr	£12 per hr
8	Time taken	1 hr	0.50 hrs
9	Overhead absorbed	£5.25	£6.00

Product Costing Statement (£'s)

		Circuits	Assembly	Total
10	Direct labour	6	3	9
	Direct materials	3	1	4
	Prime cost	9	4	13
	Overhead absorbed	5.25	6	11.25
	Total absorption cost	14.25	10	24.25

The full cost of making a mobile phone is £24.25. This is made up of direct costs £13 and overheads £11.25. The target cost for the phone was £25.00. As a result, this target has been met. If the phones were sold for £30.00, a profit of £5.75 would be earned on every phone.

Adaptations

The ten-step approach can be adapted to fit all types of manufacturing companies. There are, however, some further issues and idiosyncrasies, which need to be considered. Service departments provide services for other service departments, as well as for production departments. For example, the personnel department works for the purchasing and maintenance departments as well as for the production departments. This means some service department costs are apportioned to other service departments rather than production departments. Consider below:

Staff analysis by department

Cutting	40%	
Assembling	30%	
Finishing	20%	
Purchasing	5%	
Maintenance	5%	
	100%	

> 40% OF ALL THE STAFF EMPLOYED IN THE COMPANY WORK IN THE CUTTING DEPARTMENT

The figures above show 5% of personnel costs will be apportioned to maintenance. This can be accommodated within the ten-step method by making repeated apportionment in step 3 until all service department costs are apportioned to production departments.

Some firms make a distinction between variable overheads and fixed overheads, especially within production departments. Variable overheads increase and decrease as output changes, whereas fixed overheads do not. Examples of variable overheads include the power supply to factory machines and the usage of coolants and lubricants on factory machines. Where a distinction is made between variable and fixed overheads, unit cost calculations may take the following form:

Cost per unit

Direct labour	2.00
Direct materials	3.20
Prime cost	5.20
Variable overhead	0.50
Factory cost	5.70
Overhead absorbed	6.10
Full cost	11.80

Consequently, variable overheads can be accommodated within step 10.

Sometimes, production departments are dedicated to one product, as presented in Figure 14.3. This company has four production departments, of which the first two work on both product A and B, the third works on product A only and the fourth is dedicated to product B. This is easily incorporated into the ten-step method. The overheads per hour in P3 should be absorbed into product A and not B. The overheads per hour in P4 should be absorbed into product B and not A.

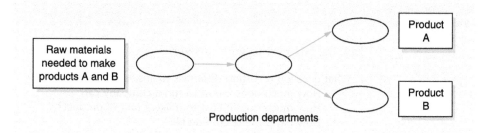

Figure 14.3 Dedicated production departments

Conclusions

Manufacturing companies have different numbers of products and different numbers of production and service departments. The approach set out here, therefore, has to be adapted to each situation. Where there are a large number of production or service departments, the calculations can become complex. The principle involved in calculating an absorption cost by dividing the overheads by labour (or machine) hours remains unchanged.

> 'The only thing that costs is labour, everything else is free.'
> A philosophical statement by Ian Mawdsley, Chartered Accountant.

Keywords

Direct costs	Any cost which can be easily identified with a unit of output.
Indirect costs	All other costs which do not go directly into making units of output. Sometimes called overheads.
Production department	A department engaged in making units of output.
Service department	Department ensuring production departments have the materials, people and equipment they need.
Cost centre	Any department consuming resources which cost money.
Allocation	Allotment of whole items of cost to cost centres.
Apportionment	Allotment of portions (percentages) of costs to cost centres.
Absorption	Charging overheads to units of output.
Prime cost	Direct labour + direct materials.
Full cost	Prime cost + overheads.
Unit of output	The goods the company produces, e.g. mobile phones.

Multiple choice questions

Tick the box next to your answer.

1. What question is costing designed to answer?
   - ☐ How much does it cost to run a company car?
   - ☐ How much does it cost to make a unit of product?
   - ☐ How big is the telephone bill?
   - ☐ How much do we spend on advertising?
   - ☐ How can we reduce the taxation bill?

2. What is the difference between a production and a service department?
   - ☐ Service departments make products
   - ☐ Production departments provide services
   - ☐ Production departments are an overhead
   - ☐ Service departments are not important
   - ☐ Production departments make products while service departments provide services

3. Overheads divided by the number of products made = ?
   - ☐ Overhead per labour hour
   - ☐ Overhead per machine hour
   - ☐ Overhead per product
   - ☐ Overhead per employee
   - ☐ Overhead per year

4. Overheads divided by total direct labour hours worked = ?
   - ☐ Overhead per direct labour hour
   - ☐ Overhead per machine hour
   - ☐ Overhead per product
   - ☐ Overhead per employee
   - ☐ Overhead per year

5. What is apportionment?
   - ☐ Splitting service department costs between production departments
   - ☐ Spreading the cost of a fixed asset over its expected life
   - ☐ Dividing overheads by labour hours
   - ☐ Portion control in a hotel or restaurant
   - ☐ Allocating costs to the right department

6. Why is overhead per *hour* more useful than overhead per *product*?
   - ☐ Because most firms have only one product
   - ☐ Because some products take longer to make than others
   - ☐ Because machine hours are better than labour hours
   - ☐ Because overheads are not direct costs
   - ☐ Because overheads only occur in service departments

7. Which of these is *not* a good way of apportioning the cost of a maintenance service department?
   - ☐ Number of maintenance visits
   - ☐ Number of maintenance hours
   - ☐ Number of machines
   - ☐ Number of employees in the production department
   - ☐ Number of emergency maintenance call outs

8. Overhead per labour hours = £10.00, labour time taken to make the product = 15 minutes; therefore, overhead absorbed = ?
   - ☐ £1 per product
   - ☐ £2.50 per product
   - ☐ £5 per product
   - ☐ £10 per product
   - ☐ £15 per product

9. Overhead per machine hour = £12.00, machine time taken to make the product = 10 minutes; therefore, overhead absorbed = ?
   - ☐ £1 per product
   - ☐ £2 per product
   - ☐ £6 per product
   - ☐ £10 per product
   - ☐ £12 per product

10. Direct labour per product = £1, direct materials per product = £2.50, overhead absorbed per product = £2; therefore, full cost per unit of product = ?
   - ☐ £1.00 per product
   - ☐ £2.50 per product
   - ☐ £3.50 per product
   - ☐ £4.50 per product
   - ☐ £5.50 per product

Multiple choice answers

	Correct answer	Comment
1	How much does it cost to make a unit of product?	Keep this question in mind when doing complex allocation, apportionment and absorption.
2	Production departments make products while service departments provide services	Service departments do not make goods. They provide the essential services, e.g. purchasing, which support the production departments.
3	Overhead per product	This is useful if the company only makes one product. Most companies make a range of products.
4	Overhead per direct labour hour	The longer it takes to make the product, the more overhead it absorbs.
5	Splitting service department costs between production departments	e.g. 50:50 or 25:75. Firms have to find a fair method of apportionment, reflecting the link between the particular service department and the production departments.
6	Because some products take longer to make than others	If a product takes longer to make, it should absorb more overheads.

7	Number of employees in the production department	All the others are a fair basis of splitting the maintenance costs. Employees in the production departments are nothing to do with maintenance.
8	£2.50 per product	15 minutes is a quarter of an hour. So, a quarter of £10.00 per hour = £2.50.
9	£2.00 per product	10 minutes is one sixth of an hour. So, one sixth of £12.00 per hour = £2.00.
10	£5.50 per product	The overhead gets added (absorbed) to the direct costs.

Discussion question

Explain in your own words why costing in a multi-product manufacturing environment is more complex than in a single-product environment. Start your answer with an illustration of the relative ease of single-product costing.

Consult the companion web site for the answer to this question.

Catatonic Computers

Catatonic Computers (CC) make printed circuit boards for personal computers. The manufacturing facility is divided into two production departments (coating and stamping) and six service departments (see below).

The selling price of printed circuit boards has fallen dramatically in recent months. The Finance Director, Ms. Neris Matthews, has been tasked with achieving a cost of £5 per unit, including an absorption of overhead. Neris now has all the information she needs to produce a full absorption cost for the next six months.

The expected overheads (fixed costs) for the next six months are:

Production departments (£'s)

Coating	4500
Stamping	5500

Service departments (£'s)

Setting up	10,000
Testing	10,000
Maintenance	10,000
Depreciation	10,000
Packaging	20,000
Planning	20,000

The work of the service departments is split as follows:

	Coating	Stamping
Setting up	10%	90%
Testing	25%	75%
Maintenance	50%	50%
Depreciation	50%	50%
Packaging	10%	90%
Planning	50%	50%

For costing purposes the production departments use an overhead absorption rate based on direct labour hours. The direct labour hours in the next six months are expected to be as follows:

Coating	2500 hrs
Stamping	2500 hrs

The variable costs (or direct costs) of producing a printed circuit board are (£'s):

Coating

Direct materials	0.5
Direct labour (0.1 hrs per unit)	0.2

Stamping

Direct materials	0.3
Direct labour (0.1 hrs per unit)	0.1

Your task

1. Prepare a product costing statement showing an absorption cost per circuit board unit using the ten-step method.
2. Compare your answer to the target cost.

Microtosh

Microtosh make PCs, monitors and printers. Split the following into direct materials, direct labour and overheads:

1. Memory boards.
2. Disk drives (A drives).
3. Wages of store person who issues parts to production.
4. Accountant's wages.
5. Factory manager's car expenses.

6. Wages of staff assembling the PCs.
7. Moving components around the factory.
8. Depreciation of welding machines used to assemble the PCs.
9. Factory telephones.
10. Repairs to the office block.

11. Running costs of the cars for the sales team.
12. Servicing the cars of the sales team.
13. Fuel for the delivery lorries.
14. The factory supervisor's wages.
15. Interest payments on borrowed money.

16. Electricity used in the office to run computers.
17. Cost of the computers used in the sales and accounting departments.
18. Oils used in the factory to lubricate the moving parts on the production line.
19. Fork lift truck hire costs.
20. Wages for the fork lift truck drivers working in the stores area.

What do you think would be the main service departments in the factory?

Whiskers Printing and Publishing

Whiskers are a publishing company specialising in glossy retail catalogues. It is a competitive market, where new business is usually won by competitive tender. A few pence can make the difference between winning a contract and losing it. Consequently, it is important to achieve accurate costings. Experience of submitting tenders suggests a price less than £5.00 per catalogue often secures the contract. The company risks losing a contract if it charges more than this.

There are two production departments: printing and binding. There are four service departments: design, maintenance, packaging and purchasing. The fixed costs relating to these departments are as follows:

	£
Printing	68,000
Binding	22,000
Design	30,000
Maintenance	30,000
Packaging	20,000
Purchasing	30,000

The labour hours worked in the factory are as follows:

Printing	20,000 hrs
Binding	10,000 hrs

The work of the service departments is split as follows:

	Printing	Binding
Design	50%	50%
Maintenance	70%	30%
Packaging	10%	90%
Purchasing	80%	20%

The variable costs (direct costs) of printing a catalogue are as follows:

                        £
Printing
Direct labour   0.40
Direct materials   0.70

Binding
Direct labour   0.60
Direct materials   0.50

Total   2.20

The time taken to make a unit of output in each of the two departments is as follows:

Printing   0.2 hrs
Binding   0.1 hrs

Your task

1. Prepare an absorption costing statement showing allocation, apportionment and absorption of overheads into the cost per unit using the ten-step method.
2. Compare the cost per unit to the target set, and calculate the profit per unit.

Spooky Dolls

Spooky Dolls manufacture doll's houses. The company has three production and three service departments. Fixed costs for a month are:

Production cost centres	Cutting	£4000
	Assembly	£5000
	Polishing and finishing	£1900
Service cost centres	Administration	£4000
	Sales	£3000
	Personnel	£2000

The service department costs are apportioned between the production departments as follows:

	Cutting	Assembly	Polishing, etc.
Administration	25%	50%	25%
Sales	30%	40%	30%
Personnel	30%	50%	20%

For costing purposes the production cost centres use an overhead absorption rate based on labour hours. Monthly labour hours are budgeted as follows:

Cutting   1300 hrs
Assembly   2300 hrs
Polishing and finishing   4200 hrs

319

The variable costs of producing a single doll's house are as follows:

Cutting	Direct materials	£15	
	Labour	£2	Labour hours worked 0.5 hrs
	Variable overhead	£2	
Assembly	Direct materials	£1	
	Labour	£6	Labour hours worked 1 hr
	Variable overhead	£0.5	
Polishing and finishing	Direct materials	£0.5	
	Labour	£14	Labour hours worked 2 hrs
	Variable overhead	£1	

Your task

Calculate the absorption cost of making a doll's house using the ten-step method.

Classical Elegant Graceful and Stylish

Classical Elegant Graceful and Stylish (CEGS) are a small clothing design and manufacturing company. They are organised into three production departments and three service departments. The production departments are:

P1   Cutting
P2   Machine sewing
P3   Finishing

The computerised accounting system shows the following cost analysis for the last quarter:

Departmental Cost Allocation Report

Cost £000's	Total	P1	P2	P3	S1	S2	S3
Wages	120	40	20	10	20	15	15
Salaries	60	10	0	5	15	15	15
Rent and rates	40	14	8	12	3	2	1
Insurance	20	5	4	2	2	4	3
Depreciation	60	25	15	15	0	0	5
Power and light	30	10	12	8			
Maintenance building	10	3	2	2	2	1	0
Maintenance plant	15	3	4	5	2	0	1
Health and safety	30	5	7	4	6	3	5
Total	385	115	72	63	50	40	45

- S1 provides services equally to all other departments, including service departments.
- S2 provides 10% to S3 and the remainder equally to production departments.
- S3 provides equally to the three production departments.

P1 is a labour intensive process, so overheads are to be recovered on a labour hour basis. P2 is machine based, so recovery is on a machine hour basis. P3 is on a labour hour basis.

The hours relating to the last quarter are as follows:

P1	Labour hours	40,000 direct labour hours
P2	Machine hours	10,000 machine hours
P3	Labour hours	54,000 direct labour hours

Your task

Establish the overhead apportionment rate (OAR) for each production department.

Solutions

Catatonic Computers

Step		Coating	Stamping
1			
2	Allocation	4,500	5,500
	Apportionment		
3&4	Setting up	1,000	9,000
	Testing	2,500	7,500
	Maintenance	5,000	5,000
	Depreciation	5,000	5,000
	Packaging	2,000	18,000
	Planning	10,000	10,000
5	Total overheads	30,000	60,000
6	Total labour hours	2500 hrs	2500 hrs
7	Overheads per hour	£12 per hr	£24 per hr
8	Time taken	0.1 hrs	0.1 hrs
9	Overhead absorbed	1.2	2.4

		Coating	Stamping	Total
10	Direct labour	0.2	0.1	0.3
	Direct materials	0.5	0.3	0.8
	Prime cost	0.7	0.4	1.10
	Overhead absorbed	1.2	2.4	3.6
	Total absorption cost	1.9	2.8	4.7

The full cost of making a printed circuit board is £4.70, which consists of £1.10 direct costs and £3.60 absorption of overhead. The target set was to achieve a full cost of no more than £5.00 per unit, which has been attained.

Microtosh

1	Direct materials	Memory boards are a component fitted in the PCs
2	Direct materials	Disk drives are components fitted in the PCs
3	Overhead	Related to stock control

4	Overhead	General administration
5	Overhead	Production overhead
6	Direct labour	Wages of the staff making the product
7	Overhead	Stock control
8	Overhead	Factory overhead
9	Overhead	Factory overhead
10	Overhead	Building maintenance
11	Overhead	Sales and marketing
12	Overhead	As above
13	Overhead	Distribution (could be a variable overhead)
14	Overhead	Factory overhead
15	Overhead	Finance costs
16	Overhead	General administration
17	Overhead	Part sales and part finance
18	Overhead	Factory overhead (could be a variable overhead)
19	Overhead	Stock control
20	Overhead	Stock control

There are many different types of overheads, including some factory overheads, which would be allocated to a production department. Some of these could be described as variable overheads, e.g. oils used up in factory machines. The service departments include:

- Stock control
- General administration
- Building maintenance
- Sales and marketing
- Distribution
- Finance costs

Whiskers Printing and Publishing

Step		Printing	Binding
1			
2	Allocation	68,000	22,000
	Apportionment		
3&4	Design	15,000	15,000
	Maintenance	21,000	9,000
	Packaging	2,000	18,000
	Purchasing	24,000	6,000
5	Total overheads	130,000	70,000
6	Total labour hours	20,000 hrs	10,000 hrs
7	Overheads per hour	£6.5 per hr	£7.00 per hr
8	Time taken	0.20 hrs	0.10 hrs
9	Overhead absorbed	£1.30	£0.70

10		Printing	Binding	Total
	Direct labour	0.40	0.60	1.00
	Direct materials	0.70	0.50	1.20
	Prime cost	1.10	1.10	2.20
	Overhead absorbed	1.30	0.70	2.00
	Total absorption cost	2.40	1.80	4.20

The full cost of printing a catalogue is £4.20, consisting of direct cost £2.20 and overheads £2.00. Overheads are absorbed on a direct labour hour basis. No specific target cost has been set, but quotations under £5 are usually successful. If catalogues were sold for £4.99 each, a profit of 79p per catalogue would result.

Spooky Dolls

Step		Cutting	Assembling	Polishing and finishing
1				
2	Allocation	4000	5000	1900
	Apportionment			
3&4	Administration	1000	2000	1000
	Sales	900	1200	900
	Personnel	600	1000	400
5	Total overheads	6500	9200	4200
6	Total labour hours	1300	2300	4200
7	Overheads per hour	£5 per hr	£4 per hr	£1 per hr
8	Time taken	0.50 hrs	1 hr	2 hrs
9	Overhead absorbed	£2.50	£4	£2

10		Cutting	Assembling	Polishing and finishing	Total
	Direct labour	2.00	6.00	14.00	22.00
	Direct materials	15.00	1.00	0.50	16.50
	Prime cost	17.00	7.00	14.50	38.50
	Variable overhead	2	0.50	1.00	3.50
	Factory cost	19.00	7.50	15.50	42.00
	Overhead absorbed	2.50	4.00	2.00	8.50
	Total absorption cost	21.50	11.50	17.50	50.50

The full cost of making a doll's house is £50.50, consisting of direct costs £38.50 and variable overheads £3.50, giving a factory cost £42.00. Fixed overheads of £8.50 have been added to the factory cost to achieve a full cost of £50.50. Overheads are absorbed on the basis of overheads per direct labour hour. If the doll's houses could be sold for £100, a £49.50 profit on each doll's house will be earned.

Classical Elegant Graceful and Stylish

The overhead apportionment rates for each production department are as follows:

Cost £000's	Total	P1	P2	P3	S1	S2	S3
Total	385	115	72	63	50	40	45
Apportion S1		10	10	10	−50	10	10
		125	82	73		50	55
Apportion S2		15	15	15		−50	5
		140	97	88			60
Apportion S3		20	20	20			−60
		160	117	108	0	0	0
Hours		40 hrs	10 hrs	54 hrs			
Overhead per hour		£4 per hr	£11.70 per hr	£2 per hr			

15 Activity-based costing

A different way of looking at the modern high technology business process.

- Flexible manufacture;
- Problems with traditional costing;
- ABC implementation;
- ABC within departments and firms;
- Evaluation of ABC.

Introduction

Importance of the subject in a global context

L evels of world trade and investment are now higher than at any time in history (www.economist.co.uk). World competition is more intense than ever before and so is the pressure to reduce costs. Within the manufacturing sector there have also been many technological advances increasing productivity, e.g. robotics. These global trends have made it more difficult to identify the cost of making a unit of product. Consequently, a more sophisticated method of calculating the cost of a product has been developed, termed activity-based costing (ABC).

Structure of this chapter

This chapter starts by examining the changing character of world manufacturing and the specific problems this causes for traditional costing (Chapter 14). ABC is then explained using a step-by-step approach. Because ABC is more detailed and complex than the traditional approach, its application to individual departments is explored before a company-wide example is attempted. Finally an evaluation of ABC is undertaken.

Activities and outcomes

A considerable amount of calculation is involved in ABC and your numerical skills will be tested and developed. Understanding the link between changes in the business environment (technology, globalisation, etc.) and accounting procedures is, however, just as important as performing the calculations correctly. Make sure you master the departmental-based examples before you tackle the company-wide exercises. Use the multiple choice questions to test your understanding before attempting the discussion and end of chapter questions. After completing this chapter you will have a balanced view of ABC and you will be able to identify situations where it can provide a solution to a business problem. You will also be able to identify situations where ABC is not the most appropriate solution.

Flexible manufacturing

The introduction of more sophisticated technology and working practices has coincided with a revolution in the way managers think about manufacturing. This revolution has many facets, which can be gathered together under the umbrella term 'flexible manufacturing'. The best way to understanding flexible manufacturing is to examine the traditional approach first.

The driving force behind traditional manufacturing was cost. Henry Ford's original Model T was the first car cheap enough to attract a mass market. Costs were low because the model T was a standard product, produced on a huge scale on a continuous production line. Work on the production line was broken down into small, repetitive tasks. At the time this 'Taylorisation' of work was regarded as an innovation. Today it is widely appreciated that repetitive work can sometimes result in a poor quality of product. The pursuit of low cost is still a widespread business strategy and one still associated, to some extent, with the Ford Motor Company.

> Henry Ford was the pioneer of what we now call the traditional approach to manufacturing. Between 1914 and 1923 production of the model T increased from a few hundred thousand per year to over two million. One of Henry Ford's main innovations was the moving assembly line. For more on this consult John Allen et al. (eds), Political and Economic Form of Modernity, Open University, 1992, p. 230. See photograph on p. 235.

Consumers today are more sophisticated: they demand a choice. Customers can choose a motor car closely reflecting their needs and tastes. Motor vehicles are now made for specific customers, an approach described as 'demand pull' (Chapter 12). Consequently, production is planned more carefully and stock levels are lower because components are delivered only when needed to make a specific car. This is termed 'just in time' production. When the car is finished it is delivered straight to the customer, rather than being held in stock.

Under this flexible manufacturing regime, team work is encouraged and staff take responsibility for the quality of work in their section or 'cell'. Production is highly automated, including some robotic processes, but human intervention is still an important part of the production process. Today there is more investment in research and development, equipment, production planning and purchasing. The key differences between modern *flexible manufacture* and the traditional approach are detailed below:

Flexible manufacture	Traditional manufacture
Toyota	Ford's Model T
Batches of one	Large batches
Demand pull	Production for stock
No stock	High stock
Supplier co-operation	Supplier competition
Quality is king	Cost is king
Autonomous cells	Taylorism

Customer choice	'Any colour, so long as it's black'
Zero defects	Quality inspections
Right first time	Reworking
Multi-skilled	Demarcation
Automated	Labour intensive

The 'flexible manufacturing' environment presents a challenge to management accountants because:

- There is a wide range of different products.
- Products utilise many common resources.
- Products consume common resources at different rates.

Overhead costs have increased considerably, particularly in the areas of research and development, purchasing, materials handling and production scheduling. The nature of these overheads is that they are not related to the volume of production or the number of direct labour hours. The costs of research and development, materials handling systems and production scheduling are largely unchanged, irrespective of whether the volume of production is 300,000 units per year or 2,000,000 units per year. The level of these overheads is more related to the number of new products developed, the number of times production is switched between products (called the number of set ups) and the number of components needed for each product. These are the types of factors governing overheads, not the level of production. Consequently, costing has to be based on those activities, i.e. activity-based costing rather than volume based.

Problems with the traditional method

The traditional method of costing is based on dividing overheads by direct labour hours (see Chapter 14). This gives overhead per labour hour, e.g. each hour worked directly on the product is the equivalent of £10 of overhead. If a product takes three hours to make, this would be the equivalent of £30 of overhead:

Overheads *divided by* direct labour hours = overheads per labour hour

In a more machine-intensive environment the logic can be extended to overheads divided by machine hours, e.g. £15 per machine hour. If a product takes two hours to machine, £30 of overheads is added to the cost of the product:

Overheads *divided by* machine hours = overheads per machine hour

Both of these approaches assume overheads are driven by hours worked. The more hours worked on a product, the more overheads it consumes.

In a continuous production line, making a standard product, this may have been correct; however, in modern flexible manufacturing overheads are different. In the modern environment overheads tend to relate to what happens before the product is made. They relate more to the planning stage. Research and development, production planning, purchasing, etc. account for much of the overhead cost in the modern environment. They are all activities that happen before the product is made. The length of time it takes to make a product may not reflect the work at the planning stage. In fact, the more work undertaken at the planning stage the *less* time it may take to make the product.

A specific problem began to emerge with traditional costing methods. Too many overheads were being charged to some products and not enough to others. Complex products, which took a long time to plan and procure, were not always charged enough overheads. Simple products, which took little planning and procurement, were sometimes charged too much overhead. The problem was often referred to as 'cross-subsidisation'.

Consider a company offering two products, one of which is standard and the other customised. For example, a computer manufacturer might offer a standard laptop and a customised version allowing the customer to choose such features as an integrated digital camera, minidisk player or satellite-based Internet connection. The customised laptop is a more complex product with potentially many more components and problems. Much of the work of the purchasing, production planning and quality testing departments will relate to the customised laptop rather than the standard. If overheads are charged to products on the basis of the direct labour time, the work done in purchasing, planning and testing is not directly charged to the customised laptop. As a result, the standard product may absorb too much overhead, and the customised laptop too little. Examine the comparison below:

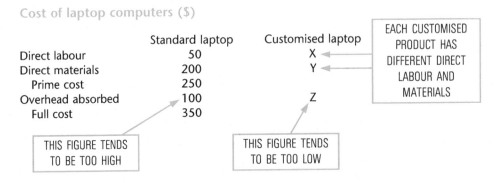

Cost of laptop computers ($)

	Standard laptop	Customised laptop	
Direct labour	50	X	EACH CUSTOMISED PRODUCT HAS DIFFERENT DIRECT LABOUR AND MATERIALS
Direct materials	200	Y	
Prime cost	250		
Overhead absorbed	100	Z	
Full cost	350		

THIS FIGURE TENDS TO BE TOO HIGH

THIS FIGURE TENDS TO BE TOO LOW

Under a traditional costing regime, the value of Z tends to be too low because it does not reflect all the activities that have gone into planning and making the customised product. On the other hand, the $100 absorbed into the standard laptop may be too high. Activity-based costing solves this problem by charging the costs of all the activities related to planning and making the product directly to the product. The extra work in the purchasing and planning departments caused by the customised laptops would be charged to the customised products and not the standard laptop.

Mechanics of an ABC system

The implementation of an ABC system should start with the identification of key activities and the costs of those activities. Next the direct causes of those activities, referred to as 'cost drivers', should be identified. Finally, cost driver rates should be established and used to charge costs back to products. The four stages in an ABC implementation can be summarised as follows:

- Activities
- Costs of activities
- Cost drivers
- Cost driver rates

Production planning is a key activity in the flexible manufacturing environment and one that could cost, say, £250,000 per year to run. The costs of production planning are driven by the number of times the production process has to be planned or rescheduled and by the number of products and components. The more complex the production process the more resource is given over to planning. The number of production schedules drawn up in a year is a good measure of the amount of production planning work done, e.g. 100 plans prepared in a year. Dividing the cost of the production planning departments by the number of production schedules prepared yields a cost per production schedule. Costs of £250,000 divided by 100 plans yields a cost driver rate of £2500 per plan. This can be used to charge the cost of production planning back to the products or departments requesting them or causing the need for them.

The first stage of ABC implementation is finding out the key *activities* that consume resources giving rise to overheads. Key activities may include purchasing, planning, maintenance and quality testing, but these are broad headings rather than detailed tasks. The specific jobs and tasks that need to be carried out on a daily or weekly basis may have to be specified in full detail. For example, in the purchasing department the work undertaken by different members of staff, e.g. sending out supplier orders or checking delivery notes, etc., may need to be recorded and measured. Conducting interviews, observing working practices, asking staff to complete time sheets, reviewing job specifications and distributing questionnaires can all help identify specific tasks.

Once the key activities are identified, the second stage is measuring the costs of those activities. This information may be readily available within a company's existing accounting system. Accounting systems, however, are often designed to show the costs of departments rather than activities within departments. The accounting system may have to be redesigned to show the costs of specific tasks and jobs. In some circumstances this can be a major project.

The third stage is identifying the causes or 'drivers' of activities. Activity costs are determined by a wide range of factors, e.g. inflation. The term 'cost driver' is reserved for factors reflecting the volume of work carried out in a department or activity. As well as being accurate, cost drivers should also be easy to measure. Measuring the number of transactions undertaken is a common cost driver, e.g. the number of invoices, delivery notes, orders and cheques. The following questions help identify cost drivers:

- What services does the activity provide?
- Who receives the service?
- What determines the number of staff required for an activity?
- What types of events or circumstances necessitate overtime?
- Are extra staff ever drafted into the activity?

- Are there idle periods in this activity?

Frequently more than one cost driver is available. In this situation the one with the most direct causal relationship with the level of work or productivity should be chosen.

The final stage is the calculation of a cost driver rate. In order to calculate a cost driver rate, the cost driver volume must be measured. The cost driver rate is calculated as follows:

Cost of the activity *divided by* volume of transactions = cost driver rate

In order to apply the cost driver rate, a system for identifying the cost driver volumes associated with each production run, batch, contract or job is needed. The ease of measuring this will be a criterion used in cost driver selection. A cost driver must have an identifiable link with a product or service.

The four stages of an ABC implementation involve collecting a considerable amount of information. It is a task likely to involve a team of people working together for a period of months. The team would be a multi-disciplinary one, involving systems analysts, accountants, personnel managers and operational managers. Because of the complexity of the implementation, an experienced project manager may be needed to oversee the work. The cost of undertaking an ABC implementation is, therefore, significant. In a large business the costs of implementing ABC could exceed $1,000,000.

> Project management is a specialised aspect of business. A project can be defined as any procedure having a beginning and an end. Implementing ABC is a good example of a project. Key features of successful project management include:
>
> 1. A clearly defined goal.
> 2. A detailed list of tasks.
> 3. A single leader.
> 4. Matching the right people to the right task.
> 5. Communication.
>
> For more on this see Fergus O'Connell, How to Run Successful Projects III: 'The Silver Bullet', Addison Wesley, 2002.

ABC in a marketing department

ABC analysis can, in theory, be applied to any area of business, for instance marketing. The types of activities and tasks carried out in a marketing department may be as follows:

- Market research
- Web site development
- Television advertising campaigns

STAGE 1: ACTIVITIES

- Newspaper advertising campaigns
- Exhibitions

The costs of running a marketing department may be as follows (all in £'s):

Staff costs	200,000
Office space	15,000
Office equipment	5,000
IT equipment	10,000
Travel	25,000
Advertising budget	100,000
Subscriptions	2,400
Training	5,000
Total	362,400

The staff costs might include a marketing director, two marketing managers and four marketing assistants.

These costs need to be broken down into more detail, identifying the cost of the key activities. Time sheets could be used to find out how much time each individual spends on each of the activities. Interviews and questionnaires could also be used at this stage. This may reveal that some activities take up little time, e.g. newspaper advertising, while others are dominant, e.g. television advertising. These investigations might reveal the following (all in £'s):

Market research	30,000	
Web site	30,000	
TV advertising	250,000	STAGE 2: COSTS OF ACTIVITIES
Newspaper advertising	22,400	
Exhibitions	30,000	
	362,400	

Possible cost drivers could include:

- Number of market research campaigns
- Number of web site updates
- Number of television and newspaper adverts
- Number of trade exhibitions

STAGE 3: COST DRIVERS

The productivity of the marketing departments could be measured as follows:

Marketing Department Activity Report

Number of MR campaigns	5
Number of web site updates	50
Number of television adverts	100
Number of newspaper adverts	25
Number of trade exhibitions	8

The Marketing Director could produce this activity report every month or quarter. On the basis of this information, cost driver rates could be calculated as follows:

Activities	Costs	Drivers	Cost driver rates
Market research	£30,000	5	£6000 per campaign
Web site	£30,000	50	£600 per update
Television advertising	£250,000	100	£2500 per advert
Newspaper advertising	£22,400	25	£896 per advert
Exhibitions	£30,000	8	£3750 per exhibition

> STAGE 4: COST
> DRIVER RATES

If the company is considering the possibility of introducing new products, it is now aware that market research will cost £6000 and updating the web site will cost £600. The cost driver rates can also be used to determine the value for money provided by the marketing department. If a specialist firm could carry out market research cheaper, an opportunity for cost savings may exist.

ABC in a personnel department

The work of a personnel department can typically be broken down as follows:

- Induction programmes for new staff
- Preparing job specifications
- Payroll liaison
- Advertising vacancies
- Interviewing candidates
- Following up references
- Annual appraisals
- Staff training
- Equal opportunities policies
- Exit interviews

> STAGE 1: ACTIVITIES

The department might typically include five people:

- Training Officer
- Equal Opportunities Officer
- Recruitment Officer
- Personnel Director
- Personnel Manager

In addition to the salary costs of these five people, the total cost of the department would also include subscriptions, office stationery, equipment, insurance, etc. The total cost of the department for a year might be in the region of £320,000. After investigation, this could be analysed as follows (all in £'s):

Induction	50,000
Job specifications	30,000
Payroll	20,000
Advertising	40,000
Interviewing	40,000
References	5,000
Annual appraisals	40,000
Staff training	80,000
Equal opportunities assessment	10,000
Exit interviews	5,000
	320,000

> STAGE 2: COSTS OF ACTIVITIES

Notice staff training is the single most costly activity. The company might consider the possibility that if the right people were recruited, the need for training might be reduced.

Possible cost drivers would include the following:

- Number of interviews conducted during the year
- Number of induction programmes organised
- Numbers of new staff recruited
- Number of training courses organised
- Number of training days
- Number of appraisals carried out
- Number of job specifications prepared
- Number of references obtained
- Number of adverts placed

> STAGE 3: COST DRIVERS

The Personnel Director could be asked to produce an activity report showing the data specified above. Likely cost driver rates would include:

- Cost per induction
- Cost per interview
- Cost per new member of staff
- Cost per training day
- Cost per appraisal
- Cost per job specification

> STAGE 4: COST DRIVER RATES

These could be charged to the departments requesting the work. When the production planning department needs a new member of staff, the personnel department charges production planning for the service provided. The cost driver rates provide a basis for assessing the value for money provided by the personnel department.

ABC in the purchasing department

Within flexible manufacturing the work of the purchasing department is essential to achieving 'just in time' production and minimising stock. A purchasing department will employ a large number of staff and other resources such as IT equipment and office space. The flow of information relating to purchasing activity takes place as follows:

- Purchase order requisition note (PORN) raised in the production planning department, alerting the purchasing department that a particular component or raw material is needed.
- Purchase order for each relevant supplier raised in the purchasing department, alerting the supplier that a particular component is needed.
- Take delivery of the goods and receive a delivery note from the supplier informing the purchasing department that the order has been fulfilled.
- Receive an invoice from the supplier informing the purchasing department how much money is owed and when it should be paid.
- Authorise payment in line with the agreed terms of business.

Even in computerised environments this activity is usually driven by paper, although the Internet may change this. The process is slowed down considerably by the need to impose proper checks and controls. The following checks and controls are recommended:

- Check the authorisation of the purchase order requisition note (PORN).
- Check the price of the goods being ordered.
- Check the quantity of goods from the delivery note back to the purchase order.
- Check the quality of goods delivered.
- Check the quantities on the supplier's invoice match the delivery note.
- Check the timing of payments back to the agreed terms of business.

If these checks are omitted, the company may pay for goods that have not been received, not been ordered or that are faulty.

Typically the activities within a purchasing department are as follows:

- Supplier audits
- Raising purchase orders
- Checking delivery notes
- Checking invoices
- Checking payment authorisation

STAGE 1: ACTIVITIES

The purpose of supplier audits is to ensure suppliers can meet the quality standards and lead times needed. They also help build a better understanding between suppliers and the purchasing team. Raising purchase orders informs suppliers about which components are needed and when. The other checks are to ensure the company only pays for what it receives and does not pay for goods that were not delivered.

In a large manufacturing company 30 to 40 people may be employed in the purchasing department. They will be paid between £15,000 and £50,000 per annum. The other costs of running the department include computers, telephones, training, stationery, insurance, recruitment, travel, etc. The total cost of the department could be around £1 million a year. The accounting department should be able to provide an analysis of the costs of running the purchasing department. Time sheet information can be used to give more detail about the work of the department. Typically the breakdown of the costs would be presented as follows (£'s):

Supplier audits	£235,000
Raising purchase orders	450,000
Checking delivery notes	110,000
Checking invoices	105,000
Checking payment authorisation	100,000
Total	£1,000,000

> STAGE 2: COSTS OF ACTIVITIES

From this analysis it is apparent that raising purchase orders and supplier audits are the key areas. The next step would be to ascertain the factors that are driving these costs. Consider the following:

Activity	Possible cost drivers
Supplier audits	Number of suppliers Number of new components Number of supplier orders
Raising purchase orders	Number of supplier orders Number of components Number of suppliers
Checking delivery	Number of deliveries Number of components
Checking invoices	Number of invoices Number of components Value of components
Checking payment authorisation	Number of deliveries Number of cheques Value of cheques

For each activity there are a number of possible cost drivers, some of which are easier to measure than others. Order documents tend to be pre-numbered and sequential and, therefore, it is easy to measure the total number of supplier orders used in a month or year. The number of components can be more problematic. Some orders relate to thousands of low-value components, while others relate to a few high-value components. The actual number of components ordered is difficult to measure and not meaningful. The number of suppliers is also difficult to measure because the list of suppliers is constantly changing.

Consequently, the number of supplier orders emerges as the best cost driver for the most costly activities. The number of supplier orders is not a good cost driver for checking invoices or payment authorisation; however, the cost of those activities is relatively small. In view of this fact, the company could adopt a single cost driver, the number of supplier orders, across all the different activities. This involves a certain loss of accuracy, but has the advantage that it would no longer be necessary to cost the five different activities. This would result in a single cost driver rate as follows:

Cost of the department *divided by* number of purchase orders raised
= cost per purchase order

If 2,500 purchase orders were raised in an average year:

$$£1,000,000/2,500 = £400 \text{ cost per purchase order}$$

Each purchase order costs the company £400 to administer. Every time a purchase order is raised, £400 is charged to the cost of the batch or contract or product. This simple approach has the benefit that both the cost of running the department and the number of purchase orders is already known. In addition to the fact that the breakdown of the costs of the purchasing department is no longer needed, cost per purchase order is readily understood and easy to calculate. Cost per purchase order is, however, simplistic and some of the detail about the work of the department is lost, e.g. the link between the number of suppliers and new components.

ABC – a whole company example

When viewed from the perspective of a company rather than an individual department, ABC calculations look rather different. The example below is intended to highlight some of the issues.

Swedish Precision Components SA

SPC manufactures four different hi-fi products: CD player (product A), DVD player (product B), combined CD & DVD (product C) and integrated compact CD DVD amplifier (product D). All the products are subject to competition from world markets and there is considerable pressure to reduce costs. The company wishes to use ABC principles where possible, but has found that machine hours-based absorption is appropriate in large areas of the business.

For the period just ended, details of production volumes, costs and times were as follows:

Product	Volume	Materials cost per unit	Direct labour hours per unit	Machine hours per unit	Labour costs per unit
A	4,000	£50.00	1.00	1.00	£10.00
B	6,000	£60.00	1.00	1.50	£10.00
C	2,000	£100.00	2.00	4.00	£20.00
D	500	£200.00	5.00	6.00	£50.00

The direct costs of each unit of product are as follows:

	A	B	C	D
Direct labour	10	10	20	50
Direct materials	50	60	100	200
Prime cost	60	70	120	250
Overheads				
Full cost				

THESE ARE THE FIGURES THAT NEED TO BE CALCULATED USING ABC

Total production overheads for the period came to £1,000,000. The issue is, how much of that £1,000,000 relates to each product?

A detailed analysis of these overheads, carried out by the ABC implementation team, revealed the following information:

Factory overhead applicable to machine activity	£600,000
Setting up production runs	£75,000
Ordering materials	£75,000
Handling materials	£100,000
Upgrades	£150,000
Total	£1,000,000

The team have found that a large portion of the overheads can be linked to product using machine hours. As a result, the total number of machine hours worked in the factory needs to be calculated. This is as follows:

Product	Volume	Per hour	Total hours
A	4,000	1.00 hr	4,000 hrs
B	6,000	1.50 hr	9,000 hrs
C	2,000	4.00 hr	8,000 hrs
D	500	6.00 hr	3,000 hrs
Total			24,000 hrs

The team have also produced the following activity report to support ABC calculations:

Product	No. of set ups	No. of material orders	No. of times material handled	No. of upgrades
A	10	20	2	1
B	15	40	2	2
C	20	50	2	5
D	30	90	10	12
	75	200	16	20

On the basis of the above, cost driver rates can be calculated as follows:

Activities	Cost	Driver	Cost driver rates
Machine-related costs	600,000	24,000 hrs	£25 per machine hour
Setting up	75,000	75	£1000 per set up
Materials ordering	75,000	200	£375 per order
Materials handling	100,000	16	£6250 per movement
Upgrades	150,000	20	£7500 per upgrade

Charging the overheads back to the products using the cost driver rates yields the following:

	£25 × 4000 HOURS		£1000 × 30 SET UPS	£375 × 90 ORDERS
Activities	A	B	C	D
Machine hours	£100,000	£225,000	£200,000	£75,000
Set up	10,000	15,000	20,000	30,000
Ordering	7,500	15,000	18,750	33,750
Materials handling	12,500	12,500	12,500	62,500
Upgrades	7,500	15,000	37,500	90,000
Total	£137,500	£282,500	£288,750	£291,250
Volumes	4000 units	6000 units	2000 units	500 units
	£34.375	£47.0833	£144.375	£582.5
	per unit	per unit	per unit	per unit

The materials handling and upgrades costs are associated closely with product D.

Finally, the costs per unit are as follows:

	A	B	C	D
Prime costs	60.00	70.00	120.00	250.00
Overheads	34.37	47.08	144.37	582.50
Total cost	94.37	117.08	264.37	832.50

Product D is by far the most expensive product to produce.

Financial services sector

The ABC technique can be usefully applied in the financial services sector, including banking, share trading, pensions, insurance and credit cards. For instance, take a collections department in a credit card company, responsible for collecting money from card holders in arrears. Staff follow set procedures for collecting the money owed, including:

- Telephone contact
- First warning letter
- Second warning letter
- Legal department warning letter
- Legal proceedings
- Seizure of assets

The first stage in an ABC implementation would be the identification of activities. The six steps above seem to capture the main activities undertaken in the department. Further investigation might reveal that some of the activities could be broken down into sub-activities, e.g. first telephone contact and then second telephone contact.

The next task would be finding the costs of the activities. The main cost will be payroll costs, but IT and office costs would also be important elements. A detailed investigation might reveal that the main cost drivers are as follows:

- Number of telephone calls
- Number of warning letters
- Number of legal letters
- Number of legal cautions
- Number of seizures undertaken

The department would produce a weekly activity report of the following nature:

Collections Department Weekly Activity Report

Number of telephone calls made	12,351
Number of warning letters issued	4,398
Number of legal letters issued	2,456
Number of legal actions started	578
Number of legal actions completed	431
Number of seizures undertaken	35
Value of goods seized	122,875
Total money collected	£1,768,943

This data can be used to calculate the following:

- Cost per phone call
- Cost per letter
- Cost per legal action
- Cost per seizure
- Cost per £1 collected

This information can provide a useful comparison for assessing the benefits of contracting out collections work. Many legal firms offer a 'collection service' and would be willing to quote for subcontracting the letters, legal action and seizures work. The cost of subcontracting this work might be less than running an in-house collection department. Many firms find ABC a useful cost reduction technique rather than a way of recharging overheads.

Advantages and disadvantages of activity-based costing

Like budgeting, ABC is a detailed accounting technique. It reveals the tasks that are undertaken in departments and the amount of time taken to carry out those tasks. It reveals the costs of those tasks and the different ways they can be charged to contracts, batches and products. It can reveal inefficiency, waste and opportunities for outsourcing. The mere threat of an ABC review could lead departmental heads to radically review working practices. ABC is, therefore, an effective tool for cost cutting and improving efficiency. The effectiveness of ABC as a method of costing, however, can be questioned.

Because ABC works at a detailed level it generates many different methods of charging costs to products. It substantially increases the number of internal recharges in the accounting system. Consequently, there may be more internal recharge transactions in the accounting system than there are sales to customers, which is illogical. As a result of ABC the costing of products will be more accurate, but the amount of work undertaken to achieve this accuracy is considerable. Companies often have to radically simplify ABC in order to make it practical. This involves a trade off between accuracy and cost. The more accurate the ABC costing, the more time, effort and cost has to go into recharging overheads.

The purchasing department case study (above) illustrates the point. After undertaking a detailed review, the costs of the department were divided by the number of purchase orders. The number of purchase orders has little direct causal effect on the activities of checking invoices and payment authorisation. The number of supplier orders is not directly related to the number of supplier audits, which was a major element of cost. The compromise of using the number of orders as a single cost driver may not be satisfactory.

ABC involves a balance between the benefit of accurate costing and the costs of achieving accurate costing. In some departments ABC can be implemented in a quick and simple way without incurring high costs. In other areas the time and costs involved in tracing the links between activities and products are too great. The SPC case study (above) illustrates this point. Most of the overheads were absorbed using a simple machine hour rate. ABC was used in specific areas where the activities were easily measured. The balance of advantage and disadvantage can be summarised as follows.

Advantages

- More accurate product costs.
- Recognises that activities cause overheads, not products.
- Can help reduce overheads by identifying the causes of and the responsibility for costs.
- Provides useful non-financial information and ratios.
- Provides a basis for outsourcing decisions and subcontracting.
- Can be implemented department by department.

Disadvantages

- Complex.
- Time consuming.
- Expensive.
- Often impossible to choose the best cost driver.
- Attracts attention away from the quality of the finished product.

Conclusions

ABC and traditional costing can be combined. ABC should be implemented where cost drivers and activities are clear. In other areas of the business more traditional approaches can still be used effectively. Alternatively, ABC can be used as a cost reduction or value for money technique rather than a technique for costing products.

Multiple choice questions

Tick the box next to your answer.

1. Which of the following is *not* a feature of modern flexible manufacturing?
   - ☐ Low stocks
   - ☐ Small production runs
   - ☐ Quality control
   - ☐ Team working
   - ☐ Large batches of standard product

2. Which of the following is *not* a key activity in a purchasing department?
   - ☐ Processing supplier orders
   - ☐ Finding new suppliers
   - ☐ Checking deliveries
   - ☐ Checking invoices
   - ☐ Preparing P&L account and balance sheet

3. Which of these is *not* an appropriate cost driver in a purchasing department?
   - ☐ Number of purchase orders
   - ☐ Number of supplier invoices
   - ☐ Number of deliveries received
   - ☐ Number of sales invoices issued to customers
   - ☐ Number of supplier visits

4. Which of these is *not* an effective way of finding key activities, and costs of activities, in a purchasing department?
   - ☐ Interview members of the purchasing team
   - ☐ Ask the team to complete time sheets at the end of the day
   - ☐ Observe the work of the department
   - ☐ Look at job descriptions and departmental structure
   - ☐ Visit one customer

5. Cost of order processing = £150,000, number of orders processed = 10,000; therefore, cost driver rate = ?
   - ☐ £15 per order
   - ☐ £150 per order
   - ☐ £150,000 per order
   - ☐ £10,000 per order
   - ☐ Zero

6. Which of these is *not* a feature of a good cost driver?
   - ☐ Easy to measure, e.g. the number of invoices
   - ☐ Increases in busy periods
   - ☐ Closely related to the work of a key activity
   - ☐ Stays the same all the time
   - ☐ Easily understood by every one

7. Which of these is *not* an example of a good cost driver?
   - ☐ Number of production runs
   - ☐ Number of inspection visits
   - ☐ Number of orders
   - ☐ Number of absence days through sickness
   - ☐ Number of set ups on the production line

8. Which of the following is not a part of ABC implementation?
   - ☐ Interviewing staff about their work
   - ☐ Reviewing job specifications
   - ☐ Producing detailed departmental costing
   - ☐ Producing departmental activity reports
   - ☐ Setting selling prices

9. What are the four steps in an ABC implementation?
   - ☐ Allocate, apportion, absorb and control
   - ☐ Cash flow, P&L account, balance sheet and ratios
   - ☐ Mirror, signal, manoeuvre and move out
   - ☐ Selling price, variable cost, fixed cost and contribution
   - ☐ Activities, costs, cost drivers and cost driver rates

10. Which of the following is a disadvantage of ABC systems?
   - ☐ Provides accurate costings
   - ☐ Have to be implemented throughout the company
   - ☐ Can be used to reduce costs
   - ☐ Provides useful non-financial information
   - ☐ Time consuming, expensive and complicated

Multiple choice answers

	Correct answer	Comment
1	Large batches of standard product	This is the traditional approach to manufacturing, e.g. Henry Ford.
2	Preparing P&L account and balance sheet	The accounting department does this, not the purchasing department.
3	Number of sales invoices issued to customers	Sales invoices are nothing to do with the purchasing department.
4	Visit one customer	Visiting a customer won't tell you anything about the work of the purchasing department, but visiting a supplier would.
5	£15 per order	Calculating the cost driver rate, e.g. £15 per order, is easier than identifying cost drivers.
6	Stays the same all the time	If a variable stays the same (constant) it cannot be driving anything.
7	Number of absence days through sickness	All the others measure the amount of work staff are doing.
8	Setting selling prices	Selling prices have to be set irrespective of the method of costing.
9	Activities, costs, cost drivers and cost driver rates	Keep these four stages in mind when tackling an ABC question. Also, think of one department, e.g. purchasing, rather than the company as a whole.
10	Time consuming, expensive and complicated	The costs of running the system may be the equivalent of the savings the system delivers.

Discussion questions

1. ABC is more effective as a method of cost reduction than a method of costing a unit of product.
2. Explain how ABC can be implemented alongside traditional methods of costing.
3. Explain why it is sometimes argued that traditional absorption costing can give the wrong costs to some products. Attempt to illustrate your explanation by using an example of your own.

Answers can be found on the companion web site.

Purchasing Department at Jenkins

The purchasing department at Jenkins, a small, UK based, sports car manufacturer, employs 15 people. The total cost of running the department for a year (including all payroll costs and travel expenses) is £575,000. The company has implemented activity-based costing in the department. The key activities have been identified as follows:

- Raising purchase orders
- Supplier audits
- Checking invoices
- Checking delivery notes
- Product development

The costs of these key activities and the respective cost drivers are as follows:

Activity	Cost	Cost driver
Raising purchase orders	£200,000	Number of purchase orders
Supplier audits	125,000	Number of supplier audits
Checking invoices	50,000	Number of invoices checked
Checking delivery notes	25,000	Number of deliveries
Product development	175,000	Number of new components
Total	£575,000	

The cost driver data is as follows:

Number of purchase orders	10,000
Number of supplier audits	250
Number of invoices checked	500
Number of deliveries	1,000
Number of new components	200

Your task

1. Calculate the cost driver rates in the Jenkins purchasing department.
2. Suggest alternative cost drivers that the company might consider.

Umbriglia SA

Umbriglia SA manufacture three products A, B and C in a large factory near Milan. The factory produced the following data relating to the preceding financial period:

Products	Output units	No. of production runs	Direct labour hours per unit	Machine hours per unit	Materials cost per unit	No. of components per unit
A	250	10	1	1	£10	20
B	250	15	2	1	£20	20
C	250	25	3	1	£30	40
	750	50				

Direct labour costs are £10 per hour and the company's management accountant has identified three overhead activities:

Activity	Cost	Cost driver
Scheduling	£25,000	No. of production runs
Set up	£25,000	No. of production runs
Material handling	£50,000	No. of components

The total number of components is as follows:

	Production	Components per unit	Total components
A	250	20	5,000
B	250	20	5,000
C	250	40	10,000
Total			20,000

Your task

Calculate the unit cost of each product using activity-based costing.

Livor Limited

Livor Limited manufacture four hi-fi products A, B, C and D in a small factory. An analysis of the costs and activities for the previous financial period revealed:

Products	Output units	No. of production runs	Direct labour hours per unit	Machine hours per unit	Materials cost per unit	No. of components per unit
A	25	3	2	2	£30	8
B	50	4	3	4	£45	5
C	200	7	4	2	£50	8
D	250	10	5	4	£75	6

Direct labour costs are £10 per hour. The management accountant has identified three overhead activities, scheduling, set up and materials handling, and has created a general costs category for all other overheads. The costs of activities and cost drivers are as follows:

Activity	Cost	Cost driver
General costs	£16,500	Machine hours
Scheduling	£7,680	No. of production runs
Set up	£3,600	No. of production runs
Materials handling	£7,100	No. of components
Total	£34,880	

Your task

Calculate the cost per unit of each product using the activity-based costing method.

Swedish Precision Components SA: The following year

Sales of two new high technology products (C and D) introduced by the company in the previous financial year have not been as high as anticipated. Sales of the traditional CD player (product A), however, remained strong. Competition from world markets is still intense. For the period just ended, details of production volumes, costs and times were as follows:

Product	Volume	Materials cost per unit	Direct labour hours per unit	Machine hours per unit	Labour costs per unit
A	7,000	£50.00	1.00	1.00	£10.00
B	4,000	£60.00	1.00	1.50	£10.00
C	1,000	£100.00	2.00	4.00	£20.00
D	500	£200.00	5.00	6.00	£50.00

The direct costs of each unit of product are as follows:

	A	B	C	D
Direct labour	10	10	20	50
Direct materials	50	60	100	200
Prime cost	60	70	120	250

An analysis of overheads revealed the following information:

Factory overhead applicable to machine-related activity	£500,000
Setting up production runs	£80,000
Ordering materials	£60,000
Handling materials	£100,000
Upgrades	£120,000
Total	£860,000

Investigation into the production overhead activities for the period identified the following totals:

Product	No. of set ups	No. of material orders	No. of times material handled	No. of upgrades
A	10	10	2	1
B	15	20	2	1
C	15	30	2	5
D	40	60	4	5
	80	120	10	12

Your task

Calculate the cost per unit for products A, B, C and D using the activity-based costing method.

Solutions

Purchasing Department at Jenkins

Activity	Cost	Cost drivers	Cost driver rate
Raising purchase orders	£200,000	10,000	£20 per order
Supplier audits	125,000	250	£500 per audit
Checking invoices	50,000	500	£100 per invoice
Checking delivery	25,000	1,000	£25 per delivery
Product development	175,000	200	£875 per new component

Other possible cost drivers might include:

• The number of components ordered
• The value of invoices
• The number of components
• The number of new products

These are all just suggestions. A detailed investigation would be necessary to ascertain the best cost driver.

Umbriglia SA

The direct costs of each unit of product are as follows:

	A	B	C
Direct labour	10	20	30
Direct materials	10	20	30
Prime cost	20	40	60

Cost driver rates

	Cost	Driver	Cost driver rates
Scheduling	£25,000	50 runs	£500 per production run
Set up	£25,000	50 runs	£500 per production run
Material handling	£50,000	20,000 components	£2.50 per component
	£100,000		

	A	B	C
Scheduling	£5,000	£7,500	£12,500
Set up	5,000	7,500	12,500
Material handling	12,500	12,500	25,000
Total	£22,500	£27,500	£50,000
Units	250	250	250
Overheads per unit	£90	£110	£200

Finally, the costs per unit are as follows:

	A	B	C
Prime costs	£20	£40	£60
Overheads	90	110	200
Total cost	£110	£150	£260

Livor Limited

The prime costs of each unit of output are as follows:

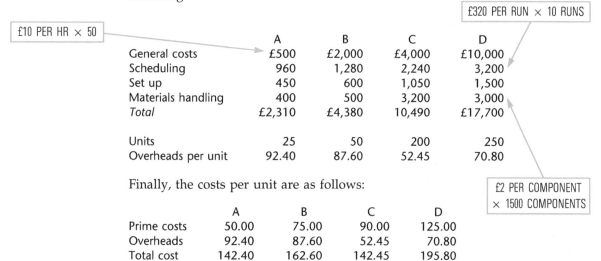

	A	B	C	D
Direct labour	£20	£30	£40	£50
Direct materials	30	45	50	75
Prime cost	£50	£75	£90	£125

`£10 PER HOUR`

The total number of machine hours and components used in the factory can be calculated as follows:

	Volume	Per hour	Total hours	Components
A	25	2.00 hr	50 hrs	200
B	50	4.00 hr	200 hrs	250
C	200	2.00 hr	400 hrs	1600
D	250	4.00 hr	1000 hrs	1500
Total			1650 hrs	3550

`8 × 25 UNITS`
`5 × 25 UNITS`

Cost driver rates

	Cost	Driver	Cost driver rates
General costs	£16,500	1650 hours	£10 per hour
Scheduling	£7,680	24 runs	£320 per production run
Set up	£3,600	24 runs	£150 per production run
Materials handling	£7,100	3550	£2 per component
	£34,880		

Charging the overheads back to the products using the cost driver rates yields the following:

`£320 PER RUN × 10 RUNS`

`£10 PER HR × 50`

	A	B	C	D
General costs	£500	£2,000	£4,000	£10,000
Scheduling	960	1,280	2,240	3,200
Set up	450	600	1,050	1,500
Materials handling	400	500	3,200	3,000
Total	£2,310	£4,380	10,490	£17,700
Units	25	50	200	250
Overheads per unit	92.40	87.60	52.45	70.80

`£2 PER COMPONENT × 1500 COMPONENTS`

Finally, the costs per unit are as follows:

	A	B	C	D
Prime costs	50.00	75.00	90.00	125.00
Overheads	92.40	87.60	52.45	70.80
Total cost	142.40	162.60	142.45	195.80

Swedish Precision Components SA: The following year

Total production overheads for the period came to £860,000. The total number of machine hours worked in the factory:

	Volume	Per hour	Total hours
A	7,000	1.00 hr	7,000 hrs
B	4,000	1.50 hr	6,000 hrs
C	1,000	4.00 hr	4,000 hrs
D	500	6.00 hr	3,000 hrs
Total			20,000 hrs

Cost driver rates

	Cost	Driver	Cost driver rates
Machine-related costs	500,000	20,000 hours	£25 per machine hour
Setting up	80,000	80	£1000 per set up
Materials ordering	60,000	120	£500 per order
Materials handling	100,000	10	£10,000 per movement
Upgrades	120,000	12	£10,000 per upgrade

Charging the overheads back to the products using the cost driver rates yields the following:

	A	B	C	D
Machine hours	175,000	150,000	100,000	75,000
Set up	10,000	15,000	15,000	40,000
Ordering	5,000	10,000	15,000	30,000
Materials handling	20,000	20,000	20,000	40,000
Upgrades	10,000	10,000	50,000	50,000
	220,000	205,000	200,000	235,000
Volume of production	7,000	4,000	1,000	500
Overhead per unit	31.42	51.25	200	470

Finally, the costs per unit are as follows:

	A	B	C	D
Prime costs	60.00	70.00	120.00	250.00
Overheads	31.42	51.25	200.00	470.00
Total cost	91.42	121.25	320.00	720.00

16 International business

International aspects of accounting and finance.

- Exchange rates;
- Currency conversion;
- Groups and joint ventures;
- Raising capital;
- Global capital markets.

Introduction

Importance of the subject

The globalisation of business is now an everyday reality. Capital to fund new businesses, as well as resources, such as materials, equipment and people, increasingly originates abroad. Consumers are based all over the world. Firms ignoring world markets may fail to compete and risk liquidation or hostile takeover.

Structure

Many firms buy goods abroad and sell to the home market, others both buy *and* sell abroad while some invest abroad. All of these activities depend on exchange rates and this is the first topic dealt with here, both in terms of buying and selling and in terms of investing. As well as considering fully owned foreign subsidiaries, this chapter considers partially owned foreign companies, sometimes termed joint ventures. Next, the opportunities for raising finance abroad are reviewed. Relations between all major foreign investment markets are explored and, finally, the concept of a global capital market is explained.

Activities and outcomes

In this chapter you will develop numerical and analytical skills. In addition to working through the in-chapter examples, take time to think carefully about the institutional aspects of international business (the different types of foreign markets). Use the multiple choice questions to check your understanding. By the end of the chapter you will appreciate the extent to which firms are impacted by world markets and volatile exchange rates.

Exchange rates

Consider visiting New York on holiday. The exchange rate between the £ and the $ will affect the cost of the holiday. The relative strength of the £ against the $

changes on a daily basis. Sometimes the £ is strong and sometimes it is weak. When the £ is strong, it may be worth almost $2. When the £ is weak, it may be worth only $1. There is, therefore, potentially a big difference in the purchasing power of the £ against the $:

Strong £   £1 = $2
Weak £   £1 = $1

Another way of expressing this is when the £ is strong, the $ is only worth 50p. But when the £ is weak, the $ is worth £1.

Many tourists visit the Empire State Building. If the cost of buying a family ticket for one day is $5 and the £ is strong, the entrance fee is the equivalent of £2.50. If the £ is weak, however, the entrance fee is equivalent to £5. This principle will apply to everything purchased; therefore, visiting New York when the £ is weak could cost twice as much as when the £ is strong.

Consider it from the point of view of American families. For them it works in reverse. They would much rather visit Great Britain when the £ is weak, because their dollars buy more goods in Britain. A weak £ means a cheaper holiday for American families visiting Britain. The best advice is to travel abroad when your home currency is strong and stay at home when it is weak.

One important sector affected by the £ to $ exchange rate is hotels and tourism. A weak £ is good for London hotels because it attracts American visitors. Similarly a weak $ benefits New York hotels. The financial press sometimes states that a strong currency is best, which is not strictly correct since it depends on the particular business or sector in question.

Consider a British company buying goods from the USA. A strong £ means that the goods are cheaper, whereas a weak £ means that the goods are more expensive:

Strong £   Good for UK firms buying in USA
Weak £   Bad for UK firms buying in USA

British firms selling goods in the USA suffer the opposite effect. A strong £ means that British goods seem expensive to American customers, reducing demand for British goods. A weak £, on the other hand, makes British goods seem cheaper to American customers, so demand for British goods increases:

Strong £   Bad for UK firms selling in USA
Weak £   Good for UK firms selling in USA

British car manufacturers have traditionally found a ready market in America. These firms prefer a weak £, because it increases demand for their products in the USA. Alternatively, an example of a British firm buying in America could be a wine, beer and spirits importer, purchasing American bottled beer, Bourbon whisky and Californian wine. This business prefers a strong £, because the goods bought in America will be cheaper. Whether a firm is *buying* or *selling* abroad and its *geographical base* will determine whether a strong or weak currency is beneficial to that company.

Foreign currency conversion

When converting foreign currency values into pounds, state the rate of exchange from the perspective of the value of the pound, e.g. £1 = $2 or £1 = €1.50. On this basis the conversion of foreign currency into pounds is straightforward – simply divide the foreign currency amount by the exchange rate. Consider a British company buying an engine from Germany. This might cost €36,000. If the exchange rate is £1 = €1.50, the conversion is as follows:

$$€36,000/1.50 = £24,000$$

So the engine will cost £24,000 at this exchange rate. If the pound (£) weakened against the euro (€), the exchange rate might change to £1 = €1.20. This would make the engine more expensive:

$$€36,000/1.20 = £30,000$$

The fall in the value of the pound against the euro has made it more expensive to buy goods in Germany.

If the British company is selling goods to Germany and the potential customers have offered €200,000 for the goods, on the original exchange rate the conversion is as follows:

$$€200,000/1.50 = £133,333$$

If the pound weakened against the euro, the conversion would be as follows:

$$€200,000/1.20 = £166,666$$

The British company benefits from the weakening of the pound against the euro. The euros it receives from the sales are worth more. Most companies selling abroad, however, insist on receiving payment in their domestic currency because this removes the exchange rate uncertainty. British companies selling in Germany will insist on payment in £ sterling.

One recurring problem is all exchange rates can be stated in two ways. For instance, the fact that £1 is worth so many $'s can be reversed to say that $1 is worth so many £'s:

$$£1 = $2$$

is the same as

$$$1 = 50p$$

and

$$£1 = €1.50$$

is the same as

$$€1 = £0.666$$

Always express the pound first and to convert an exchange rate not given from the perspective of the pound, multiply both sides of the rate by a figure that yields £1. For example, if

$$€1 = £1.50$$

multiply both sides by 0.66666 to yield

$$€0.666 = £1$$

which is the same as

$$£1 = €0.666$$

Converting the P&L account (income statement)

Many companies now make investments in foreign countries in order to gain access to local markets or manufacture goods more cheaply. These investments often take the form of a subsidiary company, wholly owned by the investor. This leads to a group structure as follows:

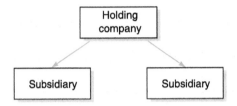

Naturally, subsidiaries transact business in local currency, e.g. an Australian subsidiary conducts business in Australian dollars. As a result, subsidiaries produce P&L accounts and balance sheets in local currency. These then have to be converted into the currency of the holding company. If the holding company is based in Britain, subsidiary P&L accounts have to be translated into £ sterling. If the holding company is based in Germany, subsidiary P&L accounts have to be translated into euros.

Different countries have different terminology and formats for presenting the P&L account, which in many countries is termed the 'income statement'. For instance, 'sales' can be referred to as 'turnover' or 'operating revenue', 'cost of sales' can be referred to as 'operating expenses' and 'profit' may be referred to as 'income'. These are just terminological differences – the concepts of profits, sales and cost of sales are exactly the same.

Consider this P&L account of an American firm that is a subsidiary of a British holding company:

Statement of Income
Year Ended December 2004 ($m)

Operating revenue	10.4
Cost of goods sold	6.2
Gross profit	4.2
General expenses	1.1
Operating income	3.1

This American-style P&L account is termed 'income statement'. The exchange rate between £ and $ changes every day, so an average figure is calculated to give a fair reflection of the movements over the year. If the average exchange rate over the year was £1 = $2, the income statement can be converted as follows:

	Dollars ($m)	Exchange rate	Sterling (£m)
Operating revenue	10.4	2	5.20
Cost of goods sold	6.2	2	3.10
Gross profit	4.2	2	2.10
General expenses	1.1	2	0.55
Operating income	3.1	2	1.55

The profit earned by this American firm is the equivalent of £1.55 million on a turnover of £5.20 million.

Next take the example of subsidiary operations in Europe:

Income Statement (€m)

Turnover	269.4
Cost of sales	151.8
Gross income	117.6
Selling expenses	44.6
Administrative expenses	27.4
Research and development	11.8
Operating income	33.8

Say the average exchange rate during the year was £1 = €1.50:

	Euros (€m)	Exchange rate	Sterling (£m)
Turnover	269.4	1.50	179.60
Less: cost of sales	151.8	1.50	101.20
Gross income	117.6	1.50	78.40
Less: selling expenses	44.6	1.50	29.73
Less: administrative expenses	27.4	1.50	18.27
Less: research and development	11.8	1.50	7.87
Operating income	33.8	1.50	22.53

The profit earned by this European firm is the equivalent of £22.53 million on a turnover of £179.60 million. The net profit % is 12.50% [(£22.53/£179.60) × 100].

The conversion of the balance sheet (sometimes referred to as the 'position statement') is the same, but for one exception. The rate of exchange for the balance sheet must be the one prevailing on the last day of the financial year, because the balance sheet reflects the assets and liabilities at that point in time. The balance sheet as at 31st December 2003 must be translated at the exchange rate prevailing on that day. The P&L account and balance sheet may, therefore, be converted at different rates of exchange because the P&L account is converted at an average rate for the financial year, while the balance sheet is converted at the exchange rate on the closing day of the financial year. In summary:

P&L	Converted at the average rate
Balance sheet	Converted at the closing rate

Usually these two rates of exchange are different. Figure 16.1 plots the exchange rate between US dollar and £ sterling over 52 weeks. The exchange rate is volatile and the average exchange rate over the year is higher than the closing rate.

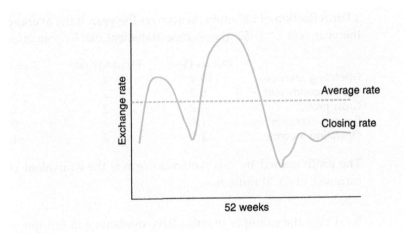

Figure 16.1 £ to $ exchange rate

Foreign currency conversion in action

Consider the situation outlined below.

Bird Watch Tobago

Bird Watch International are a medium-sized privately owned limited company which operate bird watching holidays all over the world. The group consists of a holding company Bird Watch Holdings Limited and four subsidiaries – Bird Watch Asia, Bird Watch Arctic, Bird Watch Europe and Bird Watch Tobago:

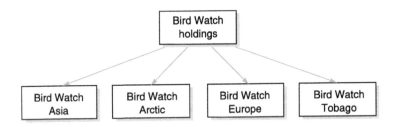

Subsidiaries are encouraged to operate autonomously. The holding company does not interfere with local managers. Rather than operate a budgeting system, the holding companies set target rates of return on capital employed (ROCE). At the moment, the target ROCE is 20%.

Trinidad and Tobago enjoys one of the most stable economies in the Caribbean. Oil, gas and tourism are the leading sectors. Unlike many Caribbean islands, Tobago is unspoilt. Bird Watch Tobago has its headquarters in attractive Scarborough. Although the US dollar is widely accepted in Trinidad and Tobago, the company keeps its accounting records in the Trinidad and Tobago dollar (TT$).

Bird Watch Tobago has just faxed the following results to the Group Accounting Department:

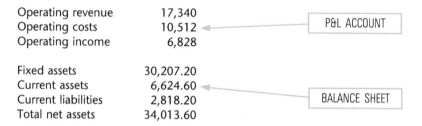

Bird Watch Tobago

Summarised Income and Position Statement
Year Ending 31st December 2004 (TT$ 000's)

Operating revenue	17,340	
Operating costs	10,512	P&L ACCOUNT
Operating income	6,828	

Fixed assets	30,207.20	
Current assets	6,624.60	
Current liabilities	2,818.20	BALANCE SHEET
Total net assets	34,013.60	

The Group Accounting Department monitors exchange rates carefully. The average exchange rate during the year was £1 = TT$12. The year end exchange rate was £1 = TT$12.20. The level of the TT$ is influenced by the world price of oil.

The income statement should be converted as follows:

	TT$000's	Average exchange rate	£000's
Operating revenue	17,340	12	1,445
Operating costs	10,512	12	876
Operating income	6,828	12	569

The position statement should be converted as follows:

	TT$000's	Year end exchange rate	£000's
Fixed assets	30,207.2	12.2	2,476
Current assets	6,624.6	12.2	543
Current liabilities	2,818.2	12.2	231
Total net assets	34,013.6	12.2	2,788

The rate of return on capital is:

Operating income (£000's)	569
Total net assets (£000's)	2788
Rate of return on capital	20.41%

Bird Watch Tobago is earning more than the required 20% return on capital.

Consider the possibility that the year end exchange rate might be lower than the average rate – for example:

| Average exchange rate | £1 = TT$12 |
| Year end exchange rate | £1 = TT$11.9 |

Showing your workings, recalculate the rate of return on capital employed:

	TT$000's	Year end exchange rate	£000's
Fixed assets	30,207.2		
Current assets	6,624.6		
Current liabilities	2,818.2		
Total net assets	34,013.6		

Operating income (£000's)	569
Total net assets (£000's)	
Rate of return on capital	

The solution is 19.9%, which is lower than the target ROCE.

Group accounts and joint ventures (associates)

When a holding company has a number of subsidiaries, the P&L accounts of all the subsidiaries are added together to form what is termed the 'consolidated' or group P&L account (see Chapter 11). The purpose of a consolidated P&L account is to show the results of the group as a whole, rather than the individual subsidiaries. Many large companies seek to establish a separate subsidiary company in each country they operate in, e.g. a subsidiary company in USA, Australia, South Africa, Denmark, etc. This results in a group with the following structure:

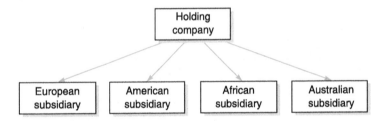

Consider the results below, referring to a company based in the USA with operating subsidiaries all over the world:

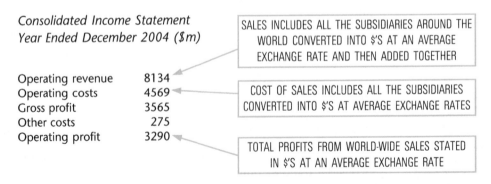

Consolidated Income Statement
Year Ended December 2004 ($m)

Operating revenue	8134
Operating costs	4569
Gross profit	3565
Other costs	275
Operating profit	3290

SALES INCLUDES ALL THE SUBSIDIARIES AROUND THE WORLD CONVERTED INTO $'S AT AN AVERAGE EXCHANGE RATE AND THEN ADDED TOGETHER

COST OF SALES INCLUDES ALL THE SUBSIDIARIES CONVERTED INTO $'S AT AVERAGE EXCHANGE RATES

TOTAL PROFITS FROM WORLD-WIDE SALES STATED IN $'S AT AN AVERAGE EXCHANGE RATE

Operating revenue includes all the companies in the group translated into $'s at an average exchange rate. Similarly, operating costs and operating profits include all the subsidiaries in the group. Changes in exchange rates and changes in the composition of the group (buying another subsidiary), therefore, affect the consolidated figures.

Most holding companies own 100% of the shares in their subsidiaries, to prevent competitors becoming involved. Only 51% of the shares in a subsidiary, however, are necessary to control it. This is because 51% is sufficient to pass any resolution at the AGM, e.g. to appoint a new Board of Directors. If the holding company owns at least 51% of the shares, the full value of the subsidiary's P&L account is included in the consolidated P&L account. The portion of the profit that is owned by another party is termed the 'minority interest'.

In some countries, laws, or accepted business practice, dictate that foreign investors do not have a controlling interest. As a result, many foreign investments are not fully controlled because only a minority of shares is held. These are termed associated companies or joint ventures. The difference between a subsidiary and an associated company is that a subsidiary is controlled (at least 51% of the shares are owned) and an associate is not controlled (less than 51% of the shares are owned). As a result, many holding companies have a mixture of subsidiaries and associates (joint ventures):

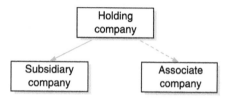

The distinction between the two has important accounting implications. Associated companies are not included in the consolidated sales and consolidated cost of sales. Rather, the holding company's share of the associated company's profits is included at the foot of the consolidated P&L account. If a holding company has a 25% share in an associated company, which has made a £1,000,000 profit, only £250,000 profit will be shown at the foot of the consolidated P&L account. The value of the company's investment, shown on the balance sheet, would also increase by £250,000. This is sometimes termed 'equity accounting'.

Consider the results of this group, which has a mixture of subsidiaries and associates:

Consolidated Income Statement
Year Ended December 2004 ($m)

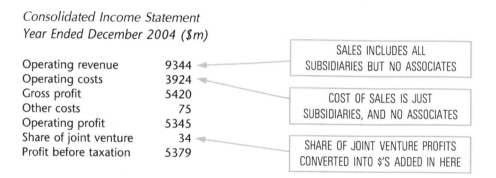

Operating revenue	9344	SALES INCLUDES ALL SUBSIDIARIES BUT NO ASSOCIATES
Operating costs	3924	
Gross profit	5420	COST OF SALES IS JUST SUBSIDIARIES, AND NO ASSOCIATES
Other costs	75	
Operating profit	5345	
Share of joint venture	34	SHARE OF JOINT VENTURE PROFITS CONVERTED INTO $'S ADDED IN HERE
Profit before taxation	5379	

The operating revenue includes all the subsidiaries but none of the associates. The share of the associate's profit is shown lower down next to the heading 'Share of joint venture'.

In summary so far, when considering consolidated P&L accounts, remember that:

- Only subsidiaries are included in group sales and cost of sales.
- Subsidiaries' P&L accounts have been translated using the average exchange rate.
- Associates are not included in sales and cost of sales, but are shown separately.

Consider a company with one subsidiary, operating in the USA, and one joint venture operating in Portugal (all in millions):

	Holding company (£)	Subsidiary 100% owned ($)	Associate 25% owned (€)
Turnover	1000	550	230
Less: cost of sales	300	120	70
Gross profit	700	430	160
Less: admin. expenses	100	27	30
Operating profit	600	403	130
Less: interest	50	25	10
Profit before taxation	550	378	120
Average exchange rate		1.55	1.67

The first step is currency conversion:

	Subsidiary (£)	Associate (£)
Turnover	355	138
Less: cost of sales	77	42
Gross profit	278	96
Less: admin. expenses	18	18
Operating profit	260	78
Less: interest	16	6
Profit before taxation	244	72

The second step is calculating the share of associate's profits:

25% of £72,000   £18,000

The third step is consolidation:

	2004	Workings
Turnover	1355	1000 + 355
Less: cost of sales	377	300 + 77
Gross profit	978	
Less: admin. & distribution expenses	118	100 + 18
Operating profit	860	
Less: interest payable	66	50 + 16
Add: share of joint venture's profit	18	25% of £72
Profit before taxation	812	

The group's profits before taxation (PBT) total £812 million from a turnover of £1355 million.

Raising finance globally

Increasingly firms are looking around the globe for the best finance deals, searching for low interest rates, moderate charges and quick and easy access to funds. Many European firms have been attracted to the USA to raise capital. The New York Stock Exchange offers access to the largest sums, and although highly regulated, is well established and relatively stable. Alternatively, NASDAQ imposes fewer rules and regulations, offering smaller sums quicker and cheaper.

In order to get the best finance deal, many companies issue bonds in foreign markets. Corporate bonds (see Chapter 12) are a means of raising large amounts of capital and differ from shares in as much as they pay the holder fixed interest unaffected by profit levels. Corporate bonds are traded in a similar way to shares and offer the investor a lower risk. For example, British companies can sell bonds in the USA. This has led to the emergence of what is termed the Euromarket. A bond issued in a country other than the country that issues the currency in which it is denominated is termed a Eurobond. For instance, a Canadian company issues bonds denominated in Canadian dollars in Europe.

The Euromarket is less regulated, cheaper and more flexible than traditional markets. As a result, it offers a better deal to firms trying to raise substantial sums. Just like shares and corporate bonds, a secondary market in Eurobonds exists. The fact that shares and bonds can be easily sold is essential to the success of new issues. If there were no secondary market for bonds, investors would be much less likely to buy them in the first place.

> The amount of money raised through the Euromarket is huge, probably in excess of $10,000,000,000,000 (ten trillion dollars).

Holding companies operating through subsidiaries also have the option of raising finance in the localities in which the subsidiaries trade. This can have the advantage of reducing the impact of exchange rate volatility. Consider a company trading in the USA, which is a subsidiary of a UK holding company. The balance sheet is set out below:

Summary Position Statement
Subsidiary Company

	$000's
Fixed assets	
Tangible	121,445
Investments	398,538
	519,983
Current assets	
Stock	158,967
Debtors	34,678
Cash	2,345
	195,990
Total assets	715,973

Exchange rates were expected to be in the region of £1 = $1.6. Imagine there was an unexpected strengthening of the value of the £ against the $, so that £1 = $2. For a company buying goods in the USA this is beneficial. The situation is different, however, for companies that already have investments in the USA. The strengthening of the £ and the weakening of the $ has the impact of reducing the value of the total net assets of the American-based subsidiary – see below:

Balance sheet conversion (000's)

Total assets	Exchange rate	£	
$715,973	1.60	447,483	AN £89,497 REDUCTION IN THE VALUE OF FOREIGN HELD ASSETS
$715,973	2.00	357,986	

The reduction in the value of the assets will feed through to the consolidated accounts. This may be interpreted by the stock markets as a form of exchange rate loss, which may, in turn, reduce the share price.

The impact of exchange rate changes, described above, is part of the additional risk of investing abroad. Borrowing in the local currency, however, can mitigate this effect. Consider the possibility that borrowing $500,000,000 in the USA had financed the assets of the American subsidiary. The position statement would then have the following form:

	$000's
Fixed assets	
Tangible	121,445
Investments	398,538
	519,983
Current assets	
Stock	158,967
Debtors	34,678
Cash	2,345
	195,990
Less: loans	500,000
Total net assets	215,973

Total net assets	Exchange rate	£	
$215,973	1.60	134,983	A £26,997 REDUCTION IN THE VALUE OF FIXED ASSETS
$215,973	2.00	107,986	

The impact of exchange rate movements is greatly reduced by borrowing in the local currency. Local financing can reduce the risks associated with foreign investment.

Another method of raising the finances for a foreign venture is linking up with a local partner(s) to form a joint venture. For example, an American firm, in partnership with a Chinese company and the Chinese government, may undertake the development of a manufacturing facility in China. Each of the three parties may take 33% of the shares. In addition to spreading the burden of financing, this has other advantages. Having government as a partner makes it easier to navigate through local regulations, laws and customs. Local partners mean that an understanding of local culture is embedded in the venture. The disadvantages are that the investor does not have control, negotiations with partners can be protracted, profits have to be shared and indigenous culture may not place a high priority on profit.

> Not all countries allow a free flow of investment, e.g. the USA limits foreigners to a maximum 25% ownership of US television and radio stations.

Global capital markets

Financial markets around the world compete to supply capital in the form of both shares and bonds of a variety of different types. Banks and venture capitalists also compete in different segments of the same market. Money is easily moved around the world and if a higher return, in terms of dividends or interest rates, is available in, say, Germany, large sums of money can quickly flow into Germany to take advantage (Figure 16.2).

To an increasing extent there is a global market for capital consisting of a variety of institutions such as the New York Stock Exchange, Euromarkets, foreign currency markets, etc. Although these institutions may be fragmented, the demands and supplies driving the market are global. One implication of this is the close relationship between world stock markets and currency markets. Across the world, stock markets show a tendency to move together. Increases on Wall Street are followed by increases in most other markets. J. Madura (International Financial Management, West, 1995, p. 490) calculated that the correlation between major stock markets is in excess of 0.50. This can be interpreted to mean that more than half the movements in the markets were closely related and less than half the movements related to country-specific factors.

Globalisation of capital markets has important implications for the modern manager. Variables such as interest rates, exchange rates and taxation have direct implications for company earnings. Increases in interest rates tend to reduce company profits. Changes in exchange rates also affect company profits by

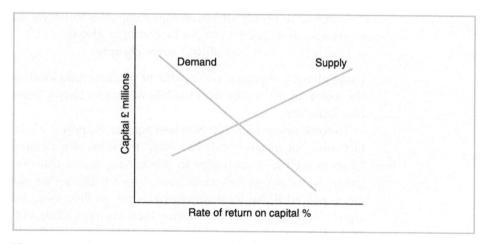

Figure 16.2 Demand and supply of capital

changing the cost of imported goods. Global capital markets increasingly determine these key variables. The machinations of these markets are complex. Consider the implications of an increase in interest rates in the USA. The first effect is to make shares and bonds seem comparatively less attractive because higher returns are available in cash deposits. The second effect will be to reduce the profits of firms that have some form of borrowing. As a result of an increase in US interest rates, share prices may tend to fall. This will in turn impact all other stock markets around the world.

Simultaneously, funds will flow into the USA to take advantage of higher interest rates. The value of the dollar will rise compared to all other currencies. A higher dollar will negatively affect firms buying in the USA, while American-based firms buying abroad will be positively affected. These firms will, in turn, start to rethink their investment decisions. The increase in the value of the $ may prompt governments around the world to reconsider their own interest rates, exchange rates and taxation.

These complex chains of events can be triggered by a number of different types of activities, such as:

- Increases in dividends
- Increases in company profits
- Increases in inflation
- Changes in taxation rates
- Currency speculation
- Trade cycle

The world financial system is constantly adjusting to changes in profits, dividends, taxation and interest rates in addition to long-term factors such as the trade cycle and inflation. This results in constant volatility in share prices, exchange rates and interest rates. Managing the risk posed by these changes is an important part of the modern management process.

Many small local businesses, which do not import or export or invest abroad, take the view that they are immune to global changes. This is not correct because:

- All businesses are affected by interest rates;
- Customers further down the supply chain may trade or invest abroad;
- Increases in profits attract foreign companies into local markets;
- Mergers and acquisitions are increasingly global;
- Competitors may buy abroad more cheaply.

Large global companies are capable of reaching into local markets anywhere in the world. In many countries the loss of smaller shops, farms and restaurants is now lamented.

To some extent there is a backlash against the power of global capital markets. In France, for instance, this has taken the form of a Campaign for Real French Food, as well as a campaign to prevent the encroachment of the English language. Some anti-globalisation protestors are angry that global capital markets are so powerful that local communities are, in their view, now powerless. They argue global capital markets destroy local business, skills and culture. They point to the fact that the most advanced countries keep on developing, while poorer countries remain stagnant.

Conclusions

Exchange rate changes make international business more risky than trading within borders. Many firms make use of forward exchange rate contracts to eliminate, or at least reduce, this type of risk. These contracts take the form of an agreement to sell or buy foreign exchange at a future date at a fixed rate. Although foreign exchange rates may fluctuate, the forward contract provides a fixed basis on which to plan foreign trade.

There are many risks involved in foreign ventures. Firms increasingly take the view, however, that ignoring globalisation is a more risky strategy than embracing it. One of the most fascinating aspects of international business, not considered here, is culture. In particular, the difference between the individualist business culture characteristic of the USA and the more team or social orientated cultures elsewhere in the world. One issue you might consider for a dissertation or a 'term paper' is the extent to which accounting-based approaches to management, e.g. budgeting, are linked to individualistic approaches to business.

Another subject you could investigate is the impact of global capital markets in your local area. This could take the form of measuring the level of investment from global sources compared to local. Alternatively, you could investigate the impact of global investment on local business, culture and society and thereby determine if the concerns of anti-capitalist protestors are well founded.

Multiple choice questions

Tick the box next to your answer.

1. If the value of the £ falls in comparison to the $, this is
   - [ ] Beneficial to UK firms selling in the USA
   - [ ] Beneficial to UK firms selling in the UK
   - [ ] Beneficial to UK firms buying in the UK
   - [ ] Beneficial to UK firms buying in the USA
   - [ ] Detrimental to all UK firms

2. If £1 = $2, $1,000,000 is equivalent to?
   - [ ] $2,000,000
   - [ ] £2,000,000
   - [ ] £1,000,000
   - [ ] $1,000,000
   - [ ] £500,000

3. If £1 = $1.5, what is $1 worth?
   - [ ] 75p
   - [ ] 120 cents
   - [ ] 66p
   - [ ] 50p
   - [ ] £1.20

4. An 'income statement' is
   - [ ] A bank statement
   - [ ] A balance sheet
   - [ ] A cash flow
   - [ ] A P&L account
   - [ ] A pension

5. Which of these encourages UK tourists to go to the USA?
   - [ ] Weak euro
   - [ ] High interest rates in UK
   - [ ] Weak $ compared to £
   - [ ] Weak £ compared to $
   - [ ] High airport tax

6. A subsidiary company has earned profits of $13,567,891 and the average exchange rate during the year is £1 = $1.66. In £ terms the profit is?
   - [ ] $13,567,891
   - [ ] £6,783,945
   - [ ] £8,173,428
   - [ ] £13,567,891
   - [ ] $8,173,428

7. What percentage of shares is needed to control a company?
   - [ ] 100%
   - [ ] 99%
   - [ ] 51%
   - [ ] 50%
   - [ ] 25%

8. Why is the average rate of exchange used to translate the foreign subsidiary P&L account, rather than the closing rate?
   - [ ] P&L account reflects the assets at the end of the year
   - [ ] Closing rate of exchange reflects movements during the year
   - [ ] Average rate reflects movements during the year
   - [ ] Profit is all earned at the end of the year
   - [ ] The closing rate is the same as the average rate

9. Which of the following is *not* an advantage of a joint venture?
   - [ ] Accesses local knowledge and skills
   - [ ] Holding company doesn't have to provide all the capital
   - [ ] Easier to put local management in place
   - [ ] Spreads the risk
   - [ ] Holding company owns 100% of the shares

10. An unexpected increase in interest rates in the USA
   - [ ] Reduces the value of the $ against the £
   - [ ] Increases company profits in the USA
   - [ ] Has no effect on stock markets
   - [ ] Increases the value of the $
   - [ ] Increases the value of fixed interest corporate bonds in the USA

Multiple choice answers

	Correct answer	Comment
1	Beneficial to UK firms selling in the USA	UK goods seem cheaper to consumers in the USA.
2	£500,000	$1,000,000 *divided by* 2.
3	66p	£1 *divided by* 1.50 = 0.666666 rec. (66p or £0.66).
4	A P&L account	Income statement is a term commonly used in the USA.
5	Weak $ compared to the £	The buying power of the £ is greater in the USA.
6	£8,173,428	£13,567,891 *divided by* 1.66.
7	51%	But there are good reasons for holding 100% of the shares in a subsidiary, e.g. to prevent competitors gaining shares.
8	Average rate reflects movements during the year	The balance sheet, on the other hand, reflects the position on the final day of the year, so the closing rate is the most appropriate. It is possible that the average and the closing rate are the same, but very unlikely.
9	Holding company owns 100% of the shares	The essence of a joint venture is that ownership and control is shared between partners.
10	Increases the value of the $	This is because money will be attracted into the USA, increasing the demand for the US$.

Discussion questions

1. Does foreign investment increase or decrease risk?
2. A quote from an entrepreneur: 'My business does not buy abroad or sell abroad. International factors therefore have no impact whatsoever on my business.' Is this correct?

These issues are further discussed in the companion web site.

Canadian Worldwide Drinks Company

A UK company is considering launching a takeover of a Canadian-based drinks company. The strategy is to use the Canadian company as a base for moving into the US market which has 250 million consumers.

Canadian Worldwide Drinks Company

Consolidated Income Statement (C$m)

	Notes	2004	2003
Net operating revenue	1	22,000	19,000
Less: cost of goods sold		7,900	6,100
Gross profit		14,100	12,900
Selling admin. & general expenses	2	5,600	5,350
Operating income		8,500	7,550
Interest paid	3	250	190
Equity income from associates	4	200	220
Profit before taxation		8,450	7,580
Taxation	5	2,000	1,900
Profit after taxation		6,450	5,680

The average exchange rates were:

2004   £1 = C$2
2003   £1 = C$2.2

Your task

1. Convert the P&L account using the respective average exchange rates.
2. Calculate the percentage increase in sales, gross profit and profit after taxation (PAT).

Wisdom of the Vine

Wisdom of the Vine is an Israeli-based, medium-sized, winemaking company. The company has been established for 20 years, during which time it has grown slowly. The company is family controlled and at the moment a new generation are emerging, eager to develop the business into different areas. The company makes large quantities of wine for the home market. If more grapes could be acquired, additional wine could be produced at little extra cost. This is because equipment, know how and labour are already paid for. These are termed 'fixed costs'.

The company, which has no foreign subsidiaries or associates, is considering starting to buy and sell abroad. It has been offered a consignment of grapes from southern Crete for 120,000 euros. The company believes it may be able to sell the extra wine manufactured from these grapes to the USA for $500,000. The company knows the potential customer will want to pay them in dollars because of the difficulty of getting an adequate quantity of shekels. The shekel is a volatile currency because of the continued instability in the region. The relevant exchange rates are 1 shekel = 0.25 euros = 0.20 US dollars.

Your task

Translate the deal into shekels and describe the type of risk involved in such transactions. If possible, suggest ways of minimising risk.

Worldwide Franchise Development

Worldwide Franchise Development has one subsidiary (100% owned) and one associated company (25% owned). The latest results, in their local currencies, are as follows:

	Holding company £000's	Subsidiary $000's	Joint venture €000's
Net operating revenue	10,000	15,000	16,320
Less: cost of goods sold	4,000	6,000	8,000
Gross profit	6,000	9,000	8,320
Selling admin. & general expenses	3,500	5,250	1,600
Operating income	2,500	3,750	6,720
Interest paid	0	750	320
Profit before taxation	2,500	3,000	6,400
Exchange rate		1.50	1.60

Your task

1. Using a three-step technique (translate, share of profits, consolidate) prepare the group accounts.
2. Write a paragraph which explains why the subsidiary's results are added to the holding company's but the associate's results are not.

Global Shop Window

Global Shop Window has one subsidiary (100% owned) and one associated company (20% owned). The latest results, in their local currencies, are as follows:

	Holding company £m	Subsidiary $m	Joint venture €m
Net operating revenue	1000	1925	8250
Less: cost of goods sold	400	875	3750
Gross profit	600	1050	4500
Selling admin. & general expenses	250	875	1200
Operating income	350	175	3300
Interest paid	25	44	300
Profit before taxation	325	131	3000
Average exchange rate £1 =		1.75	1.50

1. Using a three-step technique (translate, share of profits, consolidate) prepare the group accounts.
2. Calculate the percentage change in the consolidated PBT if the average exchange rate was £1 = $1.25.

Group Accounting Department

Company A has three subsidiaries B, C and D, which are all 100% owned. The latest subsidiary results have just arrived in the Group Accounting Department as follows (all in £m):

	Holding company A	Subsidiary B	Subsidiary C	Subsidiary D
Sales	£100	£200	£300	£400
Cost of sales	50	160	200	350
Gross profit	50	40	100	50

Your task

1. Calculate the consolidated sales, cost of sales and gross profit.
2. Recalculate the consolidated sales and gross profit on the basis that company B is only 51% owned.
3. Recalculate the consolidated sales and gross profit on the basis that company B is only 49% owned.
4. Subsidiary B is based in the USA and trades in US dollars. The figures above have already been converted on the basis of £1 = $2. What would the impact be on the consolidated accounts of a rise in the value of the $ against the £ from £1 = $2 to £1 = $1.6 (assume company B is 100% owned)?

Solutions

Canadian Worldwide Drinks Company

	2004 C$m	Exchange £1 = C$2	£m
Net operating revenue	22,000	2	11,000
Less: cost of goods sold	7,900	2	3,950
Gross profit	14,100	2	7,050
Selling admin. & general expenses	5,600	2	2,800
Operating income	8,500	2	4,250
Interest paid	250	2	125
Equity income from associates	200	2	100
Profit before taxation	8,450	2	4,225
Taxation	2,000	2	1,000
Profit after taxation	6,450	2	3,225

	2003 C$m	Exchange £1 = C$2.2	£m
Net operating revenue	19,000	2.2	8,636
Less: cost of goods sold	6,100	2.2	2,773
Gross profit	12,900	2.2	5,863
Selling admin. & general expenses	5,350	2.2	2,432
Operating income	7,550	2.2	3,431
Interest paid	190	2.2	86
Equity income from associates	220	2.2	100
Profit before taxation	7,580	2.2	3,445
Taxation	1,900	2.2	864
Profit after taxation	5,680	2.2	2,581

	2004 £m	2003 £m	%
Net operating revenue	11,000	8,636	27%
Less: cost of goods sold	3,950	2,773	42%
Gross profit	7,050	5,863	20%
Selling admin. & general expenses	2,800	2,432	15%
Operating income	4,250	3,431	24%
Interest paid	125	86	45%
Equity income from associates	100	100	0%
Profit before taxation	4,225	3,445	22%
Taxation	1,000	864	16%
Profit after taxation	3,225	2,581	25%

If the exchange rate had remained stable at £1 = C$2.2, the C$6450m PAT would translate into £2932m PAT. This is a 9% fall compared to the £3225m PAT stated above. The movements in exchange rate have a considerable impact on the translation of the company's results. This type of risk should be factored into the UK company's strategic thinking.

Wisdom of the Vine

In terms of shekels, the proposed deals translate as follows:

	Foreign currency	Exchange rate	Shekels
Sales	$500,000	0.20	2,500,000
Purchases	€120,000	0.25	480,000

The grapes are purchased for the equivalent of 480,000 shekels and generate sales equivalent to 2,500,000 shekels. This generates a profit of more than 2,000,000 shekels. There are, however, other costs that need to be taken into consideration. The costs of production may be fixed but the costs of transportation have not been allowed for. This includes the costs of transporting grapes from Crete to Israel and the costs of transporting wine from Israel to the USA. There may be other costs the company has not allowed for, e.g. insurance and import or export duty.

The benefit of establishing links with new suppliers and new customers will accrue in the long term. Measuring the profit on this arrangement is a narrow and short-term view of the matter. New supplier relationships could open up the possibility of new types of wine. The USA is a market of 250 million consumers and, therefore, represents a huge opportunity for the business. The company is perhaps overlooking the opportunity to develop a market within the European Union, which is a similar size to the USA market but more conveniently located.

One strategy the company could pursue is the acquisition of an established wine trading or winemaking company in Greece. This would give ready access to the whole EU market. The money for such a venture could be raised in euros, eliminating some of the exchange rate exposure. The company would then be in a good position to benefit from the expansion of the EU and the widening of the euro zone. Importantly, these proposed developments would reduce the company's dependence on the Israeli market, which is small compared to the EU and USA. The risk to the company of developing more international contacts may be *less* than the risk of remaining focused on Israel.

Worldwide Franchise Development

Step one: conversion

	Subsidiary	Associate
Net operating revenue	£10,000	£10,200
Less: cost of goods sold	4,000	5,000
Gross profit	6,000	5,200
Selling admin. & general expenses	3,500	1,000
Operating income	2,500	4,200
Interest paid	500	200
Equity income from associates	NA	NA
Profit before taxation	£2,000	£4,000

Step two: share of associated company profits
25% of £4000 = £1,000.

Step three: consolidation
Consolidated Income Statement (£000's)

	2004	*Workings*
Net operating revenue	20,000	10,000 + 10,000
Less: cost of goods sold	8,000	4000 + 4000
Gross profit	12,000	6000 + 6000
Selling admin. & general expenses	7,000	3500 + 3500
Operating income	5,000	2500 + 2500
Interest paid	500	0 + 500
Equity income from associates	1,000	See step 2
Profit before taxation	5,500	

The whole group has earned a profit before taxation of £5,500,000 including £1,000,000 share of associated company profits. The total group turnover is £20,000,000. All foreign subsidiary results have been converted at average exchange rates.

The subsidiary is controlled by the holding company while the associate is not. As a result, the subsidiary's results are added to the holding company's, while the associate's are not. Only the holding company's share of the associate's profits (25%) is included in the consolidated figures.

Global Shop Window

Step one: conversion

Consolidated Income Statement (£m)

	Subsidiary	Associate
Net operating revenue	£1100	£5500
Less: cost of goods sold	500	2500
Gross profit	600	3000
Selling admin. & general expenses	500	800
Operating income	100	2200
Interest paid	25	200
Profit before taxation	£75	£2000

Step two: share of associated company profits

20% of £2000 = £400.

Step three: consolidation

Consolidated Income Statement (£m)

	2004	*Workings*
Net operating revenue	2100	1000 + 1100
Less: cost of goods sold	900	400 + 500
Gross profit	1200	600 + 600
Selling admin. & general expenses	750	250 + 500
Operating income	450	350 + 100
Interest paid	50	25 + 25
Equity income from associates	400	See step 2
Profit before taxation	800	

The associated company has contributed more profit (£400m) than the subsidiary (£75m), or in fact the holding company (£325m). This is slightly worrying because the holding company does not control the associated company, e.g. it does not control its dividend policy or the composition of the Board of Directors.

Group Accounting Department

Part 1: consolidated accounts (£m)

Sales	£1000
Cost of sales	760
Gross profit	240

The four companies comprise a group.

Part 2: consolidated accounts (£m)

Sales	£1000
Cost of sales	760
Gross profit	240

Company B is still a subsidiary so it is fully consolidated despite the fact it is only 51% owned.

Part 3: consolidated accounts (£m)

Sales   £800
Cost of sales 600
Gross profit   200

Company B is now an associate or joint venture because it is 49% owned; therefore, it is not consolidated.

Part 4: consolidated accounts (£m)

Sales   £1050
Cost of sales 800
Gross profit   250

The original results in dollars from company B must have been as follows:

	$	£1 = $1.6	£
Sales	400	1.6	250
Cost of sales	320	1.6	200
Gross profit	80	1.6	50

When converted at the new exchange rate the gross profit is greater. The consolidated gross profit has risen to £250m.

In summary, changes in the composition of the group and changes in exchange rates impact the consolidated gross profit.

17 e-Business

This chapter explores financial aspects of e-business.

- Raising finance for e-business;
- Financial analysis of e-business;
- Start up costs;
- Financial and non-financial ratios;
- Breakeven analysis;
- Strategic analysis of e-business.

Introduction

Importance of the subject

Since 1995 e-business has been an exciting area of innovation and development. Internet-based companies have been formed selling books, DVDs, flights, etc. and established businesses have adapted to trading on the Internet as well as the high street, e.g. major retailers. Throughout the supply chain, the Internet has been used to plan and organise business to business (b2b) sales and logistics more effectively. Newspapers and magazines have started to run web sites parallel with their paper products, often starting with a free service and introducing charges gradually.

These developments increased the demand for web designers, software specialists and computer hardware, fuelling a rapid rise in the price of shares of Internet-related businesses. This boom came to an end in 2000 and by the end of 2002 stock markets stood 25% lower than their 2000 peak. Some e-business ventures have already gone into liquidation, e.g. Boo.com; others are still making losses but some are now starting to show profits.

Diversity

Businesses are adopting a wide variety of approaches to e-business. Where an existing business is well established, the Internet is often adapted to existing processes. Many completely new businesses, however, are being established, exploiting new ways of working and thinking. The business process can be thought of as comprising five stages: purchasing (inward logistics), production planning, production, delivery (outward logistics) and finally sales. Some businesses are adopting the Internet in all five stages simultaneously, while others adopt a more evolutionary approach, starting with Internet sales and developing into Internet logistics.

The rapid development of e-business is closely related to the willingness of capital markets to finance e-business ventures. This chapter starts with an examination of the options for financing e-business, e.g. venture capital. Next, the resources needed to start e-businesses are examined and a financial analysis of e-business is undertaken. Ratio and breakeven analyses are placed in the context of e-business and, finally, a strategic analysis of e-business, structured around Porter's Five Forces model, is developed. When you have completed this chapter you will understand the potential of and the challenges facing e-businesses, as well as the role financial management can play in successful e-business.

> New technologies do not always replace older technologies. Often new technology exists alongside the old, competing and coexisting. The Internet will not replace television or radio but will compete against it for market share.

Profits, capital and risk

Understanding the financial aspects of e-business encompasses more than just profit. Profit is the starting point for considering any business, but profit has to be seen in the light of the amount of capital necessary to earn the profit. An e-business plan may forecast £1,000,000 profit. If £100,000,000 of capital is needed to earn the profit, the ROCE is only 1%, compared to a 5% return earned by depositing the money in the bank.

Profit also needs to be considered in the light of risk. A risky company should earn a higher ROCE than a stable one, to justify the additional risk investors take. New technology is unproven and the logistical processes and extent of the market are unknown. The risks in e-business are greater than established sectors of the economy and so, therefore, should be the ROCE (see Figure 17.1).

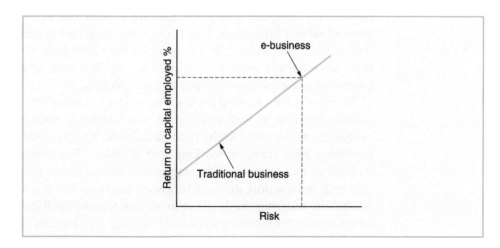

Figure 17.1 ROCE and risk

At the moment some e-businesses have not yet reached breakeven, let alone making sufficient profit to justify the capital invested or justify the risks involved.

It is difficult to imagine that, at one time, railways were a revolutionary new technology. In the nineteenth century wealthy individuals in the UK were keen to invest in the 'crazy horses'. The amounts of capital invested were substantial, around 5% of gross domestic product in some years (Bryer, 1991). In contrast with the capital invested, the profits earned were, and indeed remain, modest. It could be argued that there is a precedent for technology, which is revolutionary, but not financially viable.

Capital markets

The rapid expansion of e-business can partly be explained by the ready availability of large amounts of capital. This capital has not been supplied exclusively through traditional sources such as bank loans or listings on major stock markets. Rather, the capital has tended to be raised through business angels, venture capitalists and secondary stock markets.

Established stock markets such as the New York Stock Exchange tend to be risk averse. They are dominated by large financial institutions, selling and administering pensions and savings products requiring regular payments and receipts. These institutions require a stable and predictable dividend and, as a result, risky high technology investment is not particularly attractive to them. Although individual investors do not lead the market, they are an important force in stock market trading. These wealthy individuals do not need regular dividends, particularly as they pay the highest rates of taxation. They will often be more attracted to the possibility of taking a greater risk in return for potential long-term capital growth. For instance, rather than pay £1 for a share in an established company paying dividends of 5p per year, wealthy individuals may prefer to pay 50p for a share in a new high technology venture, which in ten years' time might be worth £20 per share.

The emergence of e-business presented an opportunity to invest at high risk but with the promise of substantial capital growth. Many wealthy individuals acted in the role of 'business angels', meaning that, at the inception of a new e-business, or at least early in its development, they bought a share of the business, e.g. 20%, in return for a substantial cash injection. One of the benefits to a new firm of business angels is that they can give a quick decision with the minimum of paper work. Business angels understand that if the business fails they will, in all likelihood, lose their money. If the business is a success, however, the value of the investment will multiply many times over. Business angels are often experienced and successful managers and entrepreneurs who can offer advice and contacts to a new venture.

Venture capitalists are professional investors acting on behalf of specialist venture capitalist companies or larger institutions that have decided to place a small proportion of their investments in higher risk ventures. Venture capitalists are highly selective, picking out only the most promising business ventures. Many companies applying for venture capital funds are rejected, wasting the company founders' time and money. Venture capitalists are interested in investing millions of pounds (or dollars) in companies which, over a period of five to ten years, can grow significantly and become listed on a major stock exchange. Venture capitalists do not become involved in day-to-day management, although they may have a non-executive role on the Board of Directors.

Venture capitalists have taken a particular interest in e-business because of the possibilities for rapid growth. They are experienced negotiators, seeking to gain the largest possible share of the company for the smallest possible investment. They sometimes try to reduce their exposure to risk by asking for personal guarantees from the company founders. Consequently, e-business entrepreneurs interested in venture capital finance need to be aware of the time, effort and dangers involved in negotiating a good deal.

> During the e-business boom (1995–2000) venture capitalists invested $4 billion per year in high technology start ups. For a few years, the supply of venture capital exceeded the demand for capital from viable new businesses.

To raise millions of pounds or dollars to start a larger e-business venture, it is necessary to involve thousands of investors. This can be achieved through an Initial Public Offering (IPO) on a junior stock market such as NASDAQ. Unlike senior markets, such as London and New York stock exchanges, no record of profits is required and the regulations and costs are lower.

The first step in achieving a successful IPO involves teaming up with a merchant bank that will guide the company founders through the process and underwrite the shares. A detailed business plan, termed a prospectus, is required, setting out in detail what is involved in the proposed venture. The next step is generating interest among institutional and private investors, involving many meetings and presentations during which the company founders, along with their advisers, will attempt to convince investors of the merits of the company. Once this is complete, the founders, working closely with the merchant bank, judge the level of interest in the company. An initial price has to be determined, reflecting the level of interest (demand) as well as the number of shares for sale (supply).

Once the initial price is set and announced, trading can begin. If the share price is too high, few shares will be bought and the capital raised will be insufficient. The merchant bank will have to step in and buy the remaining shares. If the price is too low, all the shares will be sold immediately and the price of the shares will rise sharply. Often the share price is set slightly too low in order to ensure brisk trading.

In London the Alternative Investment Market (AIM) plays a similar role to NASDAQ. AIM imposes even lower charges than NASDAQ and has even fewer rules and regulations. Nearly 300 companies are listed, some of whom have relatively small capitalisation, e.g. £2 million. Although AIM is the largest junior market in Europe, some European high technology ventures have preferred a NASDAQ listing. The prices of shares quoted on AIM are listed daily in the Financial Times, on the same page as the prices of shares on the senior market. One of the quickest ways to check the price of a share is by using a web site. Try search terms such as 'London Stock Exchange' and 'New York Stock Exchange'.

Several benefits accrue to an e-business start up when raising capital from business angels, venture capitalists or IPOs. These investors understand the high risks involved. They are aware profits may lie some years in the future and that, in the short term, losses are likely. Crucially, these types of investors do not require an immediate dividend, so all initial profits can be reinvested in the growth of the business. Bank loans, on the other hand, involve regular repayment of capital and interest, making them an unsuitable choice of financing for e-business.

Start up costs

It is commonly thought that only a modest capital investment is required to start a business on the Internet. A web page designer, for instance, could start a micro business on the Internet at very little cost. A business that seeks to compete for substantial market share, develop a brand image or provide excellent quality of service, however, will require a substantial capital sum. Customers will expect that a company operating on the Internet will have high technology manufacturing and delivery mechanisms in place, as well as sophisticated customer relations management systems.

The costs of starting a substantial e-business include the following.

People costs:

- Recruitment of experienced specialists
- Training

Legal costs:

- Copyright
- Domain name
- Terms of business
- Contracts of employment
- Lease agreements

Web design costs:

- Initial design and set up
- Regular updating

Marketing costs:

- Advertising
- Promotional activity

Flexible manufacturing systems:

- Custom-made equipment
- IT systems
- Delivery network

It is crucial to the success of an e-business start up that adequate capital is available to fund all of the above and an IPO is often the preferred means of raising capital. Existing companies can start e-business divisions or subsidiaries by reinvesting profits.

> During 1997 the whole World Wide Web crashed because of an error by an employee.

Financial analysis of e-business

e-Businesses display distinctive financial characteristics. Many e-businesses are still at an early stage in their development, have not reached profitability and are reporting disappointing sales growth. The initial enthusiasm in and excitement about the sector resulted in substantial investment and, consequently, many have large cash balances (despite the fact that they are loss making). As discussed above, the expenses involved in an e-business start up are considerable and can quickly erode this cash balance.

Consider the results set out below:

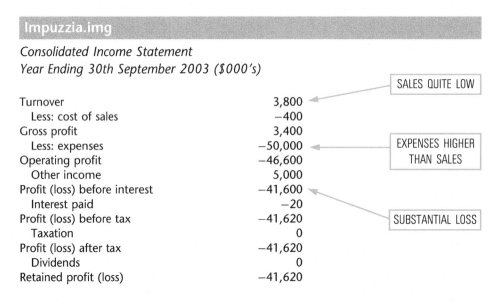

Impuzzia.img

Consolidated Income Statement
Year Ending 30th September 2003 ($000's)

Turnover	3,800	SALES QUITE LOW
Less: cost of sales	−400	
Gross profit	3,400	
Less: expenses	−50,000	EXPENSES HIGHER THAN SALES
Operating profit	−46,600	
Other income	5,000	
Profit (loss) before interest	−41,600	
Interest paid	−20	
Profit (loss) before tax	−41,620	SUBSTANTIAL LOSS
Taxation	0	
Profit (loss) after tax	−41,620	
Dividends	0	
Retained profit (loss)	−41,620	

The company has 200 employees.

In terms of the number of employees, this is a substantial business; however, turnover is only $3.8 million. Expenses are far higher than sales and, consequently, the company has made a substantial loss. Fortunately interest payments are small and the company has some 'other income', partially offsetting the losses.

The balance sheet has the following form:

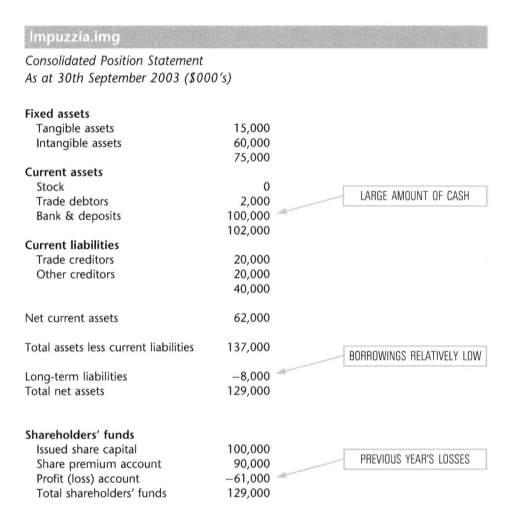

Impuzzia.img

Consolidated Position Statement
As at 30th September 2003 ($000's)

Fixed assets
Tangible assets	15,000	
Intangible assets	60,000	
	75,000	

Current assets
Stock	0	
Trade debtors	2,000	
Bank & deposits	100,000	LARGE AMOUNT OF CASH
	102,000	

Current liabilities
Trade creditors	20,000	
Other creditors	20,000	
	40,000	

Net current assets	62,000	
Total assets less current liabilities	137,000	BORROWINGS RELATIVELY LOW
Long-term liabilities	−8,000	
Total net assets	129,000	

Shareholders' funds
Issued share capital	100,000	
Share premium account	90,000	PREVIOUS YEAR'S LOSSES
Profit (loss) account	−61,000	
Total shareholders' funds	129,000	

The balance sheet indicates the company has substantial cash reserves, of $100 million, and there are few long-term liabilities. There is considerable investment in intangible fixed assets, which may have a low resale value. In summary, the balance sheet is strong, but the P&L account is weak. Sales must increase rapidly and expenses must fall.

The figures below (all in $m) relate to a larger e-business trading on lower profit margins, but with higher sales:

Income Statement ($m)
Year Ended December 2002

Turnover	602
Less: cost of sales	451
Gross profit	151
Less: expenses	
Operational overheads	302
IT costs	45
Marketing & sales	153
Operating profit	−349
Other income	0
Profit (loss) before interest	−349
Interest paid	41
Profit (loss) before tax	−390
Taxation	0
Profit (loss) after tax	−390
Dividends	0
Retained profit (loss)	−390

The summary position statement at the end of the same year is as follows:

Fixed assets		300
Current assets	1250	
Current liabilities	640	
Net current assets		610
Total net assets		910

This company displays the same three characteristics as the first. Sales need to be increased, expenses need to be reduced and cash needs to be monitored carefully to ensure it is not quickly exhausted.

Ratio analysis

Ratio analysis should be adapted to the distinctive characteristics of e-business. The unique problems posed by the sector provide an opportunity to think creatively about specialist ratios, which can assist in bringing struggling e-businesses to profit. In Chapter 10, key ratios were introduced including:

- Gross profit %
- Expense %
- Net profit %
- Stock turnover
- Current ratio
- Acid test
- Debtor days
- Creditor days
- Gearing %
- Return on capital employed (ROCE)

In the e-business context some of these will be essential and others will have no practical use. Rapid growth of sales is essential to e-business success and many firms resort to reducing prices in order to increase sales volumes. One impact of reducing prices is a corresponding reduction in profit margins. The gross profit % can be used to monitor movements in margins and can usefully identify situations in which sales are increased at the expense of margins. e-Businesses, because of their expertise in IT, should be able to design their information systems to provide the margin % on each element of the product range, as well as company-wide. This information will be useful to the marketing team, who can, for example, concentrate on promoting the products with highest margin. This type of detailed management information can be an important source of competitive advantage.

The control of expenses is a major issue for e-businesses and the expense % ratio should be monitored carefully. The expenses involved in starting a business are high and, once the business is established, expenses should fall and become more stable. Currently, many e-businesses have expenses higher than sales, yielding an expense % greater than 100%. It is essential to the profitability of e-business that the expense % is reduced to more sensible levels. e-Business managers need to be able to distinguish start up costs, which should disappear once the company becomes established, from continuing expenses. Many businesses have found start up costs higher and more persistent than they first imagined. For example, initial intensive advertising campaigns often have to be continued in order to maintain a high profile.

Many e-businesses are in a loss-making situation and consequently the calculation of net profit % is of little value. The calculation of stock turnover, however, is important in the e-business context. A well-managed e-business should use the Internet to plan and control both inbound and outbound logistics. In comparison to traditional businesses, e-businesses should, therefore, have lower stock levels. The stock turnover ratio will identify the extent to which this is achieved. The efficient management of stock has the impact of improving net cash flow. In light of the fact that many new e-businesses have substantial but finite cash reserves, this further emphasises the importance of monitoring stock turnover.

It is well known that monitoring liquidity is more important than monitoring profit in the first year (or indeed years) of a new business. e-Business is no different in this respect and the calculation of current ratio and acid test helps control the liquidity position. Debtor days and creditor days give further insight into liquidity. e-Business managers should consider calculating current ratio and acid test on a monthly basis, as well as producing monthly cash flow forecasts. These measures will provide the earliest possible warning of liquidity problems.

Adequate and appropriate sources of finance are key to business success (see above). Borrowings commit a company to specific and regular repayments and failure to meet these obligations may precipitate its demise. Many e-business start ups, however, still make use of overdraft facilities and short-term loans, because they are convenient. The gearing ratio, combined with interest cover, monitor the extent to which the company is dependent on these types of finance. Increases in gearing are a signal of increasing financial risk and, therefore, should play an important role in managing e-business. Finally, in a loss-making situation, ROCE cannot be usefully employed.

As well as adapting key ratios to the e-business context, there are some ratios that are unique to the particular sector. The financial analysis of e-business, above, revealed they often have substantial cash reserves combined with operating losses. An important issue is the length of time that will elapse before the cash reserves will be depleted. Financial analysts have started to calculate a 'cash burn rate', measuring how long it will take a loss-making company to use, or 'burn', the cash reserve. The cash burn rate is calculated as follows:

Cash *divided by* monthly losses = cash burn rate

Consider three examples of cash burn rate set out below:

	Monthly losses	Cash reserves	Cash burn rate
Micro business	£500	£6000	12 months
Medium sized	€10,000	€240,000	2 years
Global	$1 million	$42 million	3.5 years

The first company is small and, at the present rate of losses, the company will run out of cash in 12 months' time. If the losses can be reduced, the cash burn rate will be reduced, extending the life of the business. Eventually, the losses will have to be turned into profits. The second company has bigger losses, but it also has greater cash reserves. At the present rate of losses, the company will exhaust cash reserves in two years, so its liquidity position is more favourable than the first company's. The final company, which is the largest, has sufficient cash for three and a half years at the present rate of losses.

Finally, let us return to the vital question, how can e-businesses increase sales? Often customers visit a web site, but do not buy, or they buy goods once and do not return. Although increasing the value of sales is the ultimate goal, e-business managers need information on the pattern of consumer behaviour at different points in the sales process. The following information would be valuable:

- Sales by product (weekly)
- Sales by region (weekly)
- Percentage monthly increase in sales
- Market share (sales *divided by* estimated total value of the market)
- Number of visitors to the web site (weekly)
- Number of visitors who bought goods (weekly)
- Average value of a sale (weekly)
- Number of returns of goods and their value (weekly)
- Percentage on time delivery (weekly)
- Number of complaints (weekly)

This type of data provides a detailed insight into the sales process, helping identify exactly where problems lie. A range of management information is required, non-financial data as well as financial data. The use of a wide range of performance indicators is termed 'the balanced score card'. Other useful non-financial indicators include staff turnover, staff absence rates, etc.

Breakeven

Breakeven analysis is particularly relevant to e-business because it indicates what is required to eliminate losses. One of the limitations of breakeven is that it works best in a single product environment when, in practice, many Internet companies offer customers a range of products. This section first explores breakeven in a single product (or service) environment before developing it into a multi-product environment.

Many specialist newspapers, magazines and other publications are considering transferring their paper products onto the Internet, allowing more regular updating and access to a greater quantity of information. The cost savings are considerable because it is no longer necessary to print and distribute the newspapers or magazines. Consider a company publishing a weekly magazine with contribution per unit and fixed costs per year as follows:

Contribution per unit

Selling price	£2.50
Printing (variable) costs	1.50
Contribution per unit	1.00

Fixed costs per year

Distribution	£525,000
Journalists	1,030,000
Marketing	225,000
Administration	220,000
Total	2,000,000

The circulation of the newspaper is 75,000 per week, which is the equivalent of 3,900,000 per year. On the basis of the information given, calculate:

- Breakeven
- Margin of safety
- Margin of safety %
- Net profit

Fixed costs
Contribution per unit
Breakeven
Expected units
Margin of safety
Margin of safety %

Income Statement for the Year (£m)

Revenue
Less: variable cost
Contribution
Less: fixed cost
Net profit

The breakeven is 2,000,000 newspapers sold and the margin of safety of 49% suggests that breakeven is not difficult to achieve. On the basis of selling 3,900,000 papers, the company will make a profit of £1,900,000.

If the business transfers to the Internet, the situation would be very different. The web site would operate on the basis of an annual subscription, payable at the beginning of the year. All the costs would be fixed costs because, once the web site was fully functioning, there would be no additional cost associated with additional subscribers. The variable cost of an additional subscriber is, therefore, zero. The fixed costs of running the company on the Internet would be substantially less than the paper-based model because the company does not have to bear the cost of distributing the paper product. Consider the possibility that subscriptions and fixed costs were as follows:

Annual subscription	£49
Fixed costs	£1,475,000

The company hopes that all 75,000 readers will take out a subscription, because the subscription is cheaper than buying the newspaper every week and the web site has more information and links.

Internet-Based Profit Statement

Total subscriptions	£49 × 75,000	£3675m
Less: fixed costs		£1475m
Net profit		£2200m
Breakeven	1,475,000/£49	30,102 subscribers
Margin of safety %	75,000 − 31,102	60%

On every measure of risk and return the Internet-based scenario is superior. Profits, turnover and margin of safety are all higher. The calculations assume, however, all existing customers become subscribers. Some customers may prefer the paper product and may refuse the benefits of Internet subscription.

Breakeven in a multi-product environment

Most companies sell more than one product and consequently the relationship between sales and profits is not a simple one. Consider a company selling three products on the Internet:

Products	Selling price (£)	Variable cost (£)	Contribution (£)	Contribution (%)
X	1	0.75	0.25	25%
Y	5	3.00	2.00	40%
Z	10	4.00	6.00	60%

Product Z is the most expensive and delivers the highest profit, but sales of product Z will probably be low because of its cost. Product X, on the other hand, is the cheapest and likely to be the most popular. Using market research an experienced marketing manager will be able to estimate the relative proportions of each product sold within the range, e.g. X 60%, Y 30% and Z 10%. If on average the company sells 100 units of product per day, the sales would be X 60 units, Y 30 units and Z 10 units. This would deliver the following contributions:

Product	Units	Sales (£)	Contribution (£)
X	60	60	15
Y	30	150	60
Z	10	100	60
Total	100	310	135

Sales of £310 deliver a contribution of £135 per day, which represents 43%. Assuming fixed proportions between the different products, contribution will be 43% of sales. Sales of £100,000 yields £43,000 contribution. Sales of £200,000 yields £86,000 contribution, etc. On the basis of this, breakeven sales can be calculated as follows:

Fixed costs *divided by* contribution %

If fixed costs in the case above amounted to £172,000, the breakeven sales would be £400,000 (£172,000/0.43).

Take a company selling DVDs and CDs on the Internet. The selling price and variable costs may be as follows:

	CDs		DVDs	
Selling price	£10		£20	
Variable cost	£7		£8	
Contribution per unit	£3	30%	£12	60%
Sales units per week	2000		1000	

Weekly sales would, therefore, be £40,000 (£20,000 from each product) and weekly contribution would be £18,000 (£6000+£12,000) generating a contribution per cent of 45%. If total sales for the year were £2 million, a contribution of £0.90 million would be generated. If the fixed costs of running the web site amounted to £360,000, the breakeven sales would be £800,000 (£360,000/0.45).

These calculations can be represented graphically as in Figure 17.2. The horizontal axis represents sales of both CDs and DVDs in pounds rather than in units of product. The profit line is dependent on the relative sales proportions between the two products remaining unchanged. Consumer preferences, however, change quickly and, therefore, sales of each product will also change. As a result, the breakeven sales target may need regular updating. This type of breakeven graph can be used to focus employees and the management team on the importance of increasing sales to achieve breakeven.

Strategic analysis of e-business

The long-term impact of the Internet on business is difficult to assess. As a medium of communication it makes the dissemination of knowledge easier

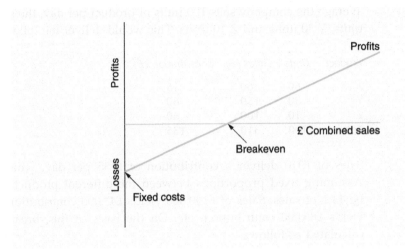

Figure 17.2 Multi-product breakeven

and the restriction of access to information more difficult. Knowledge of best practice, technical specifications, prices, processes, job vacancies, etc. is greatly increased by the Internet.

The Internet is part of a wider advance in communication technology, including video conferencing, mobile phones, electronic funds transfer, real time company news, etc., which have all helped establish a global market. These technological advances have increased world competition, causing a generalised downward pressure on prices. If falling prices are combined with a sharp downturn in the trade cycle, a damaging deflationary cycle, during which firms competitively reduce prices and profits, can occur.

Porter's Five Forces model, incorporating entry, buyer power, supplier power, rivalry and substitution, can be employed to understand different aspects of the Internet and world competition. Where knowledge is more freely available firms will be encouraged to enter new markets. The Internet allows firms to contact consumers globally, making it easier to increase market share in global markets. The Internet has proved particularly attractive to small groups of people with a common interest. It can, therefore, be employed as a marketing tool for targeting these specialist groups of consumers, facilitating entry into new markets. The Internet can also play an important role in planning and controlling inward and outward logistics on a global basis.

Buyer power arises where there are a small number of customers relative to the number of firms supplying products. e-Business makes it easier to contact customers all over the world and, consequently, it tends to reduce buyer power. Consumers, however, will be better informed about prices, service and specifications, strengthening their negotiating position.

Supplier power exists where a relatively small number of suppliers dictate the terms of trade (prices, service quality, etc.) to their customers. The Internet can be used to contact a global range of suppliers and facilitates the comparison of prices, service and products. The Internet, therefore, reduces supplier power and provides a basis for reducing the costs of materials and components.

These reductions, however, may have to be passed on to customers in the form of lower prices. Many large manufacturing firms have set up bidding or auction-type systems on the Internet, to allow suppliers from around the world to bid on line for large contracts. For more on this see J.A. Rodgers et al., Developing e-Business: A Strategic Approach, Information Management and Computer Security, Vol. 10, No. 4, 2002, pp. 184–192.

The Internet intensifies competition between existing rivals. Where firms are competing on price and quality of service, the Internet sharpens that competition by making it simpler and quicker for consumers to check prices and by increasing the importance of on-time delivery. The Internet also makes it easier for customers to seek out substitutes for products. If a consumer is experiencing difficulties booking a railway ticket, the Internet enables a consumer to switch to an airline web site and obtain a quote for flying to the particular destination. Consumers who 'surf' the net can discover substitutes they were previously unaware of. In summary, the Internet increases competition, which tends, on balance, to benefit consumers.

Conclusions

The Internet opens up new possibilities for gaining competitive advantage and reinforces the trend towards globalisation. At an operational level, e-businesses should concentrate on increasing market share, reducing overheads and monitoring cash expenses. In the longer term e-businesses should concentrate on developing brand awareness, making more information available on a commercial basis and developing closer relationships with customers.

Traditionally businesses have been secretive in an effort to maintain competitive advantage. e-Business is based more on information sharing, which tends to make the business process more transparent. In the future customers may easily be able to use the Internet to order goods manufactured to their own particular specification, track their progress through the production process and monitor delivery of those goods. This may have a profound impact on the nature of business competition. Indeed, it is possible that co-operation along the supply chain may become more important than competition. In the short run e-business intensifies competition, while in the long run it may change its whole nature.

Multiple choice questions

Tick the box next to your answer.

1. A web site costs £24,000 per year to maintain and the annual subscription is £20.
   Breakeven number of subscriptions is?
   - [ ] 24,000
   - [ ] 12,000
   - [ ] 1200
   - [ ] 120
   - [ ] Zero

2. A recently started e-business incurring monthly losses of £10,000 has a £150,000 cash balance. The cash burn rate is?
   - ☐ 24 months
   - ☐ 20 months
   - ☐ 15 months
   - ☐ 12 months
   - ☐ 6 months

3. A company with market share of 10% means
   - ☐ The company has ten customers
   - ☐ Competitors have one in ten of available customers
   - ☐ The company has 10% of the total value of the market
   - ☐ Gross profit % is 10%
   - ☐ There are ten companies competing in the market

4. Which of the following is *not* a cost of starting a retail company on the Internet?
   - ☐ Securing a domain name
   - ☐ Investing in brand recognition
   - ☐ Renting high street premises
   - ☐ Recruiting skilled web designers
   - ☐ Costs of leasing hardware and software

5. New smaller e-business ventures selling to consumers are characterised by?
   - ☐ Cash sales and cash purchases
   - ☐ Cash sales and credit purchases
   - ☐ Credit sales and cash purchases
   - ☐ Credit sales and credit purchases
   - ☐ No sales and no purchases

6. The Internet allows firms to communicate with customers all over the world. Within Porter's Five Forces model, this can be interpreted as
   - ☐ Increasing buyer power
   - ☐ Reducing buyer power
   - ☐ Increasing supplier power
   - ☐ Reducing rivalry
   - ☐ Reducing entry

7. Which of the following indicates increasing sales?
   - ☐ Reduction in market share
   - ☐ Reduction in the size of the market as a whole
   - ☐ Stable levels of repeat business
   - ☐ Sales steadily increasing month on month
   - ☐ No new products in the product range

8. Reducing selling price leads to
   - ☐ Increases in the total value of sales
   - ☐ Reduction in gross profit %
   - ☐ Increase in net profit %
   - ☐ More spending on research and development
   - ☐ Lower purchases

9. Venture capitalists are attracted to
   - ☐ High dividends
   - ☐ Companies with high borrowings (high gearing)
   - ☐ Companies already quoted on major stock exchanges
   - ☐ Risky companies with potential for high growth
   - ☐ Companies that are nearly bankrupt or in liquidation

10. The best measure of success in relation to an e-business web site is?
- ☐ The number of hits on the web site per week
- ☐ The cost of maintaining the web site
- ☐ The frequency of updating the web site
- ☐ The value of sales generated by the web site
- ☐ The number of links contained in the web site

Multiple choice answers

	Correct answer	Comment
1	1200 subscriptions	1200 subscriptions generates 1200 × £20 = £24,000. More than 1200 subscriptions are needed to generate a profit.
2	15 months	At this rate of loss all the cash will be used up in 15 months; however, losses might fall, e.g. to £35,000 per month, in which case the company can survive longer.
3	The company has 10% of the total value of the market	The more firms active in the market, the greater the rivalry in the market.
4	Renting high street premises	Firms that start up with a view to selling on the Internet do not need high street premises.
5	Cash sales and cash purchases	Selling to consumers has the advantage of being cash sales. If an e-business venture were aiming at the business to business sector (b2b) sales might have to be credit sales, which would reduce net cash flow.
6	Reducing buyer power	The company is less reliant on a small number of customers and new customers are more easily attracted.
7	Sales steadily increasing month on month	This is what most e-businesses need to achieve, but they have to compete with existing businesses to increase market share.
8	Reduction in gross profit %	Lower prices may increase the volume of sales, but looking at it £ for £, there is less gross profit in every £ of sales.
9	Risky companies with potential for high growth	Venture capitalists are particularly interested in investing at the launch and rapid growth stage of the product life cycle, particularly where there is a possibility of eventually listing on a major stock exchange.
10	The value of sales generated by the web site	The other choices are beneficial, e.g. getting more 'hits' on the web site is a good sign, but the purpose of the web site is to sell goods. No profit is earned until goods are sold.

David.img

David.img sell DVDs on the Internet. The company has been established for two years and the summary income and position statement is as follows (£000's):

	2002	2001
Turnover	775	620
Less: cost of sales	310	248
Gross profit	465	372
Less: operating expenses	540	558
Net income	(75)	(186)
Fixed assets	371	432
Current assets		
Stock	20	30
Cash	225	372
	245	402
Current liabilities	60	80
Net current assets	185	322
Total assets less current liabilities	556	754

The company predicts sales will increase by 20% in 2003, gross profit % will remain stable and expenses for the next year are expected to be £550,000.

Your task

On the basis of the summary income and position statement above calculate gross profit %, expense %, current ratio and cash burn rate. On the basis of the predictions given, estimate the net income for 2003 and write a paragraph which summarises the financial position of the company.

En-cycle-opedia.img

Income Statement ($m)
Year Ended December 2003

Turnover	801
Less: cost of sales	531
Gross profit	270
Less: expenses	
Operating costs	251
IT costs	67
Marketing and distribution	174
Operating profit	−222
Other income	2
Profit (loss) before interest	−220
Interest paid	22
Profit (loss) before tax	−242

The summary position statement at the end of the same year is as follows:

Fixed assets		301
Current assets		
Stock	50	
Cash	272	
	322	
Current liabilities	119	
Net current assets		203
Total net assets		504

The company anticipates a 20% increase in sales, a stable gross profit % and a decrease in expenses to £320m (in total) in the next financial year. Interest paid and other income is expected to be unchanged.

Your task

On the basis of the income and position statement calculate gross profit %, expense %, current ratio and cash burn rate. On the basis of the predictions given, estimate the profit before taxation in 2004 and write a paragraph summarising the financial position of the company.

Ian Tudur

Consider the data below, relating to a company with four products A, B, C and D. The company has recently closed down its retail premises and now only sells on the Internet. The fixed costs incurred by the company are much higher than anticipated:

	A	B	C	D
Selling price	£100	£200	£500	£1000
Variable cost	£90	£160	£375	£500
Contribution per unit	£10	£40	£125	£500
Contribution %	10%	20%	25%	50%
Sales units per week	2000	1000	500	100

The expected level of fixed costs for the year is £920,000.

Your task

On the basis of the proportions set out above, calculate the level of sales required to break even. Describe the effect on breakeven of selling more of the most profitable product and less of the least profitable.

Louise and Lawrence

Consider the two companies below, both selling consumer goods on the Internet. Competitive advantage is gained by low prices, speed of delivery and ease of use of web sites. Both companies are also competing against high street retailers. All data is in Canadian $m.

	Louise.img		Lawrence.img	
	2002	2001	2002	2001
Turnover	520	270	91	64
Less: cost of sales	405	201	72	51
Gross profit	115	69	19	13
Less: expenses	270	189	123	85
Profit (loss) from operations	(155)	(120)	(104)	(72)
Interest	12	18	0	0
Net profit (loss)	(167)	(138)	(104)	(72)
Number of employees	5582		1673	

	Louise.img		Lawrence.img	
	2002	2001	2002	2001
Fixed assets	325	310	120	95
Current assets	1200	1000	391	253
Current liabilities	625	725	46	77
Net current assets	575	275	345	176
Long term loans	267.0	100	0	0
Total net assets (liabilities)	633	485	465	271

Your task

Calculate key ratios using the data above as well as the % increase in sales.

Solutions

David.img

The four ratios are as follows:

	2002	2001
Gross profit %	60%	60%
Expense %	70%	90%
Current ratio	4	5
Cash burn rate	3 years	2 years

As a result of the increased turnover and reduced expenses, the loss incurred in 2002 is significantly less than that incurred in 2001. The gross profit % (60%) has remained high and, despite a fall in current ratio from 5 to 4, the liquidity position has remained strong. The cash burn rate is improving, suggesting there is no immediate danger of the company exhausting cash.

The predicted income statement for 2003 is as follows (all in £000's):

Turnover	775 × 1.20	930
Less: cost of sales	310 × 1.20	372
Gross profit		558
Less: operating expenses	£550 from the scenario	550
Net income		8

This shows that if sales continue to grow as predicted, a small net income of £8000 will be earned in 2003. In order to earn a reasonable rate of return on capital, sales will have to continue to grow and expenses reduce.

En-cycle-opedia.img

The four ratios are as follows:

	2003
Gross profit %	33.7%
Expense %	61.4%
Current ratio	2.70
Cash burn rate	1.1 years

The predicted income statement for 2004 is as follows ($m):

Turnover	801 × 1.20	961.2
Less: cost of sales	531 × 1.20	637.2
Gross profit		324.0
Less: expenses	$320 from the scenario	320.0
Operating profit		4.0
Other income		2.0
Profit (loss) before interest		6.0
Interest paid		22.0
Profit (loss) before taxation		−16.0

The company incurred a loss during 2003 because of the low level of sales compared to expenses (expense % = 61.4%). The liquidity position is mixed, reflected by current ratio of 2.7 compared to cash burn rate of just one year. At this level of losses the company can only expect to remain in operation 12 months.

An increase in sales, however, is expected in the coming year coupled with a reduction in expenses. This should enable the company to deliver an operating profit of $4m. The high level of interest payments, however, will result in the company incurring a loss before taxation of $16m in 2004. Borrowing money is not a suitable means of financing an e-business start up. The company should consider alternative forms of finance.

In the longer run, if the present rate of sales growth can be maintained, profits could become sufficient to justify the capital investment in the company and the risks involved. In a competitive market, however, continued increases in market share can be difficult to achieve.

Ian Tudur

The contribution generated in a week will be as follows:

	A	B	C	D	Total
Weekly revenue	£200,000	£200,000	£250,000	£100,000	750,000
Less: variable cost	180,000	160,000	187,500	50,000	577,500
Contribution	£20,000	£40,000	£62,500	£50,000	172,500
Contribution %					23%

Breakeven turnover = fixed costs *divided by* contribution percentage

920,000/0.23 = £4,000,000

Based on the existing product mix, sales of £4,000,000 per year will cause the company to break even. If more of the high contribution goods are sold, breakeven can be achieved at lower levels of sales. If more of the least profitable products are sold, breakeven will only be achieved at higher levels of sales. The expected profit for the year is £8,050,000.

Louise and Lawrence

	Louise.img		Lawrence.img	
	2002	2001	2002	2001
Gross profit %	22.1%	25.5%	20.8%	20.3%
Expense %	51.9%	70%	135.1%	132.8%
Current ratio	1.92	1.379	8.5	3.2
Gearing %	42.1%	20%	0%	0
Increase in sales	92%	NA	42%	NA

Both companies are making losses which, alarmingly, are increasing. The sales generated by Louise.img are far greater than Lawrence.img and the losses are also greater. Louise.img has reduced the gross profit % by 3.4% during the year, indicating that increases in sales may be at the expense of profit. Louise.img is increasing sales at a faster rate (92%) than Lawrence.img (42%).

The liquidity position of Louise.img is not as strong as that of Lawrence.img. The current ratio is less than 2, although it has improved significantly during the year from 1.3 to 1.9. The cash burn rates would be useful in this regard. Also Louise.img has high gearing and high interest payments. Lawrence.img enjoys high liquidity (current ratio of 8) and no gearing, therefore it is financially the stronger company.

18 Investment appraisal

This chapter explores a variety of decision-making techniques.

Objectives

Objectives
• Time value of money;
• Net present value (NPV);
• Internal rate of return (IRR);
• Payback period (PBP);
• Accounting rate of return (ARR).

Introducing business decisions

Importance of the subject

Managers take many types of decisions, some concerning the day-to-day running of a department or business and others of strategic importance. Strategic decisions often involve large sums of capital invested in long-term projects. Examples include buying a competitor company, launching a new product, modernising production methods and manufacturing in a foreign location. Once capital is committed to these projects it is difficult to withdraw. For instance, if a manufacturing facility has been planned, built and equipped, the only way to release the funds is to find a buyer for the new facility. This can be difficult, particularly as the most interested parties are likely to be competitors. Good strategic decision making and the careful appraisal of long-term investments is key to business success.

Time horizons

Most managerial tasks operate within a 12-month time horizon. Strategic decisions usually operate within a five to ten-year horizon, which reduces the importance of the distinction between cash and profit. Within one year there can be marked differences between cash flow and profit, because of depreciation, stock, debtors and creditors, etc. Over ten years these differences are insignificant. Consider a business start up situation in which all the equipment and materials are paid for in the first month. The net cash flow profile compared to profits might be as follows:

	Year 1	Year 2	Year 3	Total
Cash flow	−10,000	20,000	25,000	35,000
Profit	−1,000	16,000	20,000	35,000

Structure
In every year, especially the first year, there is a marked difference between cash and profit; however, taking the three years in total there is no difference. Because investment opportunities have implications stretching over a number of years, cash provides the more convenient basis for investment appraisal decisions, rather than profit. This also helpfully avoids judgmental issues such as depreciation, stock valuation, etc.

Activities and outcomes
This chapter focuses first on the 'time value of money', the essential concept in decision making. The main techniques relevant to decision making, net present value, internal rate of return, payback period and accounting rate of return, are then examined. After completing this chapter you will understand the time value of money and the cost of capital. You will be able to employ several types of investment appraisal techniques and understand different perspectives on the same investment opportunity. Use the multiple choice questions at the end of the chapter to test your understanding before moving on to the rest of the questions. You may also find the summary of key terms in the conclusions section useful as you progress through the chapter.

Time value of money

There are many different ways of investing cash, such as depositing it in a bank account to earn interest, investing in shares to earn dividends or investing in a business to earn profit. Before money can be invested in a business it first has to be withdrawn from a bank or other investment. Consequently, investing in a business means losing the interest that would have been earned. This loss of interest should be taken into account when evaluating new business ideas or investments. The profits earned from a business investment should be greater than the interest that could have been earned by keeping the money in a bank.

Consider £1,000,000 currently earning 5% interest (£50,000) per annum. The money could be withdrawn from the bank and invested in a business earning a profit of, say, £140,000. The profit is £90,000 greater than the interest, indicating the investment was beneficial. Many businesses, however, do not make a profit in the first year. If no profit was earned until the second year, two years' interest (£50,000 × 2 = £100,000) has been lost in order to earn the £140,000 profit. The business investment seems less beneficial if no profit is earned until the second year. If no profit is earned until the third year, three years' interest has been lost (£50,000 × 3 = £150,000). This suggests the business investment is a poor one, since the interest lost is more than the profit earned. This loss of interest is often referred to as the 'time value of money'. The longer a business investment takes to earn profit, the more interest is foregone and the less attractive the investment seems.

Taking into account the time value of money, i.e. the lost interest, reduces the value of cash received in the future. The further in the future cash is received, the less it is worth. This is termed the 'discounting' of future cash flows. Discount tables (see Appendix 1) are readily available showing the value of £1 in one year's time, two years' time, etc. at different rates of interest. Consider the table below which shows the value of £1 at a 5% interest rate:

Years	Cash received in the future	Discount factor from the table	Present value of future cash received
In 1 year	£1	0.952	£0.952
In 2 years	£1	0.907	£0.907
In 3 years	£1	0.864	£0.864
In 4 years	£1	0.823	£0.823
In 5 years	£1	0.784	£0.784

At 5% interest the value of £1 received in one year's time is £0.952, but having to wait five years for £1 reduces its value to £0.784. These are termed present values because they show the present value of cash received in the future. The further in the future cash is received the lower its present value (PV).

Consider a situation in which a company paid £1,000,000 for the rights to sell a branded product and earned net cash of £140,000 every year. If the prevailing interest rate was 5%, the discounting of future cash would be presented as follows:

Years	Cash payments and receipts (£)	Discount factor	Present value (£)
0	−1,000,000	1	−1,000,000
1	140,000	0.952	133,280
2	140,000	0.907	126,980
3	140,000	0.864	120,960
4	140,000	0.823	115,220
5	140,000	0.784	109,760

The discount factors have been obtained from the table in Appendix 1. The PV of the £140,000 received falls progressively, i.e. £109,760 in five years' time. The money spent on obtaining the right to sell the product is paid immediately, rather than in the future, so the discount factor is 1.

If the interest rate were 10%, the discount factors would be as follows:

Years	Cash payments and receipts (£)	Discount factor	Present value (£)
0	−1,000,000	1	−1,000,000
1	140,000	0.909	127,260
2	140,000	0.826	115,640
3	140,000	0.751	105,140
4	140,000	0.683	95,620
5	140,000	0.621	86,940

Notice the PV of £140,000 falls more quickly under a 10% discount rate. After five years, for instance, the PV of £140,000 is £86,940, compared to £109,760 under a 5% discount rate. The higher the discount rate the greater is the interest lost. Money received in the future is worth less as the interest rate increases. A high interest rate tends to reduce the amount of money invested in long-term projects and increase the benefits of keeping money in the bank. This relationship is depicted in Figure 18.1.

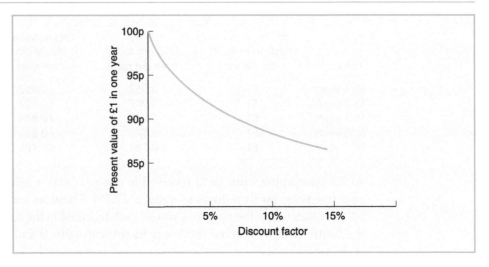

Figure 18.1 The impact of discount factors on present value

Choice of discount rate

The discount table shows a range of different interest rates, e.g. 5% and 10%. The rate appropriate for a particular investment decision depends on the risks involved and the finance deal. There are many different ways of financing business (see Chapter 12). A business financed by an individual with savings should use the rate currently being earned on the money plus a premium for the additional risk. A business financed by bank borrowing should use the rate of interest being charged by the bank. The interest rate charged by a bank on borrowings is always higher than the rate paid on deposits.

When capital is raised on a stock market, shareholders receive dividends rather than interest. Just as interest charges are the cost of using loan finance, dividends can be viewed as the cost of attracting share capital. These types of payments are often termed 'cost of capital'. Dividends can be expressed as a percentage of the initial investment, the dividends yield ratio (see Chapter 11), giving a guide to the most appropriate discount rate. In general, the discount rate appropriate to an investment decision is the cost of raising the capital.

Companies often take advantage of a range of different sources of finance, such as ordinary shares, preference shares, bonds, loans, overdraft, etc., paying slightly different costs of capital to each source of finance. A weighted average cost of capital provides a guide to the appropriate discount rate. For example, consider a company partly financed by borrowing at a cost of capital of 15% and partly financed by ordinary shares at a cost of capital of 20%. If both of these sources provide half the capital, the weighted average cost of capital is 17.5%, given by $0.50 \times 15\% + 0.50 \times 20\%$. If ordinary shares contributed three quarters of the company finances and borrowing one quarter, the weighted average cost of capital would be given by $0.75 \times 20\% + 0.25 \times 15\% = 18.75\%$.

Investors are generally risk averse and industries known to pose greater risk (see Chapter 17) have to pay a higher cost of capital to compensate investors for taking the additional risk. On the other hand, low risk sectors pay a lower cost of capital. If an investment project has a higher level of risk than the existing core business, it is likely that a higher cost of capital will have to be paid in order to attract finance for the project.

Net present value calculations

The time value of money is allowed for in investment decisions by calculating the present value of receipts and the present value of payments using a discount rate appropriate to the business. Net present value is the difference between the present value of receipts and payments:

PV of payment *less* PV of receipts = net present value (NPV)

Typically payments are made at the start (year 0) and receipts follow (year 1, year 2, etc.). If the NPV is positive the project is worthwhile and if the NPV is negative the project should be rejected. If there is a choice between a number of projects, the project with the highest NPV should be chosen.

Consider investing £1,000,000 now, in return for receipts of £300,000 in each of the next five years. On the basis of a 5% discount rate this should be set out as follows:

Years	Cash paid and received (£)	Discount factor	Present value (£)
0	−1,000,000	1	−1,000,000
1	300,000	0.952	285,600
2	300,000	0.907	272,100
3	300,000	0.864	259,200
4	300,000	0.823	246,900
5	300,000	0.784	235,200
Total			299,000

At the 5% rate this investment delivers a positive NPV of £299,000 and the company should, therefore, accept the project. Consider the possibility that the receipts are two years further in the future. The NPV would be calculated as follows:

Years	Cash paid and received (£)	Discount factor	Present value (£)
0	−1,000,000	1	−1,000,000
1	0	0.952	0
2	0	0.907	0
3	300,000	0.864	259,200
4	300,000	0.823	246,900
5	300,000	0.784	235,200
6	300,000	0.746	223,800
7	300,000	0.711	213,300
			178,400

The £178,400 NPV is positive but reduced because the receipts are further in the future. The investment opportunity is still viable and should be accepted.

Consider the same investment opportunity at a 10% rate. The NPV calculation would be as follows:

Years	Cash paid and received (£)	Discount factor	Present value (£)
0	−1,000,000	1	−1,000,000
1	300,000	0.909	272,700
2	300,000	0.826	247,800
3	300,000	0.751	225,300
4	300,000	0.683	204,900
5	300,000	0.621	186,300
Total			137,000

The £137,000 NPV is positive, but lower than that achieved under a 5% rate. The investment should, therefore, be undertaken. If the receipts are two years later the situation is different, as shown below:

Years	Cash paid and received (£)	Discount factor	Present value (£)
0	−1,000,000	1	−1,000,000
1	0	0.909	0
2	0	0.826	0
3	300,000	0.751	225,300
4	300,000	0.683	204,900
5	300,000	0.621	186,300
6	300,000	0.564	169,200
7	300,000	0.513	153,900
Total			−60,400

The combined effect of a 10% rate and receipts further in the future has delivered a negative NPV. On these assumptions the investment should be rejected.

Consider the possibility that the project presents the opportunity of making an additional one-off investment after five years, with the following net cash flow profile:

Year	Net cash flow (£)
0	−1,000,000
1	0
2	0
3	300,000
4	300,000
5	−250,000
6	300,000
7	350,000
8	400,000
9	400,000
10	0

At the 10% rate the NPV would be as follows:

Years	Cash paid and received (£)	Discount factor	Present value (£)
0	−1,000,000	1	−1,000,000
1	0	0.909	0
2	0	0.826	0
3	300,000	0.751	225,300
4	300,000	0.683	204,900
5	−250,000	0.621	−155,250
6	300,000	0.564	169,200
7	350,000	0.513	179,550
8	400,000	0.467	186,800
9	400,000	0.424	169,600
10	0	0.386	0
Total			−19,900

The extra investment after five years fails to deliver a positive NPV. The opportunity should be rejected.

Internal rate of return

The concept of breakeven (Chapter 13) is attractive to managers and can be applied in long-term decision making. Higher discount rates tend to result in lower NPVs. There will always be a discount rate yielding a zero NPV. This can be interpreted as a breakeven discount rate, termed the 'internal rate of return'. The relationship between discount factors and NPV is presented in Figure 18.2. As the discount factor increases, the NPV reduces until it falls to less than zero. The internal rate of return (IRR) is the discount factor delivering zero NPV. Larger companies monitor their cost of capital regularly. Any project with an internal rate of return higher than the cost of capital is worthwhile.

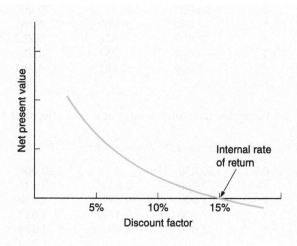

Figure 18.2 Internal rate of return

The IRR can be estimated by calculating the NPV at two different discount rates, e.g. 10% and 20%. This reveals the impact on NPV of a 10% change in discount rate and allows the estimation of the rate that yields a zero NPV. Consider the project below at the 10% rate:

Year	Cash flow (£)	Discount factor	PV (£)
0	−10,000	1	−10,000
1	4,500	0.909	4,090
2	4,500	0.826	3,717
3	4,500	0.751	3,380
Total	3,500		1,187

The project delivers a positive NPV of £1187 at the 10% rate. Consider the impact of increasing the discount rate to 20% – see below:

Year	Cash flow (£)	Discount factor	PV (£)
0	−10,000	1	−10,000
1	4,500	0.833	3,749
2	4,500	0.694	3,123
3	4,500	0.579	2,605
			−523

The NPV is now negative, −£523. The zero NPV discount rate must lie between 10% and 20%. A 10% increase in the discount rate leads to a £1710 reduction in NPV from £1187 to −£523. Every 1% increase equates approximately to a £171 fall in NPV. To reduce the original £1187 NPV to zero, divide £1187 by £171, yielding 6.94. This means a 6.94% increase in the discount rate yields zero NPV. The original discount rate was 10%, so 16.94% is the internal rate of return. If the cost of capital is less than 16.94% the project is beneficial.

Consider another project at a 10% discount factor:

Year	Cash flow (£)	Discount factor	PV (£)
0	−20,000	1	−20,000
1	7,000	0.909	6,363
2	7,000	0.826	5,782
3	7,000	0.751	5,257
4	7,000	0.683	4,781
Total			2,183

Consider the same project at a 20% discount factor:

Year	Cash flow (£)	Discount factor	PV (£)
0	−20,000	1	−20,000
1	7,000	0.833	5,831
2	7,000	0.694	4,858
3	7,000	0.579	4,053
4	7,000	0.482	3,374
			−1,884

The NPV is now negative; therefore, the zero NPV discount rate lies between 10% and 20%. A 10% increase in the discount rate leads to a £4067 reduction in NPV. Every 1% increase equates approximately to a £406.7 fall in NPV. Dividing the original NPV of £2183 by £406.7 yields 5.36. This means a 5.36 increase in discount rate yields a zero NPV. The original discount rate was 10%; therefore, the internal rate of return is 15.36%. If the cost of capital is less than 15.36% the project is beneficial.

Advantages and disadvantages of NPV

In theory NPV is the ideal technique for evaluating projects because it has a number of important advantages:

- Takes into account the time value of money.
- Based on cash, which is more accurate than profit.
- Incorporates a simple accept or reject decision rule and comparison ranking.
- Takes into account the full life of the project.

In practice many of the figures needed to calculate NPV are unknown or uncertain. The NPV technique assumes away many of the uncertainties businesses face. The technique assumes future cash flows are known, the appropriate discount rate is known, the length of the project is known and the level of risk is measurable. The initial capital cost of projects is often underestimated, consumer demand is overestimated, the level of interest rates is changing constantly and the length of the product life cycle is unknown.

Over a period of five to ten years the trade cycle can have a profound impact on risk and interest rates. During a period of expansion, investors' perception of risk reduces. They can be persuaded to invest in risky projects at relatively low rates of return. A period of recession, however, makes investors more risk averse and they have to be offered high returns on capital to persuade them to invest. As a result, it is difficult to specify a consistent discount rate over the whole life of a project. Because of these problems and uncertainties, simpler decision making techniques are also important.

Payback period

The payback period (PBP) is the time that elapses between initial investment and the date when the investment is fully recovered. Managers and entrepreneurs find the concept a useful one. Like breakeven, it is easily understood and calculated and combines elements of profit and risk. Once the payback position is reached, there is no further risk of loss and profits lie ahead.

If a company invests £2,000,000 and the resulting net cash flow is £500,000 per year, the PBP is 4 years. If the net cash flow were £400,000 per year the PBP would be 5 years. In a more complex example the following format is appropriate:

Time	Cash flows (£)	Cumulative (£)
0	−27,000	−27,000
1	3,000	−24,000
2	12,000	−12,000
3	12,000	0
4	8,000	8,000

The £27,000 initial investment is paid back within three years. Consider another example:

Time	Cash flows (£)	Cumulative (£)
0	−32,000	−32,000
1	2,000	−30,000
2	3,000	−27,000
3	4,000	−23,000
4	5,000	−18,000
5	5,000	−13,000
6	5,000	−8,000
7	6,000	−2,000
8	4,000	2,000

Payback occurs after seven and a half years. PBP can easily be adapted to the comparison of projects. Compare the payback period for the projects A, B and C below (all in £):

Year	A	B	C
0	−24,000,000	−36,0000,000	−42,000,000
1	6,000,000	2,000,000	0
2	6,000,000	6,000,000	7,000,000
3	6,000,000	8,000,000	10,000,000
4	6,000,000	10,000,000	13,000,000
5	6,000,000	10,000,000	24,000,000
6	6,000,000	12,000,000	36,000,000
PBP	4 years	5 years	4.5 years

Project A has the quickest payback. This can be interpreted to mean it carries the least risk and generates a profit most quickly. This does not mean, however, that it generates neither the largest profit nor the largest net cash flow over the whole life of the project. Sometimes projects with slower payback generate a larger profit over the whole life of the project. Although PBP is easily understood, there are drawbacks. It does not include the time value of money and it does not consider the post-payback cash profile.

Accounting rate of return

NPV, IRR and PBP are all based on cash, not profit. Yet many managers are accustomed to dealing with profit and may prefer a decision rule based on profit.

The accounting rate of return (ARR) is given by the average annual profits expected from a project, divided by the initial capital investment. When multiplied by 100, this delivers a percentage which managers and entrepreneurs can interpret. For instance, if the profits expected from a project averaged £100,000 and the initial capital was £1,000,000, the accounting rate of return would be 10%. Consider the three examples set out below (all in £):

Year	A	B	C
Initial capital	−24,000,000	−36,0000,000	−42,000,000
Profit year 1	6,000,000	2,000,000	0
Profit year 2	6,000,000	6,000,000	7,000,000
Profit year 3	6,000,000	8,000,000	10,000,000
Profit year 4	6,000,000	10,000,000	13,000,000
Profit year 5	6,000,000	10,000,000	24,000,000
Profit year 6	6,000,000	12,000,000	36,000,000
Average profit	6,000,000	8,000,000	15,000,000
ARR	25%	22%	35.7%

The figures indicate project C is the most beneficial. No account, however, has been taken of the time value of money and the figures are based on arbitrary depreciation rates. Even so, profit is a familiar concept to managers and one which readily lends itself to a percentage of initial capital.

Conclusions

Each of the different decision-making techniques has advantages and disadvantages. PBP is well suited to smaller companies needing quick payback from investments. IRR and NPV are better suited to a larger company with a dedicated team of business analysts. ARR may suit a company where profits are subject to the close scrutiny of stock markets. A sensible approach is to use all four techniques on every potential investment decision and carefully compare the results.

There are many non-financial considerations in investment decisions, including health and safety, technical specifications, market share implications and competitors' strategies. If competitors are adopting new technologies it may be necessary to follow suit, to maintain competitive advantage. If only one particular machine can deliver a required level of accuracy, financial considerations become secondary. The difficulty is integrating non-financial aspects with the financial. Companies have to choose a discount rate reflecting the level of risk they face. Analysts would make use of the PE ratio, gearing ratio and standard deviations of share price and profit to help estimate an appropriate cost of capital. Competitor analysis (Porter's Five Forces model) and consumer preferences, however, also need to be taken into account in risk analysis. Analysts have to find a way of integrating these qualitative factors into decision making.

Keywords

Time value of money	Money deposited in a bank can earn interest at low risk. This interest is lost if the money is withdrawn and invested elsewhere.
Discount rate	Lost earnings mean that cash received in the future is worth less than cash received today. In other words, future cash is 'discounted'. The extent to which future cash reduces in present value terms depends on interest rates.
Cost of capital	Companies have to pay interest and dividends to attract capital investment. This is termed the 'cost of capital'.
Present value	The value today of cash received in the future.
Net present value	The present value of receipts less the present value of payments.
Internal rate of return	The discount rate yielding a zero NPV.
Payback period	The time that elapses between initial investment and the date when the investment is fully recovered, e.g. five years.
Accounting rate of return	Average annual profits divided by initial capital.

Multiple choice questions

Tick the box next to your answer.

1. Which of the following business sectors tend to have a short-term planning horizon?
   - ☐ Pensions
   - ☐ Airports and air travel
   - ☐ Insurance companies
   - ☐ Motor manufacturing
   - ☐ Fashion

2. Within an NPV calculation what is year zero?
   - ☐ Now, the present day
   - ☐ Last year
   - ☐ Next year
   - ☐ The second year of a project
   - ☐ The tenth year of a project

3. At the 20% rate, what is the present value of £1 in four years' time?
   - ☐ £1
   - ☐ £1.20
   - ☐ £0.80
   - ☐ £0.50
   - ☐ £0.482

4. What is the present value of £1,000,000 in a year's time at the 5% rate?
   - [ ] £1
   - [ ] £952,000
   - [ ] £1.05m
   - [ ] £0.95m
   - [ ] £920,000

5. What is the present value of £1,000,000 received in one year's time at the 15% rate?
   - [ ] £1
   - [ ] £850,000
   - [ ] £1.15m
   - [ ] £0.85m
   - [ ] £870,000

6. What is the present value of £1,000,000 received in both one and two years' time at the 15% rate?
   - [ ] £870,000+£756,000 = £1,626,000
   - [ ] £1,000,000+£1,000,000 = £2,000,000
   - [ ] £1,000,000+£870,000 = £1,870,000
   - [ ] £1,500,000
   - [ ] £870,000+£862,000 = £1,732,000

7. What is the definition of net present value?
   - [ ] The initial cost of a project
   - [ ] The cash receipts generated by a project
   - [ ] The net cash flow of a project
   - [ ] The profit of a project
   - [ ] The PV of the cash receipts less the PV of cash payments

8. What is the definition of cost of capital?
   - [ ] Goods bought to sell at a profit
   - [ ] The rate of inflation
   - [ ] The return that has to be offered to attract capital investment
   - [ ] Initial costs of a project
   - [ ] Cost per unit of product

9. A company increases its cost of capital from 15% to 20%. What impact does this have on a project it is considering?
   - [ ] Increases the NPV of the project
   - [ ] Reduces the NPV of the project
   - [ ] No impact on the NPV of the project
   - [ ] Increases the life of the project
   - [ ] Reduces the initial capital needed to fund the project

10. What is the time value of money?
   - [ ] The return that can be earned simply by depositing cash in a bank
   - [ ] The working capital cycle
   - [ ] Depreciation
   - [ ] Current ratio
   - [ ] Debtor days

11. A business is evaluating a project that is more risky than its core business. The appropriate discount rate should be?
   - [ ] Lower than the normal cost of capital
   - [ ] Higher than the normal cost of capital
   - [ ] The normal cost of capital
   - [ ] The rate of interest paid on its overdraft
   - [ ] The rate of interest earned on cash deposited in a bank

12. What is the definition of the payback period?
    ☐ The number of years in a project
    ☐ The breakeven units of a project
    ☐ The margin of safety
    ☐ The length of time that elapses between initial investment and recouping the investment
    ☐ The net present value

13. Consider buying a company for £2.5m. Annual net cash flow is £250,000. What is the payback period?
    ☐ 0 years
    ☐ 1 year
    ☐ 5 years
    ☐ 10 years
    ☐ 20 years

14. A tunnelling project will cost £1.4 billion (£1,400,000,000). Net cash flow will be £200,000,000 per year starting in year 1. What is the PBP?
    ☐ 5 years
    ☐ 6 years
    ☐ 7 years
    ☐ 8 years
    ☐ 9 years

15. Competitors are introducing new technology that reduces costs and increases profits. What impact does this have on an individual company's appraisal of the new technology?
    ☐ No impact
    ☐ Less likely to introduce it
    ☐ More likely to introduce it
    ☐ Increases the length of the project
    ☐ Doubles the appropriate cost of capital

Multiple choice answers

	Correct answer	Comment
1	Fashion	This is a fast changing sector with new trends emerging all the time. The time horizon extends over months rather than years. The others are examples of long-term businesses, e.g. a pension product can run for more than 50 years.
2	Now, the present day	The discount factor in year 0 is always one.
3	£0.482	At the 20% rate, £1 in four years' time is worth less than half its present value. In ten years' time £1 will be worth only £0.162 (see present value table, Appendix 1).
4	£952,000	£1,000,000 × 0.952.
5	£870,000	£1,000,000 × 0.870.

6	£1,626,000	£1,000,000 × 0.870 + £1,000,000 × 0.756.
7	The PV of the cash receipts less the PV of cash payments	In other words the difference between the discounted receipts and discounted payments.
8	The return that has to be offered in order to attract capital investment	This can take the form of the dividends paid to shareholders and the interest paid on a bank loan.
9	Reduces the NPV of the project	The higher the discount rate (cost of capital) the lower the NPV.
10	The return that can be earned simply by depositing cash in a bank	Any money invested in business has to be withdrawn from a bank, so the interest is lost. An economist would term this the 'opportunity cost' of investment because the opportunity to earn interest has been lost.
11	Higher than the normal cost of capital	Investors will have to be offered a higher return in order to make the risky new project attractive to them.
12	Length of time that elapses between initial investment and recouping the investment	Some projects pay back quickly, but others take many years.
13	10 years	10 × £250,000 = £2,500,000.
14	7 years	7 × £200,000,000 = £1,400,000,000.
15	More likely to introduce it	Irrespective of NPV and payback calculations, the company cannot afford to lose competitive advantage.

Beverly J. Martin & Co.

Beverly J. Martin & Co. have been engaged in the production of wind instruments for 25 years. They have grown slowly, held back by competition from Japan. They are considering investing in production facilities for a new light-weight instrument with an estimated life span of four years. The fixed assets will cost £110,000 and the net cash flow will be £30,000 for each of the first two years and £35,000 for the last two years. The company's cost of capital is 10%. Calculate the NPV, comment and make a recommendation.

Three bad pennies

Consider investing £100,000 in one of three projects A, B and C under a 20% cost of capital. Cash profiles are as follows (all in £):

	A	B	C
Investment	100,000	100,000	100,000
Net receipts			
Year 1	50,000	20,000	50,000
Year 2	40,000	30,000	−20,000
Year 3	30,000	40,000	60,000
Year 4	20,000	50,000	70,000

Calculate the NPV for each project, comment and make a recommendation.

Dorothy Previous

Dorothy is considering investing in two projects with cash profiles as given below (all in £). She estimates the cost of capital at 10%. Calculate the NPV for both, comment and make a recommendation.

Year	A	B
0	−25,200	−25,800
1	0	4,000
2	4,000	6,000
3	5,000	8,000
4	8,000	10,000
5	11,000	6,000
6	8,000	3,000

First internal rate of return question

Consider a project with the following cash profile. Calculate the IRR of this project using 10% and 20% discount rates.

Year	Cash flows (£)
0	−50,000
1	12,000
2	13,000
3	14,000
4	15,000
5	16,000

Second internal rate of return question

Consider a project with the following cash profile. Calculate the IRR of this project using 10% and 20% discount rates.

Year	Cash flows (£)
0	−100,000
1	10,000
2	15,000
3	20,000
4	25,000
5	30,000
6	30,000
7	30,000

First payback question

Compare the payback period for the projects A and B below (all in £):

Year	A	B
0	−1,000,000	−1,250,000
1	400,000	250,000
2	600,000	500,000
3	700,000	500,000
4	800,000	500,000

Second payback question

Calculate the payback period for each of the three projects presented below (all in £):

Year	X	Y	Z
0	−12,000	−20,000	−16,000
1	3,000	4,000	0
2	3,000	4,000	2,000
3	3,000	4,000	4,000
4	3,000	4,000	8,000
5	3,000	4,000	8,000

Third payback question

Calculate the payback period in each of these three projects (all in £):

Year	A	B	C
0	−210,000	−180,000	−240,000
1	35,000	20,000	0
2	35,000	20,000	40,000
3	35,000	20,000	10,000
4	35,000	20,000	40,000
5	35,000	20,000	40,000
6	35,000	20,000	40,000
7	35,000	20,000	40,000
8	35,000	20,000	40,000
9	35,000	20,000	40,000
10	35,000	20,000	

Aussie Flights

Aussie Flights are considering developing a web site specialising in selling flights to Australia and New Zealand. They are in negotiations with venture capitalists keen to see profits from the venture as soon as possible. From an initial investment of £2,000,000 the following profits and losses are expected:

Year	Profits (£)
1	−310,000
2	−12,000
3	+405,000
4	+517,000
5	+650,000

Calculate the accounting rate of return.

Textpet Oil Company

Quoted on the New York Stock Exchange, Textpet oil is nervous about reporting losses. Consequently, they always include accounting rate of return in investment appraisal. A new oil field near the Caspian Sea is being evaluated. The exploration and drilling costs amount to $48,000,000. The expected profits are as follows:

Year	Profits ($000's)
1	+5,000
2	+7,000
3	+13,000
4	+15,000
5	+22,000
6	+18,000

Calculate the accounting rate of return.

Solutions

The NPV calculation should be laid out as follows:

Year	Cash flows (£)	Discount factors	PV
0	−110,000	1	−110,000
1	30,000	0.909	27,270
2	30,000	0.826	24,780
3	35,000	0.751	26,285
4	35,000	0.683	23,905
Total			−7,760

The NPV is negative, therefore the idea should be rejected. The cost of capital seems low. Most companies have to pay a higher return to attract investment. At a higher discount factor the project would be even less attractive. If the company is experiencing low profits, it might consider diversifying into a market where there is less competition.

Three bad pennies

Project A

Year	Cash flows (£)	Discount factors	PV
0	−100,000	1	−100,000
1	50,000	0.833	41,650
2	40,000	0.694	27,760
3	30,000	0.579	17,370
4	20,000	0.482	9,640
Total			−3,580

Project B

Year	Cash flows (£)	Discount factors	PV
0	−100,000	1	−100,000
1	20,000	0.833	16,660
2	30,000	0.694	20,820
3	40,000	0.579	23,160
4	50,000	0.482	24,100
Total			−15,260

Project C

Year	Cash flows (£)	Discount factors	PV
0	−100,000	1	−100,000
1	50,000	0.833	41,650
2	−20,000	0.694	−13,880
3	60,000	0.579	34,740
4	70,000	0.482	33,740
Total			−3,750

All of these possible investments show a negative net present value. Investing in any of them would, taking into account the time value of money, reduce the value of the business. Recommend rejecting all of the projects.

Dorothy Previous

Project A

Year	Cash flows (£)	Discount factors	PV
0	−25,200	1	−25,200
1	0	0.909	0
2	4,000	0.826	3,304
3	5,000	0.751	3,755
4	8,000	0.683	5,464
5	11,000	0.621	6,831
6	8,000	0.564	4,512
Total			−1,334

Project B

Year	Cash flows (£)	Discount factors	PV
0	−25,800	1	−25,800
1	4,000	0.909	3,636
2	6,000	0.826	4,956
3	8,000	0.751	6,008
4	10,000	0.683	6,830
5	6,000	0.621	3,726
6	3,000	0.564	1,692
Total			+1,048

Project A delivers a negative NPV and is, therefore, rejected. Project B, on the other hand, delivers a positive NPV indicating the project should be undertaken. The cost of capital used is a low one. The company would be advised to check capital is available at that rate of return. It is also worth checking that the cash flows are accurate estimates because once the project is started it may be difficult to release the capital invested.

First internal rate of return

At the 10% rate the NPV is as follows:

Year	Cash flows (£)	10% Discount factors	PV
0	−50,000	1	−50,000
1	12,000	0.909	10,908
2	13,000	0.826	10,738
3	14,000	0.751	10,514
4	15,000	0.683	10,245
5	16,000	0.621	9,936
Total			2,341

At the 20% rate the NPV is as follows:

Year	Cash flows (£)	20% Discount factors	PV
0	−50,000	1	−50,000
1	12,000	0.833	9,996
2	13,000	0.694	9,022
3	14,000	0.579	8,106
4	15,000	0.482	7,230
5	16,000	0.402	6,432
Total			−9,214

A 10% change in discount factor leads to an £11,555 change in NPV. A 1% change in discount factor is approximately the equivalent of £1155. The original NPV was £2341, divided by £1155 yields 2.02. The original discount rate was 10%; therefore, 12.02% should yield a zero NPV. The IRR is estimated as 12.02%. This procedure could now be repeated using 12% and 13%.

Second internal rate of return

At the 10% rate the NPV is as follows:

Year	Cash flows (£)	10% Discount factors	PV
0	−100,000	1	−100,000
1	10,000	0.909	9,090
2	15,000	0.826	12,390
3	20,000	0.751	15,020
4	25,000	0.683	17,075
5	30,000	0.621	18,630
6	30,000	0.564	16,920
7	30,000	0.513	15,390
Total			4,515

At the 20% rate the NPV is as follows:

Year	Cash flows (£)	20% Discount factors	PV
0	−100,000	1	−100,000
1	10,000	0.833	8,330
2	15,000	0.694	10,410
3	20,000	0.579	11,580
4	25,000	0.482	12,050
5	30,000	0.402	12,060
6	30,000	0.335	10,050
7	30,000	0.279	8,370
Total			−27,150

A 10% change in discount factor leads to a £31,665 change in NPV. A 1% change is the equivalent of £3166. The original NPV was £4515, divided by £3166 yields 1.42. The original discount rate was 10%; therefore 11.42% should yield a zero NPV. The IRR is estimated at 11.42%. This procedure could now be repeated using 11% and 12%.

First payback

Project A

Year	Cash flow	Cumulative
0	−1,000,000	−1,000,000
1	400,000	−600,000
2	600,000	0
3	700,000	700,000
4	800,000	1,500,000
Payback	2 years	

Project B

Year	Cash flow	Cumulative
0	−1,250,000	−1,250,000
1	250,000	−1,000,000
2	500,000	−500,000
3	500,000	0
4	500,000	500,000
Payback	3 years	

Project A pays back after 2 years compared to 3 years for B. Project A, therefore, poses lower risk and generates better short-term cash flow. The longer term benefits of projects A and B, however, are unclear. An NPV calculation would be a useful complement to the payback calculations because NPV incorporates the full life of the project and the time value of money.

Second payback

Project X

Year	Cash flow	Cumulative
0	−12,000	−12,000
1	3,000	−9,000
2	3,000	−6,000
3	3,000	−3,000
4	3,000	0
5	3,000	3,000
Payback	4 years	

Project Y

Year	Cash flow	Cumulative
0	−20,000	−20,000
1	4,000	−16,000
2	4,000	−12,000
3	4,000	−8,000
4	4,000	−4,000
5	4,000	0
Payback	5 years	

Project Z

Year	Cash flow	Cumulative
0	−16,000	−16,000
1	0	−16,000
2	2,000	−14,000
3	4,000	−10,000
4	8,000	−2,000
5	8,000	+6,000
Payback	4.25 years	

Project X has the quickest payback, 4 years. From the point of view of cash flow and low risk, project X is the best. This does not, however, take into account the full life of the project and the time value of money.

Third payback

Project A

Year	A	Cumulative
0	−210,000	−210,000
1	35,000	−175,000
2	35,000	−140,000
3	35,000	−105,000
4	35,000	−70,000
5	35,000	−35,000
6	35,000	0
7	35,000	35,000
8	35,000	70,000
9	35,000	105,000
10	35,000	140,000
Payback	6 years	

Project B

Year	B	Cumulative
0	−180,000	−180,000
1	20,000	−160,000
2	20,000	−140,000
3	20,000	−120,000
4	20,000	−100,000
5	20,000	−80,000
6	20,000	−60,000
7	20,000	−40,000
8	20,000	−20,000
9	20,000	0
10	20,000	20,000

Payback	9 years

Project C

Year	C	Cumulative
0	−240,000	−240,000
1	0	−240,000
2	40,000	−200,000
3	10,000	−190,000
4	40,000	−150,000
5	40,000	−110,000
6	40,000	−70,000
7	40,000	−30,000
8	40,000	10,000
9	40,000	50,000
10		

Payback	7.75 years

Project A has the quickest payback, 6 years.

Aussie Flights

Calculate the accounting rate of return:

Year	Profits (£)
1	−310,000
2	−12,000
3	+405,000
4	+517,000
5	+650,000
Total	1,250,000
Average	250,000
ARR	12.5%

The project delivers 12.5% average rate of return (£250,000/£2,000,000). Most of this profit, however, is earned in years 4 and 5. An NPV calculation could be used to take into account the time value of money. This would have to be based on cash flow rather than profit.

Textpet Oil Company

Year	Profits ($000's)
1	+5,000
2	+7,000
3	+13,000
4	+15,000
5	+22,000
6	+18,000
Total	80,000
Average	13,333
ARR	27.77%

The project delivers 27.77% average rate of return ($13,333,000/$48,000,000). This seems a high rate of return, but it does not take into account the time value of money.

Appendix 1

Present Value Table

	1%	2%	3%	4%	5%	6%	7%	8%	9%	10%	11%	12%	13%	14%	15%	16%	17%	18%	19%	20%
1	0.990	0.980	0.971	0.962	0.952	0.943	0.935	0.926	0.917	0.909	0.901	0.893	0.885	0.877	0.870	0.862	0.855	0.847	0.840	0.833
2	0.980	0.961	0.943	0.925	0.907	0.890	0.873	0.857	0.842	0.826	0.812	0.797	0.783	0.769	0.756	0.743	0.731	0.718	0.706	0.694
3	0.971	0.942	0.915	0.889	0.864	0.840	0.816	0.794	0.772	0.751	0.731	0.712	0.693	0.675	0.658	0.641	0.624	0.609	0.593	0.579
4	0.961	0.924	0.888	0.855	0.823	0.792	0.763	0.735	0.708	0.683	0.659	0.636	0.613	0.592	0.572	0.552	0.534	0.516	0.499	0.482
5	0.951	0.906	0.863	0.822	0.784	0.747	0.713	0.681	0.650	0.621	0.593	0.567	0.543	0.519	0.497	0.476	0.456	0.437	0.419	0.402
6	0.942	0.888	0.837	0.790	0.746	0.705	0.666	0.630	0.596	0.564	0.535	0.507	0.480	0.456	0.432	0.410	0.390	0.370	0.352	0.335
7	0.933	0.871	0.813	0.760	0.711	0.665	0.623	0.583	0.547	0.513	0.482	0.452	0.425	0.400	0.376	0.354	0.333	0.314	0.296	0.279
8	0.923	0.853	0.789	0.731	0.677	0.627	0.582	0.540	0.502	0.467	0.434	0.404	0.376	0.351	0.327	0.305	0.285	0.266	0.249	0.233
9	0.914	0.837	0.766	0.703	0.645	0.592	0.544	0.500	0.460	0.424	0.391	0.361	0.333	0.308	0.284	0.263	0.243	0.225	0.209	0.194
10	0.905	0.820	0.744	0.676	0.614	0.558	0.508	0.463	0.422	0.386	0.352	0.322	0.295	0.270	0.247	0.227	0.208	0.191	0.176	0.162
11	0.896	0.804	0.722	0.650	0.585	0.527	0.475	0.429	0.388	0.350	0.317	0.287	0.261	0.237	0.215	0.195	0.178	0.162	0.148	0.135
12	0.887	0.788	0.701	0.625	0.557	0.497	0.444	0.397	0.356	0.319	0.286	0.257	0.231	0.208	0.187	0.168	0.152	0.137	0.124	0.112
13	0.879	0.773	0.681	0.601	0.530	0.469	0.415	0.368	0.326	0.290	0.258	0.229	0.204	0.182	0.163	0.145	0.130	0.116	0.104	0.093
14	0.870	0.758	0.661	0.577	0.505	0.442	0.388	0.340	0.299	0.263	0.232	0.205	0.181	0.160	0.141	0.125	0.111	0.099	0.088	0.078
15	0.861	0.743	0.642	0.555	0.481	0.417	0.362	0.315	0.275	0.239	0.209	0.183	0.160	0.140	0.123	0.108	0.095	0.084	0.074	0.065

19 Accounting in the business environment

This chapter places accounting techniques in the broader business context.

- Application of accounting techniques;
- Creative accounting;
- Risk assessment;
- Successful business management;
- Further reading.

Introduction

Importance of integration

In this chapter an attempt is made to integrate accounting techniques, procedures and models, to develop an overview of the role of accounting and promote a broader and richer view of its possibilities. This overview will help identify which accounting technique is most appropriate in a particular business situation. In this final chapter creative accounting is also explored and the key points of risk analysis and financial management are reiterated.

Applying accounting techniques

There are a range of accounting techniques which can be usefully employed in running a business, including:

- P&L account and balance sheet
- Cash flow forecasting
- Budgeting
- Ratios
- Breakeven and margin of safety
- Costing and ABC
- Investment appraisal (NPV, IRR, etc.)

In addition to these numerical techniques there are a range of sources of finance, procedures for managing working capital and models such as Porter's Five Forces, product life cycle and supply chain. These sources, procedures and qualitative models provide a framework for interpreting quantitative data such as cash flow, P&L account, costing and ratios, etc.

Techniques can be matched up to business situations as follows:

Starting a new company	A cash flow forecast, as part of a full business plan, indicates the amount of capital needed to start the business. Breakeven could be used to identify sales and production targets for the first year. Net present value and payback period could be used to evaluate longer term investments.
Rapid growth stage of a new company	Budgeting could be used to ensure coordinated growth. Departmental managers could be made responsible for correcting budget variances. Particular emphasis should be given to cash budgets and the working capital cycle.
Direct foreign investment	Net present value, internal rate of return, payback period and accounting rate of return could all be used to give different perspectives on foreign investment opportunities.
Holding company monitoring a number of subsidiaries	Ratio analysis could be used to give an overview without generating excessive paperwork.
Preparing for a stock market floatation	A healthy P&L account and balance sheet will impress potential investors, who also pay close attention to ratios.
Keeping costs low in the face of international competition	Costing and activity-based costing.
Detailed financial control of a large organisation	Budgeting with monthly progress meetings during which variances are analysed in detail.
Selecting shares for a personal portfolio	Ratio analysis along with scrutiny of P&L account and balance sheet.

The various roles of accounting, described above, have to be adapted to the sector, size, management style and stage of growth of a particular company.

Creative accounting

There is a tendency in some accounting texts to assume all accounting techniques and procedures are beneficial. Accounting, like every other business service, needs to be rigorously analysed. The costs of implementing and operating accounting techniques should be weighed against the benefits. In Chapter 15 it was argued that the costs of implementing an ABC system are sometimes greater than the benefits. This logic can equally be applied to budgeting and investment appraisal. Some companies take the view that budgeting is time consuming and expensive and rely, instead, on ratio analysis.

To be helpful, accounting information has to be relevant, reliable and timely. This means it should be relevant to business problems and in appropriate detail. The information should be accurate, so it can be relied on when making long-term decisions. Accounting information rapidly goes out of date, so it needs to be prepared quickly. One difficulty is that checking reliability takes time and, therefore, reduces the usefulness of accounting. The key issue relating to the reliability of accounting is, however, 'creative accounting'. This is the manipulation of accounting reports to serve a particular purpose. Typically, creative accounting is employed to artificially increase profits, making the company seem more attractive to investors.

The main methods of creative accounting are as follows:

- Depreciate fixed assets over a long period, reducing expenses.
- Treat some expenses as fixed assets, spreading the cost over a number of future years.
- Failure to write off bad debts.
- Failure to write off obsolete or damaged stock.
- Failure to write off obsolete fixed assets, e.g. IT equipment.
- Overvalue stock, thereby reducing cost of sales.
- Failure to raise credit notes when customers reject goods.
- Failure to record purchases, reducing cost of sales and increasing gross profit.
- Create a non-existent customer and raise false sales invoices.

The overstatement of profits caused by these measures may go undetected for one year, but it will quickly become apparent that certain assets are overvalued or false. Some of the methods mentioned above are fraudulent, e.g. raising false sales invoices, while others are manipulations of accepted accounting practice, e.g. longer depreciation periods.

In a group of companies more opportunities for creative accounting exist. If a subsidiary is performing badly, shares can be sold so the company is no longer a subsidiary. Equally, if an associate or joint venture is doing well, shares can be acquired bringing it into the consolidated accounts. Selling goods to subsidiary companies can also create imaginary profits. Accounting rules and regulations, however, are continually being tightened, outlawing many of these abuses.

Business risk

There are many sources of business risk, including:

- Decline stage of the product life cycle
- Increasing buyer power and supplier power
- Entry of new competitors and the emergence of substitutes
- Increasing competition from established rivals, e.g. pressure to reduce prices
- Increases in interest rates

- Volatile exchange rates
- Downturn in the trade cycle
- Bad debts and slow-paying debtors
- Obsolete and damaged stock
- Obsolete fixed assets
- Increases in oil prices

A combination of two or three of these factors can result in the bankruptcy of a company. For example, a business climate characterised by rising interest rates, a downturn in the trade cycle and increased competition. When a business faces the risk of bankruptcy (liquidation), management style and processes have to be reviewed. Long-term projects should be postponed and greater emphasis should be placed on managing working capital. Cash flow forecasts should be prepared on a weekly basis.

All of the techniques studied here contribute to the measurement of risk, particularly the following:

- Fixed and variable costs
- Breakeven and margin of safety %
- Price to earnings ratio
- Interest cover
- Dividend cover
- Gearing ratio
- Gross profit %
- Market share
- Current ratio
- Acid test
- Payback period

Risk is often greatest at the launch of a new business because cash can be in short supply and it is difficult to negotiate credit. Markets and processes are untested and unforeseen problems inevitably emerge. A fast growing company can fail because it has insufficient capital to finance growth. Global companies are at risk from world events such as terrorism and the trade cycle. In fact, no form of investment is risk free because even money deposited in a bank can be eroded quickly in times of high inflation.

Successful business management

The following key points and issues have emerged:

- Profit should be viewed in relation to capital and not in isolation.
- Cash is key and needs constant monitoring and forecasting.
- Bad debts can threaten the continued existence of a business.
- Working capital management procedures are essential.
- Plan, co-ordinate and monitor on a monthly basis.
- Use a variety of flexible sources of finance.
- Minimise fixed costs and overheads.

- Understand the underlying causes of overheads.
- Use ratios to understand the relationships between figures.
- Risk takes many different forms, all of which need to be monitored and minimised.
- Carefully consider long-term investments.
- Adapt accounting techniques to particular problems and contexts.

These are the foundations of successful business management.

Conclusions

Management comprises a number of specialist disciplines including accounting, marketing, personnel, IT, operations and strategy. All of these have a role in solving business problems. A breadth of thinking is required, blending quantitative with qualitative approaches, integrating operational issues with strategic and balancing profit against risk. Accounting information is not always accurate and does not measure all the factors contributing to business success. Accounting, however, is still the single most effective tool for business management, especially when integrated with other business disciplines. Good luck with your studies.

Further reading

The following references will help you develop some of the themes introduced in this book. This will be particularly helpful if you are undertaking a dissertation or term paper.

Armstrong P. (1987), The rise of accounting controls in British capitalist enterprises. *Accounting, Organisations and Society*, Vol. 12, No. 5, pp. 415–436.

Barrow C. (2000), *Surviving the e-Business Downturn*, John Wiley.

Bowman C. (1990), *The Essence of Strategic Management*, Prentice Hall.

Bryer R.A. (1991), Accounting for the railway mania of 1845 – a great railway swindle. *Accounting, Organisations and Society*, Vol. 15/16, pp. 439–486.

Burrell G., Morgan G. (1979), *Sociological Paradigms and Organisational Analysis*, Butterworth-Heinemann.

Landes D. (1999), *The Wealth and Poverty of Nations*, Abacus.

Neimark M.D., Tinker A.M. (1986), The social construction of management control systems. *Accounting, Organisations and Society*, Vol. 11, No. 4, pp. 369–396.

Owen A.S. (2001), Finance and banking curriculum in Bosnia-Herzegovina: an application of the Ruijter and Ten Dam model. *International Journal of Management Education*, Vol. 1, No. 3.

Owen A.S. (2002), Accounting and capital: the Marxist theory of the accounting firm. *Cyprus International Journal of Management*, Vol. 7, No. 1 (Autumn). pp. 77–91

Owen A.S. (2003), Measuring large UK accounting firm profit margins, mergers and concentration: a political economy of the accounting firm. *Accounting, Auditing and Accountability Journal* Vol. 16, No. 2, pp. 275–297.

Roslender R. (1992), *Sociological Perspectives on Modern Accounting*, Routledge.

Rugman A.M., Hodgetts R.M. (2002), *International Business*, 3rd edn., Prentice Hall.

Ryan R., Scapens R.W., Theobold M. (1992), *Research Method and Methodology in Finance and Accounting*, Academic Press.

Schwartz E.I. (1999), *Digital Darwinism*, Penguin.

Smith T. (1992), *Accounting for Growth*, Century.

Tinker A.M. (1980), Towards a political economy of accounting: an empirical illustration of the Cambridge controversies. *Accounting, Organisations and Society*, Vol. 5, No. 1, pp. 147–160.

Ward K. (1993), *Corporate Financial Strategy*, Butterworth-Heinemann.

Multiple choice questions

Tick the box next to your answer.

1. Which of these is the first document to prepare when evaluating a new business idea suggested by an individual with limited capital?
   - [ ] Cash flow forecast
   - [ ] Balance sheet
   - [ ] Ratio analysis
   - [ ] Activity-based costing
   - [ ] Tax return

2. In a competitive high technology manufacturing environment which of these would work best?
   - [ ] Breakeven
   - [ ] Ratio analysis
   - [ ] Traditional costing
   - [ ] Activity-based costing
   - [ ] Payback period

3. Which of the following does *not* reflect high risk?
   - [ ] Gearing = 150%
   - [ ] Margin of safety = 5%
   - [ ] High fixed costs
   - [ ] Current ratio = 0.75
   - [ ] Margin of safety = 50%

4. Which of these do *not* reduce net profit (profit before taxation)?
   - [ ] Increasing the expected life of fixed assets, e.g. computers, 10 years (10%)
   - [ ] Treating fixed assets as an expense, e.g. software
   - [ ] Bad debt write off
   - [ ] Credit notes issued to customers
   - [ ] Stock write off

5. Which of these problems can be solved by good financial management?
   - [ ] Customers do not like the product
   - [ ] Staff are not punctual
   - [ ] Delivery to customers is too slow
   - [ ] Product is not reliable
   - [ ] Overheads (expenses) increasing rapidly

6. Low interest rates encourage?
   - ☐ Less investment in business
   - ☐ Less borrowing
   - ☐ More money deposited in banks
   - ☐ More investment in business
   - ☐ Higher internal rate of return

7. Over the product life cycle when are losses most likely to occur?
   - ☐ Initial launch
   - ☐ Rapid growth
   - ☐ Maturity
   - ☐ Steady decline
   - ☐ Losses constant throughout

8. Over the trade cycle, when are profits likely to be highest?
   - ☐ Bottom of the slump
   - ☐ Top of the boom
   - ☐ During the upturn
   - ☐ During the downswing
   - ☐ Profits constant throughout

9. In relation to companies with bank borrowings, what is the impact of a rise in interest rates on company profits?
   - ☐ Increases expenses and reduces net profit
   - ☐ Increases sales and net profit
   - ☐ Increases cost of sales and reduces net profit
   - ☐ Increases fixed assets with no impact on net profit
   - ☐ Reduces expenses and increases net profit

10. Which accounting technique complements a strict, target-led style of management?
   - ☐ Ratios
   - ☐ Traditional costing
   - ☐ Breakeven
   - ☐ Budgeting
   - ☐ Non-financial ratios

Multiple choice answers

	Correct answer	Comment
1	Cash flow forecast	Cash flow is the first document to prepare. This will identify the capital needed to start the business. After that, a budgeted P&L account and balance sheet would be useful.
2	ABC	Traditional costing can be inaccurate in this type of environment.
3	Margin of safety = 50%	A 50% margin of safety is very safe. Sales can fall by 49% and the company will still be in the profit zone.

4	Increasing expected life of fixed assets	This has the effect of reducing the annual depreciation, because the cost is spread over more years. Lower depreciation reduces expenses, and this increases profits.
5	Overheads (expenses) increasing rapidly	A budgeting system would be a good way of tackling this problem. All the others are marketing, personnel or production-type problems.
6	More investment in business	The cost of capital has been reduced.
7	Initial launch	Many of the costs are incurred at the start of the product life cycle and, as a result, losses are highest during the launch.
8	Top of the boom	The top of the boom is quickly followed by the start of the downturn.
9	Increases expenses and reduces net profit	In general high interest rates are not good for business because they increase the cost of capital.
10	Budgeting	A budgeting system establishes targets in all the main areas of the business.

Discussion question

How can managers monitor risk and what actions can they take to minimise it?

Answers can be found on the companion web site.

Index

Lightning Source UK Ltd.
Milton Keynes UK
UKOW07f1936020217

293425UK00001B/2/P

9 780750 658348